MAHAT GANDHI

Essays & Reflections

MAHATMA GANDHI

Essays & Reflections

Presented to him on his Seventieth Birthday
October 2nd, 1939

Edited by
DR. SARVEPALLI RADHAKRISHNAN
Together with a new Memorial Section

JAICO PUBLISHING HOUSE

Ahmedabad Bangalore Bhopal Bhubaneswar Chennai
Delhi Hyderabad Kolkata Lucknow Mumbai

Published by Jaico Publishing House
A-2 Jash Chambers, 7-A Sir Phirozshah Mehta Road
Fort, Mumbai - 400 001
jaicopub@jaicobooks.com
www.jaicobooks.com

© Jaico Publishing House

Complete & Unabridged

MAHATMA GANDHI
ISBN 81-7224-122-4

First Jaico Impression: 1957
Twentieth Jaico Impression (Reformatted Edition): 2012

Printed by
Snehesh Printers
320-A, Shah & Nahar Ind. Est. A-1
Lower Parel, Mumbai - 400 013

Preface to this edition

It was my desire to re-edit this volume and present it to Gandhi on his eightieth birthday, October 2, 1949. Fate decreed otherwise, and it has now become a memorial volume.

"No country but India and no religion but Hinduism could have given birth to a Gandhi," said the editorial in the *London Times* on the day after his death. It is true that we see in Gandhi the qualities we regard as characteristic of India, i.e. characteristic of India at its inspired best. Yet he belonged by right to humanity's greatest of all time. Asia has awakened under the touch of Europe, and Europe, in its present disordered and puzzled condition, is looking towards the East. To a world which is being shattered by man's selfish error and intolerance, which is questioning the divine nature of the human spirit, Gandhi's message of the life of God is the soul of man and of the way of non-violence in human conduct is of supreme value. In this hour of crisis India is proud to have made such an imperishable contribution.

A few extracts from the many and varied tributes to Gandhi after his death are reprinted in Appendix II.

Owing to the distracted condition of the world – a war in the East and a near war in Europe – and my absence from India since the end of last year, it has not been possible to get together all the persons who would have been glad to join in this world tribute to Mahatma Gandhi on his birthday.

The different essays and reflections, each with its individual character, might be expected to make the book uneven and disconnected, but I hope that it has not done so. Almost every page is knit together by a central and never-forgotten theme, the challenge and message of Gandhi to the contemporary world. By general admission something is wrong with it. We are living in a singular moment of history, a moment of crisis, in the literal sense of the word. In every branch of our activity, material and spiritual, we seem to have arrived at a critical turning-point. Those who have surveyed the scene have given us different answers about the cause and cure of our ailing civilization. Gandhi tells us that we, who constitute the social order, are the disease and we must change, if civilization is to improve.

Those who read these pages will be impressed by the fundamental unity between Gandhi's theory and practice, the exquisite harmony of his life and work, which is the very essence of sincerity. It marks him out as one of the outstanding personalities, not only of our time but of all time.

The contributions are arranged in alphabetical order. A few of Gandhi's most distinctive utterances which are of more than local and temporary importance are brought together in an Appendix.

The Editor thanks Mr. Stephen Hobhouse for his kindness in reading the proofs.

In the illuminating pages of this handy book, the enlightened reader gets a splendid opportunity to come to close quarters with Mahatma Gandhi's arresting personality and his spectacular activities.

It contains tributes to the Father of the Indian Nation, from over a hundred great thinkers from different parts of the world.

Prominent among them are: C. F. Andrews, George S. Arundale, Albert Einstein, Stephen Hobhouse, C.E.M. Joad, Salvador de Madriaga, Vincent Sheean, J.H. Muirhead, G.D.H. Cole, Aldous Huxley, E.M. Forster, Romain Rolland, Upton Sinclair, President Truman, Eamon de Valera, General MacArthur, Clement Attlee, Lord Halifax, Lord Mountbatten, S.I. Hsiung, Thakin Nu, Moustapha El Nahas, Lin Yutang, Ananda K. Coomaraswamy, Sri Aurobindo and many others.

Dr. S. Radhakrishnan's two enlightening essays further constitute a new interpretation of Gandhi's life and mission. The entire collection is a veritable depository of the greatness of the man who has influenced the modern world.

Contents

Contents   xi

MEMORIAL SECTION

Introduction

Gandhi's Religion and Politics
Dr. S. Radhakrishnan

The greatest fact in the story of man on earth is not his material achievement, the empires he has built and broken, but the growth of his soul from age to age in its search for truth and goodness. Those who take part in this adventure of the soul, secure an enduring place in the history of human culture. Time has discredited heroes as easily as it has forgotten everyone else; but the saints remain. The greatness of Gandhi is more in his holy living than in his heroic struggles, in his insistence on the creative power of the soul and its life-giving quality at a time when the destructive forces seem to be in the ascendant.

I. Religious Basis of Politics

Gandhi is known to the world as the one man more than any other who is mainly responsible for the mighty upheaval of the Indian nation which has shaken and loosened its chains. Politicians are not generally reputed to take religion seriously, for the values to which they are committed, such as the political control of one people by another, the economic exploitation of the poorer and weaker human beings, are so clearly inconsistent with the values of religion that the latter could not be taken too seriously or interpreted too accurately. But for Gandhi, all life is of one piece. "To see the universal and all pervading Spirit of Truth face to face one must be able to love the meanest of creation as oneself. And a man who aspires after that cannot afford to keep out of any field of life. That is why my devotion to Truth has drawn me into the field of politics; and I can say without the slightest hesitation and yet in all humility, that those who say that religion has nothing to do with politics do not know what religion means!" Again, "I have no desire for the perishable kingdom of earth, I am striving for the kingdom of heaven, which is spiritual deliverance. For me the road to salvation lies through incessant toil in the service of my country and of humanity. I want to identify myself with everything that lives. In the language of the Gita, I want to live at peace with both friend and foe. So my patriotism is for me a stage on my journey to the land of eternal freedom and peace. Thus it will be seen that for me there are no politics devoid of religion. They subserve religion. Politics bereft of religion are a death-trap because they kill the soul." If man as a political being has not been much of a success, it is because he has kept religion and politics apart, thus misunderstanding both. For Gandhi, there is no religion apart from human activity. Though in the present circumstances of India, Gandhi happens to be a political revolutionary who refuses to accept tyranny or acquiesce in slavery, he is far from the uncompromising type of revolutionary whose abstraction forces men into unnatural and inhuman shapes. In the acid test of experience he remains, not a politician or a reformer, not a philosopher or a moralist, but someone composed of them all, an essentially religious person endowed with the highest and most human qualities and made more lovable by the conciousness of his own limitations and by an unfailing sense of humour.

II. Religion as Life in God

Whatever opinion we may hold of God, it is impossible to deny that He means something of supreme importance and absolute

reality to Gandhi. It is his faith in God that has created in him
a new man whose power and passion and love we feel. He has
the feeling of something close to him, a spiritual presence which
disturbs, embarrasses and overwhelms, an assurance of reality.
Times without number, when doubts disturb his mind, he leaves
it to God. Was there a response from God? No and Yes. No,
for Gandhi does not hear anything said even by the most secret
or the most distant of voices; yes, because he has a sense of
reply, the appeased, satisfied feeling of one who has received an
answer. It is indeed from the nature of the reply which is so
eminently rational that he recognizes that he is not the victim of
his own dreams or hallucinations. "There is an indefinable,
mysterious power that pervades everything. I feel it though I do
not see it. It is this unseen power which makes itself felt and yet
defies all proof because it is so unlike all that I perceive through
my senses. It is proved not by extraneous evidence but in the
transformed conduct and character of those who have felt the
real presence of God within. Such testimony is to be found in
the experiences of an unbroken line of prophets and sages in all
countries and climes. To reject this evidence is to deny
oneself."[1] "It can tell you this – that I am surer of His existence
than of the fact that you and I are sitting in this room. I can
also testify that I may live without air and water but not
without Him. You may pluck out my eyes, but that will not kill
me. But blast my beliefs in God and I am dead."[2]

In consistency with the great spiritual tradition of Hinduism,
Gandhi affirms that when once we rise from the grossness to
which the flesh is prone into the liberty of spirit, the view from
the summit is identical for all. We have to climb the mountain
by different paths, from the points where we happen to be, but
that which we seek is the same. "The Allah of Islam is the same
as the God of the Christians and the Isvara of the Hindus. Even

---

1 Young India, October 11, 1928.
2 Harijan, May 16, 1938.

as there are numerous names of God in Hinduism, there are many names of God in Islam. The names do not indicate individuality but attributes, and little man has tried in his humble way to describe mighty God by giving Him attributes, though He is above all attributes, Indescribable, Immeasurable. Living faith in this God means equal respect for all religions. It would be the height of intolerance and intolerance is a species of violence – to believe that your religion is superior to other religions and that you would be justified in wanting others to change over to your faith."[3] His attitude to other religions is not one of negative toleration but of positive appreciation. He accepts Jesus' life and work as a supreme illustration of the principle of non-violence. "Jesus occupies in my heart the place of one of the great teachers who have made a considerable influence on my life." He appreciates the character of the prophet Mohammad, his fervent faith and practical efficiency, the tender compassion and suffering of Ali. The great truths emphasized by Islam – intense belief in God's overruling majesty, puritanic simplicity of life, ardent sense of brotherhood and chivalrous devotion to the poor are accepted by him as fundamental to all religions. But the dominating force in his life has been Hinduism, with its conception of truth, its vision of the soul and its charity.

All religions, however, are means to religion. "Let me explain what I mean by religion. It is not the Hindu religion which I certainly prize above all other religions, but the religion which transcends Hinduism, which changes one's very nature, which binds one indissolubly to the truth within, and which ever purifies. It is the permanent element in human nature which counts no cost too great in order to find full expression and which leaves the soul utterly restless until it has found itself, known its Maker, and appreciated the true correspondence between the Maker and itself."

3 Harijan, May 14, 1938.

There is no other God than Truth, and the only means for the realization of truth is love or ahimsa. Knowledge of truth and the practice of love are impossible without self-purification. Only the pure in heart can see God. To attain to purity of heart, to rise above attachment and repulsion, to be free from passion in thought, word and deed, to be redeemed from fear and vanity, the inconsistencies of our flesh and the discursiveness of our minds must be overcome. Disciplined effort, austere living, tapas is the way to it. Suffering rinses our spirit clean. According to Hindu mythology, the God Siva undertakes Himself to swallow the poison which comes up when the ocean is churned. The God of the Christians gave His Son in order to save mankind. Even if they are myths, why should they have arisen if they did not express some deep-seated intuitions in men? The more you love, the more you suffer. Infinite love, infinite suffering. "Whosoever would save his life shall lose it." We are here working for God, called upon to use our life for carrying out his intentions. If we refuse to do so and insist on saving our lives instead of spending them, we negate our true nature and so lose our lives. If we are to be able to follow to the farthest limit we can see, if we are to respond to the most distant call, earthly values, fame, possessions and pleasures of the senses have to be abandoned. To be one with the poor and the outcast is to be his equal in poverty and to cast oneself out. To be free to say or do the right, regardless of praise or blame, to be free to love all and forgive all, non-attachment is essential. Freedom is only for the unconfined who enjoy the whole world without owning a blade of grass in it. In this matter, Gandhi is adhering to the great ideal of the sannyasin who has no fixed abode and is bound to no stable form of living.

There is, however, some exaggeration when the ascetic code in all its fullness is prescribed, not merely for the sannyasins but for the whole of humanity. Sexual restraint, for example, is essential for all, but celibacy is only for the few. The sexual act is not a mere pleasure of the body, a purely carnal act, but is a means by which love is expressed and the race continued is not an act if it harms others or if it interferes with a person's spiritual development, but neither of these conditions is not an act of shame or sin. But when the masters of spiritual life insist on celibacy, they demand that we should preserve singleness of mind from destruction by bodily desire.

Gandhi has spared no pains in disciplining himself to the utmost possible extent, and those who know him will admit his claim that he has "known no distinction between relatives and strangers, countrymen and foreigners, white and coloured Hindus and Indians of other faiths, whether Muslims, Parsees, Christians or Jews." He adds: "I cannot claim this as a special virtue, as it has been in my very nature rather than a result of any effort on my part, whereas in the case of non-violence, celibacy and other cardinal virtues, I am fully conscious of a continuous striving for the cultivation of them."

Only the pure in heart can love God and love man. Suffering love is the miracle of the spirit by which though the wrongs of others are borne on our shoulders, we feel a sense of comfort deeper and more real than any given by purely selfish pleasures. At such moments we understand that nothing in the world is sweeter than the knowledge that we have been able to give a moment's happiness to another, nothing more precious than the sense that we have shared another's sorrow. Perfect compassion untouched by condescension, washed clean of pride, even of the pride of doing good, is the highest religious quality.

III. The Spirit of Humanity

It follows that the mark of spirituality is not exile from the natural world but work in it with love for all. *Yasmin sarvani bhutani atmaivabhut vijanatah.* Thou shalt love thy neighbour as thyself, atmaiva. The condition is absolute. There must be freedom and equality of status. Such a demand makes for the establishment of a universal community of free persons and requires those who accept it to overcome the artificial barriers of race and creed, wealth and power, class and nation. If one group or nation attempts to make itself secure at the expense of another, Germans at the expense of the Czechs, landlords at the expense of tenants, capitalists at the expense of workers, it is adopting an undemocratic method and can defend its injustice only by the force of arms. The dominant group has the fear of dispossession and the oppressed stores up just resentment. Only justice can terminate this unnatural condition, the justice which means the recognition of the equal claims of all human beings. The movement of humanity all these centuries has been towards human brotherhood. The various forward thrusts that have become manifest in different parts of the world, the ideals of justice, equality and freedom from exploitation of which men have become increasingly conscious, the demands they have come to feel are all risings of the common man against the perversions and compulsions that were perpetually developing to restrain him and hold him back. The progress of the consciousness of freedom is the essence of human history.

We are inclined to give too much importance to exceptional incidents by seeing them in distorted perspective. What we do not sufficiently realize is that these setbacks, blind alleys and disasters are only a part to be viewed in relation to the background of the general tendency at work over the centuries. If we could only get a detached view of the continued effort of mankind, we would be amazed and profoundly moved. Serfs are becoming free men, heretics are no longer burned, nobles are surrendering their privileges, slaves are being freed from a life of shame, rich men are apologizing for their wealth, militant empires are proclaiming the necessity of peace, and even dreams of the union of mankind are cherished. Yes, we have even today the lust of the powerful, the malice of knaves, the lies of the hypocrites and the rise of arrogant racialism and nationalism; yet one would be blind if one did not see the great tradition of democracy which is universal in its sweep. Unceasing is the toil of those who are labouring to build a world where the poorest have a right to sufficient food, to light, air and sunshine in their homes, to hope, dignity and beauty in their lives. Gandhi is among the foremost of the servants of humanity. He is not comforted by the prospect of the distant future when faced by the threat of immediate disasters. He joins forces with men of fixed convictions to work by the most direct means possible for the cure of evils and the prevention of dangers. Democracy for him is not a matter of phrases but of social realities. All his public activities in South Africa and India can be understood only if we know his love of the common man.

The civilized world has been stirred deeply by the Nazi treatment of the Jews, and liberal statesmen have solemnly expressed their disapproval and sorrow at the recrudescence of racial prejudice. But the strange though startling fact is that in the democratically governed countries of the British Empire and the United States of America, many communities suffer political and social disabilities on racial grounds. When Gandhi was in South Africa he saw that Indians, though nominally free citizens of the British Empire, were subjected to grave disabilities. Both Church and State denied equality of rights to non-European races, and Gandhi started his passive resistance movement on a mass scale to protest against the oppressive restrictions. He stood out for the essential principle that men *qua* men are equal and artificial distinctions based on race and colour were both unreasonable and immoral. He revealed to the Indian community its actual degradation and inspired it with a sense of its own dignity and honour. His effort was not confined to the welfare of Indians. He would not justify the exploitation of the African natives or the better treatment of Indians on account of their historic culture. While the more obnoxious of the discriminatory legislation against the Indians

was abolished, even today Indians are subjected to
restrictions which do not reflect credit on those wl
them or add to the prestige of the Government which imposes
them.

In India it was his ambition to rid the country of its divisions
and discords, to discipline the masses to self-dependence, raise
women to a plane of political, economic and social equality
with men, end the religious hatreds which divide the nation,
and cleanse Hinduism of its social abomination of untouchability. The success he has achieved in removing this blot on
Hinduism will stand out as one of his greatest contributions to
the progress of humanity. So long as there is a class of
untouchables, he belongs to it. "If I have to be re-born, I should
wish to be born an untouchable so that I may share their
sorrows, suffering and the affronts levelled at them in order
that I may endeavour to free myself and them from that
miserable condition." To say that we love God as unseen and at
the same time deal cruelly with people who move by His life or
life derived from Him is a contradiction in terms. Though
Gandhi prided himself on being a conservative Hindu, there has
been no more vigorous critic of the rigours and disabilities of
caste, of the curse of untouchability, or the vice in temples, of
cruelty to cattle and the animal world. "I am a reformer
through and through. But my zeal never leads me to the
rejection of any of the essential things of Hinduism."

Today, his opposition to the autocracy of the Indian princes is
based on his love for the millions of their subjects. Not even the
most generous observer can say that all is well with the States.
I may perhaps quote a few sentences from the *Statesman* of
Calcutta, a paper which represents British interest. "It is no
reflection upon individuals but only upon human nature to say
that in many of the States, appalling conditions prevail. The
bad landlords as well as the good ones are subject to no laws,
they have the power of life and death, there are no obstacles to
their greed or lust or cruelty, if they are greedy, vicious or cruel.

If the treaties which protect petty tyrants are never to be revised, if the Paramount Power is for ever to have an obligation of honour to defend the indefensible, then some day an irresistible force will encounter an immovable object, and according to the classic answer to this problem, something will go the smithereens." The slowness of evolution is the cause of all revolution. Gandhi, with the utmost friendship for the princes, is asking them to wake up and set their houses in order. I hope that they will realize, before it is too late, that their safety and survival are bound up with the rapid introduction of responsible government, which even the Paramount Power with all its strength was obliged to concede in the provinces.

Gandhi's main charge against the British Government in India is that it has led to the oppression of the poor. From the beginning of her history India has been known for her wealth and possession. We have vast areas of the most fertile soil, material resources in inexhaustible abundance, and with proper care and attention we have enough to go round and feed every man, woman and child. And yet, we have millions of people who are the victims of poverty, who are under-nourished and under-housed, whose lives are an unceasing struggle from youth to old age, until at last death comes to their rescue and still their aching hearts. These conditions are not due to pitiless nature, but to the inhuman system which cries out to be abolished, not only in the interest of India but of the whole of humanity.

In the broadcast address which he gave from London to America in 1931, Gandhi referred to the "semi-starved millions scattered throughout the seven hundred thousand villages dotted over a surface nineteen hundred miles broad." He said: "It is a painful phenomenon that those simple villagers, through no fault of their own, have nearly six months in the year idle upon their hands. Time was, not long ago, when every village was self-sufficient in regard to the two primary human wants – food and clothing. Unfortunately for us, when the East

India Company, by means which I would prefer not to describe, destroyed that supplementary village industry, then the millions of spinners – who had become famed through the cunning of their deft fingers for drawing the finest thread, such as has never been yet drawn by any modern machinery – these village spinners found themselves, one fine morning, with their noble occupation gone, and from that day forward, India has become progressively poor, no matter what may be said to the contrary."

India lives in the villages, and her civilization has been an agricultural one which is becoming increasingly mechanical. Gandhi is the representative of the peasant, the producer of the world's food who is fundamental in society, and is anxious to maintain and fortify this basic bias of Indian civilization. He finds that under British rule, the people are giving up their old standards and inspite of many admirable qualities they have acquired, such as mechanical intelligence, inventive skill, courage and adventure, they are worshiping material success, are greedy for tangible gains and are governed by worldly standards. Our industrial cities have lost all proportion to landscape out of which they have grown, have swollen to meaningless dimensions, and their people, caught in the entangling apparatus of money and machinery, have become violent, restless, thoughtless, undisciplinary and unscrupulous. For Gandhi, industrialized humanity has come to mean women, who for a paltry wage are compelled to work out their barren lives, babies who are doped with opium so that they shall not cry and disturb their working mothers, little children who are robbed of their childhood and in their tender years are forced into industrial works, and millions of unemployed who are dwarfed and diseased. We are being snared and enslaved, he thinks, and our souls are conquered for a mess of pottage. A spirit and a culture which had soared up in the rishis of the Upanishads, the Buddhist monks, Hindu sannyasins and Muslim fakirs cannot be content with cars and radios and plutocracy. Our vision is dimmed and our way lost. We have taken a wrong twist which has dispossessed, impoverished and embittered our agricultural population, corrupted, coarsened and blinded our workers, and given us millions of children with blank faces, dead eyes and drooping mouths. Beneath our present bafflement and exasperation, the bulk of the people retain a hunger for the realization of the old dream of genuine liberty, real self-respect; of a life where none is rich and none is poor, where the extremes of luxury and leisure are abolished and where industry and commerce exist in a simple form.

Gandhi does not aim at a peasant society which will forgo altogether the benefits of the machine. He is not against large-scale production. When he was asked whether cottage industries and large-scale production can be harmonized, he said, "Yes, if they are planned so as to help the villages. Key industries, industries which the nation needs, may be centralized. Under my scheme, nothing will be allowed to be produced by cities which can be equally well produced by the villages. The proper function of cities is to serve as clearing-houses for village products."[4] His insistence on khadi (or homespun) and his scheme of popular education centering round the handicrafts are devised to resuscitate the villages. He repeatedly warns that India is to be found not in its few cities but in its innumerable villages. The bulk of India's population must get back to the land, stay in the land, and live primarily off the produce of the land so that their families may be self-supporting, owning the implements they use, the soil they cultivate and the roof that shelters them. Not an uprooted, shiftless class of factory workers, not an unsound, rapacious, money-lending business community, but a responsible agrarian population and the stable, level-headed people of small agricultural market-towns must dominate the cultural, social, economic and noble objectives. This is not to become primitive.

4 Harijan, January 28, 1939

It is only to take up a mode of existence that is instinctive to India, that supplied her once with a purpose, a faith and a meaning. It is the only way to keep our species civilized. India of the peasant and rustic life, of village communities, of forest hermitages and spiritual retreats has taught the world many great lessons but has wronged no man, has injured no land and sought no dominion over others. Today, the true purpose of life has been perverted. How is India to get out of this slough of despond? After centuries of subjection, the people seem to have lost the will or the wish to lift themselves out of it. The forces against them seem to be too strong. To give them confidence, a prouder self-respect, a more erect carriage, is no easy task. Yet Gandhi has tried to re-kindle a torpid generation with the fire that burns in his soul, with his passion for freedom. In freedom, men and women reveal their best: in slavery they are debased. To liberate the ordinary human being from the restrictions, internal and external, which warp his nature has been the aim of freedom. As a great defender of human liberty, he is struggling to release the country from foreign control. Patriotism, when it is so pure, is neither a crime nor bad manners. To fight against the present unnatural conditions is one's sacred duty. He employs spiritual weapons and refuses to draw the sword and in the process is training the people for independence, making them capable of winning and holding it. Sir George Lloyd Lord, the then Governor of Bombay, said of Gandhi's campaign: "Gandhi's was the most colossal experiment in world history and it came within an inch of succeeding."

Though he has failed in his attempt to move the British Government, he has liberated forces in the country which will not cease to act. He has stirred the people from their lethargy, given them a new self-confidence and responsibility and united them in their resolve to win freedom. To the extent to which there is today an awakening of a new spirit, a preparedness for a new kind of national corporate life, a new social attitude in dealing with the depressed classes, it is largely due to the spiritual energy and dynamic of Gandhi's movement.

Gandhi's outlook has nothing sectional or provincial about it. He believes that the heritage of India can help the culture of the world. A prostrated India can give no hope to humanity; only an awakened, free India can give help to a groaning world. Gandhi affirms that if the British are earnest about their vision of justice, peace and order, it is not enough to put down the aggressive powers and preserve the status quo. Our love of liberty and justice must exclude the passive violence of refusing to reform a situation which is contrary to the professed ideals. If greed, cruelty and contempt of man have gone into the making of empires, we must change them before we call upon the world to rally to the forces of freedom and justice. Violence is either active or passive. The aggressive powers are now actively violent, the imperial powers who persist in the enjoyment of unjust advantages acquired from past violence are as much guilty of violence and are inimical to freedom and democracy. Until we act honestly in this matter, we cannot secure a better world-order and the world will be in a chronic state of uncertainty, full of wars and threats of wars. Self-government for India is the acid test of British honesty. Gandhi is still observing his twenty-four hours' fast every Monday to indicate to all concerned that self-rule is unattained. And yet, his is the restraining influence on an impatient India, torn between the legitimate aspirations of the people and the obstinacy of the British ruling classes. He has been the greatest force for peace in India.

When he landed in England after the South African struggle was over, he found that war against Germany had been declared. He offered to enlist unconditionally for the whole duration of the war in order to undertake ambulance work at the Front. His offer was accepted and he was placed in a responsible post with an Indian unit. But owing to over-exposure while on duty, he was taken ill with pleurisy and his life was suspected to be in danger. On recovery, he was ordered by the doctors to leave for the warm climate of India. He actively encouraged recruiting in the war – a thing which has puzzled even many of his friends. At the end of the war, the Rowlatt Act was passed against the unanimous opposition of Indians. Things were done in Punjab under martial law which shocked the country. Gandhi was one of the authors of the Congress Inquiry Report on the Punjab disturbances. In spite of it all, he recommended to the Congress at Amritsar in December 1919 that the Reforms should be accepted and worked in a constitutional manner. When in 1920, the Hunter Commission Report wavered in its criticism of official action, when the House of Lords declined to condemn General Dyer, he made the great decision of his life to refuse to co-operate with the British Government, and in September 1920, the Congress adopted the resolution of non-violent non co-operation.

It will be well to quote his own words in a letter to the Viceroy, written on August 1, 1920: "Your Excellency's light-hearted treatment of official crime, your exoneration of Sir Michael O' Dwyer, Mr. Montagu's despatch and, above all, the shameful ignorance of the Punjab events and the callous disregard of the feelings of Indians betrayed by the House of Lords, have filled me with the gravest misgivings regarding the future of the Empire, have estranged me completely from the present Government, and have disabled me from rendering, as I have hitherto whole-heartedly rendered, my loyal co-operation.

"In my humble opinion the ordinary method of agitating by way of petitions, deputations, and the like is no remedy for moving to repentance a Government so hopelessly indifferent to the welfare of its charge as the Government of India has proved to be. In European countries, condemnation of such grievous wrongs as the Khilafat and the Punjab would have resulted in a bloody revolution by the people. They would have resisted, at all cost, national emasculation. Half of India is too weak to offer violent resistance, and the other half is unwilling to do so. I have therefore ventured to suggest the remedy of non-co-operation, which enables those who wish to dissociate themselves from Government, and which, if unattended by violence and undertaken in an ordered manner, must compel it to retrace its steps and undo the wrongs committed; but whilst I pursue the policy of non-co-operation, in so far as I can carry the people with me, I shall not lose hope that you will yet see your way to do justice."

While he maintains that British rule in its present form has made India "poorer in wealth, in manliness, in godliness and in her sons' power to defend themselves," he hopes that it can be altered. Even while he continues his campaign against British control, he is not opposed to the British connection. In the heyday of the non-co-operation movement he fought stoutly against the movement for complete severance from Britain.

While he was willing to work with the British as friends and equals, he was firm that no improvement in the Indian situation was possible so long as the British adopted an unnatural attitude of patronage and superiority. Let us remember that even in moments of the greatest excitement, he did not harbour ill-will to the British. " I will not hurt England or Germany to serve India."

When by some stupid or ill-conceived measure, such as the Amritsar massacre or the appointment of the Simon Commission, India lost patience and self-control and became aflame with wrath, Gandhi was there leading the discontent and indignation into safe channels of love and reconciliation. In the Round Table Conference, he showed his indelible affection for the British and his faith in a commonwealth based not on force but on reason, and the will to promote the general good of mankind. A halting measure of self-government in the provinces was the result of the Round Table Conferences and when the majority of the people were against the acceptance and working of the Constitution, it was Gandhi again, more than any other, who persuaded the Congress to work the reforms for what they were worth. His sole concern is peace with Britain, but peace rooted in freedom and friendship. India today is represented by a leader who has no trace of racial bitterness or personal rancour; he has no faith in the use of force and restrains his people from resorting to violence. He does not desire to separate India from the British Commonwealth if only it means a fellowship of free nations. His Majesty the King, in his speech to the Canadian Parliament on the 19th of May, said that the unity of the British Empire "finds expression today in the free association of nations enjoying common principles of government and a common attachment to the ideals of peace and freedom, bound together by a common allegiance to the Crown." Gandhi demands the application of these "common principles of government" to India. He claims that the Indians should be masters in their own house, and that is neither unreasonable nor immoral. He is keen on bringing about better relations between the two camps through the co-operation of men of good will.

It is tragic that his appeal avails no more than the whistling of the wind. After years of unwearied labour and heroic struggle, his great mission remains unfulfilled, though his vision and faith are still alive. For myself, I shall hope that British public opinion will assert itself and compel its Government to set up a free, self-governing India, without bartering or niggling, without hesitation or delay, with a fine, open gesture of faith, though it may involve a little risk: for I am persuaded that if it is not done in response to Gandhi's appeal for justice and fair play, the relations of our two countries will get worse, the breach will widen and bitterness grow to the detriment and danger of both.

Whether it is the South African Government or the British Government, whether it is the Indian mill-owners or the Hindu priests or the Indian princes who are the objects of Gandhi's criticism and attack, the underlying spirit is exactly the same in all these different activities. "I recognize no God except the God that is to be found in the hearts of the dumb millions. They do not recognize His presence: I do. And I worship the God that is Truth, or Truth which is God, through the service of these millions.[5]

IV. Satyagraha

"Ahimsa or non-violence is the highest duty" is a well-known saying of the Mahabharata. Its practical application in life is satyagraha or soul-force. It is based on the assumption that "the word rests on the bedrock of satya or truth. Asatya, meaning untruth, also means non-existent, and satya, or truth, means 'that which is'. If untruth does not so much as exist, its victory is out of the question. And truth is being 'that which is' can never be destroyed." God is the reality. The will to freedom and love is in accordance with reality. When man rejects this will for his own interests, he is rejecting himself. By this act of frustration, he is setting himself in opposition to reality, is isolating himself from it. This negation represents man's estrangement from himself, his denial of the truth about himself. It cannot be final or ultimate. It cannot destroy the real will. Reality cannot frustrate itself. "The gates of hell shall not prevail." God cannot be beaten. The meek shall inherit the earth and not the mighty who will lose themselves in the effort to save themselves, for they put their trust in unspiritual or unreal things like wealth and death-dealing weapons. Ultimately, men are ruled not by those who believe in wisdom and love, in inward and outward peace.

Satyagraha is rooted in the power of reality, in the inward strength of the soul. It is not merely the negative virtue of abstaining from violence, but the positive one of doing good.

5 Harijan, March 11, 1939.

"If I hit my adversary, that is of course violence; but to be truly non-violent, I must love him and pray for him even when he hits me." Love is unity and it comes into clash with evil which is separateness, getting, despising, hating, hurting and killing. Love does not acquiesce in evil, in wrongdoing, injustice or exploitation. It does not evade the issue but fearlessly faces the wrong-doer and resists his wrong with the overpowering force of love and suffering, for it is contrary to human nature to fight with force. Our conflicts are to be settled by human means of intelligence and good will, of love and service. In this confused world the one saving feature is the great adventure of being human. Creative life asserts itself in the midst of death. In spite of all this fear and gloom, humanity is practised by all, by the farmer and the weaver, by the artist and the philosopher, by the monk and the cloister and the scientist in the laboratory, and by all young and old, when they love and suffer. Life is immense. *Frano virat.*

The advocates of the use of force adopt a crude version of the Darwinian struggle for existence. They overlook the fundamental distinction between the animal and the human worlds and exalt a biological generalization into a doctrine of human destiny. If violent resistance is adopted in a world where it does not belong, human life is in danger of being degraded to the level of animal existence. In the *Mahabharata* the warring world of men is compared to a dog kennel. "First there comes the wagging of tails, then the bark, then the replying bark, then the turning of one round the other, then the show of teeth, then the roaring, and then comes the commencement of the fight. It is the same with men; there is no difference whatever."[6] Gandhi asks us to leave fighting to apes and dogs and behave like men and serve the right by quiet suffering. Love of self-suffering can overcome the enemy, not by destroying him but by changing him, for he is, after all, a person of like passions with ourselves.

---

6 Evam eva manusyesu viseso nasti kascana. V 72, 72-3

Gandhi's acts of repentance and self humiliation are full of moral courage and atoning sacrifice.

While a few individuals here and there tried to use the method of love in their personal lives, it is Gandhi's supreme achievement to have adopted it as a plan for social and political liberation. Under his leadership, organised groups in South Africa and India have used it on a large scale for the redress of grievances. Entirely abjuring the use of any physical violence for attaining political ends, he has developed this new technique in the history of political revolution, a technique which does not insure the spiritual tradition of India but arises out of it.

It has taken different forms of passive resistance, non-violent non-co-operation, and civil disobedience. Every one of them is based on hatred of the wrong and love for the wrongdoer. A satyagrahi is chivalrous to his opponents. The disobedience to law has always to be civil, and "civility does not mean the mere outward gentleness of speech cultivated for the occasion, but an inborn gentleness and desire to do the opponent good." In all his campaigns, whenever the enemy was in trouble, Gandhi went to his rescue. He condemns all attempts to use the enemy's need as one's opportunity. We should not strike a bargain with Britain when she is in trouble in Europe. During the war he wrote to the Viceroy of India; "If I could make my countrymen retrace their steps, I would make them withdraw all the Congress resolutions and not whisper 'Home rule' or 'Responsible government' during the tendency of the war." Even General Smuts felt the irresistible attraction of Gandhi's methods, and one of his secretaries said to Gandhi; "I do not like your people and I do not care to assist them at all. But what am I to do? You help us in our days of need. How can we lay hands upon you? I often wish that you took to violence like the English strikers and then we would know at once how to dispose of you. But you will not injure even the enemy. You desire victory by self-suffering alone and never transgress your self-imposed limits of courtesy and chivalry. And that is what reduces us to sheer helplessness."[7]

Twenty years after the war, to end war millions of men are again under arms, and in peace time, armies are mobilizing, fleets are covering the seas and aeroplanes are assembling in the sky. We know that war solves no problems but only makes their solution more difficult. Many Christian men and women are tormented by the arguments for and against war. The pacifist declares that war is a crime that disgraces humanity and there is no justification for defending civilization by the instruments of barbarism. We have no right to impose suffering on men and women with whom we have no quarrel. A nation engaged in war is inspired by a grim determination to defeat and destroy the enemy. It is swept by fear and the passion of hatred. We cannot rain death and destruction on a crowded city in a spirit of love and forgiveness. The whole method of war is one of engaging Satan to reprove Satan. It is contrary to the mind of the Jesus, his moral teaching and example. We cannot reconcile killing and Christianity.

The advocates of war argue that though war is a dreadful evil, on occasions, it becomes the lesser of two evils. Practical wisdom consists in a proper appreciation of relative values. We owe obligations to the social community and the State which is its organ. As members of a society, we derive protection of person and property, education and other advantages which give our lives value and interest. Naturally, our duty is to defend the State when it is attacked, to preserve the inheritance when it is threatened.

It is this line of argument that is presented to us when we are called upon to maim and kill, to wound and destroy people against whom we have no ill will. Nazi Germany contends that

---

7 Mahatma Gandhi - His Own Story, R 247

man's principal duty is membership of his State, and his reality, goodness and true freedom the furtherance of its ends. The State has the right to subordinate the happiness of individuals to its own greatness. The great virtue of war is that it kills man's longing, in the weakness of his flesh, for personal liberty. In his speech at the twentieth anniversary of the foundation of the Fascist Party, Mussolini said, "The order of the day is more ships, more guns and more aeroplanes at whatever cost and by whatever means, even if we have to wipe out completely what is called civilian life." "From prehistoric days one cry has been borne over the centuries, 'Woe to the unarmed.' "We desire that nothing more shall be heard of brotherhood, sisterhood, cousinhood or their bastard parenthoods because the relations between states are relations of force and these relations of force are the determining elements of our policy." Mussolini adds, "If the problem is considered on the claim of morality, nobody has the right to throw the first stone." Empire building is like a game of cards. Some Powers get a good hand and play it so well that others are nowhere. When all the profits are in the pocket they turn round and say that gambling is bad and assume an attitude of amazement that others wish to play the old game. It is not right to assume that the idols of race, power and armed force are worshipped only in Central Europe.

The Archbishop of Canterbury, in his speech in the House of Lords during the debate on the 20th of March, pleaded for "the massing of might on the side of the right." "We are driven to this," he argues, "because we are convinced that there are some things that are more sacred even than peace and that these things must be defended." "I cannot believe that it is against the will of Providence that nations should defend things which are so precious to civilization and human welfare." In Gandhi we have that rarest kind of religious man who could face a fanatical, patriotic assembly and say that he would, if he had to, sacrifice even India to the Truth. Gandhi says: "Most religious men I have met are politicians in disguise: I, however, who wear the guise of a politician, am at heart a religious man."

The aim of the religious individual is not to degrade the vision to the demands of the actual but to raise the actual to the pattern of the ideal. Our patriotic allegiances disrupt the spiritual unity of the human family and we maintain our loyalty to the larger community by refusing to engage in war and our loyalty to our State by defending it on religious and human ways. The religious at least, like the Apostles, "ought to obey God rather than men." Our trouble is that society in all countries is in the hands of people who believe in war as an instrument of policy and think of progress in terms of conquest.

Man, unless he is sadistic, is happy when he is gentle and merciful. There is joy in creation and misery in destruction. The common soldiers have no hatred for their enemies, but the ruling classes, by appealing to their fear, self-interest and pride, seduce them from their humanity. People, in whom rage and hatred are fictitiously produced, fight one another because they are simple men trained to obedience. Even then, they cannot put rancour in their killing. It is discipline that compels them to do what they hate. The ultimate responsibility lies with the Governments that are implacable and pitiless. They have imprisoned simple people and diminished their humanity. Men who delight in creation are drilled to form armies, navies and air fleets that are meant for destruction. We applaud murder and make mercy a thing of shame. We forbid the teaching of truth and command the spreading of lies. We rob both our own people and strangers of decency, of happiness and of life, and make ourselves responsible for mass murders and spiritual death.

We cannot have peace until all the nations treat each other in a mood of freedom and friendliness, until we develop a new conception of the integrated social life. The fate of civilization and humanity on this planet is bound up with that deep instinct

for the universal values of spirit, freedom, justice and love of
man which form the breath of Gandhi's being. In this violent
and distracted world, Gandhi's non-violence seems to be a
dream too beautiful to be true. For him, God is truth and love,
and God wishes us to be truthful and loving, regardless of
consequences. A truly religious man takes as much trouble to
discover what is right as the prudent man does to discover what
will pay, and he does it even if it means the surrender of his
dearest interests, individual, racial and national. Only those
who have emptied themselves of all selfishness, individual and
corporate, have the strength and the courage to say, "May my
interests perish, so Thy will be done." Gandhi does not admit
the possibility that love of God and of truth and fair dealing
can hurt anyone. He is certain that against the rock of moral
law the world's conquerors and exploiters hurl themselves
eventually to their own destruction. It is not even safe to be
immoral, for the will to power is self-defeating. When we talk
of "national welfare," we assume that we have an inviolate and
perpetual right to hold certain territories; and as for
"civilization" the world has seen a number of civilizations on
which the dust of ages has settled. The jungle has conquered
their cities and jackals howl there in the moonlight.

Considerations of "civilization" and "national welfare" are
irrelevant to the man of faith. Love is not a matter of policy or
calculation. To those who are persuaded by despair that there is
no remedy against the violence of the modern world but to
escape or destroy, Gandhi says that there is another within the
reach of us all, the principle of love which has upheld the spirit
of man through many tyrannies and will uphold it still. His
satyagraha may seem to be an ineffectual answer to the gigantic
displays of brute force but there is something more formidable
than force, the immortal spirit of man which will not be
subdued by noise or numbers. It will break all fetters which
tyrants seek to rivet on it. In an interview with a New York
Times correspondent who asked him in the March crisis for a

message to the world, Gandhi recommended simultaneous disarmament on the part of the democratic powers as the solution. "I am certain," he said, "as I am sitting here, that this would open Hitler's eyes and disarm him." The interviewer asked, "Would not that be a miracle?" Gandhi replied: "Perhaps. But it would save the world from the butchery which seems impending." "The hardest metal yields to sufficient heat; even so must the hardest heart melt before the sufficiency of the heat of non-violence. And there is no limit to the capacity of non-violence to generate heat."

During my half-century of experience I have not yet come across a situation when I had to say that I was helpless, that I had no remedy in terms of non-violence." Love is the law of human life, its natural necessity. We are approaching a state when this necessity would be manifest, for human life would be impossible if men were to evade and disobey this principle. We have wars simply because we are not sufficiently selfless for a life which does not need wars. The battle for peace must be fought in the heart of the individual. The spirit in him must break the power of pride and selfishness, lust and fear. A new way of life must become the foundation of national life as well as of world order, a way of life which will conserve and foster the true interests of all classes, races and nations. It is the freed men, who have liberated themselves from submission to the blind, selfish will of avidya, that can work for and establish peace. Peace is a positive demonstration in life and behaviour of certain universal principles and standards. We must fight for them by weapons which do not involve the debasement of moral values or the destruction of human life. In this effort we must be ready to endure whatever suffering comes our way.

In my travels in different parts of the world I have noted that Gandhi's reputation is more universal than that of the greatest statesmen and leaders of nation, and his personality more beloved and esteemed than any or all of them. His name is familiar to such a degree that there is scarcely a peasant or a

factory worker who does not consider him to be a friend of
human kind. They seem to think that he is likely to restore the
golden age. But we cannot summon it, as we would summon,
let us say, a passing cab. For we subject to a thing more
powerful than any nation, more humiliating than any conquest,
and that is ignorance. Though all our faculties are designed for
life, we have allowed them to be perverted in cause of death.
Though the right to happiness is clearly implicit in the creation
of humankind, we have allowed that right to be neglected and
suffered our energy to be used in the pursuit of power and
wealth by which the happiness of the many is sacrificed to the
doubtful satisfaction of a few. The world is in slavery to the
same error to which you and I are subject. We must strive, not
for wealth and power but for the establishment of love and
huminity. Freedom from error is the only true liberty.

Gandhi is the prophet of a liberated life-wielding power over
millions of human beings by virtue of his exceptional holiness
and heroism. There will always be some who will find in such
rare examples of sanctity, the note of strength and stark reality
which is missing in a life of general good will, conventional
morality or vague aesthetic affectation which is all that many
modern teachers have to offer. To be true, to be simple, to be
pure and gentle of heart, to remain cheerful and contented in
sorrow and danger, to love life and not to fear death, to serve
the Spirit and not to be haunted by the spirits of the dead,
nothing better has ever been taught or lived since the world
first began.

Mahatma Gandhi: An Estimate
Horace G. Alexander

It is not easy to give a just measure of a great man in his lifetime. And in some ways it is even harder if you know him personally. For you must stand a little way off if you are to see a man in true perspective. I have no wish to stand even at arm's length from Mahatma Gandhi. While he lives, I find it best to try, by following his thought from week to week in his paper Harijan, to keep as close to him as possible.

However, from time to time, one must necessarily face the questions which the world asks about him, and try to answer them: and I suppose one main purpose of this volume is to show what impression he makes on some of his contemporaries.

So having made this brief apology, I will try to say how I see him in the setting of our modern world.

Our age has witnessed the revolt of the disinherited in many countries and in varied forms. The trade union movement and various brands of Socialism have proclaimed the rights of the industrial workers all over the West. Perhaps the International Labour Organization marks one first culmination of this struggle. But in Russia, it has taken another great stride: there, the industrial worker is no longer just a man to be reckoned with, one who may turn round and bite you if you treat him

too harshly; he is exalted to a specially privileged position.
Neither the I.L.O. nor the Soviet quite forgets other classes of
workers: the overworked shop assistant, the poor peasant, the
fisherman and others: but what they have done for these has
been done more or less as an afterthought.

In Germany it was not the orthodox socialists or the industrial
workers who achieved a major revolution. Another party,
clever or perhaps less scrupulous, discovered how to win the
support of another great section of the population: the *petit
bourgeoisie*. They too, were in despair: their savings having
vanished in the inflation, they were crushed between the greater
Powers above and below. If there was one class more than
another that gave Hitler the victory, it was this class of the *petit
bourgeois* – *too* often forgotten or despised by the disciples of
Karl Marx.

But Gandhi from India challenges all these Western
revolutions: industrial workers, *petit bourgeois*, intellectuals,
property-owners all these groups who are competing for power
in the West tend to forget the fundamental fact that man must
eat. He cannot eat machines; he cannot eat trade; he cannot eat
school-books; he cannot eat dividends. All those things man
can live without. He cannot do without his daily bread or rice.
And for this daily food, which civilized, urbanized man accepts
so much as a matter of course, he is dependent finally on the
hundreds of millions of silent, often semi-starved peasants or
farmers in India, in China, in East Europe, in Canada, in the
Argentine, in tropical Africa. In all these lands, the peasant or
the farmer still struggles year by year to use sun and wind and
rain (and how often they turn to mock him!) to produce the
food by which man lives. They have gone on doing this,
generation after generation, for thousands of years, while wars
and revolutions have passed over them, destroying the fruits of
their labour for the time being, just as drought and flood
destroy. And now at last they have found a voice: Mahatma
Gandhi.

Among all the millions of Indian people, it is hardly possible to find one who does not know the name of Gandhi. Even among the hill tribes or aboriginals, this friend and champion of the poor is known and loved.

Although he was trained to be a lawyer, he has become a peasant again: not only in his outward life, wearing the simple dress of a peasant, living in a remote and backward and stolidly conservative village that refuses to be cleansed and modernized even by a Mahatma; but even more in his heart and mind. He sees the world with the eyes of a peasant, shrewd, blunt, straightforward, sometimes a little rough, humorous, kindly, patient, and withal deeply religious, seeing life as a whole, aware that unseen powers are at work in ways that we cannot comprehend, though we can often sense and even apprehend them if we are willing to be silent and listen.

I shall never forget the words that Mr. Gandhi said to me when, after travelling for six months in India, I first visited him at Sabarmati in the spring of 1928. "What," I asked him, "shall I say when I get home to England?" "You must tell the English people," he replied "to get off our backs." Consider how much this means, not only of the end to be achieved but also of the way in which it can be achieved.

For it is not only the end he has in view that distinguishes Mr. Gandhi from the other revolutionary leaders of our age. Perhaps even more important are the means he adopts for that end. In his little book, *Hind Swaraj*, written in 1908, before he had taken any active part in Indian affairs, he wrote: "Kings will always use their kingly weapons. To use force is bred in them...

Peasants have never been subdued by the sword, and never will be. They do not know the use of the sword, and they are not frightened by the use of it by others." Therefore, the peasant swaraj, the peasant rule, or peasant freedom, which is Gandhi's aim, must be achieved by means consonant with the end in view. Those who aim to become rulers of men use the sword. It is the weapon of every governing class. And when Socialists or Communists or Nazis or Fascists set out to destroy the "ruling class" by using its own weapons, their success merely replaces one governing class by another. Instead of the sword remaining in the hands of the land-owning or bank-owning or factory-owning class, it passes to members of the Communist party, the Fascist party or the Nazi party. The ordinary citizen is still trampled on. A new governing order climbs on to the backs of the people.

But Gandhi wants to remove the burden of a ruling caste or class from the backs of the peasants once for all, not to push the present rulers off in order that his friends may climb up. So he has spent his life in forging a weapon that can be used by all, the physically weak as well as the physically strong. By learning from him, they learn to stand upright on their own feet, no longer bent down under great burdens.

Instead of climbing on to the people's back in order to push the other man off, says Gandhi, you must refuse to help him in any way while he remains where he is. And so, in the end, he must climb down. All his props and supports have gone. He may threaten you with every kind of punishment if you do not continue to support him. He may carry out his threats. But if you have learnt to laugh at imprisonment and death, his threats and even his sword will not move you. He cannot coerce you into action which your conscience tells you is wrong.

There are, of course, immense difficulties to be overcome before this non-violent method of action can be effectively applied. Difficult as it is to drill soldiers to stand up to machine-gun fire, even when they are free to shoot back, it is far harder to drill men to accept every kind of violence without defending themselves. Mr. Gandhi declared thirty years ago that passive resisters (or, as he would now call them, satyagrahis, those who use soul force instead of brute force) must be able "to observe perfect chastity, adopt poverty, follow truth, and cultivate fearlessness." There have been men and women in every age who have learnt the secret of this unconquerable, non-violent life. To read the letters written recently by German evangelical pastors from prison and concentration camp proves that such a character can still be developed in the West as well as in the East. If or when it can be found in multitudes, the true freedom of man, the true community of man, will be in sight.

It is noteworthy, too, that Gandhi, who relies on this tremendous self-discipline in his soldiers of peace and freedom, does not talk about "the masses". When you are thinking in terms of cannon-fodder, whether for empirebuilding or for revolution, you naturally lump human beings into an inhuman "mass". But to Gandhi, each one of "teeming millions" is an individual man or woman, with a personality as sacred as his own. He knows how to make friends with the most ignorant peasant as sincerely as with a man of his own educational level. To him, no man or woman is common or unclean. This is not a beautiful theory that he preaches: it is his daily practice.

In an age when violence has been given a fresh lease of life, when the only hope of man in the West seems to be in the "collective security" of a greater armament than the most determined aggressor can produce; when even an archbishop can only suggest that "might must be massed on the side of right" as the first step towards ultimate peace, we have before our eyes – if only we would open them and see – one man, of slender physique, precarious health and no outstanding abilities, who is demonstrating in his own life and in the magic power he exerts among his fellow-Indians, that the human spirit, when lit by a divine fire, is stronger than the mightiest armament.

The meek can still inherit the earth, if only they have faith in their meekness; if only they will cast out the fear of Hitler or of

Stalin, and look for their hope to the greatest teacher of our
age.

The Tribute of a Friend
C. F. Andrews

My aim, in this article, will be threefold. First of all, I shall try
to draw a rapid outline of the deeper religious aspect of
Mahatma Gandhi's character. In the second place, the more
directly human side of his personality will be brought into the
picture. Thirdly, a brief sketch will be given of what I regard as
the two most original contributions which he has made to the
progress of mankind in the modern age.

I

There are certain cardinal religious virtues whereon Mahatma
Gandhi lays most stress. He holds that through them an
abiding work may be done in this world by mortal man in the
fear of God.

The first is called *Satya-Truth*. This, with him, is a diving
quality, which must be made manifest, not only in word and
deed, but also in the secret chambers of the soul. Merely to
speak no falsehood is not enough, though it is an essential part
of truthfulness. The fountain-head of all truth, with him, lies in
the heart.

How great and profound is Truth may be seen from the fact
that he uses the word "Satya" for his impersonal name of God,
He constantly utters the formula, "Truth is God, and God is
Truth." And it is made clear from his daily life how fervently he
worships Truth. To swerve, in however small a degree, from
Truth, is to be cut off thus far from the divine source and as a
necessary consequence to wither away spiritually. It is to walk

in darkness instead of in the light. The daily prayer,

> *Lead me from untruth to truth,*
> *Lead me from darkness to light,*
> *Lead me from death to immortality,*

expresses this in threefold manner. Light and darkness, immortality and spiritual death, are but other aspects of this fundamental distinction between Truth and Untruth.

The second virtue which has its source in God is Ahimsa. This word may be literally translated "harmlessness," but it means for Mahatma Gandhi much more than that. It implies the positive quality of doing good. It connotes, in relation to war and bloodshed, active refusal to take part; but it also represents the will to suffer to the uttermost in order to win over those who have done us evil. In its essence, it is God's own Nature, just as Truth is. One of the most ancient and sacred texts is *Ahimsa Paramo Dharmah* – "Ahimsa is the supreme religious duty." Therefore Mahatma Gandhi spends his whole life in exploring the possibilities of this supreme religious duty and harmonizing it completely with Satya – Truth. For Ahimsa does not merely imply passive resistance in the face of untruth, but rather its active condemnation – yet without anger, malice, or violence.

The third cardinal virtue on which Mahatma Gandhi lays the greatest stress in Brahmacharya – Chastity. He points out that the very name, in Sanskrit, is derived from the word "Brahma" which means God. He holds, along with much that is very ancient in Hinduism, that by a suppression of the sex function and then its sublimation, a spiritual energy is generated which becomes a divine power, wonderful in its potency. The true follower of Satya and Ahimsa must also be a Brahmachari, i.e. one who practises complete bodily chastity. Even marriage itself is regarded by Mahatma Gandhi as a concession to human weakness. To put this in other words, complete abstinence from the sex act, together with the elimination of any thought about it, is regarded by him as one of the highest forms of spiritual life which man or woman in this world can attain. Here I cannot help feeling that the ascetic principle which is so strong in him, has carried him too far, just as I cannot understand his fasting without any limit until the object of his fast is achieved. There is something that repels me here, and I have often told him about it.

Mahatma Gandhi is essentially a man of religion. He can never think of any complete release from evil apart from God's grace. Prayer is, therefore, of the essence of all his work. The very first requirement of one who is a Satyagrahi – a striver after Truth – is faith in God, whose nature is Truth and Love. I have seen the whole course of his life changed in a few moments in obedience to an inner call from God which came to him in silent prayer. There is a voice that speaks to him, at supreme moments, with an irresistible assurance; and no power on earth can shake him when this call has come home to his mind and will as the voice of God.

More and more he finds the fullest confirmation of what he holds to be the pathway of the spiritual life in reading the Gita, which is a part of his daily act of public worship.

If I have judged him alright from long and intimate experience, there is always something of the Puritan present in his thoughts of God-"as ever in the Great Task-master's eye."

II

Let us now turn to the human side. Here there are touches which are very tender and lovable, and these should always be placed side by side with the austerity that I have pictured above.

Many years ago I had been deeply impressed by the insight of the great writer Romain Rolland, who had described Mahatma Gandhi as the "St. Paul of our own days." This seemed to me to contain an important truth; for Gandhi, like Paul, comes clearly under the category of the twice-born among men of religion. He experienced at a special moment in his life that tremendous convulsion of the human spirit, which we call "conversion". In his early days, he had followed a career at the Bar as a lawyer with great ardour. Success had been a main ambition – success in his profession; success in life as a man; and deeper down in his heart, success as a national leader.

He had gone out to South Africa on a business visit to act as lawyer in an important trial, wherein two Indian merchants were engaged in litigation. Hitherto, he had only a distant knowledge of the colour bar and had never considered what it might mean to himself if he was personally attacked and insulted. But as he journeyed from Durban and reached Maritzburg, this dreadful experience came to him suddenly in all its cruel nakedness. He was thrown out of his compartment by the railway official, though he carried a first-class ticket; and the mail train went on without him. It was late at night and he was in an utterly strange railway station, knowing no one. There, all night long, as he sat shivering with cold, after enduring this insult, he wrestled within himself, whether to take the next steamer back to India, or to go through to the bitter end, suffering what his own people had to suffer. Before the morning, the light came to his soul. He determined by God's grace to play the man. More humiliations were soon to be heaped upon him of the same character and in South Africa he was never without them. But he had put his hand to the plough and he would never turn back.

I heard him tell the story of that night to Dr. Mott last November. He made clear, as he told it, that this was the turning-point from which his own new life began.

There are other qualities in Mahatma Gandhi that have their counterpart in the rugged figure of the Apostle Paul – a faith in God that will never allow him to yield to man; a sense of the black horror of sin, especially sins of the flesh; a severity towards those whom he loves most dearly, lest 'they should fall short of his own earnest longing for them, and yet withal a pathetic tenderness of heart whichmakes him long for a touch of human sympathy whenever he is misunderstood.

There is also something more in him which comes near to St. Francis of Assisi, for Gandhi also has taken Poverty as his bride. He might truly be called today " the Little Poor Man of Segaon". For he lives there, among the depressed and poor villagers, sharing their burdens with them. On two occasions I have seen him when this likeness to St. Francis became luminously clear to me.

The former of these was in the still afterglow of a dark evening twilight at the Asram (retreat) called Phoenix, near Durban. The strain of a long day of unwearied ministry among the poor was over, and Mahatma Gandhi was seated under the open sky, tired almost beyond human endurance, but even at such a time he nursed a sick child on his lap who clung to him with a pathetic affection. A Zulu girl from the school on the hill beyond the Ashram was seated there also. He asked me to sing "Lead kindly Light" as the darkness grew deeper and deeper. Even then, though he was much younger, his frail body was worn with suffering that could never be laid aside even for a moment: yet his spirit within was radiant when the hymn broke the silence, with its solemn close.

> *And with the morn those angel faces smile,*
> *Which I have loved long since and lost a while.*

I can remember how we all sat in silence when the hymn was finished, and how he then repeated to himself those two lines which I have quoted. The other scene was in Orissa, near to the place where I am now writing. He had been very near to death; for a sudden and complete exhaustion had come over him and his blood pressure had mounted perilously high. On receiving a telegram, I had travelled all through the night to be at his side.

When I reached him, he lay there facing the sunrise after a restless night. A man from one of the lowest grades of the untouchables suddenly drew near to him in supplication just as we began our talk. In a moment his own sickness seemed to have vanished and his whole heart was torn with agony by the cruel humiliation which had reduced the man who prostrated himself before us almost to a sub-human level.

III

The two things whereby Mahatma Gandhi's name will live, hundreds of years hence, are (1) his khaddar programme, and (2) his practice of Satyagraha.

(1) He has been the first in this modern, machine age, to revive among the agricultural people of the world, on a vast scale, the practice of village industries. He had set it forward as a means of giving employment to millions of people during those seasons of the year when it is impossible for them to work in the fields and agricultural work is at a standstill. In India, this unemployment period extends to four or five months every year. In the Old days, when there was no power machinery, hand-spinning and weaving and other village industries used to occupy the time of each member of the family down to the very youngest, and very durable fabric, for everyday use, was spun and woven.

It would not be wrong to say that half, at least, of the human race has been reduced to this condition of seasonal unemployment chiefly owing to the influx of machine-made cloth, which, by its cheapness, has very gradually destroyed the home-made village industries.

Gandhi has been the first to have a burning faith that a revival of cottage industries of all kinds is still possible whereby the villagers themselves may be saved from moral as well as physical starvation. He had been able to spread in millions of human minds a new hope in this direction. His genius has not merely touched India. Already in China, under the stress of war, the peasants have started once more to grow cotton and spin and weave it into cloth. It is also quite possible that in the long, dark evenings of the winter, in the sub-arctic regions in Canada and elsewhere, similar cottage industries may be revived.

(2) By his supremely original and personal advocacy of Ahimsa, he has shown to the world that it is possible today to overcome even the violence of war by the purely voluntary suffering of corporate moral resistance called Satyagraha. In South Africa, he was triumphantly successful in this direction. General Smuts gave him all the terms he asked for, after he had led his "ragged army" of civil resisters across the Drakensberg mountains into the Transvaal. General Smuts acknowledged that such a method of moral warfare, waged without weapons of violence, was irresistible.

It is not possible to deal at length with these great subjects at the end of this paper, but others are likely to write more in this volume. Let me conclude by going back to the analogy of St. Francis that I have already mentioned. He too wore, as his daily robe, the rough home-spun of the village people. Thus in his own times, he brought the home-spun back into honour and repute before the eyes of men. St. Francis also went weaponless and ready to suffer into the armed ranks of the Saracens in order to bring peace to the warring armies by his message of suffering love. The same ideas, therefore, were in the heart of St. Francis which Mahatma Gandhi cherishes. They were thus kindred spirits. But now Mahatma Gandhi has gone further still, and his two greatest "experiments with Truth" (as he would rightly call them) of khaddar and Satyagraha have been taken up into the corporate life of mankind. They have already been put into practice on a scale never known before in human history. In this way, he has been more than any other

personality now living, a herald of peace and goodwill to
mankind.

The Essence of Gandhiji
George S. Arundale

I feel it a privilege to be asked to participate in a volume
commemorating Mr. Gandhi's attainment of his seventieth
birthday. Of course, no volume can commemorate his great and
unique services to India. Even the people of India today cannot
commemorate these. Only posterity can judge, unbiased by the
times in which Mr. Gandhi now lives. But a volume such as this
can usefully appraise various aspects of his faithfulness, even
though it be the work of his contemporaries.

For my own part, three qualities are outstanding in his life
such as I have watched it – first and most important of all, his
pure simplicity; second, his direct and keen appreciation of his
own fundamentals; third, his absolutely un-assuming
fearlessness.

There he is, wherever he is, leading a simple ordered life such
as all can live, howsoever they may be circumstanced. He lives
with the blazing light of fame ever shining upon him. In the
very midst of the glare, he lives as most of us would do well to
live. His soul is bare to the world. His habits are ever the same.
And he knows how to use the power of the Silence, as few of
the rest of us know how to use it.

His life is an example that can be followed in its details of
everydayness, for it reduces the fussy complexities of the world
into their original God-given simplicities, whereby alone shall
happiness and prosperity become restored to the human and
sub-human family.

I do not for a moment suggest we should follow the letter of his living, but I do insist that we might do well to follow the spirit of it.

Then he does somehow manage to show a way to light out of darkness. He sees where a light is, and points to it. And even if some of us be unable to see that particular light, at least we see his light; and the light of another, however different from our own, helps us to find our own. After all, there is but one light, even though each one of us brings different changes upon it.

Some of the light he sheds I am unable to use. I should look elsewhere for the laying of many of my own emphasis. But his emphasis help me to discover my own emphasis. So am I thankful for his direct and keen appreciation of his own fundamentals; for one who follows his own fundamentals, as Gandhiji follows his, wonderfully stimulates others to follow their own, possibly entirely different, fundamentals. It is not opinion that matters so much, however learned, but crystal-clear sincerity.

Finally, his what I should almost like to term casual fearlessness. I like it all the more for its casualness. There is no tremendous preparation, no girding-up of joins – he would not have much to gird up in any case – no ceremonial vigils, no tamasha of any kind. An occasion of fearlessness arises, and in instant response, the light of his fearlessness shines forth.

And what I honour most is the fact that he does not raise a great cry and summon multitudes to follow him. He may make an announcement as to the form a particular fearlessness shall take-in any case he is thinking only of something that has to be done, and that he can do no other, just as Martin Luther declared that he could do no other than that which he did, and had to do. And then Gandhiji goes ahead. If anyone follows, well and good. If nobody follows, then also well and good. So often is it true that he who knows how to go alone, which is, to say, goes alone when there are none to follow because he must go at all costs, has many more victories to his credit than he who must organize a movement before he can set going a cause.

Gandhiji's nature is to be fearless, so his fearlessness is natural. And because it is natural, it is gracious, it is chivalrous to all who are in his way, it is fearlessness which makes friends and not foes, which makes peace and not war.

I have not tried to appraise Gandhiji's political theories and activities. To tell the truth I care little what they are. After all, they are more means than ends. And I might well conceive it my duty-rightly or wrongly conceived, who can tell? – actively to oppose one or more of them in honour of my own sincerities. What I value most in anyone is his sincerity, his devotion, his courage, his selflessness, his indifference to praise or blame or to public opinion, his harmlessness, his brotherliness. He who gives these to the world gives to it infinitely more than those who give laws and schemes, doctrine and dogmas.

We need in the world today men and women afire with the spirit of universal brotherhood, afire with the nobility of their simple natures, afire with the compelling urge of ideals which mean far more to them than even fire itself. They may be right or they may be wrong. But their hearts are even beating to the mighty rhythm of Compassion. Such a man is Gandhi. Need more be said?

Gandhi, As Bridge and Reconciler
Ernest Barker

I have two memories of Mr. Gandhi. The first is of a night in November 1931, when he stayed at my house during a visit to England, at the time of the Round Table Conference. The second is of a sunny morning in the middle of December 1937, when I was driven by an Indian friend to call on him at a villa by the sea, a little to the north of Bombay, where he was recuperating from an illness under the rustle of tall palm trees.

I have vivid recollections of his visit to Cambridge. I joined with him and Miss Slade at prayers in his room; and he came down to our sitting-room, after his evening meal, and talked with us as he turned his spinning-wheel. Some of our talk was about simple things (I remember his being interested in what I had to say about the place of football in English life, and about the curious social division between the Rugby and the Association game); but we went, in the main, into deeper issues. One of our themes was Plato. I thought that he had a Platonic feeling that governing and administrative persons should live on a simple pittance, content with the opportunity of service, and not expecting great rewards. I tried to argue that government had to carry prestige, and that in order to carry prestige it must be surrounded by a certain amount of pomp and circumstance. I do not remember that we reached any agreement; but I know that I felt that I was arguing on a lower plane. Another theme which I particularly remember was the theme of the defence of India. I was arguing that peace had to be kept; that the threat of invasion or of marauding bands had to be met; that this entailed a defence force; and that, for the time being, this defence force should be guaranteed its necessary expenses, and not be made dependent on the recurrent votes, which might be adverse or at any rate exiguous, of an Indian assembly. Mr. Gandhi used a metaphor in reply. "Imagine," he said, "a village which suffers from the depredations of the animals of the jungle. A benevolent authority offers to erect a great wall of defence around the village, to secure the lives and property of the villagers. But the villagers find that the cost of the wall entails a grinding taxation which depresses their life so low that it is hardly worth living. Would they not say, 'Better the risk of the depredations, which we well know, than the certainty of a standard of life which is below our capacity of endurance?"

The two themes of which we spoke brought home to me two of the lessons which Mr. Gandhi has taught-the lesson of love, and of service rendered in love and the lesson of non-violence. I knew that I was face to face with a prophet; but I found that I could not surrender the instincts of a north-country Englishman (perhaps they are the instincts of any Englishman) – the instinct which suggests that good service deserves good payment; and is promoted by good payment the instinct which suggests that peace and order involve a struggle against war and disorder, and have to be maintained by efforts for their defence. But I could not surrender my instincts, I had to recognize the presence of something higher than my instincts – if only men were ready for its acceptance.(Perhaps if one could believe that they were ready, and could get others to agree with one's belief, they would be ready. I admitted that; but I found it difficult to summon up my own belief to the point.) After Mr. Gandhi went away, I fell to thinking about the different elements that met in him. There was the St. Francis, vowed to the simple life of poverty, in harmony with all creation and in love with all created things. There was the St. Thomas Aquinas, the thinker and the philosopher, able to sustain high argument and to follow the subtleties of thought in all their windings. There was also the practical man of affairs, with a legal training to back and strengthen his sense for affairs – the man who could come down from mountain tops to guide with shrewd advice transactions in the valley. We are all of us complicated; and Mr. Gandhi seemed to me more complicated than most of us are. He had a rich and intricate personality. It would have been a simple thing if he had just been a St. Francis. But would it have been as good a thing, or a thing so useful and so serviceable to his fellow-countrymen and the world? When I thought about the matter, I was inclined to say "No". The mixture was the essence. What he was to the world, and what he could do for the world, depended on his being more things than one.

That leads me to the final and fundamental thing which I

should desire to say. I have spoken of the St. Francis and the St.
Thomas mixed with the man of practical affairs and legal
training. I might have said, more accurately and more justly,
that the mixture was one between a great Indian tradition of
devout and philosophic religion and the Western tradition of
civil and political liberty in the life of the community. Because
there has been this mixture. Mr. Gandhi has been a great
bridge. He has been able to commend politics to his fellow-
countrymen in no secular form, and with no divorce from their
mere religious tradition; he has been able to commend himself,
and the cause of his country, to the British people, as something
far beyond the stature of a political agitator or a matter of
political agitation. Nor is it merely to his fellow-countrymen,
or to the British people, that he has presented himself as a
bridge and a reconciler. He has caught the attention and
focussed the interest of the Western peoples at large. One who
could mix a spiritual and temporal devotion, without injury to
either, could not but be a great and arresting figure of our days.

I should therefore celebrate in Mr. Gandhi the man who could
mix the spiritual with the temporal, and could be at the same
time true to both. I should also celebrate the man who could be
a bridge between the East and the West, and thereby could
render to the cause of international understanding. Nor can I
forget the man who could understand, and proclaim, the
homely and intimate necessities of his country's life. His
spinning wheel is a symbol of that understanding. To visit an
Indian village (and India is a continent of villages) is to see the
crying need of the villagers for a fuller life and a wider
engagement of faculties. If industry can be brought into
the villages (and not merely established in the cotton
mills round Bombay and the jute mills north of Calcutta), it
will be the redemption of the villages, and since the villages are
the vastly preponderant part of India, the redemption of
India-on the plane of secular economic life. It will always be
counted as one of the great services of Mr. Gandhi that

he laboured at that redemption.

These are the thoughts that come to me, from what I have seen or read or heard. I wish that I knew more. But, on such knowledge as I have, I should say that Mr. Gandhi had laboured to teach his countrymen, and had helped to teach the world at large, three things – to work in love, and for love; to work without violence; and to work with the hands, and not merely with the brain, for the building of a full life which fully engages the faculties.

"A Light upon His Name"
Laurence Binyon

I know but little of India except through her art. And since I feel that without studying her political problems at first hand in the country itself, one cannot form a judgment of any value upon the thorny tangle they seem to present, I could not presume to say anything of Mr. Gandhi's political career. I dare say that I might not be able to follow him in the details of his policy; but in a time which history will surely record as in many ways a disgrace to mankind, I feel more strongly every day that it is the things of the mind and the things of the spirit and what flows from them into the active life, that matter more than anything for this shaken and distracted world; it is for these central, permanent things that, as I conceive, Mr. Gandhi stands, and because of this there is a light upon his name.

"A Way of Living"
Mrs. Pearl S. Buck

The name of Gandhi, even in his lifetime, has passed beyond the meaning of an individual to the meaning of a way of living in our troubled modern world. In the midst of unrestrained and evil force, what for me has been of the greatest significance is the reaffirmation of this way of living. I am glad to be able to say here, upon this page, that Mr. Gandhi's steady persistence in his chosen way has given me, among millions of others, courage to resist, by that greatest of all resistances, unconquerable, unwavering personal determination, the growth of tyranny in the world. I send my thanks, and my fullest appreciation.

Mahatma
Ananda K. Coomaraswamy

The term "Mahatma" has been much abused, but has precise and intelligible meanings and a long history. Like many other of the technical terms of Indian metaphysics, the word has acquired vague or sentimental connotations; partly because in our general ignorance of all traditional philosophy and even of Christian theology we are no longer able to distinguish spirit from soul or essence from existence; and still more because of the absolute values we mistakenly attach to our boasted "personality," or rather, individuality, and consequent worship of "genius," in which we see much rather a deified humanity than the operation of an impersonal Spirit. It is with these preoccupations that we think of "Mahatma" as meaning a "Great Man" or "Great Soul," rather than one who is "in the spirit," and more than man.

At a point already far removed from the beginning we find in a Buddhist Sutra (A.I.249) the distinction drawn between the "great" and "petty" selves, *mahatma and alpatma;*[8] in another passage these "selves" of a man are distinguished as "fair" and

---

8 To make it easier for the reader, I have given all Pali words in their Sanskrit form.

"foul" (*kalyana, papa*). The foul or petty self is the composite of psycho-physical factors by which a man can be referred to as this man so-and-so and, as such, corresponds, to all that is elsewhere defined as *anatma* (not very self) and of which it is so constantly affirmed that "that is not my Self' (*na mama so atma*). The way of this petty self is mean and painful (*alpa-duhkhavihari*), it is "underdeveloped in stature, character, will and prescience." The little self is in all respects casually determined; whatever it does or wills is predetermined by what has been done or willed in a beginningless heredity of "former habitations": "we" can neither be what or as or when we will, but only what we are. The little self is mortal, subject in life to inveteracy and sickness, and destroyed without residue at the natural term of life. Our other and Eminent Self, the Mahatma, can hardly be described except in terms which are negations of all the limiting definitions by which the little self is circumscribed. In terms of our first text, a man can be thought of as "Mahatma" who is "of developed stature, character, will and prescience, un-emptied-out, and to whose way there are no boundaries" (*bhavita-kaya silacitta, -prajna, aprarikta mahatma apramana-vihari*).

The whole distinction corresponds to that of person from animal man (*purusu from pasu*) in AA. II. 3.2; to that of those who have not found the self and for whom there is therefore no motion-at-will here or hereafter from those who have found the Self and are therefore movers-at-will whether here or hereafter in CU. VIII. 1.6; to the Confucian distinction of the "Princely Sage" (*chuntzu*) from the "petty man" (*hsiao jên*); and to St. Bernard's distinction of *proprium* from *esse*. These two "selves" are again the "lives" (*anima psyche*) of John xii.25, "He that loveth his life shall lose it," one of these selves being that "life" that a man must hate if he would be "my disciple" (Luke xiv.26), the "ego" of St. Paul's *viva autem, jam non ego,* "I live; yet not 'I'" (Gal.ii.20). In "Whosoever will lose his life for my sake" (Luke ix.24) this same psyche to be lost corresponds to all that is implied by *"psyche"* in our word "psychology." To have found the *atman* is to have ceased to be anyone.

In *mahatma, maha* is simply "great," "eminent", and *atman*, like Greek *pneuma*, primarily "spirit" (as distinguished from soul and body). But because the spirit is the real being of the man, as distinguished from the accidents of this being, its temporal manifestation as so-and-so characterized by particular qualities and properties, *atman* in reflexive usage acquires the secondary value "self," whatever physical (*hylic*), psychic or spiritual (*pneumatic*) self we may intend. It is precisely at this point that the fundamental significance of the traditional and so often repeated injunction, "Know thyself," emerges, for we have "forgotten what we are," and taking pride in being "someone," are of those to whom the words of the Song of Songs, "If thou knowest not thyself, depart," can be applied. The answer to the question "Who art thou?" is the password demanded at the Gate: it is only to those who can answer in accordance with the "That art thou" of the Upanishads that the welcome will be extended, "Come in, O myself'; none who answers by a personal or family name is admitted. The condition of deification is an eradication of all otherness.

The term Mahatma as name of God, and as a designation of the state of being that can be verified only by the man who is altogether emancipated from himself is one, or one and many (CU, VII.26. 2; SB. X. 5. 2. 17) in distinction without difference, fusion without confusion. The Mahatma is the "Great Unborn Spirit" (*mahan aja atma*, BU. IV. 4. 22; *atma mahan*, KU. III. 10), the Supernal Sun (MU. VII. 11.6), the Spiritual-Essence of all that is (RV. I. 115. 1). The Great Self is the only witness, agent and knower, at the same time immanent and transcendent. To have found Him is to have abandoned all the peripheries of our existence and returned to its centre of being. Hinduism and Buddhism affirm, what is not denied in Christianity, the possibility of the attainment of perfection here and now; as must be, because the state of perfection cannot itself be connected with time. In "That art thou," the present tense is absolute; it is not the truth, but its verification that has to do with time. When the verification has been made, the relation of "individual" spirits to the spiritual Deity is that of rays to the source of illumination from or into which they can pass in or out at will. To have become such a ray of the Light of Lights is divine filiation, for the Sun's rays are his offspring.

To call a man Mahatma is then to say that he has been liberated in this life (*jivan mukta*, corresponding to the Buddhist *drste dharme vimukta*) or in some life. It is thus that the word is used in BG., e.g. VIII. 15, "these Mahatmas that have come to Me, never again return to birth, to this temporal abode of ill, they have reached the last fulfilment," and IX, 13, "Mahatmas, devoted unto Me with single mind, knowing Me the unchanging source of all beings, that have taken on the nature of God"; Krishna, the speaker, being himself the immanent Spirit (ibid., X. 20).

Our object in the present article has been to explain the word Mahatma historically. The name has been given to Gandhiji by common consent, perhaps in the general sense of "Saint". There can be no doubt that in some of its connotations, that of selflessness (with a higher sense than that of a mere unselflessness), for example, it can be properly applied to him. But we have not had in mind to discuss the applicability of the term in its full meaning to any individual for that must ever remain a secret between himself and God.

Gandhi and the Congress
Bhagavan Das

The tempestuous history of mankind during the first four decades, now closing, of the twentieth century after Christ is written around a score or so of names. Less than half of the bearers of these names are alive today. Mahatma Gandhi is not only one of these, but he is unique, *sui generis*, even among these; because he is the solitary apostle of non-violent spirituality in politics and economics. One cannot readily think of another greater or even equal moral force in Indian history since the Buddha. When the "present" has become the "past," and the overwhelming importance which the "present" always possesses has shrunk into due proportions, it is possible that the future historian may be able to mention names comparable with his; comparable on the whole, taking into account the very different settings and purposes of the different periods. Today, Mahatma Gandhi's personality stands out unique.

Naturally, therefore, the admiration with which he has inspired me is very great. I feel a great reverence also for his quality of *tapas*, his internal fire and fervour, ascetic purity, intensity of aspiration and resolve, mortification and subjugation of the flesh (all which is meant by *tapas*): such *sattvika*, refined "mortification and subjugation" as is known to ancient Indian, and also early and medieval Christian, and later Muslim, religious tradition; because that *tapas* is ennobled, rationalized, sanctified by the single-minded and unremitting employment of the soulforce, *atma-bala*, won by it, to the uplifting of India.

Thus, then, I feel great admiration for Mahatma Gandhi's marvellous political leadership of India; deep reverence for his ascetic purity and benevolence to all: and admiration as well as reverence for that astonishing self-control, that deliberate, premeditated, perpetual "self-guidance," *dhira-ta* (*dhiyam irayati*), which compels one to say of all his public actions, in all the powerfully "dramatic" situations, the trials and tribulations, which are always arising around him and for him, that

He ne'er did sordid thing or mean
On any memorable scene.

His unfailing dignity and courtesy, repose of soul, tireless activity of mind and body in the service of India, according to his inner lights-these have commanded the admiration of his greatest adversaries and often induced them to accede to his wishes.

Feeling thus, it seems to me desirable that I should not content myself with offering merely a handful of flowers on this occasion. Of such, Mahatma Gandhi may perhaps have become tired by this time. I shall, therefore, venture to record some critical observations, such as I have been placing (together with some suggestions) before him and the Indian people from time to time during the last fifteen years and more, in connection with his great work. The observations which I wish to make, in connection with the survey of Mahatma Gandhi's re-vitalization of India, are all based on traditional ancient wisdom, and do not proceed from any presumptious notion of my own superior intelligence.

The world-situation in general and the Indian situation in particular

The human world came out of a four years' terrible purgatory in 1918. But, unchastened, it is again reeling on the brink of the hell of Armageddon. Spain has been devastated by civil war which has ended with the victory of Fascism and Franco. China is fighting Japan in a life-and-death struggle. India, subjugated, impoverished, despiritualized, is engaged in a non-violent politico-economic struggle. But she also suffers from periodic communal riots which are the reverse of non-violent. This is the consequence of the machinations of malevolent religiopolitical Indian "leaders" and of the political diplomacy of Britain. Both religions have been perverted, distorted, corrupted from their true essentials by their custodians, who have made of religion a profitable profession. This root-cause has been taken advantage of by the British "diplomats." That the two communities have no common human interests, that one can profit only at the expense of the other, is only a less intelligent replica of the Western nation. That one country or nation or race can prosper only by domineering over and enslaving another country or race or nation – a notion which is the legitimate corollary of the much-boasted discovery of the Law of Struggle for existence, and of the forgetting and ignoring of the far more important and beneficent Law of Alliance for Existence. As a result, the whole atmosphere of India is pervaded by a miasma of mutual hatred and suspicion, and life is one long alarm for every honest, good peaceminded Hindu as well as Muslim. The late Hon. G.K. Gokhale pointed out, long ago, that "any two sides, taken together, of the triangle of forces, Hindu, Muslim, British, are obviously greater than the third." Accordingly, in the outcome of the three Round Table Conferences held in London (1930-1933), the malignant system of separation of the two communities was arranged by the confirmation and perpetuation of separate electorates. As a logical corollary, the evil spirit of communalism has been infused into every department of the public services, highest to lowest, by promoting the thought of communal ratios and proportions in employment. These services naturally have intelligence and information above the average of the population, and hold all the immense power of official authority in their hands; and power means almost everywhere today, power to hurt and hinder rather than to help the weak, the good, the honest.

The communal problem has become the most acute problem of India since separate electorates were instituted by British diplomacy; at first, for municipal and district boards, in the second decade of this century, and then for the legislatures, in the third.

In an interview given to an American newspaper correspondent on March 23, 1939, at New Delhi, the question was put to Mahatma Gandhi: "Is India making progress to your liking?" The Mahatma became thoughtful, and then said: "Yes, it is, I get frightened sometimes, but there is progress at the bottom, and that progress is sound. The greatest difficulty is Hindu-Muslim differences. That is a serious obstacle, there I cannot say, I see visible progress. But the trouble is bound to solve itself. The mass-mind is sound, if only because it is unselfish. The political grievances of both the communities are identical; so are the economic grievances."

It is perfectly true that these grievances are identical. Then why has he not succeeded in convincing the two communities of this, and uniting them? "The trouble is bound to solve itself." No doubt it will; but as in Spain, or peacefully? It is possible to do anything to bring about the latter form of solution? "The mass-mind is sound, if only because it is unselfish." Is not this too unqualified? The peasantry is the largest "mass" in India, as in China, Japan, and the rest of Asia. It is everywhere intensely "individualist," or "selfish." But granting that it is comparatively "sound" and unselfish," is it also duly informed and educated in respect of the essentials of religion and of the main few fundamental principles of right social organization? A peaceful solution of the trouble by itself is not likely. To some of us, it seems that only by diligent spread of knowledge of the common essentials of all religions, and of the fundamental principles of right social organization, will the solution of the communal problem be possible.

The Position of the Congress

The politico-economic struggle of the Congress, too, though largely non-violent physically, is not such psychically. Corruption of various kinds is rife within the Congress. At elections for offices within the Congress organization, ballot-boxes have been looted, burnt, carried-away, lathis have been used, serious hurt inflicted, in a number of cases; a person has been killed outright, in one or two; as in Britain more or less, until not so very long ago. Mahatma Gandhi's own writings in his weekly, the *Harijan*, amply attest this. No other evidence is needed. If it were, the speeches made in support of the "anti-corruption" resolution, passed unanimously, on December 3, 1938, at Tripuri, by the Congress in open session, supply it in ample measure. The bright side of the picture, however, is that, considering the immense areas and numbers of electors involved, and the fact that these are "first experiments," there have not been many more such regrettable occurrences.

The Cause of the Disease

Why have all the measures for awakening the mass mind which, on the whole and in the circumstances, were the best available, as proved by their marvellous success in bringing about that awakening – why have these measures of Mahatma Gandhi not succeeded as they should have ? Clearly, there has been some very serious lack in the leadership. Let it be repeated here, that the method of non-violent non-co-operation or civil disobedience, or however else it may be called, is undoubtedly the best, in India's present circumstances. By that method, Mahatma Gandhi has performed the miracle of endowing the Indian people with a will, and also a potent weapon. That method is in keeping with the ancient spirit and traditions of the people. *Dharna*, i.e. *dharana, pray-opa-veshana, upavasa, ajna-bhanga, adeshatyaga, raja-tyaga, raja tatra vigarhyate;* sitting down at the doorway of the oppressor with fixed resolve to die unless the wrong is redressed, "fasting unto death," "civil disobedience," "giving up the country," "renouncing the ruler," "public censure of the ruler," etc., are some of the non-violent forms of resisting abuse of authority, which are mentioned in the old books; though armed war is also permitted, nay, enjoined, by them, in special circumstances, after peaceful methods have failed.

It is the *lack of something more* which has caused all these noble efforts to miss their mark. Because of the lack of an indispensable ingredient, the recipe has failed to cure the disease, or even to alleviate it thus far. Mahatma Gandhi and the "High Command" never chalked out the broad outlines of any plan on which legislation could and should be conducted by the Ministries, in concert, consistently, for the promotion of the general welfare. They have been waiting for a future Constituent Assembly to do it for them. Of course, this dissatisfaction with "their own" Ministries is stronger in some Provinces than in others. But it is present in all, for one reason or another. The reasons vary with the Provinces. Some of us have been endeavouring, for many years now, to draw the attention of the "High and Low Commands" of the Congress, and of the public generally, to this great lack, and also to suggest ways for supplying it. But so far in vain. Perhaps the conflict that has arisen within the Congress now will compel the "leaders" and the public to turn their attention to it. It will have far-reaching consequences. It will ruin all that the Congress has gained by twenty years of self-denial and sacrifice, if not allayed. It can be abated, and replaced by Unity, only by supplying the great lack in the programme. So only will the newly-gained will be saved from infantile diseases, internal fevers, suicide. So only will that national will be endowed with that Unity, the absence of which is menacing it with premature death.

Of course, while it is necessary to say the above, we must not forget that the Congress Ministries are working very hard, and are making great efforts to abolish the drink evil, spread literacy, abate agricultural indebtedness, encourage local industries, improve sanitation, combat epidemics. They are not succeeding as they should, because they cannot command sufficient co-operation from the permanent services, on account of the weaknesses in the Congress ranks: and more than all else, because of the *lack of proper explanation of the word Swaraj*, "Self-Government," to the public.

Neither Mahatma Gandhi, nor Shri Jawaharlal Nehru, nor Shri Subhas Chandra Bose, nor any other member of the High Command, nor any other recognized and followed "leader" of the Congress (except CR.Das for a while), has ever tried to explain to the public what the word "Swa-raj" means. Up to 1936 or 1937, Mahatma Gandhi used to say, in effect, when occasion arose, that to him Swa-raj meant Dominion Status. In the latest interview, above quoted, he said: "I cannot exactly tell where I myself stand on that." In any case "Dominion Status" means an imitation of the British form of Government, which, styled democratic, is at bottom oligarchic; and Mahatma Gandhi has not expressed his mind about the form of social structure needed by India – something much more important than the mere form of Government. On one occasion in Poona, early in 1934, if I remember rightly, he expressly declined to consider the subject of social structure, as being a "tall order." Mahatma Gandhi has, indeed, repeatedly and frankly said such things as: "I have no prevision," "I see darkness around me," "I no longer have that confidence in myself which I formerly had," "If I had a scheme of Swaraj I would make haste to share it with the public." "The future Constituent Assembly, elected by the people, must decide." As well have let the future Constituent Assembly decide whether India should have Swa-raj or not! Mahatma Gandhi's full pronouncement on the subject is contained in his book, *Hind Swaraj*. It all amounts to this: that all that is characteristic of or peculiar to modern civilization, machinery, railways, steamships, aeroplanes, electric lights, motor-cars, post, telegraphs, printing presses, watches and clocks, hospitals, educational methods and institutions, medical systems, etc., are bad; should be given up, wholly; not simply reformed, corrected, regulated; also, apparently, by legitimate inference, much of the ancient Indian civilization too, the great temples, the beautiful carved-stone ghats and palaces, the fine arts, shawls and kam-khabs, articles of *vertu,* and varied learning and literature, all that makes the "splendour" of life, should go; and primitive agricultural life should be restored, as that is – all that God and Nature intended for mankind. But "civilization" and its arts and sciences are also the products of Nature.

The misfortune is that, as Mahatma Gandhi has, with his all-disarming sincerity, often frankly confessed, he "can only show the way to the Truth, and not the Truth itself," and he has not seen the whole Truth himself – which whole Truth the ancient Rishis of India do show, as well as the way to it. He has not seen the great Truth of their system of individuo-socialism. The element of Truth in Mahatma Gandhi's *Hind Swaraj* is a vague sensing of the fact which is expounded in the *Upanishads, Gita, Manusmriti;* the fact that all *separate individuality itself,* all this life-process, is founded upon, has its source in, the "error", the original sin, of *avidya,* the identification of the Infinite Spirit with the finite body of flesh and blood and bone; whence "egoism, selfishness, like and dislike, love and hate," and also the possibility and fact of "altruism, self-denial, philanthropy." All human sorrow finally you must give up, all joy also, and merge back into the total unconscious i.e. the Supreme Principle of Consciousness. Mere reversion to agricultural life will not suffice. You have to revert much further back. And nations, as well as individuals, have to revert thus: but in the proper time; *after* having "tasted and tested all things, and held fast by the (relatively) good;" after having equitably discharged their duties to the egoistic as well as altruistic instincts. Mahatma Gandhi has often equated Swa-raj with Ram-raj, again without precise definition. But Ram-raj, if Valmiki is to be believed, was very far from being wholly agricultural. It was largely agricultural; but it was not all villages only; it was highly urban also. Valmiki's description of Rama's Ayodhya is almost as gorgeous, though quieter, as that of Ravana's Golden

Lanka, which was predominantly "mechanical."

In the present condition of India, with her internal dissensions, the eyes of many of the educated younger generation are fixed on Russia and her Bolshevism or Socialism or Communism, though they are frightened also by its periodical bloody "purges". On the other hand, the eyes of the older generation in (as well as out of) the Congress, despite deprecations of slave-mentality, are fixed on the Democratism, or whatever it be, of Britain or its colonies, and of the US; perhaps of France also. No one in India seems overtly to be in favour of the "ideology" of Nazism-Fascism. Yet, it seems, to some of us at least, that if only all these "isms" would shed their "extremisms," and take on, instead, a little genuine spiritual religion and a few psychological principles, they would be at once shaking hands with each other, or even running into each other's arms. All these "ideologies" and "isms" have great things to their credit; all have great crimes to their debit, too. It is only lop-sided extremisms that are making them glare at each other, spend all their respective peoples' vitality on 'organizing for war" instead of "organizing for peace."

This dire jeopardy of Western Civilization, when its great sins against the weaker peoples are "coming home to roost" and its fate is hanging by a thread, this should abate, if not dispel, out "Democratist" as well as "Socialst" leaders' fond faiths in the various "ideologies" of the west, which many of the most eminent scientists and thinkers of that West itself are condemning strongly; and should induce them to give serious attention and consideraition to the principles of the ancient time-tested social structure. Some ask: If those principles were so good, why has India fallen? The answer is: Because the character of her custodians degenerated, the "spirit" changed, the 'head" went wrong, the good principles were *not* followed any longer, were *neglected, nay, were replaced by evil ones.* The custodians of the "Law" in India lost, indeed both self-denial and wisdom. Without a strong central core, a dauntless heart-

and-brain, consisting of a band of *philanthropic, self-denying and wise* persons, no nation, no people, no civilization, can flourish. A nation, a people which cannot evolve and maintain such a "heart-and-brain," must die prematurely of degeneration, or by vioent "accident," destruction by war, or become enslaved and live by sufferance. This last fate has befallen India. But it has much vitality yet left, and the strong possibility of a new lease of life, provided the needed *vidya* can be added to Mahatma Gandhi's *tapas*.

Mahatma Gandhi, our greatest *moral* force, our greatest tapas-force to-day, has only to add to that the *intellectual* force of what the ancient *vidya* teaches on the subject of *Social Organization*. He will then succeed in saving India, and will make her a shining example for the west to copy, instead of a reflection, and a pale and distorted reflection too, of that west's own features.

The work will be done if Mahatma Gandhi and the leaders of the Congress first make their own minds clear on the subject, and arrive at definite ideas as to the social structure that will best suit the Indian people; and will then organize a strong band of (Hindu and Muslim and Christian) *volunteers*, possessing the necessary spirit of self-denial, capacity for travel and hard work, and the gift of speech, and adequate *intellectual equipment*, or readiness to newly acquire it if not already possessed-volunteers who will dedicate themselves, for a while, to the work of carrying, jointly, to every corner of India (1) the good news of the traditional Scheme of Scientific Socialism, the scheme of organization devised by the ancient patriarchs, not only for the Indian people, but for the whole human race, without distinction of caste, creed, colour, race or sex and (2) the further message of all the great re-proclaimers of the one universal religion, that *all Religions are one and the same in essentials*. The Congress Committees which exist in practically every town and district, and now in a number of states also, could easily provide all needed facilities for the work of such dedicates. They would educate public opinion, tell the people that "freedom" means freedom to exercise rights and, even more, to discharge duties, as laid down in the scheme of social organization for the different vocations.

Gandhi's Statesmanship
Albert Einstein

Gandhi is unique in political history. He has invented an entirely new and humane technique for the liberation struggle of an oppressed people and carried it out with the greatest energy and devotion. The moral influence which he has exercised upon thinking people through the civilized world may be far more durable than would appear likely in the present age, with its exaggeration of brute force. For the work of statesmen is permanent only in so far as they arouse and consolidate the moral forces of their peoples through their personal example and educating influence.

We are fortunate and should be grateful that fate has bestowed upon us so luminous a contemporary – a beacon to the generation to come.

Gandhiji As a Social Scientist and Social Inventor
Richard B. Gregg

Because of his widely misunderstood attitude towards machinery, Gandhiji is regarded in the West as almost the antithesis of a scientist, but that is a mistake.

He is a social scientist because he follows social truth by the scientific method of observation, intuitional and intellectual hypothesis, and experimental test. He once told me that he considered Western scientists not very thorough because not many of them were willing to test their hypothesis on themselves. He, however, always makes the first test of an hypothesis on himself, before he asks anyone else to try. That is so, whether the hypothesis relates to a matter of diet, sanitation, spinning wheel, caste reform, or Satyagraha. The title he chose for his autobiography was *My Experiments with Truth*.

He is not a mere scientist : he is a great scientist, in the realm of social truth. He is great because of his choice of problems, because of his methods of solution, because of the persistence and thoroughness of his search, and because of the profundity of his knowledge of the human heart. His greatness as a social inventor is shown by the close adaptation of his methods to the culture and modes of thought and feeling of the people and to their economic and technological resources. This greatness is also shown, I think, by his discrimination in choosing what to try to discard and what to try to conserve. Again, it is shown by the rate at which he applies and pushes reforms. He knows that in any society there is an organic rate of change peculiar to it at that stage. He knows that while certain processes in gestation may come suddenly to birth, other changes will require at least three generations to bring about the complete change, to slough off old inherited habits and attitudes and master the new with its major implications. Another mark of his greatness in social invention is that whenever he proposes a social reform he creates an effective organization to accomplish it. He is a master of all the details of both organization and administration. The results of his work in numerous fields have already proven him surpassingly great, and history will, I believe, prove his greatness in places where his work has just begun.

The widespread and difficult social problems on which he has especially worked are: (1) poverty, (2) unemployment,

(3) violence-between individuals, groups, and nations,
(4) disunity and friction between social groups, (5) education,
(6) to a lesser extent, sanitation and public health, nutrition,
and agricultural reforms. That these are great problems, all will
admit. Let me discuss them in reverse order.

In the field of sanitation and public health, Gandhiji realizes
that many of the problems cannot be solved until the poverty of
the people can be mitigated. Yet he has tried out and put into
practice in his ashrams many simple measures of sanitation
which are within the means of the peasants who form the bulk
of the population. He has trained many workers in these
measures and they are gradually being put into effect in
numerous places.

Gandhiji has made great strides in persuading separated social
groups to harmonize their differences, especially in the instance
of Harijan reform. I know of no country where there has been
so great a voluntary and therefore real (inner as well as outer)
movement of social unity as in this instance. The problem of
Hindu-Muslim friction is largely due to outside political factors
which neither Gandhi nor any Indian can control. Yet it will be
solved when India wins her freedom, and Gandhiji's method
will count largely in the solution.

In the realm of popular education Gandhiji has recently
initiated a scheme in which all education will come to the
pupils through some handicraft – all desirable knowledge being
related to or implied in the processes and relationships of that
particular handicraft. In the economic stresses probably lying
ahead for all of us, this scheme has high promise. Not only will
it enable students to earn their tuition as they go, and thus
make education available to the masses with a minimum of
state aid, but it will also prune off much useless frippery and
make education relevant to life. Furthermore, it is wholly
consistent with the close dependence of mind upon hand and
eye throughout the evolution of the human species.

The problem of violence and Gandhiji's method of solution I have considered in my book, *The Power of Non-violence,* and I will not attempt to discuss it further here. While his method has not yet won freedom for India, it has made great advances and altered the political and social attitudes of practically the entire population. Most of them have lost their former inferiority complex and have instead hope, self-confidence, political energy and demonstrated power of a new sort. I am confident that Gandhiji's method will win India freedom. Not only that, it will alter the entire world.

Gandhiji's solution for the problems of poverty and unemployment is the revival of hand-carding, hand-spinning and hand-weaving of textiles and the re-development of other handicrafts. The validity of this proposal is so widely and deeply decried in the West, and in India, too, by Indians educated in Western and urban modes, that I would like to discuss in terms of Western concepts some reasons for its soundness.

It is realized well in India, but hardly at all elsewhere, that because of the Indian climate, with its concentrated short rainy season and its long period of heat and dryness, there are periods ranging from three to six months all over India when the peasants are completely idle. During the worst of the heat, they cannot cultivate the hard soil nor can they sow or reap. As there are approximately 120,000,000 actual workers in field and forest in continental India, the extent of this seasonal rural unemployment every year is tremendous, both absolutely and relatively to the total population of the country. The economic losses are excessive. The psychological and moral depression and deterioration caused by it is appalling. Before the advent of mill-made cloth from the West, the peasants used this idle time to spin and weave their own clothes and to work at other supplementary handicrafts. Even today, about one-third of the cloth used in India is woven on hand-looms. Cotton grows in practically every province in India. The cost of hand-tools for this work is within the low financial means of the peasants. The traditions of handicraft are not yet lost. The market cost of hand-made cloth is not much above that of mill cloth, and for those who spin their own yarn it is less. In most parts of the population, clothing cost amounts to form one-fifth to one-sixth of the total cost of living. For people close to the margin of subsistence, a saving of one-tenth of the total cost of living, as is attainable without strain this way, would be vital. Such handiwork is not only economically valuable; it is subtly but powerfully restorative of hope, initiative, self-respect, and self-reliance which are all so badly damaged by prolonged unemployment and poverty. This curative power of handicraft is well recognised by modern psychiatrists, and handicraft, under the name of "occupational therapy" is widely used for the cure of mental disease, especially depressive insanities. For these reasons, the proposal to revive this industry as a remedy for Indian unemployment is not so absurd as would at first seem.

But, even so, many laugh the idea to scorn and say it is going backward, an anachronism, an attempt to turn back the clock, an abandonment of the immensely fruitful principle of the division of labour, a discarding of machinery and science.

A technological system exists presumably for the benefit of the entire mass of people who live under it. If the given technology does not benefit a considerable minority, it is not folly for that minority to adopt any other mode of technology which will really improve their economic condition. When for millions of people, a given technology no longer provides their material needs, it is for them a blind alley, and it is silly of them not to retrace their steps until they can find a real way out – a way subject to their own control. For them, the economic clock has stopped. To adopt any technology which will actually provide, at whatever rate of speed, one of their chief material needs is not putting the clock back, but starting it again. Modern war will turn the clock back more effectually than the adoption of hand-machines, yet the statesmen are devoting vaster and vaster sums to war, with the approval of most engineers and other "educated" people.

Modern industrialism has reduced the social function of work to a rather more primitive stage than it was when handicraft prevailed. Our actual practice of moral unity has not got much beyond, if at all, what it was at the handicraft stage. The only "going back" was when our grandfathers and we were so unintelligent as not to realize and act on the conviction that human society is a unit, and to choose methods and tools and media of exchange which would express that unity in detailed daily transactions and work.

Adopting handicrafts would not be an abandonment of the principle of division of labour. In some respects that principle has been outmoded by automatic and semi-automatic machinery. In other respects, the previous intense application of the principle can no longer operate effectively because of a change in two necessary factors – a shrinkage of previously large markets and a weakening in the complementary co-operation, interdependence and harmony between labour, management and capital. Division of labour has its limits of advantage and those limits have recently shrunk.

Gandhiji's proposal does not discard machinery or science. It brings simple machinery to a now unused reservoir of man-power – the unemployed. The use of that particular type of machinery will not create too difficult additional social and economic problems at a time when difficulties are already very great.

In all countries, there is now a steady increase in the amount and proportion of state funds devoted to military equipment and activities, and thereby a steady lowering of the common standard of life and reduction of public services like education, public health, and so on. The economic system is in a period of decline. In the West, anyhow, there is a steady social deterioration and disorganization, marked by increases in the rates of insanity, suicide and crime. If another world war comes, mankind will need occupational therapy on a large scale. Khaddar and handicrafts of all kinds will become still more valuable to people everywhere – valuable both economically and therapeutically.

Then, too, we must not overlook the fact that all industrialized countries are on the brink of rapid and great decreases in population. The evidence has been detailed by such authorities as Carr-Saunders, Kuczynski, T. H. Marshall, Enid Charles, H. D. Henderson, Arnold Plant, and Hogben. The vast economic and social effects of this drop in population, especially in the West, will be tremendously difficult and will be felt all over the world. For this reason again, handicraft activity, especially khaddar, will become extremely helpful.

These considerations, among others, convince me that Gandhiji is a great social scientist and social inventor. His achievements remind me of the old Sanskrit saying: "Magic powers do not come to a man because he does things that are hard, but because he does things with a pure heart." That is, miracles can be accomplished by lofty, single purpose and utter devotion. Thank God for Gandhiji!

The Hour and the Man
Gerald Heard

When the Western world began to imagine that to be rich was to be civilized, it assumed that as its mechanic skill would inevitably increase, its welfare would also be equally increased, its prosperity would become permanent, all men would be equal because equally supplied with indefinite goods, and progress would be infinite.

Now that this brief occidental myth is vanishing, it is possible

to say that all men are not equal – there are great men and
small, by natural spiritual endowment – and also that
civilization does not progress inevitably but is capable both of
collapse and also of sudden new mutations under the
inspiration of a single creative mind.

This discovery has come not a moment too soon. For as the
Western world imagined that it was preparing for itself a future
of infinite comfort, ease and plenty, it was in point of fact, not
only failing to solve its fundamental problem, but steadily and
rapidly aggravating this issue. That problem and issue is the
search for a real sanction of law and order, and how, if violence
is the only method of preserving peace and justice, peace and
justice are not to be destroyed by their preserver. This question
had been confronted by all great reformers. Jesus had declined
the sword, but his followers had taken it up as soon as they
were given civil authority. Mohammed also began by preaching
a faith to be spread by persuasion, but subsided into
persecution as the quickest propaganda. Yet warfare is not
efficient, let alone the question whether it can ever be righteous.
With every mechanic invention, arms have become increasingly
instruments of imprecision. It is not merely that "He, who's
convinced against his will, is of the same opinion still." War
hits inaccurately and blindly, so injuring many who were at
first completely outside the original dispute and bringing them
in against the aggressor. War is not an "instrument of policy":
it is a disease of society.

Hence many original minds, wishing to advance their
purposes, have sought, at first hardly knowing what they were
at, and then with increasing realization, to create an instrument
and to train a "Force" which would be apt, appropriate,
precise, effective. One such outstanding effort was the Society
of Jesus of Ignatius Loyola. Here were selected men, trained not
only in the intelligence but also in the deep will by careful if
rudimentary psychological exercises; organized on military lines
as far as discipline and obedience to superiors are concerned;

denied all distractions of home, wife, children, property or rank; and so trained, equipped and mobilized, sent out under the orders of a General to recapture for the Roman Church what it had lost in the first flood of the Reformation.

The next stage in the development of a new unarmed Force came, not with an order attempting to re-establish a religion, but from specific achievements in solving particular problems which, till then, had successfully resisted the accepted method of making them yield to violence. With the rise of the new psychiatry treatment of lunacy a local but very definite and unexpected victory for non-violence was achieved, a victory which meant, with the triumph of the "open-door method," a power to cure lunacy and to reduce the incidence of madness, a power which the old, mistaken, conventional method of violence had never had. The extension of this method of trained, reassuring initiative, spread to the contacting of backward peoples (the anthropological approach), the educational training of wild animals, and the re-socialization of the criminal.

Yet all these remarkable results in dealing with particular classes of men and animals unamenable to violence – results which in single cases had already been frequently demonstrated even in the West by such consistent religious individuals as the quakers – were isolated discoveries, so isolated that the practitioners of these methods did not even themselves realize the relevance of their particular discovery, technique and success to the general problem of war and peace, general social order and international relationships.

Meanwhile, warfare itself had been developed until it had reached a pitch of potential destructiveness never before thought possible, and, as often happens with mankind, as the thing increased both in horror and in ineffectiveness, as men had failed to rid themselves of such a madness, they attempted to make what had once been a means into an end; and what had been defended as an unavoidable necessary effectiveness, they now advocated as a ghastly idolatry, as a supreme good in itself.

To meet such a convergence of two madnesses – the blind submission of free men to the powers of murderous machines and then to the dictates of a group – folly as blind as and even more destructive than the murder-machines themselves, there was needed a man as ingenious as the inventors of the diabolic instruments of destruction and as dynamic as the demonic leaders who were stampeding their peoples into mutual massacre.

There can be little doubt that this man will be recognized by historians as M. K. Gandhi. At the time when Europe, Asia and Africa were being drawn as never before into a tri-partite, bewildered, chaotic contact, India gave this man to Africa that there he might make his first great demonstration against (or perhaps it would be truer to say with) Europe. For his technique of non-violence was and is by its nature one to educate its opponents, as much as to succour those whose cause it advocates. Springing from India, it was nevertheless right that its first demonstration should be in Africa, for this method belongs to mankind and indeed is the one valid approach and link between not merely all the races of mankind but between man and all sentient beings. India, which had sent out this man, then, in turn, became the centre of his next great campaign in which he strove, through the long life which now reaches its crown, to teach that great country, which is in its situation and in its contents an epitome of all mankind's peoples and problems, how it might win its freedom by training itself in a practical way to implement the teaching which had been the core of all the instruction of all the sages of India.

What the future may hold we cannot see, but it does not seem to be hazardous either in time or space to foretell, that in this coming generation, and in India itself, will be worked out the final contest between the forces of destruction, urging their case by telling the timid and the rich that they alone can give these people security, and the forces of construction whereby a trained, disciplined, informed new order of the Saviours of Mankind will take the field and strive to give mankind the only victory which will not mean ruin, not merely of man's goods but of his very race. We cannot tell how that issue will turn. It is not in us to command success, but we can say that whether it succeeds or fails, it is the one path for those who care for their fellows; and that that path is open today is due, more than to anyone, to the man who today stands at the summit of his life and service to mankind.

M.K. Gandhi: Apostle of Light and Truth-Force
Carl Heath

In the history of humanity, the apostolic man must always face a tremendous struggle. "I am come like light into the world," said one. But the children of light are never welcome, for men love darkness rather than light. The clouds of ignorance, prejudice and indifference are even felt as protective. The apostolic man must break through and overcome.

All his life, this breaking through darkness and this overcoming of ignorance and prejudice have been the mark of M.K. Gandhi's character. That is why today, when he shines, not alone as the foremost spirit of India, but as an inspiration to all generous humankind, he has behind him a long record of suffering and struggle, of strenuous prayer and many fasts. He could not be great were it otherwise.

Mohandas Karamchand Gandhi long ago learnt the secret of patience. Indeed he has discovered the truth of the saying of Thomas a Kempis: "Thy peace shall be in *much* patience."

They who study his life and watch him closely in his public actions and relationships cannot but be impressed by the fact that whilst the excitement of other men may dangerously increase his blood-pressure, it does not affect his characteristic patience – patience with opponents, patience with an alien Government, patience with his endless visitors, and patience with his own, at times, disturbing disciples. Perhaps this patience is his because, in spite of much furious wrong and exasperating happenings, he is so deeply aware in his own soul that "the mills of God grind slowly." M.K. Gandhi works in those mills.

And then with no pretensions to infallibility and through making mistakes for which he has from time to time with a rare courage done public penance, he is the devotee of truth. "Now-a-days," he wrote three years ago, "nothing so completely describes my God as Truth." This, be it noted, has led him not to a world of speculative verities, but to a devotion in service. "To be true to such religion one has to lose oneself in continuous and continuing service of all life." This is not, however, the service of benevolence from above. It is "a complete merging of one-self in, and identification with this limitless ocean of life." It "must be taken to include every department of life." So he makes truth a concrete realism.

And hence in M.K. Gandhi is to be found an integration of life. He is never standing apart, the spiritual superior-aloof. If he is a Mahatma or great soul, he is also a man of the people amongst the people. Clear sighted, keeping much silence before God, humbleminded in the essential sense, the spiritual man of prayer and vision; he is also the man of much physical work, very approachable, lovable and humorous – and right in the thick of the human struggle, moral and religious, social and political.

Subtle as he sometimes is, he is to be loved for his simplicity and clarity of soul – for he has gone through much cleansing of the spirit; also for the material simplicity of his existence that attracts men and women of all nations and multitudes of his own. For he has divested himself possessions and knows, like Thoreau, the joy of possessing all and owning nothing. And, in this condition, of serving all life for a great interior end, becoming for millions of striving men and women a sustaining centre – Gandhiji!

Consider his struggle for his fellow-nationals in South Africa, for the untouchables of his own Hindu community – his harijans; for the peoples of India and their freedom; for the village life of the plains with its bitter economic want and its deep need for education; for the tribesmen of the mountain frontiers; for Moslem-Hindu unity; for the prisoners; for men and women of all classes, creeds, castes and races; for the sub-humans expressed in "cow protection"; and for the great creative idea of non-violent resistance to evil, itself a veritable world of life and direction for those who struggle with the war spirit all round the world. And in all this, his ever-persistent rejection of the spirit of ill-will toward any, justifying his proud claim to be "a humble servant of India *and humanity.*"

That M.K. Gandhi should hold with such strength to the doctrine of Satyagraha is fitting, for he is himself an incarnation of soul-force. Above all his political and social activity, he remains always the man of the soul. And as such he speaks to the modern world as a challenging man. That is his greatest virtue and prophetic value. Thwarted and imprisoned, derided and scorned, he has but stepped higher and higher in the scale of human life.

His humanity to men and to all living things has given him multitudes of friends in every place and nation under the sun. There is in his mind no distinction in his attitude to Hindu or Moslem, Christian, Buddhist, Parsee, or Jew, or men of any other faith. All are his friends and parts of the family of Truth, and Truth is God. In all relations with humans, as with sub-humans, ahimsa rules his life. For this age he is *the type* of the civilized and humanized man.

On Freedom and Belonging
William Ernest Hocking

One way among the many ways in which Gandhiji has instructed our times in respect to the dilemma which confronts every man, as he realizes how his local belonging, and all his social ties, limit his freedom of action and even of thought.

Perhaps the first effect of reflection on our institutions is to make one aware of their defectiveness; it becomes hard for the educated man in our Western communities to belong to a Church, since he can accept no one of the creeds as it stands: or to a political party, since they are all tainted with stupidity and self-interest. The study of philosophy has a strong tendency to detach a man from these ties, and also from the ties of family and country. The philosopher must be no partisan; he must be "above the battle." Religion carries the detachment a stage further: in union with the One, all differences vanish, and one becomes the universal being in principle. At the same time, one also becomes useless and meaningless.

Gandhiji has called his deity by the name of Truth; this principle is universal, and above all creeds. He also calls him by the name of Rama. He finds his way, in politics, to the One; he has a platform of conversation with men who differ most widely from him in policy and interest. Yet he is man with a party; almost one might say, he is a party in himself; he defines issues, makes definite proposals, continues argument in their behalf through the proposals, continues argument in their behalf through the *Harijan* and other organs: he is the reverse of useless and meaningless.

In brief, he has shown how the detachment of the sannyasi may contribute to the effectiveness of the statesman; and how the acceptance of local mission and of manifold belonging may contribute to the maximum of personal freedom. For no one I have ever met so impressed me as doing the things, each day, which he most wanted to do and most enjoyed doing.

This is a simple matter – to him – and yet the lack of clearness on this one thing is at the root of much of the unhappiness and confusion of the world. Our own community in America is full of men who are seeking freedom by escaping from belonging and its obligations, from the family tie which they have assumed, from the melee of political action, from organized religion, and in the end from their own empirical being with its local insertions.

Democracy falters because reflection robs it of the services of those who might best bear its burdens. We have still to learn the "glory of the imperfect": and that he who wins release by putting off the particular and local is winning release from existence itself, since existence is particular.

Gandhiji teaches us that there is no greatness except greatness within one's own kind; no universality except the universality within one's own province; no freedom except the freedom within one's own belonging.

The Nature of Gandhi's Greatness
John Haynes Holmes

It was nearly twenty years ago that I declared to the American public that "Gandhi is the greatest man in the world." My countrymen did not know of Gandhi at that time – his name had scarcely found its way into our Western world ! But since that time, his name has become as famous as that of any other living man, and Americans know that I was right in hailing him as "the greatest."

Gandhi's pre-eminence in this age is due to nothing that is ordinarily accounted genius or glory. He commands no armies and conquers no territory. He is not a statesman in high office, ruling the destinies of nations. He is not a philosopher or sage – has written no great books or poems. He does not even possess those elements of conspicuous and dominant personality which make a man outwardly at least an impressive leader. His genius lies where he would have it – in the realm of the spirit. It is his "soul-force" which has raised him to a position of unparalleled influence and leadership, and achieved things beyond the reach and range of all but a few of the greatest characters of history.

To Gandhi, more than to any other Indian, will be attributed the independence of India when this independence is at last won. To him also will be attributed the vast achievement of making his people worthy as well as capable of independence by reviving their native culture, quickening their sense of personal dignity and self-respect, disciplining their inner lives to self-control-making them spiritually as well as politically free. Added to this is his great work of delivering the Untouchables from their bondage to affliction-a work destined to be for ever memorable as the greatest single act of human emancipation known to history. Lastly, there remains Gandhi's supreme achievement of taking the principle of "non-violent resistance" and transforming it into a technique for the accomplishment of liberty, justice, and peace upon the earth. What other men have taught as a personal discipline, Gandhi has transformed into a social programme for the redemption of the world.

Gandhi is great among all the great of ages past. He is great with Alfred, Wallace, Washington, Kosciusko, Lafayette, as a nationalist leader. He is great with Clarkson, Wilberforce, Garrison, Lincoln, as an emancipator of the enslaved. He ranks with St. Francis, Thoreau, Tolstoy, as a teacher of what the

Christian scriptures call "non-resistance," and better the "love that never faileth." He holds his place with Lao-tse, Buddha, Zoroaster, Jesus, as one of the supreme religious prophets of all time. Best of all is the man, on whom I wrote in my recent book, *Re-thinking Religion:*

"He is modest, gentle, unfailingly kind. His sense of fun is irresistible, his simplicity of manner captivating. Quiet, almost soft in his ways, he has an indomitable will and an iron courage. His sincerity is transparent, his devotion to truth inexorable. Having nothing to lose, his position is impregnable to attack. Sacrificing everything himself, he can ask anything of others. Material considerations, worldly cares and ambitions, have long since vanished from his life. The spirit, as manifest in truth and love, possesses his utterly. 'My creed,' says Gandhi, 'is service of God and therefore of humanity... and service means pure love.'"

A South African Tribute
Alfred Hoernle

It is fitting that among the tributes from all over the world to Gandhi's spirit and ideals there should be at least one from a White South African.

For it was in South Africa, as far back as 1893, that Gandhi first became the champion of an Indian community. It was in the "Fort" at Johannesburg, which I pass every day on my way to University, that, later, he and many of his followers were imprisoned with hard labour. It was with General Smuts, colonial secretary after the restoration of self-government to the Transvaal, that he negotiated for the future of the Indian community in South Africa. It was as leader of his people in the struggle against discriminating legislation that he first experimented with the technique of passive resistance. In many

Indian homes in South Africa, and in all public buildings owned by the Indian community, the picture of the "Mahatma" occupies a place of honour. There are still many men and women-both White and Indian – in South Africa who fought and suffered at Gandhi's side. One of his sons has remained in the Union as editor of *Indian Opinion*, which his father founded and which is still published at Phoenix, Natal, the Indian settlement brought into being to realize one of Gandhi's dreams for the advancement of his people. Yes, Gandhi had made for himself a never-to-be-forgotten place in the history of South Africa, before he passed on to devote his gifts of leadership, spiritual and political, to the land and the people of his birth.

Reading the account of his South African life, written by one of his White friends and supporters, Rev. Joseph J. Doke, Baptist Minister at Johannesburg *(M.K. Gandhi: An Indian Patriot in South Africa),* and seeking there the secret of the hold he had over his people and of the deep impression he made even upon many of his White opponents, I am struck by the following things.

First of all, there is the strength of mind which enabled him to practise his belief in non-violence even under provocations which would have aroused the fighting fury of other men to the point of meeting violence with violence. More than once he was the victim of kicks and blows and verbal indignities from Whites who thought thus to demonstrate the superiority of their race and teach this "coolie" his place. He never retaliated by force. He refused to prosecute the sentry who kicked him off the footpath in front, of President Kruger's house. When he suffered the most brutal assault of all – this time from opponents among his own people – and lay bleeding and helpless, he pleaded with the police not to punish his assailants: "They thought they were doing right," he said, "and I have no desire to prosecute them." Clearly, one clue to the secret of his power over others is his power over himself.

Again, when arousing and organizing the South African Indians to resist legislation, the aim of which was to make them outcastes in South Africa – aliens barely tolerated under severe restrictions and debarred in principle from citizenship – he was not content merely to demand abstract rights: more important was it for him to build up their self-respect. He found them dispirited and sunk in apathy, accepting their depression without protest: he recalled them to a sense of their manhood as a moral basis for demanding to be treated as men by White South Africa. His dream for the future of the Indian community, so Rev. Doke tells us, was: "An Indian community in South Africa, welded together by common interests and common ideals, educated, moral, worthy of the ancient civilization to which it is heir; remaining essentially Indian, but so acting that South Africa will eventually be proud of its Eastern citizens, and accord them, as of right, those privileges which every British subject should enjoy."

Thirdly, he knew how to combine leadership with humility. To the wealthier Indians he set the example of public spirit: what he received, he spent unstintingly in promoting the interests of his people. Among the poor, he moved as one poor himself. Son of a prime minister in his home state; sprung from a family accustomed to position, influence, power, culture; trained for, and called to, the Bar in England; able to meet cultured Europeans on equal terms, he yet never sought privileges for himself, but preferred to be treated like any other Indian. When the law required all Indians to register their fingerprints for identification, though he might have claimed exemption, he made a point of being the first to comply, as an example to the rest of his people.

And, fourthly, in the midst of his struggle for Indian rights, he always insisted that those who claim to deserve citizen-rights must be ever ready to substantiate that claim by voluntarily playing their part in the hour of need, even when no participation in communal effort is demanded of them. For the fighting in Natal, during the Anglo-Boer war, he offered to organize and equip a corps of Indian stretcher-bearers. After initial refusals, the offer was accepted, and the Indians rendered valuable service: General Robert's son, mortally wounded, was carried by Indian bearers seven miles to the base hospital at Chieveley. This service was repeated in the last Zulu war of 1906. And, but for Gandhi's prompt action, the outbreak of plague in Johannesburg, in 1904, might have been far more destructive of life than it was.

Such were the character and spirit of the man who first used the weapon of "passive resistance" in a situation of racial conflict, refusing, as he put it, to submit to a law which offended Indian consciences, but still, as a law-abiding subject of the state, accepting the penalties imposed by the law. At the same time, he knew, and said, that the phrase "passive resistance" expresses only half the ideal: "It fails to convey all I mean. It describes a method, but gives no hint of the system of which it is only a part. Real beauty, and that is my aim, is doing good against evil." In that spirit, he claimed that the Christian command to love one's enemies and to do good to them that hate and persecute one, is in accord with the deepest wisdom of Indian thought and religion.

May I conclude by a few reflections on what I have just now called the "weapon" of passive resistance?

It has, clearly, come to stay. In various forms of application, men have experimented with it since then and will continue to do so. Individuals (e.g. conscientious objectors in war-time) can use it as individuals. Groups, powerless in a political and military sense, can fall back on it as their only possible weapon. As a *moral*, not a *physical*, weapon, it raises political warfare to a higher plane. It involves self-chosen suffering and humiliation for the resisters, and thus demands in them unusual resources of self-mastery and strength of will. If it is effective, it is so by working on the consciences of those against whom it is being used, sapping their confidence in the exclusive rightness of their case; making their physical strength impotent; and weakening their resolution by insinuating a sense of guilt for the suffering they have a part in causing. Whether it is an effective weapon against opponents who have no conscience to appeal to I am inclined to doubt. Gandhi's recommendation, reported in the Press, to the Jews in Germany to defend themselves by passive resistance, might, if adopted, merely reveal that Nazi storm-troopers and their leaders have no consciences open to this sort of moral pressure.

Moreover, just because passive resistance is a moral weapon, men will rarely in the mass be able to rise to or maintain themselves for long, on the plane of selfless devotion on which instinctive pugnacity, anger, and resentment are transmuted into patience, forbearance, and love. It is not a "method" which can be practiced apart from the "system of which it is part;" that is, divorced from the spirit of love for your enemies and requiting evil with good.

If a mass of men is to rise to such heights, it needs a leader even more than men always need a leader for concerted action – a leader, moreover, in whom the required courage and moral conviction are so incarnate that by practice and precept he can communicate them to his followers, without needing the devices of high-power propaganda or the support of the bludgeons and bayonets of storm-troopers. Such leaders are rare: a Gandhi does not arise even once in a lifetime.

It is interesting to recall that, at the time, White South Africans criticized Gandhi, because they feared that the example of Indian passive resistance would be imitated by the natives who were, and are, by law and custom kept in a position inferior even to that of the Indians, in order that South Africa may be a "White man's country." Characteristically, Gandhi's reply was that a moral weapon is preferable to rioting, violence, and bloodshed; that the use of a moral weapon presupposes a just cause: and that, if the cause of the natives is just and they are sufficiently high in the scale of civilization for the method of passive resistance to be usable by them, they will *ipso facto* have become fit for the franchise and for a voice in the determination of their place in the multi-racial structure of South Africa.

Thirty years have passed since then. The Indians in South Africa still cherish the memory of Gandhi's leadership, but they have not used the weapon of passive resistance since he returned to India. As for the natives, considerable as has been their development in spite of all obstacles, no one can confidently predict when, if ever they will be ready for the use of a weapon which makes such exceptional demands on the users. Disarmed as they are, divided among themselves, helpless, their ultimate hope lies in this weapon alone. But the day of a native Gandhi is not yet. It may not come at all, but the continued efforts of the White minority in South Africa to entrench for all time its political, social and economic ascendancy are likely to unite against it all non-European sections of the population. In that event, it may happen that the Indian community will provide from its ranks, and with Gandhi's tradition behind it, a leader in passive resistance for a united non-European front.

Gandhi in South Africa
Hon. Jan H Hofmeyer

During his recent visit to India to attend the Tambaram Conference, that great missionary statesman, Dr. John R. Mott, called on Mahatma Gandhi at Segaon. One of the questions put by him was "What have been the most creative experiences in your life?" The Mahatma's reply may fittingly be quoted here:

"Such experiences are a multitude. But as you put the question

to me, I recalled particularly one experience that changed the
course of my life. That fell to my lot seven days after I had
arrived in South Africa. I had gone there on a purely mundane
and selfish mission. I was just a boy returned from England
wanting to make some money. Suddenly, the client who had
taken me there, asked me to go to Pretoria from Durban. It was
not an easy journey. There was the railway journey as far as
Charlestown and the coach to Johannesburg. On the train, I
had a first-class ticket, but not a bed ticket. At Maritzburg,
when the beds were issued, the guard came and turned me out,
and asked me to go into the van compartment. I would not go
and the train steamed away leaving me shivering in the cold.
Now the creative experience comes there. I was afraid for my
very life. I entered the dark waiting-room. There was a white
man in the room. I was afraid of him. What was my duty, I
asked myself. Should I go back to India, or should I go
forward, with God as my helper and face whatever was in store
for me? I decided to stay and suffer. My active non-violence
began from that date."

It is not pleasant for a South African to recall this incident, yet
it does serve to emphasize the importance of South Africa in
Mr. Gandhi's life history. For it was in South Africa that the
doctrine of *Satyagraha* was conceived, that the weapon of non-
violent resistance was forged. Often, there is justice in the
working of history. India, though not of its own volition, had
given to South Africa one of the most difficult of its problems.
South Africa, in its turn, likewise not of its own volition, gave
to India the idea of civil disobedience.

The Indian had come to South Africa because it was deemed
to be in the white man's interest that he should. It seemed to be
impossible to exploit the Natal coast-belt adequately without
indentured labour. So the Indians came and brought prosperity
to Natal. Many remained, welcome contributors to the colonys
welfare, and others followed, both free and indentured
immigrants. But in due course, the Indian, with his lower

standard of living, began to threaten the European in some of the occupations of which he had previously had a monopoly. This was sufficient to arouse colour prejudice – and the Indians came to be regarded, in Lord Milner's phrase, as "strangers forcing themselves upon a community reluctant to receive them." It was this prejudice that was brought home to the youthful Gandhi on Maritzburg Railway Station – as a reaction to it, *Satyagraha* was born.

There is no need here to tell the story of the Mahatma's life and work in South Africa. It was a long struggle, in the course of which Gandhi's chief opponent was another of the great world figures of to-day, General J.C. Smuts. The two men had much in common. Some years ago, I visited, in the company of a high Government official, a reformatory for Indian and native boys just outside Johannesburg, which had once been a prison. My companion pointed out to me the room in which Gandhi had been incarcerated thirty years ago and recalled how he, then a junior magistrate, had taken to him books on philosophy, the gift of his ministerial chief, General Smuts. Happily, the bonds of mutual respect and friendship between the two men pre-vailed over all disruptive forces, and are still effective links today.

What did Gandhi achieve in South Africa? He was unable to prevent Smuts from gaining his main objective, which was to terminate Indian immigration into South Africa. But Gandhi secured that Indians were spared the dishonour of being named specifically in the immigration law, and he also obtained the redress of several minor grievances of Indians already resident in South Africa. If he hoped, as he doubtless did, when he left South Africa, that the settlement arrived at between Smuts and himself would lead to the disappearance of anti-Asiatic prejudice, he was destined to be disappointed. The prejudice is still a powerful force in South Africa today, and some of its manifestations are not to South Africa's credit.

Yet Gandhi's leadership has left an abiding mark on the Indian community in South Africa. He enabled it to triumph over the disabilities resulting from the low-caste origin of most of its members, and he gave it a consciousness of pride of race which has never been effaced. The Indian community in South Africa is prepared to resist the stigma of segregation as firmly today as ever it fought under Gandhi's banner against dishonouring legislation. But most important of all was the fact that during the years when Gandhi defied the law, crossing provincial boundaries without registering fingerprints, going into gaol and out of it, he was in fact perfecting the creed of self-abnegation, and learning its power and effectiveness as a weapon.

So then it can be said that South Africa played a big part in the development of the man who was to be not only India's Mahatma, but also one of the great spiritual leaders of the world, although its white rulers can hardly recall with satisfaction the specific circumstances which brought that about.

Gandhi's Satyagraha and the Way of the Cross
John S. Hoyland

At Madras,[9] in the late autumn of 1938, there was held a gathering of Christian statesmen, coming from all parts of the world, but especially from the young Churches of Africa and the East, for the consideration of the problems of the modern world in the light of the message of Christ. Before the meeting of the Madras Conference, a unique event took place. A number of these distinguished Christian leaders, men of world-

---

9 Much of the following material has been taken from Harijan (published at Poona) for December 10 and December 24, 1938.

wide influence in opulent and imposing sections of the Church, travelled long extra distances in order to visit, and sit at the feet of a Hindu leader, Mr. Gandhi. Their object was to gain from him advice as to how they might learn to follow Christ better. It may safely be affirmed that at none of the long series of oecumenical councils held in the past have the Christian leaders done such a thing. That they have done it now shows on the one hand how widespread and deep-going is the conviction that Christianity has gone wrong (largely as a result of its compromise with modern industrialism and modern imperialism) and on the other hand how profound is the belief that this great seer of India has come nearer than we have to the discovery of the mind of Christ and to the practising of the way of Christ.

In the extremely important conversations which he held with these Christian leaders, Mr. Gandhi dealt first with the question of money. He put his convictions in a nut-shell, as follows: "I think that you cannot serve God and Mammon both, and my fear is that Mammon has been sent to serve India and God has remained behind with the result that He will one day have His vengeance... I have always felt that when a religious organization has more money than it requires, it is in peril of losing its faith in God, and pinning its faith on money. You have simply to cease to depend on it.

"In South Africa, when I started the *Satyagraha* march, there was not a copper in my pocket, and I went with a light heart. I had a caravan of 3,000 people to support. "No fear," said I. "If God wills it, He will carry it forward." Then money began to rain from India. I had to stop it, for when the money came, my miseries began. Whereas they had been content with a piece of bread and sugar, they now began asking for all sorts of things!

"Then take the illustration of the new educational experiment. The experiment I said must go on without asking for any monetary help. Otherwise, after my death, the whole organization would go to pieces. *The fact is, the moment financial stability is assured, spiritual bankruptcy is also assured"*

Nothing could be more characteristic of Mr. Gandhi's idealism than this last statement. He has insisted over and over again that the possession of invested funds, or secure economic resources, spells spiritual ruin to a living movement. Those who have been willing and self-sacrificing volunteers become grafters, who are in the movement for what they can get out of it. Those who have been helped and ennobled by it become pauperized. The movement and its funds become a cow to be milked, and to be milked more adroitly and plenteously by oneself than by other people. Inevitably, corruption and degeneration set in. Every type of hypocrisy and falsehood is encouraged.

The present writer has had some experience of the distribution of relief funds in various countries, after pestilence, famine and war; and is convinced that Mr. Gandhi is right. A really living spiritual movement will dispense with funds to the utmost possible degree, and will be infinitely the stronger for so doing. Mr. Gandhi's views in this matter are derived from his convictions regarding the principle of non-possession, which may be closely compared with the Franciscan principle of the subduing of the "proprium" – the sense of personal possession. The thing is summed up thus by one of Mr. Gandhi's closest disciples: ''Money will come for an object to which you are prepared to give up your life, but when there is no money, you will not miss it, and the object will be carried on, perhaps all the better for want of it."

Another very urgent-topic discussed by Mr. Gandhi with the Christian leaders on this occasion was what to do with ''gangster" nations. It is well for us British by the way, when we discuss such questions, to recognize that many of the peoples of the earth regard us as amongst the gangster nations. The fact that we finished compiling our swag in 1919, when we added nine new mandates to the British Empire, and have been fairly quiet and satiated since then, does not make these other nations feel that we deserve the title "gangster nation" any less than more recent aspirants after international loot. Those who find themselves in the uncomfortable position of being subject – peoples within the British Empire are especially eager that as our consciences become healthily uneasy with regard to international gangsterdom, we should not solely be concerned with the gambollings in this field of Germany, Italy and Japan.

Mr. Gandhi was insistent that those who believe in and have learnt something of the practice of non-violence should recognize that even this extremely unpleasant and dangerous phenomenon of modern international gangsterdom can and must be met by the methods of non-violence. "Ultimately," he declared, "force, however justifiably used, will lead us into the same morass as the force of Hitler and Mussolini. There will be just a difference of degree. Those who believe in non-violence must use it at the critical moment. We must not despair of touching the heart even of gangsters, even though for the moment we may seem to be striking our heads against a blind wall."

A little later, the discussion turned to the type of creative experience which is likely to prove decisive in making a life effective for non-violent action against wrong. Mr. Gandhi recounted one such experience which fell to[10] his lot seven days after he had arrived in South Africa, in the last decade of the nineteenth century.

This episode brings out clearly two fundamental elements in Mr. Gandhi's achievement. In the first place, his conquest of fear. Those living in a more or less homogeneous population in a Western country can perhaps have but little idea of the fear

---

10 This is the incident of the ejectment from a train, followed by an assualt by a coachman, quoted at length in Mr. Hofmeyer's article on pp. 91-92.

with which the average Indian regards – or rather used to
regard – the white man. He seemed to the peasant a being from
a different planet, a being endowed with almost supernatural
powers over the forces of nature, a being to be regarded with
an awe which often became servility, a being to be trembled
before and implicitly obeyed. It has been well said that the
greatest single gift which Mr. Gandhi has conferred upon his
fellow-countrymen is the power of conquering this fear
complex in the presence of the white man. He has taught the
Indian, and especially the Indian peasant, to stand erect, to
look the white man in the face undismayed, and deliberately to
disobey his orders, if he believes them to be disastrous for the
well-being of his country. Fear is infectious. But so also is
fearlessness. Mr. Gandhi has in himself a spirit of fearlessness
which he has the faculty, superlatively, of transmitting to other
people. He has put courage into Indian peasants to refuse to
pay unjust land-taxes, in spite of all that district officials might
do against them. To those who know India, this in itself will be
sufficient proof of the extraordinary quality of his personality
with regard to the conquest of fear.

In the second place, that youthful episode on the railway
station at Maritzburg brings out Mr. Gandhi's life-long practice
of the belief that suffering can be used creatively for the
redemption of others. The incident of the ejectment from the
train, and of the assault by the coach driver, may seem trivial.
But the indignity and pain was endured, by a shrinking and
sensitive boy, courageously *for the sake of other people*. Here
was born, in practice, lot merely in theory, the idealism of Mr.
Gandhi's *Satyagraha*, the idealism which says, "Don't run from
a situation of suffering: plunge into it boldly, not out of
bravado or asceticism or self-martyrdom, but because if you
bear it in the right spirit for the helping of other people, such
suffering becomes creative for the righting of wrong." The gay
enthusiasm with which two hundred and fifty thousand Indians
were to go to gaol, some thirty years ater, so as to win a better

future for their country, was in a sense due to the courage with which the lad in Natal had gone through with his rough experience. There is *no* experience of suffering or humiliation which may not if accepted in the right spirit, be turned to good in this way for he sake of others. For *Satyagraha* is not merely a dramatic method of winning freedom and unity for one's country, or conquering militarism and warfare, or improving a vicious social and economic order. It goes deeper still. It is the principle of the eternal Cross, the principle which says with St. Paul, "I fill up the sufferings of Christ." The man who understands something of this true neaning of *Satyagraha* looks backward down the long vista of history, and sees everywhere, all through the slow upward evolution of the race, progress for the type that is destined to survive bought by the sacrifice and suffering of innumerable individuals. He sees a great principle like that of parent-love, or later social co-operation, coming into action, at first feebly and tentatively, later with decisive effect, but always working by the self-subordination of the individual, through suffering and death often voluntarily chosen, in order to promote the well-being of others, of progeny (for instance) or later of fellow-tribesmen. As he looks at the history of humanity, he sees the same principle more and more clearly blazoned forth, as the centuries go by. And the whole great key-principle of history and progress is summed up in the Cross of Christ. "He set his face steadfastly to go to Jerusalem." "If it be Thy will, let this cup pass from me."

Thus the student of *Satyagraha* is brought to recognize how in leading his fellow-countrymen in a movement for the voluntary taking upon them, non-violently, of suffering on behalf of others, Mr. Gandhi has had the genius to bring out into the open, once more, a world-principle which the selfishness, the hot-water-bottle luxury, the profit-hunting spirit of Western civilization has obscured from our eyes. Pietistic Christianity has preached much about the Cross during the century and a half since the industrial revolution effectively began. But under the drive of an all-permeating spirit of competitive selfishness, the Cross has in reality receded into the background, to become a mere dogma or instrument of purely individual and personal salvation. The great task of our generation and unless it is accomplished, ours may be the last generation of civilized humanity – is the rediscovery of the Cross, not as a dogma, but as a living and eternal principle for the ending of wrong, warfare, violence. We have to learn afresh that Christ really meant what he said when he pronounced the solemn words, "Take up thy Cross and follow me." We have to learn afresh that he meant us to take upon ourselves, of our own free will, privation, suffering, even death itself, in the manner in which he was taking these things upon himself. That is, we must do it redemptively – for the sake of saving mankind from sin and wrong-and non-violently, without trying to pay him back in his own coin. Above all, we must do it humbly, patiently, in the spirit of friendship and goodwill.

But with Christ himself, and in his intention with his followers also, this taking up of the Cross depended upon a new consciousness of God. Mr. Gandhi's message today rings with the same conviction. We are to awaken once more to the fact of God. God himself works in this way, the way of non-violence, the way of the Cross. That way of the Cross is not a freakish notion of a few wild-eyed pacifist fanatics. It is the will of the Eternal and Living God, of all effective conquest of sin and righting of wrong. The Cross flings its shadow across all history, and across every individual life. It is God's will in action on the human stage. Christ teaches that God is above all like the father of the Prodigal Son, who welcomed the wrong-doer home again generously and without reproaches, and like the Good Shepherd, who for the sake of one lost sheep leaves home and safety, and goes out upon the wild mountains, amongst darkness, storm, and danger, in order that he may find it and save it. That kind of action against wrong is the will of God, the way of God, the very nature and being of God. God is

Love like that, He is the Love that is seeking, saving, redemptive goodwill, which takes upon itself of its own free motion suffering, danger, death for the sake of this sufferer and that, till all a suffering world is saved.

That is the God with whom we have to reckon: with whom mankind has to reckon if warfare and poverty and the other curses of humanity are to be conquered in time. We must awaken to Him.

Mr. Gandhi was asked by a distinguished Christian leader (Dr. John R. Mott) what had brought deepest satisfaction to his soul in difficulties, doubts and questionings. He replied, "Living Faith in God." God reveals Himself to men not through individual vision or exclusive personal interview (as it were) but through action: in this connection Mr. Gandhi spoke of the experience that had come to him in relation to his three weeks' fast for the removal of untouchability. If we are dedicated to doing the will of God, God will Himself give us all the guidance we need in His own way. Christ said once, "He that doeth the will of God shall know the true teaching." And when Christ instituted the great, but forgotten, sacrament of menial and manual service, on the occasion just before his crucifixion when he washed his disciples' feet, he said to them, "If I, your master, have *done* this for you, you also ought to *do* the same. If you understand the example which I have set you, happy are you if you *act upon it*." It is in *action* of Christlikeness that we reach the fulfilment of our individual life's purpose, and come into harmony with the master-purpose of the universe.

Mr. Gandhi also laid emphasis upon the necessity of much silence in a man's life, if that life is to be genuinely efficacious for the conquest of evil. He spoke as follows: "I can say that I am an everlastingly silent man now. Only a little while *ago* I remained completely silent for nearly two months, and the spell of that silence has not yet broken... Nowadays I go into silence at prayer time every evening, and break it for visitors at two o'clock. I broke it today when you came. It has become both a physical and spiritual necessity for me. Originally the step was taken to relieve the sense of pressure. Then I wanted time for writing. However, after I had practised it for some time, I saw the spiritual value of it. It suddenly flashed across my mind that that was the time when I could best hold communion with God. And now I feel as though I was naturally built for silence."

Nothing could indicate more clearly than these words the deep-lying spiritual basis of the effective power for righteousness which works through Mr. Gandhi. It is in these unhurried periods of silent communion with God that he gains the almost uncanny quality of prophethood and seership which gives him so extraordinary an authority over those who love him and follow him.

On a subsequent occasion, Mr. Gandhi discussed with some others of the Christian leaders, who had just been gathered in conference at Madras, various aspects of the problem of the rescuing of humanity from the impending international crisis which threatens to plunge us into war-fare once more, and thus into an orgy of hatred and violence. How can civilization be saved from the "humiliation of impotence" which is gnawing at its roots today? It has had the message of Christ for nearly two thousand years and yet Western civilization has never been able to enforce or implement that message, and is therefore breaking down before our eyes at the present time. There is a profound disquietude all over the West with regard to what is happening, and the prospects for the future. It was fitting therefore that these Christian leaders should come to the man who has outspokenly based his life-work on the attempt to make the central principle of the Christian Gospel – the Cross of self-chosen, unresisting, redemptive suffering – live once more; and has brought thereby regeneration to an ancient world-order which had become, in many ways, effete. Before our own eyes, the Cross has come to live again, in creative triumph, amidst a non-Christian environment, through the efforts of this man.

Is there not a hope, then, that even in the West, hardened though it is by the generations of unrestricted profit-hunting since the Industrial Revolution began, there may come a creative recovery of the message of the Cross: and that this recovery may come in time to save us from the disaster of wholesale mutual destruction which we see looming ahead?

Mr. Gandhi was asked by one of his visitors what was the fundamental motive in the work which he had done for India. Was it social, or political, or religious? His activities have spread so widely into all three spheres, and have exercised so deep an influence both on the fundamental structure of Hindu society and on the political status of India, that such a question is natural. Mr. Gandhi replied as follows: "My motive has been purely religious... I could not be leading a religious life unless I identified myself with the whole of mankind: and this I could not do unless I took part in politics. The whole gamut of man's activities today constitutes an indivisible whole. You cannot divide social, political and purely religious work into watertight compartments. I do not know any religion apart from human activity. It provides a moral basis to all other activities which they would otherwise lack, reducing life to a thing of "sound and fury, signifying nothing.""

Mr. Gandhi was asked, in this connection, whether his service was done through love of the cause for which he worked, or for love of the people whom he served. He replied unhesitatingly, that his motive was love of the people. To serve a cause without serving persons was a dead thing. He instanced the manner in which he began in early life to sympathize with, and try to improve the position of the Untouchables. His mother had one day forbidden him to play with an Untouchable boy. This awakened questioning in his mind, "and from that day my revolt began."

Asked to explain in more detail his attitude to non-violence,

which, it was observed, does not seem to be likely to be
adopted very widely or effectively in the West, Gandhi said: "In
my opinion non-violence is not passivity in any shape or form.
Non-violence, as I understand it, is the most active force in the
world... Non-violence is the supreme law. During my half-
century of experience I have not yet come across a situation
when I had to say that I was helpless, that I had no remedy in
terms of non-violence.

"Take the question of the Jews, on which I have written. No
Jew need feel helpless, if he takes to the non-violent way. A
friend has written to me a letter objecting that I have assumed
that the Jews had been violent. It is true that the Jews have not
been violent in their own persons... But they have not been
actively non-violent or in spite of the misdeeds of the dictators,
they would say, "We shall suffer at their hands: they knew no
better. But we shall suffer not in the manner in which they want
us to suffer." If even one Jew acted thus, he would save his self-
respect and leave an example which, if it became infectious,
would save the whole of Jewry, and leave a rich heritage to
mankind besides.

"What about China? you will ask. The Chinese have no
designs upon other people. They have no desire for territory.
True, perhaps, China is not ready for such aggression; perhaps,
what looks like her pacifism is only indolence. In any case,
China's is not active non-violence. Her putting up a valiant
defence against Japan is proof enough that China was never
intentionally non-violent. That she is on the defensive, is no
answer in terms of non-violence. Therefore, when the time for
testing her active non-violence came, she failed in the test. This
is no criticism of China. I wish the Chinese success. According
to the accepted standards, her behaviour is strictly correct. But
when the position is examined in terms of non-violence, I must
say it is unbecoming for a nation of 400 million, a nation as
cultured as China, to repel Japanese aggression by resorting to
Japan's own methods. If the Chinese had the non-violence of

my conception, there would be no use left for the latest machinery of destruction which Japan possesses. The Chinese would say to Japan, 'Bring all your machinery, we present half of our population to you. But the remaining two hundred million won't bend the knee to you.' If the Chinese did that, Japan would become China's slave."

Mr. Gandhi could not have given a more uncompromising statement of his fundamental belief about non-violence. The trouble with the war-method of righting wrong, even the kind of wrong which China is suffering today, is that it attempts the task of "casting out Satan by Satan." It is the use of iniquitous methods of action, the burning, shooting, maiming, torturing of human beings, in order to repel other human beings who are using those methods of action. Such a process can never end the evil will which has made the first aggression possible. It merely makes that evil will more determined and more dangerous. The only effective method of righting wrong is not the foolish and essentially abortive attempt to cast out Satan by Satan, to end violence by means of more violence, but the good-will which voluntarily takes upon itself suffering for the sake of changing the spirit of aggression into the spirit of friendship.

Mr. Gandhi then quoted Shelley's great lines from the Mask of Anarchy, lines which should be far better known than they are:

> *Stand ye calm and resolute*
> *Like a forest close and mute,*
> *With folded arms and looks which are*
> *Weapons of unvanquished war.*
>
> *And if then the tyrants dare,*
> *Let them ride among you there,*
> *Slash, and stab, and maim, and hew –*
> *What they like, that let them do..*

With folded arms and steady eyes,
 And little fear, and less surprise,
Look upon them as they slay,
Till their rage has died away.

Then they will return with shame
To the place from which they came,
And the blood thus shed will speak
In hot blushes on their cheek.
Rise like lions after slumber
In unvanquishable number –

Shake your chains to earth, like dew
Which In sleep has fallen on you –
Ye are many, they are few.

The discussion then turned to another branch of the same subject. Mr. Gandhi said: "It has been objected, however, that non-violence is all right in the case of the Jews, because there is personal contact between the individual and his persecutors; but in China, Japan comes with long-range guns and aeroplanes. The person who rains death from above has never any chance of even knowing who and how many he has killed. How can non-violence combat aerial warfare, seeing that there are no personal contacts?

"The reply to this is that behind the death-dealing bomb, there is the human hand that releases it, and behind that still is the human heart that sets the hand in motion. At the back of the policy of terrorism is the assumption that terrorism, if applied in a sufficient measure, will produce the desired result, namely, bend the adversary to the tyrant's will. But supposing a people make up their mind that they will never do the tyrant's will, nor retaliate with the tyrant's own methods, the tyrant will not find it worth-while to go on with his terrorism. If sufficient food is given to the tyrant, the time will come when he will have had more than a surfeit...

"I learnt the lesson of non-violence from my wife, when I tried to bend her to my will. Her determined resistance to my will on the one hand, and her quiet submission to the suffering my stupidity involved on the other, ultimately made me ashamed of myself and cured me of my stupidity in thinking I was born to rule over her; and in the end, she became my teacher in non-violence. And what I did in South Africa was but an extension of the rule of *Satyagraha* which she unwittingly practised in her own person."

Here is another exceedingly important principle in regard to *Satyagraha*. It is a movement, a principle of action, in which women can take an equal share with men. Not only so. It is a movement in which women are peculiarly fitted for leadership. For untold centuries, the sovereign weapon of womanhood has been patient suffering, combined with an outspoken and fearless witnessing against violence arid oppression. Now she is called upon to take the lead in making this same spirit and method the key-principle for the saving of the world.

Let us remind ourselves of the four fundamental ideas of *Satyagraha*.

First, there is wrong loose in the world.

Second, wrong must be overcome.

Third, wrong cannot be overcome by violence, which only makes the evil-will deeper and firmer, and renders it inevitable that some day that evil-will, however remorselessly suppressed, will break forth again with tenfold violence.

Fourthly, wrong can be overcome by patient suffering, which in the spirit, of good-will voluntarily takes the pain inflicted by wrong upon itself, even to death. For such a spirit there is inevitably Resurrection, even though the individual *Satyagrahi* has given his life for the truth.

It is clear that in relation to all four of these fundamental ideals, womanhood has from time immemorial known and practised *Satyagraha*. The fact of wrong has been forced upon woman's consciousness by the tyranny under which she has herself suffered. Gradually, she has come to the knowledge and to the determination that, at any cost, this tyranny must be ended. She cannot end it by violent methods, and has already too much good sense ever to suppose that the use of such methods can solve the problem of the relationship of the sexes. She has turned to another way of action, unflinchingly courageous protest against tyranny, whether in her own home or in the sphere of national politics. She has coupled therewith-in the case not only of the leaders of the woman's movement but oftens of thousands of inconspicuous individuals – a redemptive bearing of the worst that tyranny can do, in the spirit of self-chosen suffering on behalf of others. The elementary biological facts of human nature, the way in which children are brought into the world and reared, make women not merely acquainted from within with the principles of *Satyagraha,* but actual practising *Satyagrahis,* though they may never have heard of Jesus Christ or of those, who in our own day, have tried to make his Cross a loving power once more. Every baby that is born into the world is born through self-chosen suffering, and brought up through the love which bears all things for the sake of others.

Therefore, this modern call, which has come to us through Mr. Gandhi, that we should make the principles of thd Cross of Christ really operative in the affairs of men, even on the widest possible stage, is in reality a call to womanhood to step forward into what may be called a world-wide leadership of ideas, for the ending of the great curses which afflict mankind-poverty, oppression, warfare.

The fact that we men have life at all in the world means that our mothers practised *Satyagraha*, walked the way of the Cross, not merely in the pangs through which we were born, but in a thousand forgotten incidents in the everyday life of our childhood. They suffered for us, willingly and joyfully, because they loved us. The call to us is that we should go forth in the same spirit of joyful endurance for the saving of all mankind. If we have any sense, we men will recognize that in this task the women have already gone much further than we and can therefore guide us and inspire us. Without their leadership we shall inevitably fail.

One of Mr. Gandhi's visitors then confronted him with the problem of dictatorships which seem completely impervious to any kind of moral appeal. Would it not be playing into the hands of these dictators if those whom they threaten were to confront them with non-violence? Since dictatorships are unmoral by definition, can it be expected that the law of moral conversion will hold good in their case?

Mr. Gandhi stated his opinions very impressively here also. "Your argument," he said, "presupposes that the dictators are beyond redemption. But belief in non-violence is based on the assumption that human nature in its essence is one, and therefore unfailingly responds to the advance of love. It should be remembered that these dictators have up to now always found ready response to the violence that they have used. Within their experience, they have not come across organized non-violent resistance on an appreciable scale, if at all. Therefore, it is not only highly likely, but I hold it to be inevitable, that they would recognize the superiority of non-violent resistance over any display of violence that they may be capable of putting forth. Moreover the non-violent technique does not depend for its success on the good-will of the dictators; for a non-violent resistor depends upon the unfailing assistance of God, which sustains him throughout difficulties which would otherwise be considered insurmountable. His faith makes him indomitable."

Here again we may notice how fundamentally religious is

Mr. Gandhi's idealism of *Satyagraha*, as was Christ's idealism
of the Cross. We must start, not from human suffering under
tyranny and oppression, bitter as this may be. We must start
from God. The first question for us to answer is this. What do
I believe to be the will of God, and what kind of a God do I
believe Him to be? If our answer to that question is that He is
a God of good-will, who works by freedom and justice and
who means His will of freedom and justice to become
dominant in human affairs, then all we have to do is to catch
hold of the hand of this Father – God – and we Christians can
sum up His nature by saying that He the God and Father of our
Lord Jesus Christ. If we thus hold His hand (and we shall soon
find that it is rather a case of, His holding our hands), we shall
be led forward along the way of the Cross, that is, the way of
non-violent self-chosen bearing of the worst that tyranny and
wrong can do against the good-will which is God's will, in
order that others may be freed from tyranny and wrong.

We start from God. At the back of all our discussions, all our
plantings, there is to be the fact of God. If we leave Him out of
count, we shall fail indeed. And, if He is a Living God, He
must, as Mr. Gandhi teaches, be sought in silence, because what
matters is not that we should say things to him, even in the
most splendid of liturgical forms, but that He should make
known His will to us, and show us His way. Such guidance,
with the power which comes from laying our own wills in line
with the Divine will, can come to us only as we wait silently
before Him, and listen for His voice.

Then as we return to God and know His will in power, we
shall become, as Mr. Gandhi says, inspired by an indomitable
faith, which will help us to surmount all obstacles.

But we must begin with God: return to Him: that our policies
and enterprises may be not our own, but His.

Pursuing the subject of right action against the dictators, one
of the Christian visitors asked Mr. Gandhi what attitude,

should be adopted in the face of aggression which does not trouble actually to use force, but employs the overwhelming threat of it in order to obtain what it wants.

Mr. Gandhi replied as follows:

"Suppose they come and occupy mines, factories, and all sources of natural wealth belonging, e.g. to the Czechs. Then the following results can take place:

(1) The Czechs may be annihilated for disobedience to orders. That would be a glorious victory for the Czechs and the beginning of the fall of Germany.

(2) The Czechs might become demoralized in the presence of overwhelming force. This is a result common in all struggles; but if demoralization does take place, it would not be on account of non-violence; but it would be due to absence of or inadequacy of non-violence.

(3) The third thing that can take place is that Germany might use her new possessions for occupation by her surplus population. This again could not be avoided by offering violent resistance, for we have assumed that violent resistance is out of the question.

"Thus non-violent resistance is the best method under all circumstances.

"I do not think that Hitler and Mussolini are after all so very indifferent to the appeal of world-opinion. But today these dictators feel satisfaction in defying world opinion because none of the so-called Great Powers can come to them with clean hands, and they have a rankling sense of injustice done to their people by the Great Powers in the past. Only the other day, an esteemed English friend owned to me that Nazi Germany was England's sin, and that it was the treaty of Versailles that made Hitler."

In this connection, the present writer has vivid memories of

walking through unending wards of children's hospitals in
Vienna, during the period of starvation just after the peace of
Versailles, before the American child-feeding schemes had taken
full effect. In those hospitals, one saw the twisted and tortured
bodies of innumerable little children, the Victims of our
Blockade, and of the horrible diseases to which it gave rise. It is
estimated that one million German and Austrian women and
children died as a result of that supreme international crime.
When Bismarck took Paris in 1871, he rushed food-trains into
the starving city at the first possible opportunity. We
deliberately starved Germany and Austria for eight months
after the Armistice, in order to force from our beaten enemies
the kind of Peace we wanted. We got it; and a fundamentally
bad Peace it was; but no insults or injustices in the Peace itself
(not even the war-guilt clause or the statement regarding
German colonial incapacity) were anything like so iniquitous as
the manner in which we obtained it, the Blockade. I remember
saying to myself at the time, as I saw those suffering children,
"There will be a long bill to pay for this some day." That day
has now come. The survivors amongst those children, and
those who were of the same age at the time, are now the
spearhead of the Nazi forces. It is amongst them that the Nazi
ideology finds so many fanatical devotees. We, the victorious
Allies, made Mussolini by the way in which we treated Italy
after the war. Britain, for instance, took nine of the fourteen
new mandates, and Italy got none. We made Hitler by the way
in which we treated Germany and Austria during the period of
the Blockade and by the Peace of Versailles. You cannot
perpetrate international crimes on that scale without sowing
the seeds of a formidable reaction later on. If history teaches
anything at all, it teaches this.

But amongst the Nazis, as they look back on that period of
torture and of humiliation, the legend is inculcated that the
Jews were responsible. It was the Jews, so the fantastic story
goes, that stabbed the German armies, in the back whilst they

were still unbroken on the field, by bringing about revolution at home. Therefore, they are the first enemy to be punished. Hence the sufferings of the Jews in Germany today are the result of the bitter reaction against our international sins, in the Blockade and the Peace. It is not for us to condemn the Nazi policy towards the Jews, for we are the people who brought that policy about. It is for us, in the first place, to blame ourselves: and in the second place, to do all that we can for the relief of the Jewish sufferers.

One of the visitors then asked: "What can I as a Christian do to contribute to international peace? How can international anarchy be broken down, and non-violence made effective for establishing peace?"

It must have been a somewhat interesting spectacle to see these Christian leaders, chosen apostles of the Prince of Peace, gathered from all parts of the world, after two thousand years of failure, to apply Christ's method of the Cross to the problems of war, consulting Mr. Gandhi, who prides himself upon being a convinced Hindu, upon the right method of making operative the fundamental principle of their own Christianity!

Mr. Gandhi replied:

"You, as a Christian, can make an effective contribution by non-violent action even though it may cost you your all. Peace will never come until the Great Powers courageously decide to disarm themselves. It seems to me that recent events must force that belief upon the Great Powers.

"*I have an implicit faith – a faith that today burns brighter than ever, after half a century's experience of unbroken practice of non-violence – that mankind can only be saved through non-violence, which is the central teaching of the Bible, as I have understood the Bible.*"

When Mr. Gandhi says "non-violence" or *Satyagraha*, he

means the method of the Cross. That is why, when he visited our Settlement in Birmingham, he chose the hymn "When I survey the wondrous Cross," as expressing for him the very heart of universal truth. Here then is his testimony that mankind is only to be saved by the Cross, and by our taking the words of our Master literally, "Take up thy Cross and follow me."

When shall we learn what our own religion means? It is profoundly to be hoped that the words of the great Hindu-and far more than his words, his own living practice of the principles in which he believes – may bring the day of awakening nearer in Christendom. Already in the most populous Christian country of Europe, the Church is persecuted: and there are urgent rumours of far more bitter persecutions to come, in a vast new Kulturkampf against the Christian Church. Will the German Christians rise to their opportunities for the revitalizing of Christianity as a whole, and perhaps for the saving of civilization, by facing their troubles in the spirit of the Cross, by "entering prisons as palaces," by rejoicing that they are counted worthy to suffer for Christ Jesus? And in our own problems, especially those of the combat against warfare and against poverty, are we going to live by the same principle? For the Cross is not only to be borne in periods of active persecution. It is the living principle of self-identification with the needs and sufferings of those everywhere who are "God's little ones" because they are hungry and naked, sick and oppressed.

Mr. Gandhi then described what he had recently seen of the progress of the spirit of non-violence amongst the wild fighting races of the North-West Frontier:

"I was not prepared for what I saw. They are in dead earnest about the thing, and there is a deep-rooted sincerity in their hearts. They themselves see light and hope in non-violence... Before it was all darkness. There was not a family but had its blood feuds. They lived like tigers in a den. Though the Pathans used to be always armed with knives, daggers and rifles, they use to be terrified of their superior officers, lest they should lose their jobs. All that has changed now with thousands. Blood feuds are becoming a thing of the past among those Pathans who have come under the influence of Khansaheb's non-violence movement and instead of depending for their livelihood on paltry jobs, they have turned to the soil for cultivation, and soon they will turn to industry if their promise is kept."

These last remarks illustrate Mr. Gandhi's belief in hard work especially hard work on the land. When he was amongst us in England in 1931, he laid great stress upon the necessity for communal land settlements as a means both of solving the problem of unemployment and of refounding a Christian civilization. The same has been his message in India, and with it the insistence on the daily giving of a generous measure of time to hard work with the hands at other forms of handicraft, especially the spinning of yarn.

It may be well for us to remind ourselves that when the old classical civilization crashed in the fifth century, it was slowly and arduously re-created by small, bodies of men who went out into the ruined wastes that had once been fertile, and there, in the name of Christ, founded tiny communal land settlements, the primitive cloisters. The early monks, who brought back scientific agriculture and then education, religion, refinement, were primarily Digging Men. It was by the Spade, swung not for private profit butfor the community, for Christ and for his suffering war victims of the barbarian invasions, that these heroic pioneers built up the great civilization of the Middle Ages, a civilization in many ways far more creative and infinitely more Christian than our own.

It is at least possible that in our own time, civilization, such as it is, with its militarism and its industrial competition, may again crash, through a new world war. If this is so, there will be crying need once more of Digging People, who will have the courage to build for Christ by working with their spade not for their own advantage but for the community, for the war victims, and for their Master.

But, if this is to be so, we must prepare now: That is one reason why the extensive growth during recent years of unemployed men's allotment associations up and down England and Wales is of such importance: and it is also a reason why it is needful that members of the more fortunate classes should go, in larger and larger numbers, to share in, the work of such associations, as has been the practice for a number of years with the Work Camp teams.

The discussion between Mr. Gandhi and the Christian leaders then turned back to the subject of religion. He was asked what was his method of worship. He replied: "We have joint worship morning and evening at 4.20 a.m. and 7 p.m. This has gone on for years. We have a recitation of verses from the Gita and other accepted religious books, also hymns of saints, with or without music. Individual worship cannot be described in words. It goes on continuously and even unconsciously. There is not a moment when I do not feel the presence of a Witness, whose eye misses nothing, and with whom I strive to keep in tune. I do not pray as Christian friends do" (presumably Mr. Gandhi is here referring to liturgical prayer); "not because I think there is anything wrong in it; but because words won't come to me. I suppose it is a matter of habit... God knows and anticipates our wants. The Deity does not need my supplication; but I, a very imperfect human being, do need His protection as a child that of its father... I have never found Him lacking in response. I have found Him nearest at hand when the horizon seemed darkest – in my ordeals in goals, when it was not all smooth sailing for me.

"I cannot recall a moment in my life when I had a sense of

desertion by God."

To those of us who remember the attitude in earlier days of some of these Christian leaders who interviewed Mr. Gandhi in this fashion, the conversation summarized above has an extraordinary interest. One of the most distinguished of them came to Cambridge when the present writer was a student there, and spoke with measured and dynamic eloquence on the Evangelization of the World in this Generation. Confidence and ordered certainly were the key-notes of that remarkable address. We Western Protestant Christians (especially perhaps the Presbyterians among us) had the truth. The only problem was to get it across to the rest of the world in time to avert disasters in the East, due to the absence of the Truth there!

Then came the Great War. And now how greatly is the situation changed! We have discovered that one who prides himself on being a Hindu is far nearer the Truth of Christ, the Truth of the Cross, than we are; and, rightly and wisely indeed, our leaders – these same leaders – go to sit at his feet and learn from him what Christianity means, for in the last analysis Christianity is the Cross of Christ.

Ex Oriente Lux.

An Indian Statesman's Tribute
Sir Mirza M. Ismail

It gives me very great pleasure to respond to the invitation kindly extended to me by Sir S. Radhakrishnan to send a contribution to the volume of Essays and Reflections on the life and work of Mahatma Gandhi which is to be presented to him on the occasion of the seventieth anniversary of his birthday.

The completion of "three score years and ten" of his life is much more than a matter of gratification to Mahatma Gandhi's

innumerable friends and admirers, among whom I am happy to
have the privilege of counting myself. Every birthday of his is
looked upon as an event for country-wide rejoicing, and his
seventieth birthday will doubtless evoke unfailing enthusiasm
throughout India.

To me it is a matter of deep personal interest to recall the
circumstances in which I have been brought into close touch
with this great man, who is both teacher and leader.

In 1927 or so, when Mahatma Gandhi's health was failing he
turned to the salubrious climate of Bangalore and the bracing
air of the Nandi Hills, for the change which he so much
needed. It was then that an opportunity presented itself to me
of coming into close personal contact with him. The few weeks
that he stayed in our midst have left behind some of the
happiest memories in the minds of the people of Mysore.
During those days I met the Mahatma as often as I could, and
the reverence, love, and affection which he then inspired in me
have formed the basis of a friendship which I have cherished
and valued ever since.

It is a matter of peculiar pleasure to me to recall the very
interesting time I spent in London during the sessions of the
Indian Round Table Conference; notably in connection with the
second session, in which the Congress participated and was
represented by Mahatma Gandhi as its sole delegate. He was
without doubt the most distinguished of the members from
India. He electrified us by the remarkable speeches that he
made in the course of our deliberations. The second session of
the Conference was made memorable to me personally by the
support, though qualified, which I received from Mahatma
Gandhi for the scheme which I had the honour of placing
before the Federal Structure Committee providing for the
creation of a Federal Council as the Second Chamber of the
Federal Legislature, to be composed of the representatives of
the Governments of the Federating Units. Mahatmaji, who was

all along opposed to the creation of a bicameral legislature, was prepared to modify his attitude and accept the proposal adumbrated in my memorandum, if the Federal Council was allowed to become an advisory body. Indeed, as I had occasion to acknowledge in one of my addresses to the Mysore Representative Assembly, "I personally found in the Mahatma a powerful ally at the Second Round Table Conference when voicing my criticisms of the feature of the White Paper Constitution which seems to me to be most open to criticism, that is, the composition of the Upper Chamber." The subsequent course of events is a matter of history, but I recall this circumstance as an illustration of Mahatma Gandhi's keen desire to help in the efforts to devise a sound constitution for India.

Let me turn from these personal reminiscences to the significance of the life and work of this great son of India not merely for his own country but also for the world at large. It is often said that it is a hazardous thing to predict immortality for one's contemporaries because posterity makes its own choice. But in prophesying immortality to the name of the Mahatma, there is little possibility of one's prophecy being falsified by the verdict of history. Contemporary opinion is unanimous that he is one of the greatest Indians ever born. He is unquestionably the most important living Indian and, as I had occasion to say some years ago in a public address, "he may be said to represent the spirit of India and to voice her sentiments as probably no one else can do." He has captured and won the hearts of his countrymen by his universal sympathy and his most passionate allegiance to his high ideals. He is revered by all those to whom the spirit of service makes a strong appeal. Truly one of the most outstanding personalities in the world to-day, Mahatma Gandhi occupies a position in the national life of India which is unique, and he has used this unique position for the benefit of his Motherland. To judge from the extraordinary influence he wields over the minds of the great mass of the

Indian people, Mahatma Gandhi may be reckoned as one of the most powerful personal forces in the British Empire today.

There is a touch of cynicism, but a substratum of truth in the remark that politics is a sordid game, and that its exigencies often demand a compromise with conscience. Success in it, so it is said, generally goes to the man who is not much encumbered by scruples. But here is Mahatma Gandhi, who is the most conscientious, scrupulous and principled of Indians and yet is the most successful politician of them all! He is the eternal enigma of India. A man of rare moral elevation, of unimpeachable private life, of transparent sincerity of conduct and of a strongly religious bent of mind, he recalls to our mind great spiritual leaders and saints. On the other hand, as the inspiring leader of a resurgent India who has given Indians a new spirit, a sense of self-respect and a feeling of pride in their civilization, he is something more than a mere politician. He is a great statesman, a man of vision. Indeed, as Richard Freund has remarked in the Spectator, "Unsteadily, tentatively but already visible in outline, an Indian nation is emerging and Mr. Gandhi is its maker."

It is this combination of Saint, politician and statesman which appears so intriguing to the Englishman but which is accepted, if not understood, by his Indian followers. Mahatma Gandhi is among the great men of the world whom all praise but few understand. He has imported religion and ethics into politics and has forged strange moral weapons to fight material forces in the political arena for the achievement of practical results. If he has brought religion into politics and has spiritualized it, he has likewise brought politics into religion and has secularized many an issue which orthodox Hinduism regarded as purely religious in character. The emancipation of Harijans is easily the most outstanding of such issues on which he has led the revolt of intellectual India against the forces of Hindu orthodoxy. But in fairness to him it must be said that his move to eradicate the evil of "untouchability" from the land is dictated as much by his genuine humanitarian impulse as by his reformist zeal and political insight.

Mahatma Gandhi has immense faith in himself – a faith which has increased with his mystical confidence in the efficacy of spiritual force and which sometimes borders on inspiration. He rules and is ruled more by his heart than by his head, by intuition rather than by intellect. He has often been known to explain to himself and his followers a most puzzling piece of advice he has had to give them or most inexplicable conduct in particular circumstances by a simple but mystifying reference to "my inner voice." "Plain living and high thinking" is his maxim of life, and the degree to which he has disciplined his emotions, his conduct and his very physiology is at once the admiration and despair of lesser men. "Gandhi feels that if you control yourself you can control politics." He does not make any weak concessions to the flesh and is Spartan in his tastes and habits. Truth and Non-violence are the fixed stars by which he steers his own barge and by which he has tried to guide the ship of the Congress and of the nation over the stormy sea of Indian politics.

If I am asked to explain the secret of his immense hold upon the imagination of the Indian people I should not think so much of his ability – consummate as it is – as a politician or of the degree of success which has attended the application of his methods to the solution of India's problems. Indians, as a race, are peculiarly sensitive to character and are more responsive to moral than to intellectual leadership. And it is the Mahatma's absolute sincerity of purpose and purity of motives combined with a sterling personal character that have won for him the confidence and affection not only of his own political followers but of many people outside the Congress organization who neither share all his views nor subscribe to his political doctrines and methods.

It was a little over five years ago that I said, in the course of my address to the legislators of Mysore: "There is one man above all others who can help us towards a reconciliation of our difficulties, and towards that new phase of character that is the groundwork of self-government. I am not one of those who wish Mahatma Gandhi to retire from politics. There never was a time when India so badly needed the guidance of a genuine leader, and in him we have one who holds a unique position in the country and is not only a convinced lover of peace and an ardent patriot, but also a far-seeing, sagacious statesman. I feel that he is qualified far better than anyone else to reconcile the conflicting elements in the country and to induce them all to march together to a further stage along the road that leads to self-government. He also has it in his power, as no one else has to establish the happiest relations between India and Great Britain. I feel sure that the Government has in him a powerful ally and Great Britain a true friend. If he should retire from politics at this juncture, there are indications that the arena would, in all probability, be occupied by demagogues and vain visionaries, who are out to mislead themselves and the country by meaningless shibboleths."

A great deal has happened since I uttered these words. Ministries responsible to legislatures have come into being in all the Provinces. The problem of an Indian Federation has come to the foreground of discussion. Gandhiji, as he himself has said, "has ceased to be in the Congress but continues to be of it." But nothing has as yet happened which would induce me to retract or even modify the sentiments to which I then gave expression. With the exception of Mahatma Gandhi who is still the dominant force-as dominant, I should say, as ever-the country has no one else to turn to for ultimate guidance. The Mahatma is a force for moderation, for reason, for practicality in politics. And India can ill-afford to do without him either now or for as long a time as one can foresee.

If Mahatma Gandhi is so full of meaning and value to us in India, it is no less true that his life and work possess a meaning to the world outside, which, at the present time, is so much distracted by wars and threats of war. His political technique, which is essentially pacific in conception, and his philosophy of political conduct, based on the triple maxim of Love, Truth and Non-violence, furnish ample food for reflection to nations whose mutual relationships are at present regulated by diplomacy, hatred and war.

Let me conclude by heartily congratulating Mahatma Gandhi on his seventieth birthday, and by wishing him many years of health, happiness and fruitful activity in the service of India in particular and of the world in general.

The Authority of Detachment and Moral Force
C.E.M. Joad

In what consists the most characteristic quality of our species? Some would say, in moral virtue; some, in godliness; some, in courage; some, in the power of self-sacrifice. Aristotle found it in reason. It was by virtue of our reason that, he held, we were chiefly distinguished from the brutes. Aristotle's answer gives, I suggest, part of the truth, but not the whole. The essence of reason lies in objectivity and detachment. It is reason's pride to face reality, when the garment of make-believe, with which pious hands have hidden its uglier features, has been stripped away. In a word, the reasonable man is a man unafraid; unafraid to see things as they are, without weighing the scales in his own favour, allowing desire to dictate conclusion, or hope to masquerade as judgment.

The reasonable man, then, is detached: detached, that is to say, from the subject-matter which his reason investigates.

Is he also detached from himself? I think that he is not. I have

known men of the highest intellectual ability who swore like
"nitwits" when they broke their bootlaces, and lost their
temper when they missed their trains. Great scientists and
mathematicians are not remarkable for serenity of mind, while
philosophers, who should be equable, are peppery;
philosophers, indeed, are noted for the irritability of their
dispositions. Hence I think that Aristotle's pronouncement
hints at the truth rather than states it. The truth is that the
characteristic virtue of humanity lies in the extension to the
self, its passions, temptations, hopes and desires, of that
attitude of objective detachment which the man of reason
applies to the subject-matter which occupies the attention of
the intellect. To combine non-attachment to the self with the
passionate apprehension of certain truths and the disinterested
attachment to certain principles, is to generate what I take to be
the most distinctive virtue of humanity-moral force.

It is in the possession of the virtue of detachment from self
that, I suggest, lies the source of Gandhi's authority. A
superficial expression of his detachment is his control over his
body. The detached man has power over his body because,
having effected its separation from the true self, he is enabled to
use it as an instrument for the purposes of the self. Thus, it is
no accident that Gandhi can sleep at will, at a moment's notice,
for any period that he likes to prescribe, no accident that he can
deliberately lose or gain weight without altering his diet.

Another expression of the same virtue is the combination of a
fixed resolution in regard to ends combined with a maximum
adaptability in regard to means. The detached man is not a
fanatic; he is never so attached to his way that he is not
prepared to abandon it and substitute for it another way.
Provided that the end remains clearly in view, he will approach
it by whatever road events and circumstances suggest. Hence
the combination of the politician and the saint in Gandhi,
which has so puzzled observers; the adroitness in negotiation,
the childlike simplicity which is seen in retrospect to have been

the most astute political wisdom, the aptness at and the readiness for compromise are characteristics of a man who, firmly fixed in regard to his end, can be non-attached in regard to the means to that end. Thus Gandhi, the instigator of Civil Disobedience as a political weapon, feels no scruple at calling it off, the moment it seems unlikely to succeed; thus Gandhi, the saint who fasts for the good of his soul, is perfectly ready to make use of his fasting as a bargaining counter, and to begin to eat again, when fasting has served its political turn; thus Gandhi, the implacable opponent of the Constitution, is now prepared to co-operate in working for the Constitution which he so strenuously opposed, provided only that the representatives of the native states are elected by the peoples and not, as the Constitution at present envisages, nominated by the Prince; and thus, finally, Gandhi, the lifelong enemy of the British in India, is now rightly regarded as the best friend of the British in India, a friend whose authority alone prevents not only a resumption of Civil Disobedience, but a resort to the more familiar methods of revolutionary agitation. Will the British, one wonders, extend before it is too late the small concessions that are now asked, extend them voluntarily and with a good grace, or must India become another Ireland, driven by their refusal into an intransigence which refuses to accept the concessions which would now content her?

To return to detachment. Detachment, I am suggesting, is one of the most potent ingredients of that power so easy to recognize, so difficult to define that we call moral force, a power which men, alone of sentient beings, possess.

Physical force affords no problems and raises no questions. A man is physically stronger than you and accordingly, he has his way with you, either directly through the compulsion exerted by his superior strength, or indirectly through fear of the pains and penalties he may inflict upon you, if you thwart his will. It is the compulsion of direct physical force that throws one man over a precipice; it is fear of indirect physical force that causes another to deny himself in this life that he may please God and escape eternal torment in the next. Physical force bestows power, which may be defined as the ability to make other men do your will for fear of the consequences, if they do not.

But moral force can command no such penalties. If I resist moral force, I do not suffer. Why, then, do I obey it? It is difficult to say. I recognize its authority, and, even if I resist it, I know that it is right and I wrong, and I recognize and know these things because I am myself a spirit, acknowledging the superior spirit of another. Thus, moral force exerts not power but influence, which may be defined as the effect produced by one human being upon the mind and actions of another, not through fear of punishment or hope of reward, but by virtue of the latter's intuitive acknowledgement of intrinsic superiority.

It was by moral force that Gandhi induced thousands to besiege the gaols, demanding that they should be arrested; it was by moral force that he caused thousands to allow themselves to be beaten to pulp without lifting a hand in self-defence.

The experiment of Civil Disobedience, inspired by moral force, has an immense significance for the contemporary West. Is it only by devoting all its savings to equipping itself with the instruments of slaughter, is it only through the willingness of its members to use these instruments, whenever the Government of the State to which they belong deems the mass-murder of the citizens of some other state to be desirable, that a modern community can hope to survive? Is there no way for a nation engaged in dispute to demonstrate the superior rightness of its cause, except by killing off as many members of the opposing nation as it can contrive? These are questions which insistently demand an answer in the Western world, and unless our generation can find some other answer than the one which has been traditionally given to them in the past, its civilization is doomed to destruction.

To Gandhi belongs the supreme credit of having had the wit to suggest and the courage to act upon another answer. Christ and Buddha, he has said in effect, are right. It takes two to make a quarrel, and if you resolutely refuse to be the second, nobody can quarrel with you; refuse to resist by violence, and you will not only gain your ends more effectively than by violent resistance, but you will defeat violence itself by demonstrating its non-effectiveness. It is this method, theoretically as old as human thinking, which Gandhi sought – it is his supreme claim to our gratitude – to apply to the conduct of human affairs. He is a man who has shown himself persistently willing to take the risk of the noblest hypothesis being true. No doubt, the method he advocates is in advance of the times; no doubt, therefore, his thought appears shocking and subversive to the conventional many. Inevitably, it challenges vested interests in the thought of the present, unsettling men's minds, alarming their morals, and undermining the security of the powerful and the established. Hence, like all original geniuses, he has been abused as an outrageous and often as a blasphemous impostor. Heterodoxy in art is, at worst, rated as eccentricity or folly, but heterodoxy in politics or morals is denounced as propagandist wickedness which, if tolerantly received, will undermine the very foundations of society; while the advance on current morality, in which the heterodoxy normally consists, is achieved only in the teeth of vested interests in the thought and morals it seeks to displace. Thus, while the genius in the sphere of art is usually permitted to starve in a garret, the genius in the sphere of conduct is persecuted and killed with the sanction of the law. An examination of the great legal trials of history from this point of view would make interesting reading. Socrates, Giordano Bruno, and Servetus were all tried and condemned for holding opinions distasteful to persons in authority in their own day, for which the world now honours them. One of the best definitions of a man of genius is he who, in Shelley's words, "beholds the future in the present, and his thoughts are the germ of the flower and fruit of latest time." To put the point biologically, the genius is an evolutionary "sport" on the mental and spiritual plane, designed to give conscious expression to life's instinctive purpose. He represents, therefore, a new thrust forward on the part of life and destroys the prevailing level of thought and morals as surely as he prepares for a new one. The thought of the community as a whole presently moves up to the level from which the genius first proclaimed his disintegrating message, and we have the familiar historical spectacle of the heterodoxies of one becoming the platitudes of the next.

It is in this sense that Gandhi is a moral genius. He has announced a method for the settlement of disputes which may not only supersede the method of force, but, as men grow more powerful in the art of destruction, must supersede it if civilization is to survive. No doubt his method has for the moment failed; no doubt he has promised more than he can perform, but if men had never promised more than it was possible for them to perform, the world would be poorer, for the achieved reform is the child of the unachieved ideal. Because Gandhi has believed, he is himself believed, and his authority in the world, though unbacked by force, is greater than that of any other man.

Mahatma Gandhi and Soul Force
Rufus M. Jones

Anyone who has had the privilege, as I have had, of visiting Mahatma Gandhi and his fraternal community in his Ashram in Ahmedabad, would welcome, as I do, the opportunity to contribute an Essay to the volume of Reflections on his seventieth birthday. He has had a profound influence on my own philosophy of life and on my actual way of life, and I am glad to give public testimony to my debt to this wonderful man, who fortunately for me lived in my lifetime.

Francis of Assisi has been one of my supreme heroes since I began the study of his life in 1905, and Gandhi has always seemed to me to be more like Francis than anybody else whom I have ever known. I was very much surprised at the time of my visit in 1926 to discover how little acquaintance Gandhi had at that time with the "poor little man" of Assisi. I sat by him and told him a number of stories from *The Little Flowers of St. Francis.* I told him the finest one of all, the one on "Perfect Joy", and the one which tells how Brother Giles and Saint Louis, King of France, met and embraced and kissed one another and then knelt in a long silence and separated without speaking any words, which seemed to both of them unnecessary, for as Brother Giles put it, "We read one another's hearts far better than if we had spoken with our mouths." Brother Giles's experience of reading hearts without the need of words was very much like mine, as I sat there with a modern saint, sitting on the floor, who certainly had no royal robes such as Louis IX often wore.

I also discovered that Gandhi knew very little about another man whom he very much resembled in spirit. John Woolman, the most remarkable and the most saintly of all the Quakers of the eighteenth century and a striking example of "soul-force." Woolman heard that the Susquehanna Red Indians were on a warpath and were scalping the colonial settlers in the west. He felt "a pure moving of love" to visit these Indians, to endeavour "to feel and understand their life and the spirit they live in, if happily," he wrote, *"I might receive some instruction from them,* or they might be in any degree helped forward by my following the leadings of truth among them."

He found the Indians in war with paint and feathers on the march. He got them together in a meeting in which they sat in deep inward stillness, and then Woolman, in much tenderness of spirit, told the Indians why he had come to visit them, and finally he offered a brief prayer. After the meeting was over, one of the Indians was heard to remark: "I love to feel where words come from". It is a perfect account of the way Mahatma Gandhi works and touches hearts far beyond and far deeper then the words he speaks or writes, because people "feel where the words come from."

We often speak of his principle of *life-Satyagraha* – *as* "non-violence," but that is a negative phrase; while his principle of life is gloriously positive. Gandhi told me that he owed a debt of gratitude to a Quaker, Michael Coates, who, in the early days of the former's life in South Africa, was his intimate friend and the person who introduced him to the Sermon on the Mount and brought him into a sympathetic understanding of Christ's spirit and way of life and gospel of heroic love, which deepened his insight and his faith in impalpable forces. The influences which shaped his life and thought were numerous, and he has always counted Tolstoy, Ruskin, Thoreau and Edward Carpenter in his most intimate list of guides on the way.

What he really means by *Satyagraha* is the manifestation of an energy no less real than that which breaks through a dynamo and operates with notable effects. The dynamo does not *create* the energy; it lets it "come through." Somewhat so is the person who exhibits "soulforce," the organ of a deeper Life than his own tiny, limited, finite sources of strength. The man's soul, in its depth-life, opens into boundless reservoirs of larger Life and Power, inexhaustible fountains of Love and Truth and Wisdom which under right conditions may stream out through him. The Upanishads speak of "the infinite personality of man" and imply a beyond always within the person.

The person who finds out how to draw upon these deeper life-energies becomes not only a centre of repose and serenity, but at the same time, a centre of heroic love, of adventure and of creative activity. Something like this is what Gandhi means by "soul-force," and his life is a unique demonstration of it. It is "heroic passivity" but it is vastly more.

I asked him once, if after all the complications of the difficult world and all the frustrations he had experienced, he still believed in "soul-force." "Yes," he said, "faith in the conquering power of love and truth have gone all through my inmost being, and nothing in the universe can ever take that faith out of me." As he said these words, he ran his fingers down his lean sides, over his protruding ribs, and one knew that he was not thinking of the energies of that poor, thin, undernourished body, but of the depth-life of the soul opening into uncounted resources of Love and Truth.

I want to illustrate this gospel of heroic love, this way of life which rises infinitely above violence, in persons who were unknown to Gandhi, but who walked this same path of forgiveness and humility. I shall speak first of James Nayler, the seventeenth-century Quaker who was punished with outrageous severity as a "blasphemer." He had his tongue bored through with a red-hot iron. He was set in a pillory for two hours. He was whipped at a cart-tail through London streets by a hang-man. His forehead was branded with the letter "B". It was further decreed that he should ride through Bristol on horseback, facing the horse's tail, be whipped in the market place and then be imprisoned in Bridewell in solitary confinement, without ink or paper, until released by Act of Parliament.

This man who thus suffered man's inhumanity gave this testimony to the world that had wronged him: "There is a spirit which I feel, that delights to do no evil, nor to revenge any wrong, but delights to endure all things, in hope to enjoy its own in the end; its hope is to outlive all wrath and contention, and to weary out all exaltation and cruelty, or whatever is of a nature contrary to itself. It sees to the end of all temptations. As it bears no evil in itself, so it conceives none in thought to any other. If it be betrayed it bears it; for its ground and spring are the mercies and forgiveness of God. Its crown is meekness, its life is everlasting love unfeigned; it takes its kingdom with entreaty, and not with contention, and keeps it by lowliness of mind. In God alone it can rejoice, though none else regard it, or can own its life. It is conceived in sorrow and brought forth without any to pity it; nor does it ever murmur at grief and oppression. It never rejoiceth but through sufferings; for with the world's joy it is murdered. I found it alone, being forsaken; I have fellowship therein with them who lived in dens and desolate places in the earth, who, through death, obtained this resurrection and eternal holy life."[11] That is a memorable instance of "soul-force."

William Law was the outstanding English mystic of the eighteenth century. He did not suffer to the extent that Nayler did, but he too had his own hard winepress to tread and he expressed in unforgettable words of beauty this same gospel of soul-force. Here is one of his many interpretations of it.

"Love does not want to be rewarded, honoured, or esteemed; its only desire is to propagate itself and become the blessing and happiness of everything that wants it. And therefore, it meets wrath and evil and hatred and opposition with the same one will as the light meets the darkness, only to overcome it with all its blessings. Did you want to avoid the wrath and ill-will or to gain the favour of any persons, you might easily miss of your ends; but if you have no will but to all goodness, everything you meet, be it what it will, must be forced to be assistant to you. For the wrath of any enemy, the treachery of a

---

11 Little Book of Selections from the Children of the Light, by Rufus M. Jones pp. 48-9.

friend, and every other evil, only helps the spirit of love to be more triumphant, to live its own life and find all its own blessings in a higher degree. Whether, therefore, you consider perfection or happiness, it is all included in the spirit of love and must be so – for this reason, because the infinitely perfect and happy God is mere love, an unchangeable will to all goodness; and therefore every creature must be corrupt and unhappy so far as it is let by any other will than the one will to all goodness. Thus you see the ground, the nature and perfection of the Spirit of Love."[12]

Robert Browning, in his *Instans Tyrannus,* has given a strikingly vivid picture of "soul-force," arrayed against a menacing tyrant who is in the process of crushing a poor defenceless man. This is what happens. The tyrant is speaking:

> *When sudden...how think ye the end?*
> *Did I say, "without friend"?*
> *Say rather, from marge to blue marge*
> *The whole sky grew his targe*
> *With the sun's self for visible boss,*
> *While an Arm ran across*
> *Which the earth heaved beneath like a breast*
> *Where the wretch was safe pressed!*
> *Do you see? Just my vengeance complete,*
> *The man sprang to his feet,*
> *Stood erect, caught at God's skirt and prayed*
> *So I was afraid!*

---

12 Selected Mystical Writings of William Law. Edited by Stephen Hobhouse, pp. 140-1.

Gandhi's Achievements for the British Commonwealth

A. Berriedale Keith

To some of us, the significance of Mahatma Gandhi's career lies essentially in the fact that it represents the deliberate pursuit of an ideal despite the innumerable difficulties which such action inevitably presents in a world refractory to the embodiment of idealism in concrete activities. For the history of the Commonwealth, prime importance must attach to his services in South Africa to the cause of recognition of the value of the human personality. In a country wherein the doctrines of the Afrikaans-speaking element formally denied equality in Church or State to those not of European race, he stood out for the essential principle that men qua men are equal, and that artificial distinctions based on race and colour are both unreasonable and immoral. When the enormous strength of the forces of opposition is realized, it will always stand out as among the highest of his achievements that he greatly improved the position of his people, and placed the problem of their status in the Union of South Africa in a new light. That since his departure, a narrow-minded racialism has once more gained increasing power, is a matter for deep regret but the resisting power of the Indian community has enormously increased since the Mahatma inspired it with the sense of its own dignity and negatived the idea that any man or group of men could be properly exploited by others as an instrument for their aggrandisement. Submerged as that ideal may be for a time, it cannot be supposed that it will wholly disappear. In Kenya and Zanzibar also, the principles of his teaching have had results in mitigating the efforts of the British members of these communities to take advantage of their influence in England to secure the administration of these territories without due regard for India's rights. Nor has his effort been confined to the welfare of Indians; the doctrines which he has preached are equally applicable to the future of the Africans, and he has given no excuse for the growth of the doctrine that Indians should be content to claim equality of treatment for themselves because of their historic culture, and to join with Europeans, in treating as inferiors and suitable for servile conditions, the native inhabitants of African lands.

In India, the Mahatma has taught a doctrine which demands admission of the equality of man no less from Indians than from Europeans. If he has thus created serious difficulties for his fellow-Indians, whose sacred texts seem, as is the case with all ancient codes of every land, to give divine sanction for human inequality, he has removed the greatest of all barriers to the recognition of the right of Indians to self-government, the argument that regard for the interests of the humbler ranks of the people forbids that their destinies should be handed over to those whom the Aitareya Brahmana pronounced to be destined to be the servants of others, liable to be driven from their homes at pleasure and even to be slain. The stand made for the untouchables by the Mahatma, and its success in arousing all that is best in Hinduism, are features of his career, which, in the course of time, will perhaps stand out as the most salient of all, matters in which unalloyed satisfaction can be felt by all students of significant moments in historical development.

The doctrine of non-violent non-co-operation with government has had a more controversial history. It is a creed which demands more than normal human nature can afford, for man is essentially by instinct combative, and those who began as advocates of non-violence have often yielded to more primitive feelings. Yet, it is idle to deny that history shows that, for some psychological reason difficult to understand, British Governments will readily concede to opposition, which hampers administration, demands ignored so long as they were presented on grounds of reason alone. If then, the Mahatma adopted a technique which involved the risk, and in practice the certainty, of acts of violence, he must be admitted to have had the excuse that thus only could he further the attainment of the ends which he regarded as vital for India. While others, both among the living and the dead must share the credit, there is no one who, in equal degree, is responsible for what is one of the most remarkable achievements in the history of the Commonwealth, the effective operation of responsible government in the provinces of India. It is indeed a *monumentum aere perennius.*

Sanskrit literature is singularly rich in pregnant stanzas, which in youth are learned by every schoolboy introduced to the sacred speech. One, it is permissible to think, became engraved on the memory of the young Gandhi, for it expresses the ideal to which his whole life has been consecrated.

> *ayam nijo paro veti ganana laghucetasam*
> *udaracaritanam tu vasudhaiva kutumbakam.*

"Only base minds reckon whether one be kin or stranger. Men of noble conduct take the whole world for their home."

Gandhi's Place in World History
Count Hermann Keyserling

We are living in an age of the most powerful and most encompassing tensions that have ever characterized any period in the history of man. The conquest of space and time has rendered illusory the mere idea of seclusion; the rise of the masses, or at any rate of immense majorities (as opposed to the minorities which up to the world war actually ruled all countries, whatever may be the theories professed), to political and social power has made of the mere number a formidable force, representing, moreover, a definite quality. And since life means an ever unstable equilibrium between opposing and contending forces, of which many are polar in quality-(like the electric energy which manifests itself in the correlation of positive and negative electricity, one pole evoking and even creating its anti-pole) the changes outlined above have led to a state of things where, on the psychical and spiritual plane, currents of unheard – of powers, comparable to the strongest imaginable electric currents, act in correlation to each other. The definite ideas attached to definite movements matter little, and they are always misleading, for firstly, each of them contains and unifies many more components than is indicated by the name given to it, and secondly, the real power behind a "name and form" has, in the long run, as all history shows, very little in common with the latter. A movement, which began its career with one definite aim in view always grew, as life proceeded, into something different. Accordingly, I do not, in the very least, believe in the accuracy of any of the current designations for world movements; no nation in the world really means what it says when pretending to struggle for Democracy or Socialism or Freedom or Godlessness. In reality, all of them grope in the dark for a goal as yet unknown to them, which will reveal its final outlines only after the embryo, that each is now, not only has been born but has grown up. And no single one of the causes that men fight for in our days can possibly achieve final victory: the world of man being divided into gigantic fields of tension, centres of formidable power, only a harmonized synthesis of all that survives – a distant synthesis very difficult to reach – will eventually produce a relatively stable equilibrium.[13]

And there is one more difficulty to consider: it is not easy to foretell which of the existing great forces will remain one for long, and which other force, hardly existent as yet, may, in its turn, become a world power. But here two principles, the

---

13 See the development of this trend of thought in the chapters "Tension and Rhythm" of the author's book, The Recovery of Truth (London: Jonathan Cape)

importance of which are seldom understood, can if intelligently observed, help one to arrive at a relatively correct prophecy. The first of these principles has been formulated by ancient China. According to it, each historic happening really takes place about twenty-five years before it becomes visible, the idea being that the children and not the grown-ups of today will rule the world in a quarter of a century; thus, the character of that future can be anticipated by a correct estimation of the spirit really alive among the children.[14] The second principle in question relates to the law of polarity:[15] each acting force of necessity constellates – to use a very good astrological term – its polar opposite. A very strong thesis, owing to its very strength, creates and vitalizes the corresponding antithesis. The more one-sided a movement is, the greater the chances of a correspondingly one sided counter movement. It is from this viewpoint alone, in my opinion, that the exact historic importance of Mahatma Gandhi can be anticipated with some degree of probability; and precisely from this vantage-point, the importance appears very great indeed. This age of ours is one of accepted violence as no previous age ever was, for this time, the majorities of absolutely all countries inhabited by white men are in some form or other in its favour, as are equally the majorities of most coloured races. Owing to this, it seems to me quite out of the question that this movement, demanding change by means of force, should end before having exhausted all its chances and possibilities; there will be wars and wars, struggles and struggles, in some place or other of the earth for many centuries to come. But precisely because that is and will be so, a movement inspired by the apparently merely negative idea of non-violence can gain a vital and a historic importance

---

14 See the developement of the trend of thought in the chapters "Politics and Wisdom" of the author's book, Creative Understanding (London: Jonathan Cape).

15 See the chapter "The Mystery of Polarification" in the author's book The Art of Life (London: Selwyn & Blount).

that it could never have – and as a matter of fact never has – gained under other circumstances. All the more so, as the polar tension between the ideal of non-violence and its opposite implies another polarity: that of the supremacy of the importance accorded to the means employed versus the supremacy of importance accorded to the ends attained. And it is this latter polarity which, in my opinion, guarantees the immortality of Gandhi as a symbol, whatever may be the eventual success of the movement initiated by him on the plane of facts. Indeed, as long as the Jesuit maxim, "the end sanctifies the means" (a maxim really also accepted by the Puritans in their dealings with Red Indians), prevails, a real and permanent betterment of the world's condition seems out of the question: destructive means employed engender corresponding counter-means and so forth ad infinitum. As the Buddha put it: "If hatred responds to hatred, when and where will hatred end?"

Gandhi is not the only living symbol of that counter-pole to modern aggressive expansionism, which today characterizes most vital peoples, and will, as time proceeds, characterize ever more peoples. Just as peaceful China has, in self-defence, become aggressive, similar changes are very likely to happen in India, which includes, among others, many warlike races and tribes. But Gandhi is the most visible, most spectacular, most singleminded and most pure-hearted symbol of the aforesaid counterpole, and he alone, so far, stands for an existing mass-movement. For ahimsa really corresponds to the most vital, because deeply rooted, ideals of the Hindus. And finally Mahatma Gandhi will remain – personally I am convinced of this – a very great historical figure for still another reason: that he stands precisely and exactly on the threshold between two very different ages. On the one hand, Gandhi incarnates India's traditional ideal of a saint, but on the other hand, he belongs to the most modern type of mass-leader. To that extent, his historical position seems similar to that of John the Baptist. Very likely, the one-sided type of saint will no longer play a part in that future state of man which I have often described as the "oecumenic" state,[16] the part he has played in the past: a new synthesis of the Cross and the Eagle[17] will be its cardinal sign. The new examples of man will be the complete man in whom the forces of the spirit and the earth balance each other. But the advent of this new example will have been prepared, more than by any other living man, by that great dweller on the threshold, whose name is Gandhi.

Gandhi's Faith and Influence
Professor John Macmurray

In the last generation an English poet could write:

East is East and West is West

And never the twain shall meet

At the time when this couplet was written, it expressed a view which could be seriously discussed. Today, this view has become so patently preposterous that it is almost a standard jest. To a large extent, the development of communications is responsible for this rapid unification of mankind. One of the effects has been the ease with which individuals in all parts of the world become news and are developed into international celebrities. One finds oneself wondering how many of these modern reputations will stand the test of time; how many of these international personalities will hold their place in the

---

16 See in particular the second chapter of the author's World in the Making (London: Jonathan (Cape).

17 This synthesis has been described in anticipation in the chapter "Suffering" of the author's last book, From Suffering to Fulfillment (London: Selwyn & Blount). A fragment dealing in particular with the polar correlation of Eagle and Cross has been published in the Indian magazine, Prabuddha Bharata, and in the volume dedicated to the centenary of Ramakrishna's birth.

minds and hearts of future generations as significant figures in world history. In a few cases, is it possible to feel any certainty? The one case in which I feel it impossible to have any doubts is the case of Mahatma Gandhi.

Human greatness has many dimensions. What determines its permanence is its depth. The very greatest men in history are men whose significance for the world rises from the very depths of human personality. One of the characteristics of such men is the way in which they lend themselves to the most diverse and incompatible interpretations. The greatness of Socrates, for example, reveals itself with peculiar force in the fact that a generation after his death, there existed quite a number of rival schools of philosophy, all at loggerheads with one another, and all claiming to be the heirs of the true teaching of Socrates. These men, characteristically, are not writers of books; neither are they men of action, in the ordinary sense of the term. They act in both fields through others. The impact of their personality upon other people is itself a creative energy. The mere fact of their being in the world as the kind of human beings they are, transforms the world so that it can never quite be the same again. Mr. Gandhi is a man of this kind. His influence depends almost wholly upon the integrity of his own personality, and exhibits itself in its effect upon others, in a transformation of their outlook and a heightening of their human capacities. He might be interpreted as a mystic, as a statesman, as a pacifist, a democrat, a social revolutionary, a conservative of the most reactionary colour. A case could be made out for all those views of the significance of his life work. Yet none of these interpretations would touch the secret of his influence. Their incompatibility would merely reveal that the significance of his influence lay deeper than the level at which any such classification can reach.

My own respect and admiration for Mr. Gandhi does not rest upon agreement with his views or his policy. It rests rather on the recognition that in face of such a man, questions of agreement and disagreement, whether about theories or practice, are ultimately irrelevant. He is perhaps *the* man in our world who has once again demonstrated, on an immense scale, the creative power of saintliness and of faith in the reality of moral principle. In an age when Western civilization is disintegrating through its belief in material force, in which men have come to look upon the principles of human community as noble ideals which are powerless in the face of the grim realities of material force, Mr. Gandhi took his stand upon the power of moral principle to defeat the organised forces of money and armaments. It is too early to estimate his success or failure. But it is not too early to assert that by his faith he has integrated the millions of India, while the civilization that claimed to dispose of the destinies of India was disintegrating through losing its hold on just such a faith. Wielding, like Rousseau's legislator, "an authority which is no authority," he has created a general will, and made India a nation. By the sublime simplicity of his moral courage he restored to the masses of his fellow-country-men their self-respect and a belief in their own humanity. And in doing so, he has changed the course of history and decided the future of a great part of the human race.

The Need of a Life Instilled with Unity
Don Salvador De Madariaga

Mankind may some day look at our age as that in which the most difficult of human arts – and the last to be adumbrated by man – emerged from the cavern age. All that lies behind us, as well as all that lies under our eyes, in the art of government is barbarous; even, if I may venture this paradoxical statement, the idea itself of the art of government – which may after all be but a cave-dwelling anticipation of something as yet but half guessed amongst men: the balance of collective and invividual trends in human life.

The taboos of primitive races and the tyrannous practices of their chiefs; the glory of the old Asiatic potentates; the purple splendour and bloody horror of the Roman emperors; the blessing hand and the grabbing hand of the Popes of Rome; the knightly and the infamous wars of the Middle Ages; the daring and sordid adventures of the *Couquistadores* and of empire builders; the gradual evolution of law from command to consent and from consent to common sense; the civil wars of industry with their rough and ready methods of strike and lockout by which the whole community is paralysed to solve a small conflict in a corner of it; the rise and the first – though not the last-fall of the League of Nations; the rise and the first – though not the last-fall of Marxism; the appearance of Fascism-Nazism as the mechanization of tyranny – all this seen from the future, all these struggles, and many more which the nets of mental attention have left uncaught, are but passing forms, imposed by the circumstances of time and place, of the one and permanent problem of human communities – the adjustment of collective and individual trends.

That neatest of all frontiers, the skin, leads man into the error of imagining himself an autonomous, nay, an independent being. We Europeans are far more given to falling into this error than are orientals, but all men in different degrees and shades tend to believe themselves individually defined. Yet, a little reflection suffices to show that even on the merely physiological plan, a man is but a tree with nomadic instincts which has packed up its earth and roots and hidden them away inside its trunk in order to be able to move. As for other than physical aspects of life, man is unthinkable without men, as much as the coral without a reef, or the bee without a swarm. Man is essentially a unit of a congeries.

But the main point is that this congeries has a double finality. We are not, so far at any rate, able to discern the point of view of the single bee from the point of view of the bee swarm; but we believe – and whether we are right or wrong in this belief matters but little – that there is a final point of view in individual man. This makes the life of man an immense problem indeed; for if all that must be considered were the interests of the congeries, the solution, though still difficult, would be, so to speak, only difficult in one dimension; but when we have to consider the final interests of the individual human cells who compose the congeries as well, then our difficulty is raised to the square power.

In short, the problem of collective life comprises two rhythms:

The rhythm of the individual, measured in years: three score and ten;

The rhythm of the congeries, measured in centuries; and two poles of finality:

That of the individual, who is, or believes he is, an end in himself;

That of the congeries, which is, or believes itself to be, an end in itself

Nor have we yet exhausted the complications of this system. For there are a number of kinds of congeries to which human cells belong, and amongst them one which is, at any rate today, predominant to the point of oppression. The nation is, nowadays, the form of community endowed with the greatest vitality amongst men. Its life wave-length is measured in centuries. But it is not the longest-lived of all human forms of life. Obviously the longest-lived is mankind itself, the community formed by all the human beings inhabiting the earth; for this community is the most clearly defined of all human congeries, since it occupies all the space and all the time there is.

Therefore our system of rhythms and finalities will have to be completed as follows:

Finality:	*Rhythm:*
Man	Man
Nation	Nation
Mankind	Mankind

All history may be read as the struggle of this system towards its own balance. Civil wars and revolutions, under the banner of liberty, assert the rhythm and the finality of man; reactions and oppressions under the banner of dictatorship assert here and there the finality and the rhythm of the nation. International wars assert the rhythm and the finality of nations over other nations. The never-interrupted struggle towards the higher forms of peace and towards either spiritual or material unity, or both, assert the rhythm and the finality of mankind.

Why is this struggle more acute than ever in our day?

The answer must be found precisely in the fact that while the third terms of the series, mankind, has come to the fore in our time at a quicker pace than ever before in history, it has nevertheless evolved much more rapidly along the material than along the spiritual avenue of progress.

Mankind progressed first towards its own fulfilment through its spiritual avenue. The results were disastrous. By a strange inversion of its most sacred tenets, religion led everywhere to strife, division and bloodshed. Mankind then sought to fulfil itself by what is called free thought, the intellectual approach, that which during the nineteenth century used to be called the religion of science. This time its success was complete – but equally disastrous.

Complete because, by giving up all its ideals of unity in order to save scientific truth, whate'er betide, mankind did effect its own unity nevertheless, thanks to the all but miraculous control which it acquired over the forces of nature. Mankind has never lived in its own presence and hearing to the extent it does today. Its numbers had already increased *arithmetically* as a result of the first wave of inventions in the first part of the nineteenth century: nowadays they have increased *virtually* by becoming endowed with so high a degree of mobility as to amount almost to ubiquity. This increase in both numbers and motion is equivalent to an increase in density. The human congeries has more *body*; it has also, though to a much lesser extent, grown more conscious of itself.

But the progress has nevertheless been disastrous because the other two terms of the series – the nation and man refused to acknowledge this change and remain attached to a conscious or subconscious conception of unlimited finality for the individual and for the nation, as if mankind was no concern of theirs whatsoever.

Such is the cause which makes the balance between the three forms of human life – individual, national and universal so difficult of adjustment in our day; but the problem is in itself permanent in the history of human societies. As a makeshift, which threatened by a lack of balance which may endanger one or other of the finalities which constitute them, societies evolve systems of force. Thus, by a curious aberration, men are led to mistake strong for healthy societies, or perhaps better, coercive and authoritative for strong societies. Yet, it is obvious that in a society, progress is always accompanied by a gradual reduction of force or, in other words, that a society evolves towards perfection as the role of coercion in its midst becomes less and less important for its healthy working.

Force in a society, is therefore like a surgical contrivance in a human body, an artificial prop to do for a time what life is, for that time, unable to do.

It is obvious that the problem can only be solved on the basis of balance. Defined as is the adjustment of the three finalities –

individual, national, universal, neither Liberalism nor Statism (whether Communists, or Fascist, it is all one) nor universalism can in themselves meet the needs of the case. Mankind will not emerge from the present barbarous stage in our history until enough men in enough countries have realized that Liberalism, Communism-Fascism and Universalism must all emerge into a higher conception rooted on the sense of the organic unity of the whole.

In its essence, therefore, the problem of our day is less in the doing than in the being. We need not act differently; we must become different. Such is the evolution we must set going if we are to change the world – as change it we must, or else it die, and we with it.

Two conditions must be fulfilled towards this aim – that the trend of the evolution become clear and conscious in the leading men of the universal society; and that the sense of it be conveyed to vast fields of human life. The first is a slow process, predominantly, but by no means solely, intellectual. We are witnessing it under our own eyes all over the civilized world, including, despite appearances, the totalitarian countries. The second is more difficult, because the living sense of things can only be conveyed by life: a life instilled with unity is needed to convey the living sense of unity to others. Such a life is Gandhi's. And that is why the Mahatma is perhaps the most symbolic man of our day, for he is not so much a man of action or a man of thought as a man of life.

The Power of Non-violence
Miss Ethel Mannin

In penning this brief tribute to Mahatma Gandhi, I do so in all humility, as one who has never had the honour to meet him, but as a pacifist who sees in his gospel of non-violent resistance the only practical solution to the problem of peace and war, and the only sane tactic in the social struggle. In the civil, Disobedience Campaign of 1930, Gandhi demonstrated the living power of non-violence, a magnificent example to a world that increasingly understands no power but the sword, and which is seemingly incapable of learning that violence never defeats violence but merely begets it.

I am well aware that the Mahatma did not invent the principle of non-violence, that it has existed in India for centuries as a religious tenet, but Gandhi, as Brailsford has said, reaffirmed it "against the drift of Western teaching and example," and rose to his tremendous moral power as a leader of his people through this reaffirmation. During the nationalist struggles of 1930, he gave to his millions of followers not merely a political tactic but a profound religious faith such as Christ gave to those early Christians who faced martyrdom for their inspired interpretation of Truth.

He revealed to the masses a power not of rifles and machine-guns, such as their oppressors used, but the power innate in each individual unit of the great mass, a power which this war-haunted world has yet to realize, and which, exploited to the full, can make war impossible. There is something which the politicians and warmongers overlook in their propaganda for methods of violence in achieving their ends, and that is the indestructibility of the human belief in freedom. In a word, rifles and machine-guns will not destroy a man's soul, nor a nation's. A nation may be crushed and enslaved, but the jackboots of might cannot stamp out the living spirit of freedom; they may succeed in driving it out of sight, underground, for a period, but in darkness and in secret, it grows to power again, and the day comes when once more it blazes forth, a light to lead mankind.

There is no enslaving the man who is master of his own soul; to destroy his body is merely to give the greater power to his spirit. Christ upon the cross was infinitely more powerful than the Christ who rode in triumph with palms spread in his path and Alleuias sounding in his ears.

To give back violence for violence is to sink to the level of the tyrant, who understands power only in terms of death and destruction; the power of non-violent methods of resistance is the power of life, of the unquenchable spirit. By his teachings, Gandhi may be said to have liberated the "soul" of India; from abject and servile slaves they became men again, their heads held high, a light of faith and hope in their eyes, a people capable of marching on to their ultimate liberation as a nation, without recourse to the degrading tactics of their oppressors. Women laid aside their veils, symbols of their servitude, and marched as the equals of men in the bloodless struggle for freedom, proudly humble, humbly proud, their self-respect restored, free because of the pure flame of freedom which burned within them. Men and women of all ages began to realize that life is indeed a "pure flame" and that "we live by an invisible sun within us," and in the light of that realization there is no defeat.

Nationalist India in 1930 effectively demonstrated the power of non-violence as a practical political tactic; but it was also a demonstration of the triumph of the human spirit. The fact that thousands were flung into gaols and subjected to all manner of brutalities could not stem the tide of this great moral renaissance surging through the Indian masses.

It is essential to appreciate the value Gandhi attaches to asceticism in order to understand non-violence as more than a political tactic; it should be clearly understood that Ahimsa is inextricably bound up with the philosophy of love and the pursuit of Truth, that, indeed, Ahimsa is love universally applied. It is no new gospel, this subordination of the flesh and cultivation of the spirit; it was a part also of the teachings of Christ; Gandhi demonstrates it in relation to contemporary life, and therein lies his power and his saintly greatness.

It is an important part of his teaching that the more one takes to violence as a means of settling a dispute, redressing a wrong, the farther one recedes from Truth, for the attack on the enemy without, he says, leads to the neglect of the enemy within. "We punish thieves because we think they harass us," he observes, "for the moment they leave us alone; but they only transfer their attentions to another victim. This other victim, however, is ourselves in another form, and we are caught in a vicious circle. In due course, we see that it is better to endure the thieves than to punish them. The forbearance may even bring them to their senses. But enduring them, we realize that thieves are not different from ourselves, they are our blood-brothers and our friends, and may not be punished."

Therein lies the essence of the philosophy of non-violence, ethically and as it may be applied to war and the social struggle for freedom. For Gandhi there is no separating Ahimsa in daily life from its application to world problems. The path of Ahimsa, he acknowledges, may entail continuous suffering and the cultivation of endless patience, but he goes on to point out that its reward is an increasing peace of mind, and greater courage; we learn to distinguish what is of value, what is everlasting, and what is not. For Western civilization it is a difficult ethic, this saintly asceticism controlling daily life, as difficult as Christianity – not to be confused with Paulianity – which it closely resembles. Yet only by casting out hate and replacing it by universal love, only by the total rejection of violence, will struggling humanity ever achieve that peace which is not merely absence of war in its social midst, but that inner peace essential to the well-being of mankind.

Mahatma Gandhi must be saluted as the twentieth century saint who stands uniquely alone, and who, both by teaching and example, points the way to salvation in a world which, if it heed him not, is doomed to self-destruction. He should be regarded not as a political leader, despite his immensely valuable services to the Indian Nationalist movement and the political repercussions of his fasts, but rather as a spiritual leader and teacher, his so called political activities merely as the logical outcome of his ethics and philosophy.

It is not necessary to endorse, personally, the ethics of a saint in order to respect and admire his saintliness. If much in Gandhi's interpretation of Ahimsa seems, to the opposing materialist philosophy, anti-life, it has to be acknowledged that on the spiritual plane, which is Gandhi's chief concern, it is very much the reverse, and as Gandhi himself has pointed out, all faiths have produced great men and women. For the world today, it is the living exponent of the power of non-violence that Mahatma Gandhi shines in our midst like a beacon light. "Others abide our question; thou art free...out topping knowledge."

Yet his wisdom is for all men, for all time.

Gandhi and the Child
Dr. Maria Montessori

We Europeans see quite a different Gandhi from the one that is known to those who live near him. So, if we look at the sky at night we see a star as a very tiny thing, shining and twinkling. But, if we were near, it would not appear either small or solid, we should see an immense extension of colour and light, devoid of material substance.

To us, Gandhi appears merely a man. A very small man, wearing only a loin-cloth. Everybody knows him, even the smallest children, in every corner of Europe. Everyone, when he sees his picture, exclaims in his own language. "That is Gandhi!"

And what do they think of him, our people who live so far from him, in a civilization so different? They know him as a man who preaches peace. But not a pacifist like those in Europe. Our pacifists argue and hurry about; they have to attend meetings and write in the papers. Gandhi does not hurry, and he is sometimes in prison where he does not speak and hardly eats. And yet millions of men in India understand and follow him because they are aware of his "spirit"

His spirit is like a great energy that has the power of uniting men because it effects some inner sensitivity and draws them together. This mysterious and marvelous energy is called Love. Love is the only force that can bring about a real union between men. Without it, they are drawn into a superficial association by force of external circumstances and the pursuit of material interest but this association without love is insecure and leads to dangers. Men should be united in both ways – by a spiritual force attracting the soul, and by material organization.

I felt this very deeply when Gandhi paid a short visit to Europe some years ago, and stayed a few days in Rome on his homeward voyage. I then felt that there emanated from Gandhi a mysterious power. During his stay in his honour, and while he sat on the floor and spun, they sat round him, serene and silent. And all the adults also who attended this unforgettable reception were silent and still. It was enough to be together; there was no need of singing, dancing or speeches.

But I was still more impressed when some society ladies went to Gandhi at half-past four in the morning to see him pray and to pray with him. Another remarkable fact is that during his stay in Rome, where he was living in a country house in complete retirement, a young lady came walking along the path to the house one morning because she wished to speak to Gandhi alone. She was Princess Maria, the youngest daughter of the King of Italy.

We must think about this spiritual attraction; it is the force that can save humanity, for we must learn to feel this attraction to each other, instead of being merely bound by material interests. How can we learn this? These spiritual forces always exist around us, just as the cosmic rays exist in the universe, but they are concentrated by special instrument, through which we can detect them. These instruments are not so rare as might be thought: they are Children! If our soul is far from the child, then we see only his small body, just as we see the star in the sky as a little shining point where really there is an immense extension of heat and light. We must be nearby to feel the greatness of the mysterious energy radiating all round. The art of spiritually approaching the child, from whom we are too far, is a secret that can establish human brotherhood, it is a divine art that will lead to the peace of mankind. The children are so many, they are numberless, like the Milky Way, that stream of stars that passes right across the heavens.

On his birthday, I ask Gandhi to give honour to the child in India and in the world and to give his followers, who believe in him and in the power of the spirit, faith also in the child.

The Evolution of Mr. Gandhi
Arthur Moore

Mr. Gandhi, at seventy, is younger in spirit than many men of forty, because he is still a learner and an experimenter. He has, it is true, been identified with a body of doctrine, but its boundaries have never been rigid, and I should judge that he has always regarded it as his principal business to seek truth. Giving it out and leading others have come second. And for long intervals he is prepared to retire from leading, while he seeks for more light.

I first met him in Delhi in September 1924. He had

undertaken a twenty-one-day fast for Hindu-Moslem unity. His friends, were greatly concerned for his life, and Mohamed Ali telegraphed to everyone he could think of to come to Delhi and attend a "Unity Conference," in order that Mahatmaji should be at least sustained by the knowledge that his fast had immediately produced an unusual effort to bring the two warring communities together. The summer had been marked by a series of communal riots. I was one of those who responded to the summons, and in the early morning after my arrival, Mohamed Ali appeared in my hotel bedroom and told me that he proposed to take me at once to Mr. Gandhi. I found him weak but smiling, lying on his bed in Sultan Singh's house on the Ridge, with the faithful C. F. Andrews and others in attendance. We talked for a time, but Mr. Gandhi was not able to talk very much and I do not remember what was said. But the picture remains vivid and the contract was intimate and pleasant. Since then, although over the years the actual number of times when I have had the opportunity of conversation with him does not amount to more than six or seven, I have always retained that sense of friendship and intimacy that he diffused. As a journalist, and for a time an M.L.A. in a different camp, I had often to criticize his policy and to do what I could to oppose him, particularly during the period from 1930-32, but nothing affected that personal relation. Sometimes, we have exchanged letters, very frankly expressed on my side, volumes of his autobiography appeared, and it fell to me to write extensive notices of them. Bound in *khadi* and beautifully clearly printed at his own press in Ahmedabad, these two green volumes *(The Story of My Experiments with Truth)* form a great literary work of absorbing interest, and after reading them I felt my knowledge of what had been a baffling personality greatly deepened. The workings of his mind are far from simple or easy to follow, but his prose in these books is lucidity itself. Moreover, his simplicity and directness in action and his candour in statement are as remarkable and invaluable on many occasions as are his subtlety and intricacy of thought and argument on others.

The Mahatma has led a kind of double life, that of a political leader and a religious leader. As a nationalist and a head of his people, he set himself to rouse their national instinct, stiffen their morale, school them in self-respect and the spirit of willing sacrifice. With this, he combined an appeal to the popular mind based on his own asceticism and renunciation of wealth, which is very powerful in an Eastern country, and notably in India, where poverty and the abolition of desire have long been taught as steps to the path of enlightenment. In his book, he tells us that his political experiences have for him not much value, whereas in the spiritual field his "experiments with truth" have made up his real life. The narration of his painful life's journey up to 1927 was in one sense, a confession of failure. For thirty years, he had been starving and pining to achieve self-realization, "to see God face to face, to attain Moksha." For this, he has experimented with non-violence, celibacy, vegetarianism, with every kind of renunciation, and has walked a path "narrow and sharp as the razor's edge," yet at the end of these years all he laid claim to have had was "faint glimpses of the absolute Truth, 'God'." He had not found God of realized Truth, though he had reached complete certainty that God exists and is the supreme reality.

Mr. Gandhi is a Puritan who is firmly convinced, as he tells us, of the truth of the doctrine of original sin. Life presents itself to him, as to all ascetics, as a series of taboos, and not as a thing to be thankfully savoured and enjoyed for the greater glory of God. Sex, of course, is the chief root of the trouble, and of Mr. Gandhi's attitude to sex and his chapters on *brahmacharya*, all that can be said is that he is more completely opposed to the point of view of modern psychology and medicine than one could have imagined it possible for any man to be. Repression, repression, and more repression is his cure for human instincts that he regards as entirely shameful. "There

is no limit to the possibilities of renunciation," and Mr. Gandhi
was evidently seriously perturbed because he could not yet give
up milk, which he regarded as a dangerous and passionate
drink that made the *brahmacharya* vow difficult to observe.
Fresh fruit and nuts are "the *bramachari's* ideal food," but best
of all is fasting, so long as it can be endured.

With ideals so far removed from those of the mass of
humanity, it would not have been strange if Mr. Gandhi had
become, as have some Christian ascetics, intolerant and a
persecutor. But nothing of the sort has happened, and despite
the inhibitions with which he seems to have made life such a
difficult business for himself, his character retains the simple
lovableness which has given him such power. Besides his thirst
for some pure vision of truth, he has that most warming of
qualities, a genuine love for his fellow men. He hates, on the
one hand, cruelty and oppression, and on the other, dirt and
disease. But asceticism held him always in the past from setting
his feet in a large room, and in his story of his early days,
continually we see him refusing experience and shrinking from
life.

His student days in England deepened and strengthened the
hold of his ancestral religion, and it was there for the first time,
through Sir Edwin Arnold's translation, that he made the
acquaintance of the Gita.

Now even as I write, something very significant has happened.
Mr. Gandhi seems to be entering a new phase.

Lately, Mr. Gandhi intimated that he had received "new light"
as a result of his experiences at Rajkot. The nature of the light
is now revealed and very important it is. For no one can
seriously question the influence that Mr. Gandhi has now for
many years exercised over the Hindu masses and the part that
he has consequently been able to play in the modern history of
India. He was the author of two all-India civil disobedience
movements, separated by an interval of years, which threw, the

country into turmoil and caused the authorities grave concern. In addition, each of those movements left consequences which continued after they had ceased, and are at work today. A basic alteration in Mr. Gandhi's creed and teaching, given in his mature age, at a moment when he has just demonstrated afresh his unchallengeable hold over the Congress organization and the mass mind, is therefore a first-class event. It affects more than India, for Mr. Gandhi has his followers elsewhere, and is in fact world news.

In common with others, I have criticized the high spiritual claim made for the theory of non-violent non-co-operation, because it drew a spiritual distinction between physical and mental violence. It is a method of fighting which is open to unarmed people, and is on a par with the boycott and the strike, which are indeed part of its technique. It can fail or prove effective, according to the superiority of organization on one side or the other and the importance of the particular issue at stake. But it is not a distinctively spiritual weapon any more than is armed rebellion or war. For Christians, the teaching is plain. It is the thought in the mind, the desire in the heart, that constitutes transgression. The deed is only the expression. In order to gain impetus for a non-co-operation campaign, Mr. Gandhi himself has to encourage violent thinking, to denounce the British, to preach against foreign imports. His followers, of course, went to all lengths in rousing racial hate, and the general result was that probably nowhere in the world was such unrestrainedly violent vituperation to be found, as in the Press and on the platforms of India during a "non-violent" campaign. Actual violence naturally resulted also. That was all in the day's work, and the British did not complain of the form that the war took – for a form of war it was – but what they rejected was the claim that this kind of non-co-operation was on a high ethical plane, was in fact applied Christianity or something nobler still. Bluntly stated, the economic object of boycotting Lancashire goods was to provide work, wages and food for one set of people in India and to deprive another set in England of work, wages and food. Between starving and killing there is no notable moral difference. No honest Englishman would claim that the naval blockade of Germany during the war, designed to bring pressure upon suffering German civilians as well as soldiers to end the war, differed ethically in kind from trench warfare. Or, if it did, it might conceivably be held the lower of the two.

When violence, clearly attributable to his non-co-operation movement, broke out, Mr. Gandhi's remedy was to undertake a personal fast. He believed that his eight-day fast for Chauri Chaura, in some way, atoned for the crimes committed there. Later, he extended the scope of the objects of his fasts. In 1924, he carried through a twenty-one-day fast for Hindu-Moslem unity. When sent to prison in the second phase of the last civil disobedience movement, he obtained release by fasting, and he also undertook a fast to procure a modification of the Communal Award. His later fasts, indeed, including that at Rajkot, seemed to have lost the character of atonement and were criticized by many of his own followers as being of a coercive character.

To criticisms of the spiritual value, both of non-violence when added to non-co-operation, and of his fasting method, Mr. Gandhi formerly seemed impervious. He spoke as if he knew some inner experience that he was right in giving them this spiritual value, and that even where to all appearances they were failures they were in fact successes. And a host of imitators fasting against this or that, or starting "non-violent" *satyagraha* against this or that, sprang up all over India.

But now there is a change. Mr. Gandhi has had new light. He has come to suspect his own motives, to think that after all he was working for political and secular ends when he believed himself to be carrying out a spiritual work. He has told us that his fast at Rajkot was "tainted with *himsa*" and that he has now laid down all his weapons. If after all his efforts at purification, his years of ascetic renunciation, his efforts to love his opponents, he now judges that he is still unfit to use these methods, how much less likely is it that there was ever any hope that multitudes could be fit or that those who now attempt them are so? But more important than this consideration is the great advance which Mr. Gandhi himself appears to have made, and which may well have tremendous results both in India and elsewhere. Mr. Gandhi has been very near to the acceptance of Christianity for many years. His latest utterance shows a new understanding of the inner grace of Buddhism and Christianity alike. The grace of "non" is not abounding, and there is more virtue in co-operation than in non-co-operation. The world is sore beset by violence, and some new dynamic to change men's hearts is not only solely needed, but also consciously needed. In all countries, there is a demand for it and there are movements which may preclude its arrival – "when man's need is greatest." It may be that Mr. Gandhi's development is symptomatic of much else.

One of the most perplexing moral problems of our time is the attitude towards war. Many Christians, Buddhists, and sincere people of no professional religion hold that to take part even in a defensive war is wrong, that the Christian rule of resisting not evil applies to a nation as well as to an individual. To me – I must frankly say – the Tolstoyan doctrine, which Mr. Gandhi adopted, has always appeared to be philosophic anarchism. I see no answer to the argument that if we must abolish defensive forces we must also abolish the police. An individual, who from genuine love of his oppressor accepts injury, may well end by conquering the heart of the oppressor. If the individuals composing a nation, having themselves suffered no personal injury, allow an aggressor nation to injure individuals amongst themselves as much as it likes, their action seems to me unlovely. By a kind of moral passion, as dangerous as moral indignation, those who preach this doctrine seem to be trying to impose upon others a certain conduct instead of being content to cultivate true humility in themselves individually. The man full of moral indignation against aggressors who forgets humility and finds it impossible to remember the common humanity of the aggressors, and the man so full of moral passion for humility that he spends more time on urging those whom he can approach to humiliate themselves before aggressors in general than in cultivating his own personal loving acceptance of injury in actual daily life – these two (and they represent most of us at one time or another) are not essentially dis-similar. In either case we fail, and are theorists rather than realists. The missing essential for both at the times when they are carried away by moral indignation or moral pacific fervor is the sense of oneness with humanity. If the morally passionate for collective non-resistance to evil had their way, evil would have its sway, and the grandchildren of the morally passionate would be not saints but merely slaves. Not humility, but servility, would flourish. Only the rarer spirits in a subject race become lights for the world. The mass have to cultivate the arts of flattery, concealment, and duplicity.

The "pacifist" argument always seems to me to have been finally refuted on the highest plane long ago in the *Bhagavad Gita* by Krishna in his exhortations to Arjuna. Three years ago I tried Mr. Gandhi on this, but his view, as far as I understood it, seemed to be that the war story in the Gita was symbolic and not actual, and that the argument did not apply to physical war and actual taking of life.

But since Rajkot there seems to me to be a new Mahatma. We must all revere a man who has throughout a life of devoted service persisted in the sternest self-discipline, the most exacting renunciations, the passion for self-purification. If he has reached a new illumination, then the light will shine brightly indeed from a mirror to the making of which so many years and so much effort have gone. From every country comes the recognition that the hope of the world lies in the individual soul of man. Each has to begin on himself. But we need a power to produce the silence when we can hear our own owls speak. Otherwise we may go sadly astray. Some already, carried away by moral passion, are very noisy about their quiet times, and seem more anxious to make converts than to listen in. In India, at least, Mr. Gandhi could produce a stillness in which true peace might be born.

The Hindu Idea of Truth
J.H. Muirhead

It is a high privilege to have the opportunity of contributing, even though it be only a few lines, to a volume in honour of one who has given lustre to contemporary history in a way that none other has – the man who, in Romain Rolland's words, "has raised up three hundred millions of his fellow men, shaken the British Empire and inaugurated in human politics the most powerful movement that the world has seen for nearly two thousand years." At the time when leaders in other lands were either challenging the existence of any such thing as human justice or of any moral governance of the world, or were seeking to do justice to one class of society by the persecution of another, Gandhi was engaged in a crusade for the deliverance of India from bondage to another nation and of any class in India to other classes, in the name of the unity of mankind and of a kingdom not of this world. Besides all this, and likely to count for even more in centuries to come, not only in India "that timeless land", but throughout the world, he has given living witness to the best that philosophy has had to say upon the object towards which all religion that is worthy of the name is directed, and upon the echo which it summons to seek perfection in the individual soul.

I am not likely, in these few lines, to say anything that is not better said elsewhere in this volume, but there is one word, central to the teaching of Hinduism in general and to Gandhi's interpretation of it in particular, which on account of its ambiguity, is apt to form a stumbling block to the ready acceptance of it on the part of those who are imbued with the scientific and practical spirit of the West, and on which I should like to use this opportunity to a short comment.

It was suggested to me on the occasion of the first lecture recently given by Sir Sarvepalli Radhakrishnan at a meeting of the British Institute of Philosophy under the Subrahmanya Iyer Foundation, the object of which is to promote the study of "Ultimate Truth." In the introductory lecture, Chairman drew attention to the difficulty some have in reconciling the founder's idea of truth with the ordinary philosophical one of it as "the agreement of opinion with fact." In contrast to this definition of the word, it seemed in the above title to be used in a vague sense, which not only included the totally different idea of moral goodness and social justice, but assumed that it was possible to attain some ultimate, completely satisfactory expression of truth. In reply to this criticism, the lecturer had no difficulty in showing that, whatever can be said in favour of the philosophical definition and limitation of the idea of truth, Western literature itself recognizes another wider use of the word, as we have it over and over again in the Prophets and most clearly of all in the great Gospel saying, "Ye shall know the Truth and the Truth shall make you free". While one could see that the audience was deeply moved by the speaker's eloquent exposition of the Hindu doctrine, one could not help thinking that there were some who still felt that something remained to be said about the source of this difference and about the relation which the two meanings bore to each other. "Could it be," I asked myself, that with all its subtlety, Indian thought had failed to make clear the distinction, which we have inherited from the Greeks, between Knowing and Being – reality as it presents itself to our minds, and reality as it is or would be to the divine mind?" I did not believe that so fundamental a distinction had been missed by the great Indian thinkers, but it might, I thought, be that in more popular statements (as for instance in Gandhi's "Truth is that which *is*; error that which *is not*" "Hinduism is the religion of truth, Truth is God," "There is no other God than Truth") this difference was ignored. Anyway, it seemed worthwhile to experiment by substituting in all such passages "reality" for "truth" and noting how far this would clarify the situation.

If this were done, it might, in the first place, be possible to define truth in the narrower sense as the reflection or expression of reality in the mirror of the human mind. In religious language, truth would then be "the Word of God." ("O God," exclaimed Kepler, "I think Thy thoughts after Thee.") But in the second place, it would leave it open to us to find other expressions of reality in other forms of experience besides thinking. Why may not the Real Mirror itself in what we do as well as in what we think? In the good will as well as in the true thought? Is there anything that seems to give more of reality to our willed actions than the sense of their being in agreement with what our world, taken in its widest scope, requires of us – once more in religious language, of their being one with the Will of God? Or again, since mere right action is not in itself enough, but the doing of it must spring from right feeling, may it not be in love of our fellows that the reality, both of ourselves and of them, comes home to us most simply and vividly? Widen your idea of fellowship and take in all living things, as Gandhi does ("Thou shalt love thy neighbour as thyself. Yes, but who is my neighbour?" To which he replies, "Everything that lives is thy neighbour") – do this and do you not come nearer the heart of things ("Nature or God") through love of them than through anything else? "He prayeth best who loveth best both man and bird and beast."

Yet when all is said than can be said in favour of the above substitution, it still may be asked whether the habit which prevails even among philosophers, of using truth and reality as interchangeable terms may not have its justification from the side of knowledge – theory itself. Plato distinguished different levels of knowledge according as it was of things of sense and imagination, as in ordinary life, or, as in science, of things with their causes or reasons. Of the former, the rising of the sun might be an instance, of the latter, the revolution of the earth on its axis and its turning to the sun. In both these, we distinguish between our knowing and the fact known. But there is a higher level still, Plato held, in which these two are united but also transcended in a sense of an immediate vision and absorption in what is seen, and the mind seems at home with the very being of things. Such we may conceive was the vision which Kepler had when he seemed to see the sun and the planets as they are to God or which the poet has when he seems to live in the things he depicts and they in him. While to Western readers this doctrine has often proved a stumbling-block and rock of offence, to Eastern readers it is more likely to seem to be "telling them their own dream," and to be something verifiable in the everyday experience not only of the philosopher and the poet but of the saint. For my part I think that their dream has come to them through the "horn-gate"[18] and is a true one.

Gandhi's Spiritual Authority
Gilbert Murray

In a world where the rulers of nations are relying more and more upon brute force and the nations trusting their lives and hopes to systems which represent the very denial of law and brotherhood, Mr. Gandhi stands out as an isolated and most

---

18 According to the Greek poets fales dreams were sent from Heaven to men through a gate of ivory and true dreams through one of horn.

impressive figure. He is a ruler obeyed by millions, not because they fear him but because they love him; not as the master of wealth and secret police and machine-guns, but as holding that spiritual authority which, when it once dares to assert itself, seems to reduce almost to impotence the values of the material world. I say "seems": for against purely material force, untinged by conscience or pity, it would be helpless. It only wins its battles because of its secret appeal to the spiritual element in its enemy, that humane element from which man, in his utmost effort to be brutal, cannot quite shake himself free. "A battle of the unaided human soul against overwhelming material force; and it ends by the units of material force gradually deserting their own banners and coming round to the side of the soul!" So I wrote about Mr. Gandhi twenty years ago.

We cannot, of course, assume that a spiritual authority is always right in its guidance. Its claims and professions can seldom be proved or disproved. It is directed by human beings, who are subject to ordinary human frailties and as liable as other autocrats to be corrupted by power. But among spiritual rulers, as among rulers in general, Mr. Gandhi stands out as almost unique. In the first place, he utters no dogma, no command, only an appeal; he calls to our spirits; he shows what he holds to be the truth, but does not exclude or condemn those who seek the light in some other way.

In the second place, he is unique in his manner of fighting, as was shown best in his fifteen years' struggle for the rights of Indians in South Africa. He and his followers were repeatedly imprisoned, herded with criminals, treated as sub-human creatures, yet whenever the Government which oppressed him were weak or in trouble, instead of pressing his advantage he turned and helped them. When they were involved in a dangerous war, he organized a special corps of Indian stretcher-bearers to help them; when, in the midst of a non-violent strike by his Indian followers, the Government were suddenly

threatened by a revolutionary railway strike, he immediately
gave orders for his people to resume work until his opponents
should be safe again. No wonder that he won the day. No
genuinely human enemy could hold out against that method of
fighting.

Thirdly, perhaps the hardest point of all for a leader who is
worshipped and idealized by immense multitudes, he never
claims to be infallible. I see that at this moment he is calling a
pause in his "non-co-operation" campaign, in order that he, as
well as his opponents, may wait and think.

The spiritual authority of one unarmed man over great
multitudes is in itself wonderful, but when that man not only
abjures violence and helps his enemies in their need, but also
recognizes his own human fallibility, he claims unanswerably
the admiration of the whole world. From a distant country,
from a quiet alien civilization, with different views from his on
many practical questions, out of the careworn and striving
movements of thought in Europe, where the human conscience
and intellect seem for the moment to stand helpless under the
bludgeons of ignorance and brute force, I gladly give this great
man the title his disciples claim for him and hail with reverence
"Mahatma Gandhi".

A Visit from the Far East
Yone Noguchi

Leaving Nagpur for Bombay towards the end of December
1935, I stopped over at Wardha, an insignificant country town,
but the spiritual center of the Gandhi movement. I was glad to
see Gandhi with a fitting background in his Ashram, a
monastery or refuge, where unlike the ancient ascetic, this
modern prophet responds to every pulsation of hope or pain in
his nation's life. In view of his illness, he was lying down in a

tent pitched upon the flat roof of a two-storeyed concrete house, square in form with a yard in the center. I found him with a saintly little smile revealing his broken teeth, stretching out his bare legs, as lean as a cricket's and as stiff as steel wire, which one of his disciples was shampooing. I found difficulty in connecting this seemingly simple and unaffected man with the heroic fasts that had made the mammoth soul of England once tremble in fear. Noticing that he put on his head something wrapped in cotton cloth, I asked him what it was. He said that it was wet earth which, according to his doctors advice, was good for a man like him whose blood pressure was high. Then with a smile in which cynicism and philosophy commingled, he explained: "I sprang from Indian earth. So it is Indian earth that crowns me."

After a little talk, I bade him farewell and descended the stairs to meet three or four of his disciples, who were waiting to take me round the Ashram. Passing by a place containing beehives, I was taken into a shed to see a bull turning a stone mortar and making oil out of rape seeds. Then I went to another place where paper-making experiments were in progress. One of the disciples said: "How simple it is to make paper! If this paper-making becomes popular in our country as a subsidiary industry, we shall be able to keep a great deal of money at home." It need hardly be said that the spinning-wheel, the Charkha, holds an important position in the Ashram. A little flat wooden box was brought out, which revealed, when uncovered, a miniature wheel invented by Gandhi himself during his leisure moments in prison. The explainer said: "You can put it even into a handbag and carry it in the train to fill the vacant hours by turning it.

Then he said further: "Gandhi is remarkably scientific. And his patience always brings his inventive mind to complete success. Had he been a watchmaker he would have the best watch in the world to his credit. As a surgeon or a lawyer, he would also fill the highest place. But describing himself as a

farmer and a weaver by profession at his trial in 1922, he
pledged himself to the sacredness of manual labour. Among the
various kinds of such work, he regards weaving most highly
because it gives one a habit of exactitude and a mental training
in keeping strictly to the law of economy. Gandhi hates waste
more than anything else. Believing that manual labour alone
can give a new life to India, he makes the Charkha his own
symbol and calls the people to the holy banner of an
independent life." It is only incidental that his movement
appears to be a rebellion against the British yoke, because,
while seeking to save India from corruption, it would also save
the other countries of the world through its great lesson of
creative energy, the propagation of life close to the soil. The
importance of service within one's immediate surroundings as
against a groping after distant ideals, is not limited to India
only: the manliness of the "self-supporting and self-sufficing"
Swadeshi spirit must be recognized through all time and
throughout the world.

Gandhi cannot find any higher way of worshipping God than
by serving the poor and identifying himself with them. When he
goes on a railway journey, for instance, he always takes a third-
class ticket, reminding himself that he also belongs to the lower
orders of mankind where humanity and love are found to be
the richest. As one who has spent the best part of his life with
working-class people and has shared joys and sorrows with
them equally, Gandhi offers to his friends the spinning-wheel as
an inspiration of the "self-supporting and self-sufficing" life.

Lying alone in my compartment of the train for Bombay, I
could not put away from my mind, for some time, the image of
Mahatma Gandhi. Once I had the pleasure of reading his little
essay entitled "Voluntary Poverty," in which he expressed his
joy at discarding the things that belonged to him before. For
anybody in a country like India to live with anything more than
bare necessities, he believes, means living like a robber. Unless
you be like one who sleeps outside with nothing on his body,

you have no right to declare that you can save India and the Indians. I am told that even the cloth with which Gandhi covers his loins is reduced to the very minimum. It was natural that Gandhi should advance from this eulogy of poverty into asceticism through which one's five senses are to be controlled as a method of self-purification.

A warrior in combat near Heaven with a prospect of unseen victory,

Blowing a bugle that rings to the last gulf of Hell,

A lonely hero challenging the future for response.

Withered and thin,

But with a mammoth soul shaking the world in fear-

Through this man, love, profaned and ignored,

Through this man, life's independence, shattered and fallen.

Through this man, body-labour bereft of honour and prize,

Cry rebel-call against tyranny; to God's justice be praise!

A sad chanter of life close to the mother-earth,

(Where is there a more burning patriot than this man?)

A lone seeker of truth denying the night and self-pleasure,

(Where is there a more prophetic soul than this man's?)

A pilgrim along the endless road of hunger and sorrow.

Gandhi in His Many Aspects
B. Pattabhi Sitaramayya

I. Gandhi the Avatar

"Be careful in dealing with a man who cares nothing
for sensual pleasures, nothing for comfort or praise
or promotion, but is simply determined to do what
he believes to be right. He is a dangerous and
uncomfortable enemy because his body which you
can always conquer gives you so little purchase over
his soul.

—Professor Gilbert Murray

The world has produced great men from time to time. Each
nation has produced its own saints, martyrs, and heroes, its
own poets, warriors and statesmen. In India, we call our great
men *avatars*, men who descend on earth from on high
embodiments of the Divine, in order to protect and punish vice.
We have in our midst an avatar in *Gandhi* who has worked out
the gospel of perfect non-violence in the work-a-day world.

II. Gandhi-the Sthitaprajna

In Gandhi's view, Swaraj is not the replacement of the white
bureaucracy by the brown. It is the total recasting of life,
indeed a reconquest of India. To reunite the various fragments
dismembered territorially into provinces and states, cut up
communally into Hindus and Muslims and Christians, divided
professionally into rural and urban folk, and split up diagonally
into excluded and included areas, that is the problem envisaged
by him. The other part of the task is to restore the culture of
the nation and charge it with all that is worth copying in
modern life, to resuscitate the ideal of service, to supplant the
selfishness fostered by the new civilization by a feeling of pity

for the poor, to level up the low, instead of suffering society to be composed of tall oaks and short-poppies, to ensure food and raiment to all, to lower, if need be, the standard of life on the average instead of raising it for a few. To this end, he has evolved a new synthesis in his own life and has combined in himself the four varnas and the four asrams of Hindu society. He fulfils the role of a Brahman and is the law giver, he is Ksatriya and is the chief constable of India. As a Vaisya he mobilizes the wealth of the country and as Sudra he has produced food and raiment. In the great trial he said, "I am a weaver and farmer". And then although a grihastha, he leads a life of celibacy like a Brahmachari, serves mankind along with his wife like a vanaprastha and is finally a true Sannyasi, having given up his all in his ministry to mankind. All the while Gandhi is essentially a man with no superhuman touch or pretensions about him. He is a business man, a man of humour, wit and wisdom, a child amongst children, a "jolly good fellow" among the grown-ups, and a saint and sage amongst mankind, a guide, philosopher and friend to all. He has a beaming countenance with a pair of scintillating eyes and a laugh which lays bare his whole heart from within. He is frank to a degree and never believes in hearing charges behind people's backs, but always puts them to the accused in the presence of his accusers. He accepts your explanation, takes your word for truth. He is precise in his talks and expects his statements to be understood both with reference to his subjectives and his principal clauses. Most people have taken the latter and ignored the former and therefore expected objective results without bearing subjective burdens. His style is all his own, composed of short sentences, shot out like veritable shrapnel in a *feu de joie* at a new-year parade, dynamic in force and devastating in effect. Gandhi is the full man – the Purna purusa of the Upanishads whom it is a privilege to know and a blessing to work with. He is the *Sthitaprajna* of the Bhagavadgita, who, by his self-control and renunciation, has conquered himself and conquered the world.

III. Gandhi-His Dual Programme

As a satyagrahi, Gandhi knows no defeat. If the nation is tired of the offensive, it is at once put on the constructive programme. From the fast pulley to the loose, the belt in the workshop does not glide with greater ease than Gandhi's power belt from the destructive plane of fight to the constructive. With equal swiftness and suddenness does he switch on the aggressive programme of Civil Disobedience and it develops momentum with the vehemence and rapidity of a tornado of a tidal wave. What his offensives are like, the world knows only too well. A moral issue is always involved in his campaigns which are seemingly insignificant in character but single-pointed in aim and far-reaching in results. Here it is the Amritsar massacre for which an apology is demanded. There it is the Khilafat wrong, remote in its seat and scene but proximate in its effects and influence. Elsewhere it is the salt tax, trivial in incidence but sinful in its yield. When the world thinks that Gandhi has sustained defeat, he converts that defeat by a sentence into victory.

Gandhi's constructive programme has met with a mixed reception in the country, has not, even now, captivated the imagination of the bulk of the population. His Khaddar is the poor man's panacea, the new economic talisman, the hope of the widow and the orphan, the maimed and the blind; a collateral industry that serves as a staff supporting the peasant weighed down by an unbearable burden of indebtedness and taxation. The revival of Khaddar stands for a whole cult, for it reacts against the backstroke of machinery which is a good servant but a bad master. Khaddar symbolizes the revival of the creative genius of India, the sense of freedom and ownership that has always animated the Indian craftsman, the atmosphere of purity and family compactness in which the Indian arts have all along thriven. Khadi is the uniform of the Indian patriot, and the badge of national emancipation. The first five years of

Gandhi's ministry were devoted to the task of placing Khaddar on a stable basis so that it might lead the way to other village industries and home crafts and retract all machinery, which is merely *violence in motion*, to its strict limits in life. Gandhi's constructive programme is a three-fold one-*Economic* in Khaddar, *Social* in the removal of untouchability and *Moral* in the abolition of drink. After achieving the first, he addressed himself to the second and the story of his fast unto death in September 1932 is now a chapter of the world's history. The third, prohibition, is being implemented as a part of the ministerial programme under the scheme of provincial autonomy. Only a few weeks ago, did Gandhi express his sad disappointment at the slack pace at which this reform is being achieved by his trusty colleagues; for three and a half years is the limit he has set for the complete eradication of drink from India. The fourth item is cultural and relates to *national education*, for which an All-India Board has been formed at Haripura and under its auspices, a system of primary education, known as the Wardha scheme, is being propagated with the object of linking up the child's education with the life of the nation. There remains but one great reform to achieve namely *communal* unitY-notably Hindu-Muslim unity. The draft formula is all but ready and the process of unification contemplated is not one of bargains in proportions but of appeal to the good sense and the better selves of the two great communities of India. When thus the nation's activities and attention are directed now to the preparation of men and munitions and now to war, or vice versa, not one can speak of success or failure. In Gandhi's judgment, the fight with Britain is essentially a moral fight: for the seven citadels constructed by the British are moral (or immoral) *prakarams* (or protection walls) round their central authority. These are the Services, the Legislatures, the Law Courts, the Colleges, the Local Bodies, the Commerce and the Titled Aristocracy. Gandhi's programme of non-co-operation is simply aimed at destroying each of these in turn and all in the end. The triple boycott of councils, courts

and colleges is a part of this plan. At one time, there was even
a call to the services and the Army to give up their bondage. It
was thus that the charm of British rule in India and its
invincibility was broken.

IV. *Gandhi and Satyagraha*

Satyagraha in an age of violence and warfare is as strange a
weapon as a steel knife in the Stone Age or the petrol engine in
the midst of single-bullock carts. People simply cannot
understand it, do not believe in it, will not look at it. When
Transvaal is quoted, they brush it aside as an event that was
possible on a small-scale, short-range fight-not applicable to a
continent like India. Champaran, Kaira and Borsad are equally
readily dismissed as essays in miniature which cannot be
reproduced on a nationwide scale. Today all doubts have
disappeared and all difficulties have dissolved. The problem is
to keep Satyagraha within the limits of Satya and its
concomitant ahimsa. Truth and non-violence, which constitute
the two component factors of the new technique are not
passive, much less negative forces, they are positive, aggressive
forces investing the programme with all the attributes of war
on the violent plane. In confounding and demoralizing your
enemies and ultimately conquering them by converting them, in
engendering a rigid sense of discipline amongst its adherents, in
working upon the mind and the emotion of the votaries of the
new technique, in invoking courage, sacrifice and endurance, in
mobilizing a destructive armoury, Satyagraha operates as a
positive and irresistible force to whose efficacy experience has
borne ample testimony.

Gandhiji's conception of *Truth* and non-violence is known to
few. It has a double aspect in respect of both, one a positive and
the other a negative. When the Collector of Champaran wrote
to him a stiff letter which he later decided to withdraw and
asked for its return, and when the young followers of Gandhi

began to copy it, Gandhi admonished them and said that, if they kept a copy, the letter could not be said to have been withdrawn. That was a new definition of Truth which was repeated during the Gandhi-Irwin pact when the Home Secretary, Mr. Emerson's insulting letter was, on second thoughts, withdrawn and we have not got a copy of it in the archives of the Congress-for the same reason, that to keep a cppy of a letter that is withdrawn is to harbour it, in your files as well as your breast, and that is untruth as well as anti-non-violence.

The subtlest incitement to violence is not tolerated by Gandhi. In the year 1921, when Gandhi agreed that the speeches of the Ali brothers lent themselves to such a misconstruction, he secured from them a statement repudiating any such intention on their part. But when the same Ali brothers were being prosecuted for their Karachi speech in October 1921, he repeated it in Trichinopoly and caused the whole of India to repeat the same from thousands of platforms. To him the one test is – is the speech non-violent through and through? If it is, his challenge is as ready as his apology. As that is the view he takes of non-violence, he was shocked when, in the Civil Disobedience movement of November 1921, during the visit of the Prince of Wales, 53 people died and 400 were wounded! At this distance of time, the five days' fast by way of Penitence then undertaken by him appears as a trifle compared with his later fasts extending over 21 days and 28 days and his last "fast unto death."

Gandhi's non-co-operation has always been intended and embarked upon for co-operation, but he has never surrendered his first principles of Truth and Non-violence, as is borne out by his letter to Lord Reading dated February 1,1922:

"But before the people of Bardoli actually commence mass Civil Disobedience, I would respectfully urge you, as the head of the Government of India, finally to revise your policy and set

free all the non-co-operating prisoners who are convicted or
under trial for non-violent activities in the country, whether
they be regarding the redress of the Khilafat or the Punjab
wrongs or Swaraj or any other purpose, and even though they
fall within the repressive sections of the Penal Code or the
Criminal Procedure Code or other repressive laws, subject
always to the condition of non-violence. I would further urge
you to free the Press from all administrative control and restore
all the fines and forfeitures recently imposed. In thus urging, I
am asking your Excellency to do what is today being done in
every country which is deemed to be under civilized
government. If you can see your way to make the necessary
declaration within seven days of the date of publication of this
manifesto, I shall be prepared to advise postponement of Civil
Disobedience of an aggressive character till the imprisoned
workers have, after their discharge, reviewed the whole
situation and considered it *de novo."*

V Gandhi-His Inconsistencies

Gandhi has been charged with the impracticability of his ideals
by the moderates, with the moderation of his programme by
the extremists, with inconsistencies of conduct by both; and in
the midst of these conflicting assessments and appreciations of
his life and work, he has stood unmoved like a rock and
allowed the flow of praise and blame to pass him unaffected.
The one guiding principle of his life is the verse in the
Bhagavadgita which says:

"Happiness and misery, gain and loss, victory and defeat – do
thou treat them alike and gird thyself for battle. Thus wilt thou
not incur sin."

In 1896, Gandhi visited Poona and learnt his first lessons in
politics at the feet of Tilak and Gokhale. The former appeared
to him, he said, like the Himalayas – great and lofty, but
unapproachable, while the latter appeared like the holy Ganges

in which he could confidently take a plunge. In 1939, Gandhi has risen to the heights of Himavan but is easily accessible and has fathomed the depths of the Ganga and is ever purifying.

Few people understood what Satyagraha was when it was crudely known by the name of Passive Resistance. It was defined by Gokhale as follows (in 1909):

"It is essentially defensive in nature and it fights with moral and spiritual weapons. A passive resister resists tyranny by undergoing suffering in his own person. He pits soul force against brute force; he pits the divine in man against the brute in man; he pits suffering against oppression; he pits conscience against might; he pits faith against injustice, right against wrong."

In 1939, Satyagraha has become a household word and the universally acknowledged strategy of oppressed citizens whether of British-India or of the Indian States and is warmly recommended to the Jews against the German pogroms and the Chinese against the Japanese inroads. At Karachi in 1913 the Indian National Congress voted its admiration "for the heroic endeavours of Gandhi and his followers and their unparalleled sacrifice in their struggle in South Africa for the maintenance of the self-respect of India and the redress of Indian grievances." The resolution was passed by the unanimous vote of the House. And in 1931, at the forty-fifth session of the Congress held again at Karachi, Gandhi won the admiration of the nation for his heroic endeavours not on behalf of a handful of men in South Africa but on behalf of the whole nation of 350 millions whose emancipation was successfully inaugurated on the same vital and abiding principles of Satyagraha.

In 1914, Gandhi was a loyal citizen of the British Empire and helped in recruiting for the Great War even as he had organized Red Cross units in the Zulu Rebellion and the Boer War early in the twentieth century. His attitude, however, to war has veered round from one pole to the other. Though even as late as in August 1918 he had stood for unconditional help to the British in recruitment, still in September 1938, when the war clouds were lowering over Europe, he stood four square against any proposal to exploit the war situation for the benefit of India or to participate in the apprehended war in any measure. The two pictures may be studied in closer detail.

In 1919, Tilak was served with an order prohibiting him from lecturing without the previous permission of the District Magistrate. Only a week before, we are told, he was engaged in a recruiting campaign, and as a guarantee of good faith, he had sent to Mahatma Gandhi a cheque for Rs. 50,000, the amount to be forfeited as penalty if certain conditions were not fulfilled by him. This was in the nature of a wager. The wager was that Tilak undertook to recruit five thousand persons from Maharashtra if Gandhi could secure a promise from the Government before-hand that Indians would get commissioned ranks in the army. Gandhi's position was that the help should not be in the nature of a bargain and therefore he returned the cheque to Tilak.

In September 1938, the Working Committee of the Congress was sitting from day to day at Delhi to deal with the war situation in Europe. There were two schools of thought in the country – those who would negotiate India's rights with Britain and then agree to help her and those who would not help in the prosecution of a war under any conditions. Gandhi belonged to the latter group, and he was, in 1938, as clearly against participation in war on any conditions as he was for helping Britain in 1918 unconditionally.

In 1918, Gandhi was engaged in a multiplicity of activities of which the most notable was directed against the Rowlatt Bills. Today, he is engaged in fighting against similar laws operating with full force and vigour in the various States of India- Travancore, Jaipur, Rajkot-Limbdi, Dhenkanal and so on. No better testimony can be cited to his plan and purpose than was placed on record by the author of *India (1919)* – *a* Government of India publication:

"Mr. Gandhi is generally considered a Tolstoyan of high ideals and complete selflessness. Since his stand on behalf of the Indians in South Africa, he has commanded among his countrymen all the traditional reverence with which the East envelops a religious leader of acknowledged asceticism. In his case, he possesses the added strength that his admirers are not confined to any religious sect. Since he took up his residence in Ahmedabad, he has been actively concerned in social work of varied kinds.

"His readiness to take up the cudgels on behalf of any individual or class whom he regards as being oppressed has endeared him to the masses of his countrymen. In the case of the urban and rural population of many parts of the Bombay Presidency, his influence is unquestioned, and he is regarded with a reverence for which adoration is scarcely too strong a word. Believing as he does in the superiority of 'Soul Force' over material might, Mr. Gandhi was led to believe that it was his duty to employ against the Rowlatt Act that weapon of Passive Resistance which he had used effectively in South Africa. It was announced on 24th February that he would lead a Passive Resistance of Satyagraha movement if the Bills were passed. This announcement was regarded as being of the utmost gravity both by the Government and by many of the Indian politicians. Some moderate members of the Indian Legislative Council publicly affirmed their apprehension as to the consequences of such a step. Mrs. Besant, with her remarkable knowledge of the psychology of the Indian temperament, warned Mr. Gandhi in the most solemn manner that any such movement as he contemplated would result in the release of forces whose potentialities for evil were quite incalculable. It must be clearly stated that there was nothing in Mr. Gandhi's attitude or pronouncements which could have justified the Government taking any steps against him before the inception of the movement. Passive Resistance is a negative and not a positive process. Mr. Gandhi expressly condemned any resort to material force. He was confident that he would be able, by a process of passive disobedience of Civil Laws, to coerce the Government into abandoning the Rowlatt Act. On 18th March, he published a pledge regarding the Rowlatt Bills which ran as follows: 'Being conscientiously of opinion that the Bill known as the Indian Criminal Law Amendment Bill No.1 of 1919 and the Criminal Law Emergency Powers Bill No.2, 1919, are unjust, subversive of the principles of liberty and justice and destructive of the elementary rights of an individual on which the safety of India as a whole and the State itself is based, we solemnly affirm that in the event of these Bills becoming Law and until they are withdrawn, we shall refuse civilly to obey these Laws and such other as the Committee hereafter to be appointed may think fit and we further affirm that in the struggle we will faithfully follow truth and refrain from violence to life, person and property.' "

In 1919 (July 21st) Gandhi accepted the advice of the Government and friends and suspended Civil Disobedience, and in 1934 (April) again he had occasion to suspend Civil Disobedience except in his own person. "I have been accused of throwing a lighted match," said he in 1919. "If my occasional resistance be a lighted match, the Rowlatt Legislation and the persistence in retaining it on the Statute Book is a thousand matches scattered throughout India. The only way to avoid civil resistance altogether is to withdraw that legislation." In 1934, in his Patna statement, dated April 7th, he said on the eve of suspending Civil Disobedience once again:

"I feel that the masses have not received the full message of Satyagraha owing to its adulteration in the process of transmission. It has become clear to me that spiritual instruments suffer in their potency when their use is taught through non-spiritual media. Spiritual messages are self-propagating.

"I must advise all Congressmen to suspend civil resistance for Swaraj as distinguished from specific grievances. They should leave it to me alone. It should be resumed by others in my lifetime only under my direction, unless one arises claiming to know the science better than I do and inspires confidence. I give this opinion as the author and initiator of Satyagraha. Henceforth, therefore, all who have been impelled to civil resistance for Swaraj under my advice directly given or indirectly inferred will please desist from civil resistance. I am quite convinced that this is the best course in the interests of India's fight for freedom.

"I am in deadly earnest about this greatest of weapons at the disposal of mankind."

In 1934, in the same Patna statement, he bemoaned that "the indifferent civil resistance of many, grand as it has been in its results, has not touched the hearts either of the terrorists or the rulers as a class." But today, he has the satisfaction of over 2,500 of these friends having been released from internment and avowed their faith in non-violence, while as a crowning piece of the victory of non-violence over violence, Sardar Pridhwi Singh, who was taken for dead, while really he had been moving freely between India and Europe for over seventeen years, after jumping out of a running train while in custody and transfer, delivered himself into the hands of Gandhi who in turn committed him to the care of the British jails in India and is striving hard for his release.

After the suspension of Civil Disobedience in 1919, Gandhi, knowing the happenings in the Punjab, was doubtless greatly shocked by the unexpected turn that events had taken and admitted that "he had made a 'blunder of Himalayan dimensions' which had enabled ill-disposed persons, not true passive resisters at all, to perpetrate disorders."

When the Reform Act of 1919 was enacted, Gandhi advocated the view that, despite the unsatisfactory and inadequate nature of the reforms, the Congress responding to the sentiments in the Royal Proclamation, should express the "trust that both the authorities and the people will co-operate so to work the reforms as to secure the establishment of Responsible Government". Compare with this his attitude in 1937 asking for assurances from the Government regarding the non-uses of the special powers and the non-interference by the Governors in the day-to-day administration of the Provinces and the enforced implementing of the same by the Government in the matter of the release of political prisoners accused of violence, of the appointment of the Governor of Orissa and the drastic revision of the Zamindari and the Land Revenue Laws of the country and the return of the confiscated lands to the peasantry of Bardoli.

At the Amritsar Congress, Gandhi pleaded "for the return of the madness of the Government with sanity but not to return madness with madness". Today, he assures the country that in Rajkot and in the states where the governments are going mad, once again success will be the people's, if only they observe non-violence and return madness with sanity.

Gandhi's passage from the wholly humanitarian to the purely political field was imperceptible and even involuntary not that he was not aware of it, but he could not resist it; and when he joined the All-India Home Rule League and became its President, he felt a call to duty on his terms. Those terms, he said, were "strict adherence to truth and non-violence in the promotion of the causes in which he had specialized, namely Swadeshi Communal unity, Hindustani as the lingua franca and a linguistic re-distribution of the Provinces". The reforms were to him secondary. From social service to politics was then an easy glide to him, through the passage of religion. Today, he reverts to social service from politics through the same passage. Indeed, to him, both are the same, as they constitute but the two sides of a coin, the medal itself being composed of the sterling material of *Satya* and *ahimsa* which form the basal principles of all religions.

To Gandhi, non-co-operation is not an end in itself but is a means to an end. His outstretched hand of co-operation is always open to the grasp of his opponent provided national honour is not imperiled. That was his position in 1920 and that is his position today. In 1920, it was spurned, in 1939 it is warmly sought after by the Government.

Another study in contrast is furnished by Gandhi's attitude towards complete Independence in 1921 and 1929. In 1921 he stated at Ahmedabad:

"The levity with which the proposition has been taken by some of you has grieved me. It has grieved me because it shows lack of responsibility. As responsible men and women, we should go back to the days of Nagpur and Calcutta."

In 1928, when the question of Independence was once again brought to the fore, Gandhi made the following characteristic observation:

"You may take the name of Independence on your lips as the Muslims utter the name of Allah or the pious Hindu utters the name of Krishna or Rama, but all that muttering will be empty formula if there is no honour behind it. If you are not prepared to stand by your own words, where will Independence be? Independence is a thing, after all, made of sterner stuff. It is not made by the juggling of words."

And in 1929, he closed his conversations with Lord Irwin, on December 23rd, with the virtual challenge that he would organize the nation for complete Independence.

In 1920, the Government expressed their trust and belief that "the sanity of the classes and masses alike would reject non-co-operation as a visionary and chimerical scheme, which, if successful, could only result in widespread disorder, political chaos and ruin of all those who have any real stake in the country." "The appeal of non-co-operation is to prejudice and ignorance," they said, "and, its creed is devoid of any constructive germs." Today this very Government is anxious to negotiate a treaty with the founder of the movement and the residual legatee of its best asset, namely Civil Disobedience.

In 1921, when Lord Reading opened negotiations with Gandhi – and they failed owing to a slight mischance in that Gandhi's telegram reached Lord Reading in Calcutta a little late – everyone thought that Gandhi was an impracticable man, yea, an impossible man, but when Lord Irwin, releasing him and his twenty-six comrades from jail opened negotiations with him in 1931, a decade later, everybody praised him for his qualities of give and take, for his sense of proportion, propriety and perspective-qualities equally in evidence and equally effective in the gentle negotiations between Gandhi and Lord Linlithgow in June 1937 which resulted in official acceptance by the Congress.

In 1922, the Chauri Chaura tragedy in which twenty-one constables and a sub-inspector were burnt alive, and with them the police station where they were penned, made Gandhi go back upon the whole programme of Civil Disobedience, while in 1939, the murder of Bazelgette in Ranpur (Orissa) has compelled him to tender the same advice to the people of the States of the Eastern Agency in Orissa. Prestige has never stood in the way of the paramouncy, of non-violence. On Gandhi's release in 1924, he made a declaration in the course of which he observed that he "retained his opinion that council entry is inconsistent with non-co-operation." Yet it was he, who in 1934 endorsed council entry when Civil Disobedience was suspended and worked it up to its logical conclusion of official acceptance under conditions which have enabled the Ministers to work the Reform Act not as the British would have them do but as the nation would desire and demand.

In 1934, in his famous Patna statement, April 7th, he referred to the states and declared that "the Policy advocated by some in regard to the states was wholly in difference from what I have advised. I have given many an anxious hour to the question but I have not been able to alter my view."

In 1939, he has altered his view altogether only because the conditions in the states have entirely changed. The new awakening amongst them has roused his sympathies to the point of inducing him to offer his utmost support to the cause of the states' people, so that today Mrs. Gandhi is in jail in Rajkot and Gandhi has said that the Princes must either confer on their people responsible government of the states or undergo extinction.

VI. Gandhi – His Instinct

Truth and non-violence are higher experiences of man which require a trained sensibility to appreciate them even as music and mathematics or Khaddar fabrics and communal unity. Trained sensibilities develop direct intuitions, and Gandhi always judges by intuition and not by reason. It is the attribute of virtue to perceive truth instinctively. So does this embodiment of virtue, while those who follow in his footsteps have the duty laid upon them of being the exponents and interpreters of his teachings in terms of the ethical laws and the social conventions of their age and clime. It was thus that he decided upon the great resile at Bardoli in 1922, upon Salt Satyagraha in 1930 upon the suspension of the Civil Disobedience movement in 1934, and on the States' policy in 1939. Light dawns upon him suddenly. Oftentimes did he say that he saw no light and was praying for it. And when he sees the light it appears strange to his people, for his remedies are unprecedented and awe inspiring. When a madman disturbs a meeting of the A.I.C.C., he stops the volunteers trying to remove him bodily and asks the whole house of three hundred members to adjourn. The disturber is paralysed. When a municipality is imposed upon the people of Chirala-Perala by force, and against the people's will, his remedy is that they should quit the place; and quit they did like the Tartars of old who revolted against Zebech Dorchi. In the No-tax campaign of Bardoli and Chersada, the peasants were asked to leave their homes and hearths and migrate to the neighbouring state of Baroda, thus making the puissant British Government with their mighty cohorts hors de combat. When the people of the Nilgiri state in Orissa have been oppressed by their Prince, an exodus is the ready and ancient remedy prescribed and followed to bring round an erring ruler to his senses. The success in these cases depends upon the endurance of the people as well as their purity of heart, Gandhi's following, however, does not always see eye to eye with him. They often resisted his decisions. They stoutly opposed the Bardoli resile in 1922 (February) and praised the spirit behind the crimes of anarchy. When the Serajgung resolution was once again voted upon at Ahmedabad at the All Parties' Conference in the autumn of 1924, Gandhi wept in the open meeting; he wept because some of his own devout followers voted on the side of praising the young man who had committed the crime.

Gandhi's habit is to play with fire – yet he always emerges unscathed from this risky game. He has been arrested several times. Every time the ordeal of fire has burnished the metal of his frame. He expressed regret times without number over the madness of his people, and insisted on the Congress doing so as well. He has agreed to the postponement of his cherished schemes of mass Civil Disobedience time after time merely because violence broke out at some place or other, however remote it might be.

Gandhi works more effectively upon the country when he is silent than when he talks, when he is out of the Congress than when he is in. People may have forgotten the fact that at Cawnpore in the year 1925, he took a vow of political silence which he broke at Gauhati in December 1926. But to him such periods of silence, physical or political, are periods of incubation when huge plans mature in his mind and are, after full gestation, given birth to as well-thought-out programmes and formulae. One such long interval was the period between the Cawnpore Session (1925) and the Calcutta Session of 1928 which were followed by the Lahore (1929) challenge on the ticket of complete Independence. Gandhi resists his own following and tries their mettle as much as he does his opponents. If they stand his test, he takes up their ideas and makes them his own. If they fail, they go by the board. It was thus that he dealt with the problem of Civil Disobedience first, then of complete independence and finally of the states. Today he is vehement on the question of the States much to the surprise of his colleagues and the chagrin of his opponents. The younger Congressmen suspect his bona fides and have publicly charged him with being engaged in making a compromise with the British on Federation. They loudly proclaim their determination to destroy the edifice of Federation which is a two-storeyed structure. The youth direct their guns at the top storey. Gandhi is already pulling down the first floor and pillars thereof. These pillars are the States without which there is no Federation, and the Provincial apartments of the ground floor are threatening to collapse since the pillars that support the top floor are fast crumbling. Gandhi's strategy is truth. His armoury is non-violence. He means what he says and does what he means. When he declared at the Second Round Table Conference that he would *"fight with his life"* the dismemberment of the Hindu Community by Government fixing separate electorates for Harijans, he meant it. He confirmed it on the Azad Maidan on his return from England (December 28, 1931). He committed it to writing in March 1932 in a letter to Sir Samuel Hoare and he began his "fast to death" on September 20, 1932. Today he is taking another fateful vow on the question of the states and he will break Federation. "What is more, if God so wills it, I feel I have enough strength and energy in me to lead a battle much more strenuous than any I have fought." Gandhi's life and career furnish a study in contrasts, which are but seeming and imaginary, being the necessary attributes of a character deeply religious and intensely practical. To combine the ideal with the real, daring with caution, the spirit of revolution with a sense of conservatism, a dash for the future with a bias for the past, the fulfilment of nationalism with the preparation of the nation for universal humanity, in one word to reconcile liberty with fraternity, and evolve from both humanity, is to tack on the brake to the engine in a well-formed train and run it on its rails with its stops and starts, with its steady ascents and rapid descents, with its level and linear movements and its uneven and gradient curves. India has the glory of being led by one who is a man amongst men and yet, what is a puzzle to the contemporary world, has developed into a miracle, a frail being who is a real phenomenon, a Sthithaprajna, yea, an avatar, one who has elevated politics to the sublimity of a religion, charged the conflicts of society with a high ethical and humanitarian touch, and strives to hasten the advent of that far off divine event, the Parliament of Man and the Federation of the World.

Gandhi's Message to the Whole World
Miss Maude D. Petre

I, an Englishwoman, am about to speak a few words on the career of one who has not spared the character and conduct of my own land; who has, to a large extent, lived and worked in opposition to her.

And yet, when I was offered the opportunity of adding my contribution to this volume I embraced it fearlessly, for I know that, if Mahatma Gandhi had devoted his life to the cause of his own people, he had also stood for a wider cause, a more far-reaching cause, the cause of humanity itself. And thus I felt that essentially, he had worked for the ideals of every country that is conscious of the part it has to play in the destiny of the world as large as well as in the conduct of its own affairs. For, like the individual, every nation has a twofold vocation: the call to live its own life and direct its own affairs to the best for its own welfare, and the call to live its life as an organ of the great community of all nations and all mankind.

Now it is because the Mahatma has been a prophet and leader in this second and greater vocation of every human soul and every human society that the purely political side of his career seems to me relatively unimportant; and that I can venture to concentrate, as, I believe, posterity will concentrate, on the lesson he has persistently inculcated of human disinterestedness and universal charity.

As he himself has said:

"If I seem to take part in politics it is only because politics to-day encircle us like the coils of a snake from which one cannot get out no matter how one tries. I wish to wrestle with the snake... I am trying to introduce religion into politics."[19]

Now what is to be expected of a life whose main direction is the moral regeneration of human society as a whole; the metamorphosis of selfishness, rivalry and cruelty into mutual forbearance and fraternal co-operation? The expectation of wise men in such a case is an expectation of disappointment, of humiliation, of failure. And I venture to say that we have, in Gandhi, an example of heroic failure in spite of all that he may have achieved. Reformers must ever be prepared to leave their bodies by the way-side, for like Moses, they may see the land of promise, but not enter.

"I have caused thee to see it with thine eyes, but thou shalt not go over thither."

---

19 Quoted in Mahatma Gandhi, R. Rolland. (George Allen & Unwin).

For, in Gandhi's own words, "a reformer's business is to make the impossible possible by giving an ocular demonstration in his own conduct"; and when he thinks of his own "littleness and limitations," he is "dazed."[20]

For, once great spiritual aims become the objects of concrete work and effort, the perennial struggle of body and spirit comes into play; the purity of spiritual effort is tarnished; the aim is blurred and obscured; the prophet is dragged down into the arena of human passion; his wisest measures are executed by the unwise, his purest efforts get tainted, in the course of fulfilment, by human passion and selfishness.

Yes, it has been a losing battle, but one whose losses in their final sum are, like the stones rejected of the builder, the corner stones of a new Jerusalem. Moses did not enter the promised land, but he saw it, and the land was there; his own presence or absence therefrom did not affect the future of Israel; others would sit down in peace within the borders in front of which he died.

And so it seems to me that, in enumerating the chief efforts of this life, we are also enumerating its chief failures; failure inevitable, but failure also fruitful.

Here are some of the battles in which he has been worsted, but the lesson of whose story will outlive the defeat.

First of all, the battle with the machine, against which he advanced, armed with no sword or gun, but with the spinning-wheel. A pathetic effort indeed; as many of his own followers told him. An effort doomed to failure. And yet the spinning-wheel has hummed a word of truth; of soul-searching truth, that only too many of us have long and sadly recognised.

The machine has exercised a de-humanizing influence on life; it has got the better of us; and all the hand-spinning of India

---

20 See Young India

will not avail to conquer it. But the hand-spinning of India may avail to make us realize our servitude; and the call to a simpler and more human life may, at last, rouse men to assert their own primacy; to reduce the monster to his rightful dimensions; to make it the servant and not the master of the human soul; to hold it in check and deny even its temporary material advantages when they run directly counter to the true welfare of body and soul.

A second battle against cruelty to man and beast. And here he has had to contend with his own people at least as much as with others. He has urged man "to look beyond his own species, and realize his identity with all that lives."

And, while he has upheld the doctrine of the sacredness of life, his heart has bled over the sufferings of dumb creatures that were not, indeed, slaughtered, but that were, indeed. neglected.

The third and greatest battle has been against the spirit of domination and violence, and he has gone forth, even more totally disarmed than David, against the Goliath of human force and passion, for he has carried but one weapon, that of non-violence.

He has been worsted again and again not only by his foes, but, what is more bitter, by his friends. And he has come up hard against the unsolved pacifist problem, of how the non-violent are to survive in a world of violence; of how non-violence itself is to survive in a world wherein violence predominates.

Let anyone run through the pages of Young India if they would realize the persistent problems that have beset the Mahatma's career.

And it is on this point that the Mahatma best shows forth the triumph of failure. For he maintains that the doctrine has never really been put into practice.

"Try it," he says, "for we can never truly estimate the strength of the soul until we have ceased to defend it by bodily means.

"I seek entirely to blunt the edge of the tyrant's sword, not by putting up against it a sharper-edged weapon, but by disappointing his expectation that I would be offering physical resistance. The resistance of the soul that I should offer instead would elude him. It would at first dazzle him and at last compel recognition, which recognition would not humiliate, but would uplift him. It may be *urged that this is an ideal state. And so it is.*"[21]

Here we have faith coupled with open-eyed recognition of failure: of belief in the policy proposed coupled with certainty that the moment has not yet come, even if it be coming, for its perfect fulfilment.

Are we then to regret, as one great poet regretted, that Gandhi has brought his teaching and ideals into the arena of human life and passion in such fashion as to manifest their present, at least partial, failure? Yes, and No!

Yes, because one hates to be convinced of the bankruptcy of some of the noblest human ideals.

Yes, because one hates to see a prophet dragged about in the melee, not living above it as some have done.

No, because the very brutality of the contest has forced men to open their eyes to ideals which might otherwise have been preserved, in calm dignity, but only in the minds of a thinking minority. The Jews had to look on the face of Christ before they struck it; and men must listen to the message of meekness and charity before they can deny it.

We cannot fight without receiving scars; nor can we even fight without, in our turn, striking where blows were unmerited.

---

21 See Young India, October 8, 1925.

And so there has been both good, and evil in the Mahatma's political struggle.

But through the hubbub of passing rivalries and dissensions has sounded the human message, the message to all mankind. A message to both East and West, a Hindu message, but mostly uttered in the language of Christianity.

And this is why I dare, with humble apologies, to neglect all that is local and purely national in the policy of Mahatma Gandhi, and to appropriate his person and mission in the name of my own and all countries of the world.

The Wisdom of Gandhiji
Hy. S.L. Polak

It is not by chance that Gandhiji was included, some years ago, in a series of addresses at the guildhouse, during Dr. Maude Royden's ministry, on "Makers of Modern Thought." When the time comes to assess the great men of today and to discuss their contribution to the world's thought and practice, probably no name will stand out more significantly and constructively than that of India's foremost leader.

There are other leaders in the world whose names are more frequently on men's lips. They are leaders, not of life, but of death; they are leaders towards the abyss and not towards the heights; they are leaders of hate and of violence, not of love and of non-violence; they are leaders back to barbarism, not forward to the nobler civilization; they are leaders of a doctrine of "superiority" of race, raised to the rank of a false divinity, not of the fellowship of man within the Fatherhood of God.

But who, looking back into the mists of history, absorbing its lessons and watching its results, can doubt that, in the long run, it is Gandhiji's teaching of Ahimsa that will triumph and not the resort to violence of these new Caesars? His conquests are in the realm of the spirit, sowing the seed of the regeneration of mankind; theirs are in the world of matter, and their paths are strewn with blood and tears. He would win his opponent by self-suffering; they would add to human suffering by the remorseless destruction of whatever and whoever stands in their way.

Many years ago, Gandhiji said to me: "Men say that I am a saint losing himself in politics. The fact is that I am a politician trying my hardest to become a saint." That is a humble, homely and modern confession of human imperfection seeking to evolve, positively and by self-discipline, towards the higher levels of perfection. It explains the faults of action and the errors of judgment that he has repeatedly admitted during his fifty years' pilgrimage as a "truth-seeker". One need not agree either with his interpretation of a situation or of the best method of dealing with it to recognize that he has never failed in his steady insistence that "There is no Religion higher than Truth". To hold the vision steady, to keep the faith – what more can one demand of a man? If he should at times stumble and falter – what are these but human experiences on the Path? And Gandhiji asks us to believe that he recognizes them as warning signs, so that he may retrace his steps, and march the more unerringly towards the Goal that he has marked out for himself.

In the course of his pilgrimage, he has learnt many lessons, and he has acquired a store of practical knowledge that is the common treasure of all who pass along the same road. Mere mumbling of *mantras* has no attraction of him; they must have a meaning adaptable to the ordinary activities of human life and need. Moreover, they must, in his view, be universally applicable, or they are substantially untrue. We need, therefore, not be surprised to read the following interpretation of his doctrine of *Ahimsa* as a practical rule of life:

"If one does not practise non-violence (which, elsewhere, Gandhiji speaks of as the "maturest fruit" or Truth) in one's personal relations with others, and hopes to use it in bigger affairs, one is vastly mistaken. Non-violence, like charity, must begin in the home. And if it is necessary for the individual to be trained in non-violence, it is even more necessary for the nation to be trained likewise. One cannot be non-violent in one's own circle and be violent outside it. Or else, one is not truly non-violent even in one's own circle; often the non-violence is only in appearance. It is only when you meet with resistance...that your non-violence is put on its trial...Living among decent people your conduct may not be described as non-violent. Mutual forbearance is non-violence. Immediately, therefore, you get the conviction that non-violence is the law of life, you have to practise it to those who act violently towards you, and the law must apply to nations as to individuals. Training is, no doubt, necessary. And beginnings are always small. But if the conviction is there, the rest will follow." All of which is but an old saying of his – "fix your standards; sooner or later you will attain to them" – writ large.

A teaching of this kind – ancient in India (and in Palestine) – must sound sheer madness to the dictators whose power-politics are menacing our world with the destruction of the noble things that it cherishes, sheer madness to the terrified victims of violence and cruelty and to those threatened by the ruthlessness and greed of modern conquest. Yet, may it not be that Gandhiji and his spiritual forbears, who taught that hate is conquered by love, that man should love his neighbour as himself, that we are all members one of another, are right? And that in this world of rapid communication and swift transport, of growing interchange of thought and recognition of mutual interdependence, the only chance of the survival of man and of the higher values is to put into practise this ancient teaching voiced in modern language by this new prophet.

Whilst others are described as "leader", it is not for nothing that Gandhiji (much to his regret) has been given the title of "Mahatma". It was a great soul who, thirty years ago, wrote with insight: "Soul-force is matchless. It is superior to the force of arms. How, then, can it be considered merely as a weapon of the weak. Men who use physical force are strangers to the courage that is requisite in a passive resister ("Satyagrahi")... Who is the true warrior – he who keeps death always as a bosom-friend?...Control over the mind is alone necessary, and when that is attained, man is free... and his very glance withers the enemy." No wonder, then, that he declares positively and unhesitatingly: "My confidence is unshaken, that if a single satyagrahi holds out to the end, victory is absolutely certain."

Nowadays, sabre-rattlers shout orders to the world through microphones and punctuate their commands with the dropping of bombs or the spraying of poison-gas. They brag of their victories over other nations and strut among the ruins of freedom. The people are at the same time the instruments of their pride and the victims of their violence. How different from the mild accents, the emphasis upon man's spiritual powers, the recalling of the ancient message of peace, and love, and brotherhood, by this Indian teacher of today. As ever, the message of a new age is given to us from the East. Have we the wit to listen and the wisdom to learn? Gandhiji does not pretend to originality. In his *Autobiography* he recalls: "The sage who realized truth found non-violence out of the violence raging all about him, and said: 'Violence is unreal; non-violence is real'.

It is once more the fashion among the younger folk, as it was a generation or so ago, to mock at religion and to reject it as a superstitious remnant of human ignorance and folly, if not something baser still. I have no doubt that in India, too, the same false philosophy is abroad and that many young men and women are trying to "throw away the baby with the bath-water," to use a homely Western phrase.

They would do well to ponder over the sayings of their great sages and to seek to discover anew the true meaning of the ancient lore. But if they are unwilling to learn from the wisdom of the past, let them at least heed the wisdom of their own great national leader, when he says authoritatively:

"Religion is a thing not alien to us: it has to be evolved out of us. It is always within us; with some, consciously so, with others quite unconsciously, but it is always there. And whether we wake up this religious instinct in us through outside assistance or by inward growth, no matter how it is done, it has got to be done, if we want to do anything in the right manner, or to achieve anything that is going to persist."

So, too, he tells us that "Ahimsa" is the soul of Truth and that non-violence is the highest religion. And he adds – whether we can believe it or not – "If you express your love – Ahimsa – in such a manner that it impresses itself indelibly upon your so-called enemy, he must return that love."

It is good to live in a time that has produced another great "lover of mankind," following so soon after Tolstoy. How the sages and saints, the prophets and devotees, major or minor, do purify the atmosphere and spread light "amid the encircling gloom!" What should we do without these spiritual "sweepers," who help us, from age to age and from generation to generation, to cleanse our souls, so that we may realize anew our Divine nature and, encouraged once more to enlarge our capacity for endeavour, climb with resolute courage the heights that still remain for us to read?

In one of Olive Schreiner's prose-poems, she pictures the adventures of the seeker after the "bird of Truth," of which he had once had a vision, and she leaves us with him, dying on a mountain top, clasping to his breast one feather that had fallen from the bird. The message that Gandhiji, in his seventieth year, leaves with us may well by such a feather, and we shall be fortunate indeed if, at our own death, we have clasped it to our bosom and made it our own.

The Triumph of the Spirit
Llewelyn Powys

A confirmed rationalist and lover of earth life, it is no easy task for me lucidly to present the ideas suggested by the appearance of such an extraordinary being as Mahatma Gandhi. It is clear that his presence amongst us offers a difficult challenge to explain away. In our handy-dandy-market-place world, we feel the irresistible attraction of the man. The mere sight of his picture in any of the daily papers ruffles our customary soul sloth as he peers out from the common commercial page with a look of pure wisdom. I have been told that there exist in certain parts of China white bats, and the photographs of this rare man seem scarcely less strange than do the faces of such unusual creatures, equipped as he is with eyes that seem to penetrate deep into life's darkest secrets, and with ears that by their generous habit testify to an essential sweetness of nature such as is seldom to be met with either in the Orient or in the Occident. No human being in our time has more successfully vindicated the power of love, not, be it understood, the natural love of vineyard and cornland, but the ideal love of the mystics, of the Christian and of the Hindu, a love that goes clean contrary to our animal inheritance. To people sceptical of supernatural rumours, much of Mr. Gandhi's thought cannot fail to be meaningless, made up as it seems of the veriest illusions, or often enough of trite moral preconceptions whose roots, when closely examined, are seen to go not much deeper than those inculcated everywhere by priests eager to find divine sanctions for the more serviceable contracts of society. Not for nothing as a young man was this serpent-phobe to be found at prayer meetings and hymn-singing parties in England and South

Africa, as well as in India. But if his head appears often easily turned by the airs of heaven, it is otherwise with his heart which remains always sane, sunny, humane and honourable.

To read the autobiography of Mr. Gandhi is truly a revelation as to the triumph of the spirit over the body. Somewhere he tells us that he has always striven to attain "fineness and rarity of spirit". How narrow are the horns of the dilemmas upon which he balances, like one of the Schoolmen's angles poised upon the point of a bodkin! Quaint enough to a free mind are the conundrums that keep entering into this pious head so much to be revered. Gandhi takes a pledge not to drink the milk of the cow, and then is full of scruples when he sips a little goat's milk, lest this beverage might have been included in his original vow. He sees a calf suffering from an incurable malady – is he justified in killing it out of compassion? How were the monkeys "those wily and intelligent cousins of ours" to be kept away from the cultivated cousins of ours" to be kept away from the cultivated grounds of the peasantry without violence? It will be noticed that these nice problems may be associated with the Hindu doctrine of cow worship, a doctrine which for Mr. Gandhi has the widest possible significance, nothing less, in fact, than the religious recognition by the human race of a moral obligation to shelter and protect, and never to kill, other creatures that breathe upon the earth's surface, however unassuming and lowly. Mr. Gandhi's ethical sensibility may be exacting, but it is also very sure, and never does he condemn the gross turpitude of the West with more passion than when he has occasion to refer to vivisection, that dark abomination still palliated by Governments that are sentimental as they are cynical, and morally blind as they are lacking in magnanimity.

The treatment that this "well-descended spirit" has so often received at the hands of Europeans must remain a matter for the heaviest shame. Insulted and buffeted, threatened and beaten, and on one occasion nearly lynched by a white mob in Durban, he has not been embittered but has merely continued following his fairy fancies with dedicated, resolute steps. How comes this little body, this habitation of brittle bones, can house so mighty a spirit? The applause of the noisy world seems to affect him as little as does its hatred. His personal dignity is of a kind so supreme that he can suffer the most mortifying physical indignities and remain unviolated and inviolable. Harried here and there, now being pulled through the window of a crowded train, now bending his spine to sweep up the dung of indentured labourers, now serving "untouchables" as though they were of his nearest kin, his perfect simplicity and perfect goodness appear utterly unaffected. It is impossible to associate him with the sort of spiritual vanity that so infects our own idealists; whether secular or clerical. His genius is free as a cloud and he will change notion or custom overnight if he hears a true word. This Ariel breaks asunder all chains save those placed on his heels by the great Prospero of his life-long allegiance. Mr. Gandhi, for all his high principles and high thoughts, possesses a remarkable store of practical good sense. It is this, combined with an utter selflessness in all his approaches to life, which has rendered him so invincible in his various struggles against wrong-doing and oppression. Wherever he goes all falls before him, as though his brown spinning hand held between finger and thumb a goblin's wand.

If ever the secret of Jesus has been practically proven it has been so by this saintly Hindu. This is perhaps why the words of Jesus are so often upon his lips though he is far too clear a thinker, and has a far too honest a mind, to accept the dogmas and theological inventions of our Western faith. "My reason was not ready to believe literally that Jesus, by his death and by his blood, redeemed the sins of the world. Metaphorically, there might be some truth in it." He was always strongly attracted to the Christian ideal of self-sacrifice and the sermon on the Mount, with all its manifold implications, made a deep impression on him. Nietzsche uttered once the piercing paradox, "There has been only one Christian and he died on the cross." Perhaps if the frenzied philosopher had lived long enough to observe the manner of life of this other Guru, he would have qualified his celebrated quip.

With a noble tenderness and devotion, Gandhi cared for the sick and wounded in that unforgivable "manhunt" known as the Zulu Rebellion, and as he marched through "those solemn solitudes" of the African hinterland, he decided, he tells us, to observe the vow of Brahmacharya. Did not Jesus also turn away from his family believing like Gandhi that "he who would be a friend with God must remain alone?" Listen, too, to the following rash pronouncement: "God helps us when we feel ourselves humbler than the dust under our feet. Only to the weak and helpless is divine succour vouchsafed."

It is difficult to foresee the influences that will shape our human destiny here on earth. Perhaps, "metaphorically speaking," these two heroes, so sinless and so sin-obsessed, have fallen upon an unexpected clue by which "the old Dragon underground" may be bound in straiter limits. If it is found that happiness, as in the golden age, can be charmed back to earth by the gentle persuasions of their magical manners, blessed will it be indeed for the race of turbulent mortals so long abused. It is impossible not to respond to the story of Mr. Gandhi's four Indian clerks who, when they were asked whether they would come with him to nurse men stricken with the plague, with the terrible black death, answered simply, "Where you go, we will go also."

If Gandhi's inspired gentleness gives to us English contrite and broken hearts for the horrible atrocity – "a monstrous progeny of a monstrous war" – committed by General Dyer at Amritsar, he will have done a most valuable service for our native land. He will have proved once again that FEAR does not rule the world and that there is a power greater than the bloody triumph of the sword.

Ha! Monsieur Maggot and my Lord Rat,
Here's something for you to squinny at!
We pine and pine-but by Holy Rood
There's something here not understood
And we are not the Devil's food.

How can we suffer the good name of our island race to be dragged down, down to the dust, "through the brute and boist'rous force of violent men!" Gandhi, with the eye-balls of the God Siva, sees through the frivolity of our Western culture, with its confidence in machines, with its lust for gold, with its lust for power, with its thoughtless acceptance of life's more trivial and more obvious values; with its reciprocity with nature acquired through killing innocent wild creatures – a culture that knows nothing of meditation, a culture that prompts us to reduce to the level of the humdrum all the poetry that surrounds us, common as the grass of the field.

At Chauri Chaura, in 1922, there occurred upon the Indian side a shameless example of mob violence. Gandhi at once stopped his movement of civil disobedience and imposed upon himself an arduous fast. This conduct was typical of the Mahatma, typical of the great soul. In Piers Plowman, the sturdy little religious political book of the fourteenth century, there occurs a sentence which I have for long regarded as one of the most beautiful to be found in our literature. I think it can be placed with propriety at the end of this faltering appreciation. "Never lighter was a leaf upon a linden tree, than thy love was when it took flesh and blood of man, fluttering, piercing as a needle-point.

Homage from China
M. Quo Tai-Chi

The processes of social and political regeneration all over China in our own times work in all the countries of Asia; and to serve and direct these processes, a surprising group of leaders has been vouchsafed. Two of them have supremely embodied the greatest need of our continent, that moral prestige shall ever dominate high political acumen, whatever the diverse ways by which national regenerations are being worked out. As a devoted follower of Sun Yat-sen, I count it a privilege to offer my word of homage to Mahatma Gandhi on the occasion of his seventieth birthday.

A Statesman in Beggar's Garb
Sir Abdul Qadir

Some years ago, I was on a visit to Vienna – the old, gay Vienna before the Anschuluss. I went to one of its big restaurants for my mid-day meal. It was a busy hour and the place was crowded. I had some difficulty in finding a vacant table. A waiter came to me, and instead of asking what I required, he said:

"Do you come from the country of Gandhi?"

"Yes, I come from India and have seen Gandhi and spoken to him on a few occasions."

He was pleased to hear this and said: "I am so glad, I shall now be able to say I have met someone who had met Gandhi."

Aware as I was of the fact that the fame of Gandhi had spread far and wide, I had not realized that even the man in the street, in countries not connected with India and parted from it by land and sea, had come to know him and respected him.

This leads my thoughts back to the year 1931. I was then in London and Mahatma Gandhi came there to attend the second Round Table Conference. Some people in India were of the opinion that he lost in prestige by that visit to England and made a mistake in attending the Conference. I do not agree with that view. I think he made a great impression on thinking people in England and created a friendly atmosphere in this country, in spite of the fact that in all his public utterances in London he made no secret of the fact that he desired the fullest political liberty for his country.

His dress elicited some mild criticism in certain quarters, but such criticism did not matter to Gandhi, and his personality and the significance attached to his participation in the conference conquered it.

One of the strong points of Gandhi's character is his supreme indifference to what people say about any course of conduct which he has decided for himself, for good reasons that satisfy his conscience. He, therefore, continued to wear, during his last visit to England, the dress he had adopted for years past. A loin cloth round his waist, his legs bare, and a sheet of home-spun cloth or a blanket round his shoulders, according to the season being hot or cold – this is now his dress, and he was not deterred from sticking to it, while travelling through France, where he received ovation, or attending a big function in London or in the sitting of the Round Table Conference itself. These sittings were not open to the public, as the hall in the palace at St. James's, where the Conference was held, was not large enough to allow the admission of visitors. I learnt, however, that they could occasionally allow someone to occupy a secretary's seat for a short while as a special case, and I managed to go in one day. Lord Sankey was in the chair. On his right sat Sir Samuel Hoare, the secretary of State for India, and Parliamentary representative, and on the left the first place was given to Gandhi and then followed other Indian delegates, who occupied also the seat opposite the Chair. The deference that Lord Sankey appeared to pay to Gandhi was remarkable.

The climax of Gandhi's freedom from convention in the matter of dress was reached when I saw him mounting the carpeted stairs of Buckingham Palace to greet the King and Queen, with his blanket round his shoulders, at the Royal Party in honour of the Conference Delegates and other visitors. I do not think the Palace had seen a visitor in that costume before, nor is it easy to conceive that anyone else would have been allowed the same freedom.

Two interesting questions arise in this connection. Firstly, why has Gandhi adopted this garb and secondly, what is it that has earned him the towering position in which the observance of established conventions can be waived in this case?

Those who have read Gandhi's own story of his life, styled *My Experiments with Truth,* know that when he first came to England to qualify for the Bar, he was familiar with the life of a man of fashion and wore suits made by West End tailors. After being called to the Bar and returning to India, he went to South Africa in connection with a law suit and decided to stay on there. It was then that the serious purpose of his life took shape. It was there that he began to make sacrifices for the welfare of his countrymen settled there. It was the contact with their troubles and sorrows which brought about a change in him. The story of his useful work there is too well known to require recapitulation here. When he returned to India and began to take part in the struggle for Indian freedom, he gave up all ideas of practicing as a lawyer, and dedicated himself to the work of political and social reform. It was at this stage that he adopted the loin cloth, as a voluntary act of self-denial, reducing his standard of life to the minimum. There is nothing to distinguish Gandhi's garb from that which is worn by the poorest people. He tells us in the story of his life that "the idea of Renunciation appealed to him greatly, even when he was a student in London, as the highest form of religion." That early seed in his mind has now grown into a tree and borne fruit.

By the answer to the first question about the garb assumed by Gandhi, the second question has also been practically answered. His strength lies in his not wanting anything for himself. In his varied career, in the course of which intervals of hardship, detention and imprisonment have alternated with triumphal processions and enthusiastic shouts of Jai (Victory) in his honour, there has been no question of "Self," of office or rank or emolument. It is this aspect of his life that has touched the hearts of friends and foes alike.

He has been invited by Governors and Viceroys to have frank talks with them about problems affecting the future of our country. Princes have consulted him and Ministers have sought his advice. A well-known verse of our famous Indian poet, Sir Mohammed Iqbal, fits in with a case such as this:

> Dil-i-shah larza girad zi gada-i-be-niaze.

> "The heart of a King trembles at the sight of a beggar who begs not."

It is this "begging not," this rising above personal want, which has given Gandhi the marvellous influence he possesses.

During his stay in England, Mahatma Gandhi stayed at Kingsley Hall, in the East End of London, spending any time that could be spared from the work of the Round Table Conference among the poor. He is always happy when associated with them and enjoys the kinship of spirit between them and himself. He could have stayed at one of the palatial hotels of London if he had wished. He could have stayed with some of his friends in a well-furnished and comfortable home, but he preferred the invitation of Miss Muriel Lester of Kingsley Hall in Bow. This establishment provides a club for the working people in that area, where they have a social and intellectual center and hold their meetings. It has some residential accommodation also, where one can live in a simple way on less than one pound a week for board and residence. Gandhi occupied one of the small rooms in this house, while he was representing India at the conference. I have seen that room. The management of the place are proud of their association with Gandhi and gladly point out to visitors the room which is now called by Gandhi's name.

Gandhi has the rare gift of inspiring love wherever he lives. He collected round him a band of devoted men and women, including some Europeans, when he fought the battle for the rights of Indians in South Africa. He attracted a still larger number of zealous co-workers when he changed his sphere of work to a bigger field in India, and during his brief visit to England in 1931, he added a number of friends and admirers to those he already had. When he had to go to jail, on his return to India, his jailers felt drawn towards him, and when he was ill in hospital his nurses became so fond of his genial temperament that they were sorry when he recovered and left the ward. This is all the more remarkable, as his charm comes simply from the beauty of his soul and does not depend for assistance on charms of personal appearance. Gandhi's love has its source in a strong belief in God and in his deep spirit of religion. His autobiography is full of passages showing his belief. For instance, referring to the ideal which he wishes humanity to follow, he observes: "Infinite striving after perfection is our human right. It carries with it its own reward. The rest is in the hands of God." In the same book he tells us that "the religious spirit within him became a living force" at an early stage of his career in South Africa. Those, who have watched his life since, know that it is the same spirit which has been at work throughout his career and has made it possible for him to climb the great heights of patriotic fervour which he has reached and kept.

On his attaining the seventieth year of a life devoted to the

service of the motherland and to the cause of religion and
humanity, he will receive numerous tributes. Most of them will
be from persons who have worked with him and have not
always agreed with him in matters of policy or about methods
of work, but my appreciation of his lofty personal character
and of his lifelong services to India is as sincere as of those who
have had a closer and more intimate touch with him. The great
awakening that we see among the masses of India owes more to
his labours and influence than to any other living man. He
stands as a demonstration of the power of the spirit, of what he
calls "soul force," in the sceptic and materialistic world of
today, and has thus earned for himself the title of Mahatma, or
"the great soul," which has been conferred upon him by his
countrymen.

India's Debt to Gandhi
Rajendra Prasad

Mahatma Gandhi's contribution to Indian politics has been
immense. The Indian National Congress had been in existence
for thirty years when he returned to India finally from South
Africa in 1915. The Congress had aroused and organized
national consciousness to a certain extent; but the awakening
was confined largely to the English-educated middle classes and
had not penetrated the masses. He carried it to the masses and
made it a mass movement. Mahatma Gandhi's movement
operated both horizontally and vertically. He took up causes
which were not entirely political but which touched very
intimately the life of large masses of people. His successful
Satyagraha in Champaran on behalf of the cultivators and
labourers, who had suffered for a century or more under an
iniquitous system of the forced growing of indigo for the
benefit of planters, at once, extended the sphere of Congress
activity to the proportions of a mass movement. His equally

successful Satyagraha in Khaira for a revision of revenue assessment which was considered unjust had a similar appeal to the masses of the district. Congress politics was no longer confined to demanding a larger share in the higher public services of the country or seats on the Executive Councils of Governors. It identified itself with the sufferings of the toiling masses and, what was more, succeeded in securing relief for them. Since these early movements of 1917 and 1918, there have been others of a similar kind, and in all of them, the objective has been the securing of benefit not for a small class or group but for masses at large. Fight for relief has not been directed only against the British interests or the British Government. It has unhesitatingly attacked Indian interests and prejudices with equal vigour. Thus the unsatisfactory conditions under which Indian labourers have to work in factories have not escaped his vigilant eyes and one of the earliest things he did was to help workers of Ahmedabad to secure better conditions. The miserable lot of the depressed classes has necessitated a relentless drive against the vicious and wicked custom of Untouchability among the Hindus, and Mahatma Gandhi has carried it on even at the risk of his life. The Congress organization has also spread and expanded, covering the entire length and breadth of this vast country, and has got today millions of men and women on its rolls. But the influence of the Congress extends far wider than its mere numbers would indicate. The depth of that influence has been tried and tested as people have passed through the fiery ordeal of suffering and sacrifice at its call.

Mahatma Gandhi's greatest contribution, however, does not consist in making the masses of India politically self-conscious and organizing them on a scale they had never before been organized. To my mind, his greatest contribution to Indian politics and perhaps to suffering humanity in the world at large lies in the unique method which he has prescribed and employed for fighting wrongs. He has taught us how it is

possible for us to successfully fight the mighty British Empire
without arms; he has given us and the world a moral substitute
for war. He has lifted politics from the plane of sophisticated
and untruths, where at its worst it degenerated into low
intrigue and at its highest could not rise beyond diplomatic
circumlocutions and secret diplomacy, to the pitch of a high
idealism in which the end, however noble, can in no
circumstances justify recourse to means which are not pure and
immaculate. He has placed truth on its pedestal of glory even in
politics, no matter how harmful its effect appears to be at the
moment. His frankness and deliberate exposure of ugly or
weak spots in ourselves to our so-called enemies has
confounded both friends and opponents alike. But he considers
our strength lies not in concealing our weakness but in
knowing and combating it. The rigorous observance of non-
violence, even where temporary advantages may apparently be
gained by ignoring or mitigating it, has been recognized by
experience to be not only the straightest course but also the
wisest policy. It was the moral and spiritual fervour of his
teaching which at once caught the imagination of the people,
who saw and recognized that when all was dark around he
showed us the way out of our misery and slavery. When we
were feeling utterly helpless, he made us realize our own
strength through Truth and Non-violence. Man, after all, is not
born with arms and weapons. He does not possess even the
claws of a tiger or the horns of a wild buffalo. He is born with
a soul and a spirit. Why should he depend upon these
extraneous things for his protection and uplift? Mahatma
Gandhi has taught us that death and destruction await us if we
rely upon them – that life and liberty are ours if we rouse the
spirit within us. No power on earth can keep us under
subjection once that spirit is roused, once that dependence on
extraneous things and circumstances is given up and once
self-confidence and self-reliance are created. India is gradually,
but none the less surely and steadily, getting that self-confidence
and is in the measure of that self-realization becoming

irresistible. God grant that she shall not be deflected from the strait and narrow course of Truth and Non-violence which she has selected under the guidance of Mahatma Gandhi! That is Mahatma Gandhi's greatest contribution to Indian politics and that will be India's contribution to the deliverance of the world.

The Fool of God
Reginald Reynolds

> *His fools in vesture strange*
> *God sent to range*
> *The World and said: "Declare*
> *Untimely wisdom; bear*
> *Harsh witness and prepare*
> *The paths of change."*

These are the opening words of W.G. Hole's poem, The Fools of God, which I discovered in the Visva-Bharati Quarterly in 1929, a few months before I went to India. It is not a well-known poem, but I doubt if anything I have ever read made a more profound or lasting impression on my mind. This was due not merely to the intrinsic merit of the verse, but to the fact that they proved prophetic.

The poem tells of God's instructions to His Fools: "Be deaf; defer to none, and ever perversely shun the prudent way." They depart

> *And proffering toil and thirst*
> *To men in softness nursed,*
> *Today by all are cursed,*
> *Tomorrow blessed.*

In their quest they scorn

> *The comfortable ways*
> *Of men's consent and praise.*

But "faith-befooled" they claim

> *To see the light that rings*
> *Men's brows and makes them kings*
> *With Power to do the things*
> *Of righteousness.*

Within a few months of my discovering that poem, I met – may I say it with all respect – Public Fool Number One, Mahatma Gandhi. And it did not take me long to discover that the vivid description in the lines that had so moved and inspired me fitted this man to the last detail.

In spite of all that has been argued to the contrary, I do not think Gandhi is a clever man. Since I first came to know him, ten years ago, I have often felt extremely critical of his words and his actions. I am not among those blind venerators to whom the Mahatma can do no wrong. I regard him neither as a Messiah nor as an Avatar. His claim to greatness would, in my mind, be a slender one if it had to rely upon his political sagacity. It is by other standards that he must be judged.

To explain the full and true significance of Gandhi, it would be necessary to trace the whole history of Hinduism, from its earliest roots, laying stress upon those numerous reform movements which have their place in the development of every religion. For it is in the nature of organized religion to decay, and in its decay to throw out continually new seeds of life in which the spirit lives while the old husks die and the dead boughs wither.

I once heard a formidable American Christian catechizing one of Gandhi's disciples. He asked what book had most deeply influenced the Mahatma. Pencil and notebook were ready and we all knew what answer he hoped to receive. But the reply was : *The Gita. The New Testament*, together with the writings of Tolstoy and Ruskin, played its part. But primarily Gandhi is a Hindu reformer.

And yet Gandhi is not merely a Hindu. His true proto-type was Kabir, who first achieved honour as a saint among both Hindus and Mohammedans. He was the great prophet of Hindu-Moslem unity, a Moslem himself and disciple of the Hindu teacher Ramanand. Rabindranath Tagore has given us a beautiful English translation of Kabir's sayings from which it is possible to illustrate this historical link.[22]

Put thy cleverness away: mere words shall never unite thee to Him.

Do not deceive thyself with the witness of the scriptures:

Love is something other than this, and he who has sought it truly has found it.

Here in three lines is the very essence of Gandhi's teaching as a religious leader and it is as a religious leader that I wish to consider him at the moment.

When an Indian scholar once wrote an article entitled 'Does the *Gita* support Orthodoxy?" (it was published later in The Aryan Path of March 1933), he sent it to Gandhi for his perusal. The Mahatma's reply-dated, January 11, 1933 from Yeravda Central Prison was characteristic:

"I have now carefully read both your articles on the *Gita*. I have found them to be interesting.

"I observe that you have reached the same conclusion that I had by a different method. Yours is the learned way. Not so mine."

---

22 All quotations from Kabir are from Kabir's Poems, translated by Rabindranath Tagore and published by Macmillan (5 s. net)

Needless to say, the conclusion of both the scholar and the
Fool of God was that the *Gita* gave no support to orthodoxy.
But Gandhi had not reached his standpoint through
"cleverness."

Kabir might well have been writing about Gandhi when he
said:

"It is a hard fight and a weary one, this fight of the truth-
seeker; for the vow of the truth-seeker is more hard than that of
the warrior, or the widowed wife who would follow her
husband.

"For the warrior fights for a few hours, and the widow's
struggle with death is soon ended:

"But the truth-seeker's battle goes on day and night, as long as
life lasts, it never ceases."

Or again, when Kabir speaks of life and death, the spiritual
heritage of Gandhi is manifest:

"If your bonds be not broken whilst living, what hope of
deliverance in death?

"It is but an empty dream that the soul shall have union with
Him because it has passed from the body:

"If He is found now, He is found then,

"If not, we do but go to dwell in the City of Death."

Something equivalent to the Catholic and Protestant traditions
in Christianity can be traced in most religions. Each tradition
has its typical faults and its high peaks of achievement, and the
apex of Protestantism is to be found among the finest of its
Puritans. In our age, we are inclined to see nothing in the
Puritan but his intolerable negations: it is too easy to forget
what Puritanism in its inception had to contend with. In his
right place, the Puritan is but a stern physician who prescribes
abstinence and a strict regimen for a patient who is sick from a

surfeit. That may not be the conscious purpose of the Puritan: it is his historical function.

Wherever great movements of social reform or revolution are found, a strain of Puritanism can be discovered. It is part of the discipline of men and women who have to give up much in order to concentrate their energies upon one thing. That the leaders of modern India should be Puritans and the chief of them all a rigorous ascetic is therefore no accident. A revolt against imperialism could make no headway unless it struck at the fetters and blinkers which kept the people of India ignorant, indolent, caste-ridden and superstitious. Gandhi was able to lead the movement for political emancipation because he opposed the power of the priests, the evils accepted by the orthodox, "untouchability," the inferior status of women, child-marriages, neglect of public hygiene, religious intolerance, wasteful expenditure on marriages, the use of opium – in short, the social corruption which had produced political inertia.

Once more, we shall find that a long tradition had existed in India, with intermittent manifestation of considerable interest, which helps to explain the success of Gandhi's work in opposition to the conservative main current of Hindu orthodoxy.

Long before Gandhi's time there were "Fools of God" in India. In Bengal, the Bauls (the name signifies "madcaps") included both Moslems and Hindus, chiefly of the lower castes. Spiritually, their affinity with Kabir has been noted. They rejected scriptural authority and the sacredness of temples, for, as one of their songs complains:

> *Thy path, O Lord, is hidden by mosque and temple:*
> *Thy call I hear, but priest and guru bar the way.*

They believed involuntary poverty, in self-respect and self-knowledge. Their God was the "inner guru," the "Man of the Heart".

And it was a Baul who said – as a warning to myself and others who with our little learning try to appraise the incalculable –

A goldsmith, me thinks, has come into the garden:

He would appraise the Lotus, for sooth,

By rubbing it on his touchstone.

Judged by the standard of the goldsmith, the lotus was valueless. Our familiar measurers may often prove equally deceptive when human wisdom sits in judgment over the Fools of God.

Homage from a Man of the West to Gandhi
Romain Rolland

Gandhi is not only for India a hero of national history whose legendary memory will be enshrined in the millennial epoch. He has not only been the spirit of active life which has breathed into the peoples of India the proud consciousness of their unity, of their power, and the will to their independence. He has renewed, for all the peoples of the West, the message of their Christ, forgotten or betrayed. He has inscribed his name among the sages and saints of humanity; and the radiance of his figure has penetrated into all the regions of the earth.

In the eyes of Europe he appeared at a moment when such an example seemed almost a miracle. Europe had barely emerged from four years of furious war, of which the ravages, the ruins and the rancours were persisting, sowing the seeds of fresh and even more implacable wars, conjoined with the overturning of revolutions, with their fatal train of social hatreds, which was gnawing the heart of nations. Europe was under the weight of a heavy night, pregnant with misery and despair, without a single ray of light. The appearance of Gandhi, this feeble and nude little man, who repudiated all violence, whose only arms were his reason and his love, and whose humble and stubborn gentleness had just achieved its first victories, seemed a paradoxical defiance hurled in the face of the politics and the thought, traditional, accepted, and unquestioned, of the West. But it was, at the same time, a beam of health which shot through the despair. One could hardly believe it...And it was some time before one could be convinced of the reality of such a prodigy... who knew this better than I, who was one of the first in the West to discover and to spread the message of the Mahatma?... But in the degree that the certainty of the existence and the constant, patient and progressive activity of the spiritual master of India made itself felt, a torrent of recognition and of faith flowed from the West towards him. For many, he was like a return of Christ. For others, for independent thinkers, disturbed by the disordered movement of the civilization of the West, whose direction was no longer governed by any moral principle, and whose marvellous genius of discovery and invention is monstrously distorted towards its own ruin. Gandhi was a new incarnation of Jean-Jacques Rousseau and of Tolstoy, denouncing the illusions and the crimes of civilization, and preaching to men the return to nature, to the simple life, to health. Governments pretended to ignore and despise him. But the peoples felt him to be their best friend and their brother. I have seen here, in Switzerland, the pious love that he inspired in humble peasants of the countryside and the mountains.

But if his message of wisdom and love, like that of the Master of "The Sermon on the Mount," has touched the hearts of countless good people, he did not depend upon it (any more than he would have counted on that of the Master of Nazareth) to change the course of destiny of a world which was itself dedicated to war and to destruction. To be applied to politics, the doctrine of Non-violence requires a very different moral climate from that which pervades the Europe of today; it demands a total, immense and unanimous sacrifice of self, which has no present chance of success, in the face of the growing ferocity of the new systems of totalitarian dictatorships, which have been established in the world, and which have left their pitiless traces in the blood of millions of men. The radiance of such sacrifices has neither the possibility nor the hope of exerting a victorious influence except at the end of a very long period of trial for the peoples. And the latter cannot find the heroism to support them unless they feel sustained and exalted by a faith like that of Gandhi. This faith in God is lacking in the majority of men in the West, among the people as much as among their leaders. And new faiths (nationalist or revolutionary) are progenitors of violence. The most urgent task for the peoples of Europe is to defend by all means their liberties, their independence and even their lives, menaced by the devouring imperialisms of allied fascist and racist states. Their political abdication would inevitably lead to the servitude of humanity, perhaps for centuries. In these circumstances, we cannot recommend the practice of Gandhi's doctrine, however much we may respect it.

It seems to us that it is called to play in the world the role of those great monasteries of the Christian Middle Ages, wherein were preserved, as on an islet in the midst of the surging ocean, the purest treasure of moral civilization, the spirit of peace and of love, the serenity of the spirit. Glorious and sacred role! May the spirit of Gandhi, as aforetime that of the great founders of the Christian orders, of St. Bruno, of St. Bernard, of St. Francis, maintain, among the raging torments of the age of crisis and of transformation which the human race is traversing, the *Civitas Dei*, the love of men harmony!

And we, intellectuals, men of science, men of letters, artists, we who are also working, within the limits of our feeble strength, to prepare for the mind that "City of all men, where reigns the 'Truce of God'" – we who are "the third order" (to use the language of the Church) and who belong to the panhumanist confraternity, we offer our fervent homage of love and veneration to our master and brother, Gandhi, who is realizing, in the heart and in action, our ideal of humanity to come.

The Fruits of True Leadership
Rt. Hon. Viscount Samuel

From time to time, Gandhiji does things and says things that exasperate me. They seem to me unreasonable and perverse. Seldom I feel myself to be his opponent and not his supporter. Yet all the while, I am sure that here is a man who, with utter sincerity and utter self-sacrifice, is striving passionately, by this road or by that road, towards good ends.

Let the world recognize its great men. Let the world show gratitude to its great servants. "To the dead the roses; to the living the thorns," has been said in irony. Let us sometimes offer roses, when well deserved, to the living also.

In his long life, Gandhiji has rendered many services to India and through India to mankind. Three are outstanding.

He found a people whose characteristic was "oriental submissiveness". To be conquered, to be ruled, to be backward, uneducated, superstitious, poverty-stricken – this was accepted, for the countless masses of the Indian people, as the destined lot commanded by the history of the past and imposed by the irresistible conditions of the present. Gandhi came forward as a leader of the movement, then small and precarious, to change all that. His qualities soon gave him pre-eminence. He had that combination of spiritual enthusiasm with shrewd practical judgment which, when rarely it appears, moves masses and wins resounding triumphs.

He taught the Indian to straighten his back, to raise his eyes, to face circumstance with a steady gaze. It has been said that "Life can only be understood backwards, but it must be lived forwards". Gandhi taught his people to study their past, not so as to be absorbed by it, but in order to learn its lesson; he inspired them to grasp the present with strong hands, in order that they might actively mould the future. He taught them to "live forwards." And in this fuller dignity, in this stronger striving, he showed it to be vital that the women of India should also share.

The British are a self-respecting people. For that very reason we respect self-respect in others. I do not hesitate to say that in spite of all the controversy and all the conflict of recent years there is more true esteem among the British people for the Indian people today than at any previous time in all the centuries of their contact.

A sixth of mankind dwell in the territories of India. Gandhi, more than any other one man, has helped to raise the status, to uplift the spirit of this great section of the human race. India should be grateful to him for it. And Britain should be grateful. And the world at large, which indirectly and ultimately shares the benefit, should be grateful.

The movement was stained by some terrible crimes and outrages. But never at Gandhi's instigation. They were committed in open disobedience to his earnest appeals.

The second great achievement which makes his name illustrious is that he successfully combined liberty as the aim with non-violence as the method. Protest, persuasion, disobedience if need be; but not force, not killing of opponents, not outrage, not rebellion – that was, and is, his message.

In India, such a policy fits the character of the people. It calls for much self-sacrifice, which they are always ready to give, and it conforms to their sense of what is right. It is a conduct that is essentially religious, in the best sense of that often misused word. And it has proved effective. Non-violence, coupled with energetic effort on the part of great masses of the people, has overcome a short-sighted, but not unnatural opposition far more speedily and far more completely than the contrary policy could ever have done.

Gandhi's third great service has been to take up, with vigour and power, the cause of the depressed classes; to bring it into the forefront of Indian politics; and to set it well on the road to success.

The treatment of the outcastes – it must be frankly said by all who are true friends of India – is a dark blot upon her social and religious history. What kind of religion is it which first degrades, and then keeps them under, for no other reason than that they are degraded? True religion must ever seek to liberate and uplift, never to oppress, the human soul.

Gandhi has realized all this with keen, direct insight. He has felt it deeply. In face of an obstinate, obscurantist resistance, he has striven, incessantly and indefatigably, to raise these millions of suffering people; and, by freeing India from this disgrace, to bring her towards her rightful place in the forefront of civilization. And now he is able to see this movement also steadily gaining ground; he is able to feel the certainty of its ultimate success.

What other living man, looking back on the record of seventy years, can survey achievements such as these leadership in uplifting the spirit and exalting the dignity of a vast nation; leadership in showing the world of today and of tomorrow that the greatest results in the field of public affairs can be won by the sheer power of the human spirit, without the brutality of force; leadership in rescuing from a degradation, that has lasted through century after century, tens of millions of the victims of injustice?

Gandhiji, at this moment of retrospect, may well feel content with the survey. Let others, too, bring him their tribute. He has often been picked and scarred by the bitter thorns. Let us offer him now the roses of our gratitude.

The Poet's Verdict
Rabindranath Tagore

Occasionally, there appear in the area of politics, makers of history, whose mental height is above the common level of humanity. They wield an instrument of power, which is almost physical in its compelling force and often relentless, exploiting the weakness in human nature – its greed, fear, or vanity. When Mahatma Gandhi came and opened up the path of freedom for India, he had no obvious medium of power in his hand, no overwhelming authority of coercion. The influence which emanated from his personality was ineffable, like music, like beauty. Its claim upon others was great because of its revelation of a spontaneous self-giving. This is the reason why our people have hardly ever laid emphasis upon his natural cleverness in manipulating recalcitrant facts. They have rather dwelt upon the truth which shines through his character in lucid simplicity. This is why, though his realm of activity lies in practical politics, peoples' minds have been struck by the analogy of his character with that of the great masters, whose spiritual inspiration comprehends and yet transcends all varied manifestations of humanity, and makes the face of worldliness turn to the light that comes from the eternal source of wisdom.

Gandhi: A Character Study
Edward Thompson

I admit a disability at the outset. I do not know Mr. Gandhi well; and his recent phase, and reports that come from India, fill me with disquiet. Fortunately, he has already done enough to be part of history, and in a series of autobiographical books of often startling frankness, has himself provided the materials for a study of his character and purposes.

He is a Gujarati, one of a race that is unwarlike and has been often overrun and pillaged, especially by the Marathas. His origins are rarely mentioned in the West, which does not understand their significance, but they are rarely forgotten in India. He has laid himself open to the retort (and it is part of his moral courage that he is aware of this, and does not let himself be deflected by awareness) that his emphasis on *ahimsa*, "non-violence," is a badge of his unmartial origins. The Marathas, I think, rarely forget that they are Marathas, and that he is a Gujarati; among them his vogue has been fitful and wavering. It has been the same with the Rajputs, another warlike nation. "To me, as a Rajput," said a Central Indian Prince to me, "the doctrine of *ahimsa* is inconceivable! It is a Rajput's *duty* to kill and to be warlike!" Nevertheless, ahimsa is the core of Mr. Gandhi's teaching, and though he has had to force it upon so many reluctant converts, it has been the cause of his remarkable victories. I shall have to return to this, and to show that it is so.

One does not get away entirely from one's race and beginnings, and there may be a debit side sometimes to the fact that he came from an unpolitical and unmartial nation, and from a small and unimportant state inside that nation. The ideal that the ruler should be personally accessible to his subjects whenever they suffer oppression has lived on in India. But, until the Governments of the world, and their whole social and financial and political systems, change radically, it seems, in practice, to belong to a vanished age. It might have been conceivable in the Athens of Pericles, where everyone of any distinction was known by sight and the free population was not large – or in the Porbandar (the small Gujarati State) of

Gandhi's childhood. Mr. Gandhi's politics are often inadequate to questions that fall outside a village economy – the defence of India, for example, in a world beset with totalitarian – owers. He thinks in terms of small and primitive units, and seems not to see the modern world's complexity (except as something to be dreaded and warded off – how one wishes this were possible!). He is busy always *with the individual* and while, if you must be in extremes, this is infinitely better than the opposite attitude, which sees men in the mass, as trees from which taxation can be shaken down, as cannon-fodder, and "reserves of manpower" (from which a few thousands or even a few hundred thousands can be shot away or killed out of "economic causes"), yet, if India is to be saved, the piecemeal individual process will have to be supplemented by large-scale planning and action. God has been very good to India, following a Gandhi by a Nehru. The younger man can be trusted to conserve all that is great and effective in his predecessor's work, and yet to have the courage to carry that work into a world that the older man distrusts.

Partly because of this restricted outlook, at the Round Table Conference, Mr. Gandhi showed at a disadvantage, and never got on to the plane of his opponents, who envisaged men in groups and masses. He is at a disadvantage today, in a world where nation after nation is being welded into a club of destruction to strike down other nations. His *ahimsa* weapon, which in his hands was so sharp and strong, is blunted. The simile was used, in a discussion in my own house, that it was a pair of scissors, needing two blades, his own and his opponent's. It succeeded in India, because it was used against a Government that – however imperfectly recognized that the game of insurrection and repression had rules; his enemy had streaks of humanity and liberalism. The Government, therefore, found itself ultimately helpless when line after line of Nationalists stood up fearlessly to be struck down by the *lathis* of the police, while British spectators were overcome with shame and American *journalists* hurried off to cable home their indignation. It was a world in which, if you had strength to endure to the end, you were sure to be saved, and to see your cause saved also!

All that world has passed away, and it is hard to be sure that we saw it in operation! Mr. Gandhi has said that, if the Abyssinians had practised strict non-violence, they would have won, and when the scissors simile was used to him (in pre-totalitarian days, when no one even dreamed of the monstrous figures that haunt our contemporary vision) he rejected it. But surely his idea of *ahimsa*, like the long-bow, now belongs to history? If he had been confronting a Fascist or Nazi Power, or if India were to find herself invaded by one of these armies that pitilessly lay waste whole cities from the air and sweep all their prisoners before firing squads, should we not realize its limitations? Is it strange that in the National Congress now there is the sharpest division of opinion concerning it, and that the young think this weapon is a museum piece, like the arquebuses and scimitars of a bygone day?

All this, however, means only that Mr. Gandhi is a consistent pacifist, and that I am not. I know that a hundred years from now, men will still be puzzling over his personality, although Book Societies will be recommending *The Riddle of M. K. Gandhi, The Secret of Mr. Gandhi, The Man Who Fought an Empire,* and reviewers will be declaring that this or that biographer has at last "unveiled" his "mystery!"

Ten years ago, at the height of his fame, too much attention was focussed on him as a picturesque figure. This distracted notice from his actions, but served to bring out his lovableness and naturalness. There is no question that he enjoyed the fun of it all; and he has never been taken in by his own legend. "Your Majesty, I myself was never a Wilkesite," John Wilkes told George III. Mr. Gandhi has never been a Gandhiite; he has preserved a cool and slightly contemptuous attitude towards his

own sillier entourage, and is well aware that many of his
votaries have not helped his cause. Among his engaging
personal qualities is impishness, and his sense of humour brings
him constant happiness. You get on far better with him if you
preserve self-respect, and he does not resent it if you keep the
conversation light. He arrogates no dignity to himself (though
he possesses plenty), he will "pull your leg" and enjoy having
his own pulled in return.

He has a dry suspicion of the imaginative and "literary". He
will smilingly dismiss an unwelcome opinion, with "Ah, but
you see, you are a poet!" – in a manner that leaves the quite
clear impression that what his courtesy implies but forbids him
to say outright is "Ah, but you see, you are a half-wit!" The
relations between him and Rabindranath Tagore, men whose
mutual respect has been deep and unshaken, yet men utterly
unlike each other, have been fascinating to watch. India has
watched them for years, and the spectacle has been a
considerable part of that country's rich public education! It has
ministered to pride to realize that your land possesses two men
so great, yet so different and so well aware that each is essential
to the nation-building work that both have at heart!

"He can be *exasperating!*" Every one of us who has had to do
with him has said this at one time or another, and said it with
affection! He will send a wire that brings a friend or colleague
a thousand miles, on presumably important business, and he
will break off discussion and use up what may be the only time
available, because the exact minute has arrived when he gives
his patients enemas! I use a mild example of the kind of thing I
mean, because one should always aim at understatement! I
watched him once (at the discussion I have mentioned earlier)
while for three hours he was sifted and cross-questioned by a
group which included the Master of Balliol, Gilbert Murray, Sir
Michael Sadler, P.C. Lyon. It was a reasonably exacting ordeal,
yet not for one moment was he rattled or at a loss. The
conviction came to me, that not since Socrates has the world

seen his equal for absolute self-control and composure; and once or twice, putting myself in the place of men who had to confront that invincible calm and imperturbability, I thought I understood why the Athenians made "the martyrsophist" drink the hemlock. Like Socrates, he has a "daemon". And when that daemon has spoken, he is as unmoved by argument as by danger. I can still hear Lindsay's desperate tones, as he cited Cromwell's appeal to the Presbyterian ministers – "In the bowels of Christ, I beseech you to think it possible that you may be mistaken!" – and added. "Mr. Gandhi! think it *possible* that you may be *mistaken!*" Mr. Gandhi did not think it possible. For, like Socrates, he has a daemon"; and, when that daemon has spoken, death may thrust his fangs into Mahatmaji's face, or a whole University bring its arguments, but Gandhi is immovable.

Perhaps, his unsurpassed command of English idiom comes partly from this perfect control over his mind. The hardest thing in our language for a foreigner is our prepositions. I never met an Indian who had mastered them as Gandhi has. I learnt this during the Round Table Conference, when two or three times he asked me to draft some statement for him. If you are a professional writer, you try to be careful about your prepositions, and I admit that I took a deal of trouble over this drafting. Mr. Gandhi would glance over my work, and would make just one subtle prepositional change – you might (if you did not know English from the roots of your mind) think the change was a trifle. But it did its work. Perhaps it left a loophole (and politicians are suspected of linking loopholes). Anyway, it changed my meaning into Mr. Gandhi's meaning. And our eyes, as they met and each of us smiled at the other, showed that we both knew that this had happened.

Yes, he is a lawyer; and lawyers can be most exasperating – as the League of Nations discovered when Britain was represented there by lawyers! When revolution comes in any land, and the people take charge of their affairs at last, the first reform is always the execution of all the lawyers. It is often the only reform that subsequent ages do not regret.

And what was the British Government in India to do, when it was confronted by a lawyer, who in his battle with it, gradually mastered the subtlest shades of meaning in English words, who not only was without fear or care for self, but could not be put out by the most unexpected turn in argument? And, what made it worse, the man's sense of humour made him willing to concede to you his own insignificance, so that you could not strike him through himself! And what made it worst of all was that here was Antaeus again, whose strength was invincible when it touched his Mother Earth! Gandhi rested always on the patience of the East, its utter indifference, its tested methods of resistance.

As a matter of fact, India's only chance in those days was by strict practice of *ahimsa*, "non-violent non-resistance," and it was a flash of inspiration when Gandhi saw this, sooner than anyone else. *"In hoc signo vinces."* Of course! Granted an opponent who did not expect this kind of attack, who would be bewildered by it, who would vaguely feel that he could not strike down an enemy who refused to strike back, you had found a weapon indeed! *And India, weak and disarmed, had no other!* It is silly to take up bows and arrows against machine-guns, if bows and arrows are all you have! You merely give the enemy justification for using machine-guns "in self-defence," whereas otherwise he may be ashamed to use them! "Non-violence," however ineffective today, did its work in its time.

And with this inspiration, born out of helplessness and desperation, came another. "Sit *dharna!*" the spirit of India whispered. I think it was Rushbrook Williams who first traced Mr. Gandhi's political action to the ancient practice of "sitting *dharna*". This practice, which was a nuisance in India of John Company days, was one whereby a creditor at an obstinate debtor's door, an aggrieved person at the door of an oppressor or enemy, sat fasting until death or redress released him. If it was death, then the ghost sat on eternally, an implacable shadow, now beyond the reach of appeal or repentance. This was Mr. Gandhi's action, an action magnificently vernacular. He has been, with intervals, sitting *dharna* at the British Empire's threshold for close on forty years. Once or twice, we have come very near to having his ghost on our hands. "Non-violent non-co-operation." Young India watched with absorbed interest when Young Ireland handled bomb and revolver, shot from behind hedges and derailed trains. But all India watched with a more poignant interest yet, when MacSwiney, the Lord Mayor of Cork, hunger-struck until he died. In 1929 an Indian student, accused of a political murder, did the same, and the passage of his body home from the Punjab to Calcutta was pageant which will not be forgotten. The Alien Government was being fought to the death, with Indian weapons. Those weapons had already been imported into the West, and had succeeded there. Witness the Non-conformist Passive Resisters, then the Suffragettes (who had gone one better, by thinking of the hunger-strike – but perhaps they were not strictly "non-violent"), then Ireland. Here was "non-violence," even unto death!

"He is moral, but not spiritual," a great Indian once said to me of Gandhi. Another Indian said, "He is *elusive*, but there is no doubt that he is capable of the very highest forms of truth." I come home to this. He disappointed some who met him in London during the Round Table Conference; they said in surprise, "He is not a saint!" Well, I do not think he is a saint; and, to be frank, I do not care whether he is or not. I think he has been something far harder, and something which the desperate nature of the times through which we have lived has needed far more than it has needed saints. "He is capable of the very highest forms of truth." He is; he can rise to extraordinary heights of nobility. The whole of that South African struggle, where he was the focus and spearhead (and everything else) of

Indian resistance to intolerable injustice, is an episode too great
for any praise of mine. And not only was his courage
tremendous; so was the man's generosity. The magnanimity of
Indians fills me, every minute of my life, with astonishment.
They have shown, as individuals and as a race, that they can
rise above resentment, as I the Englishman feel I could never
rise above it, if I were in their shoes. Gandhi *ought* to have
hated every white face to the end of his life – yet he did not!
Indeed, as Edmund Candler noted long ago, he rather likes
Englishmen. Then, there came what was called a Zulu rebellion
in Natal, which began with the hanging of twelve Zulus, and
passed into a ghastly tale of shooting and flogging. Gandhi, to
show that he was not anti-British and that he and his fellows
were willing to take their share of work when trouble was
ablaze, volunteered for ambulance work. By a refinement of
stupidity (this is all I will call it) they were given the care of the
bodies of Zulus which had been lacerated by whippings
inflicted under martial law. It was a good training, if it was
meant to harden these Indians to the anticipation of what
Governments can do when they are frightened! It did harden
them in this way, but not in another; Gandhi kept his belief
that the Englishmen can be touched by reason and an appeal to
his sense of fairness. In April 1919, General Dyer shot down
nearly two thousand people in the death-trap of that sunken
garden at Jalianwala, in Amritsar, where the wounded were left
all night to crawl and cry out. There followed the provocation
of infamous debates in both British Houses of Parliament, and
of the mean agitation that whipped up a subscription of
GBP26,000 to the Dyer Testimonial Fund. Gandhi and Jayakar
were deputed to draw up the National Congress's own report
on the Punjab disturbances. Detailed and circumstantial
evidence (readily believed in the misery and humiliation of the
time) was pressed upon them, to show that General Dyer had
deliberately "lured" the crowd into the sunken garden, so as to
make a slaughter of them. The evidence had behind it the

impetus of uncontrollable passion and suffering. Mr. Gandhi brushed it aside, brushed aside the insistence of his own people. "I do not believe it," he said, "and it shall not be set down in the Report."[23] Never was his self-possession more triumphant; and self-possession in such circumstances is a high moral victory. If you lived through the war, you know how difficult it is to be shaken by indignation and patriotism and yet remain just. Gandhi achieved this, and achieved it under humiliation that has never been the Englishman's experience, that of belonging to a beaten-down nation. This is "the highest form of truth" – truth of action, not mere truth of speech.

My last example is his trial, in 1922, an episode honourable to him and to his opponents – unusual, and perhaps unique, in the high quality of human "decency" that showed in it, and made it, when there was so much to cause conflagration, a revelation of the honesty and fairness on both sides. That trial began a genuine change (I will not say of heart, but) of attitude in the British community in India. They had already learnt to respect Mr. Gandhi, however much he exasperated them, and now they saw, in the dramatic (it was this, without passing into that further phase when we condemn the striking by styling it theatrical) minutes of the trial, the man's queer, ironical, entirely honourable, and magnificently unworldly and valiant spirit. How much more we saw I cannot say. I can speak only for myself, the typical John Bull; I began to see that he challenged, not so much the British dominion, as a thing that many of us longed to dare to challenge, the whole modern world, that has mechanized and arrested human life. His quarrel with us was a deeper and wider thing than we had thought!

He was released early, because of his operation (January 12, 1924) for appendicitis. The Jail Governor offered to let him have in his own ayurvedic physician or any surgeon he chose.

---

23 My informant was M.R. Jayakar.

Not to be outdone in courtesy, Mr. Gandhi left himself in the Governor's hands, and claimed no special privilege. The surgeon used an electric torch, which fused halfway through the operation; the nurse held a hurricane lantern till it was finished. Had the patient died, we know what India and the world would have said. Miss Mayo has given a sneering account of this episode, of which Mr. Gandhi speaks as "a sacred" experience, creditable to his jailors, "and, I trust, to myself" It was; and in a world where so many unpleasant things happen, here is something of another kind.

I have no time to speak of his cult of the spinning wheel, which I have come to see was wise and justified, though it was sometimes taken to absurd extremes, as when he wanted Tagore to do spinning daily. Or of that harmless touch of masochism in him, which makes him, as a penance for wrong done by his countrymen to outcastes or milch cows, deliberately do with his own hands the dirtiest scavenger work he can find, in his outdoor hospital, and drink only goats' milk (as a protest against the cruel *phooka* method of forcing more milk than a cow can really give).

He is a superb judge of other men. His humanity is one of the profoundest things that history has seen. He has pity and love for every race, and most of all for the poor and oppressed. He is genuinely *nishkam*, desireless. All India knows that he regards all men and women equally, his own son being no more to him than the son of a sweeper. He is without fear or care for self. He is humorous, kindly, obstinate, brave. India was fissured and split-cracked, shattered, and patched – as no other folk on the earth's surface. For the first time since Buddha, she knew a stirring that spread to her remotest places, a breath and voice felt and heard everywhere, even though the words were not always understood. The Nationalist Movement has had more eloquent men, more learned men. But one man only who has convinced men and women in India that he is of the same flesh and blood as they are. He has held up a hope before the outcaste; the Dom and the Hari have begun to dream that they come within the category of human. He has set in action emotions and hopes that are far wider than any political grouping. He has definitely shifted the course of a people's way for the future.

He has done more than even that. I have criticized him as a politician. But, as I have said elsewhere, "he will be remembered as one of the very few who have set the stamp of an idea on an epoch. That idea is 'non-violence', which has drawn out powerfully the sympathy of other lands". It also – and this no one seems to have noticed – set "a reciprocal quality on the British Government's repression'. The struggle in India has been accompanied by bloodshed and savagery. Yet, when all has been said by the extreme protagonists of both sides, its conduct justifies a guarded belief that its outcome may be a sane and civilized relationship between the two countries."[24] If that should come to pass, when the insanity now ravaging the world has passed away, then my own country, as well as India, will look on this man as one of its greatest and most effective servants and sons. He has kept the quarrel between England and India what it is in essentials, a quarrel inside a family. Families often behave very badly, but their quarrels are rarely implacable.

The Path of Satyagraha
Srimati Sophia Wadia

Gandhiji is a practical mystic whose philosophy of life and whose political programme are, at once, an inspiration to thousands and a puzzle to millions. While his philosophy of

---

24 Thompson and Garratt, The Rise and Fulfilment of British Rule in India. P. 655

Soul-life can be understood in theory by any intelligent individual, and its principles practised by the ardent and resolute aspirant, his political programme will remain a riddle until he is perceived as a figure evolving very naturally out of the long, long past of India, and in a real sense, embodying the forces which are moulding its present history.

Present-day India is not a new civilization on an ancient soil, like Iran or Egypt. The living stream of Indian consciousness in the twentieth century is a continuity, the same stream which has been steadily flowing for millennia. Even the results of archaeological excavations in India take on a new meaning and come to possess a new value unlike any other finds, except perhaps those in China. For example, the Pyramids speak of the glory of an Egypt that is gone; not so, let us say, Mohenjo-Daro, which is not a relic, but an organism in the living culture of India.

In reality there is no modern India in the sense in which we speak of modern Iran or modern Egypt; it is not modern even in the sense in which Japan is, i.e. the same old people metamorphosed into modernity. Modernized India exists only in large cities, and even there, but very partially. There is a tendency in a not negligible portion of English-speaking India to "go modern"; that tendency unfortunately seems to be gathering force, though it is being checked by the writings and activities of Gandhiji. Modernized India will come into existence only when his influence is rejected and his political methods have fallen into desuetude. That would be, for India as well as for the world, an even greater catastrophe than was India's rejection of Buddha's doctrines. That rejection was bad and injurious, but did not kill India's culture, though it stemmed its rising tide and deprived her of the opportunity of serving the world at large on as great a scale as she might have done.

It is necessary to view Gandhiji's life activities as a developing and an unfinished chapter of Indian history. Our Indian history has been primarily made by spiritual individualities. Great kingdoms with arts and literature of monumental proportions grew naturally from the roots of spiritual culture embodied and taught by those individualities. For example, the Empire of Asoka and the art of Ajanta are fruits of but a single branch of a giant tree; that branch is Gautama Buddha. There are numerous branches of that tree whose trunk represents the indivisible culture of the previous Buddhas, including the Vedic seers and singers; its roots are buried in still more ancient soil known in Puranik lore as *saka dwipa and sveta dwipa*. It is necessary to view Gandhiji as a living central figure on the twentieth-century canvas of Indian history, which presents in its background, details covering millions of years.

The mighty spiritual individualities who have played the leading role in our history have always been integrated beings. They integrated themselves by disciplining their warring members. The more complete the harmonious fusion of the activity of the hands, the head and the heart, the greater the individuality. Not by outer opulence but by inner enrichment have they served their beloved Motherland. When necessary, they have worn a royal garb, as in Rama's case; in another era Siddharta, also a Prince, exchanged his sceptre for the begging-bowl of the Buddha; both were integrated individualities. There have been others – poets, seers, sages, all of them different in their outer appearance and working in environments which were different, but all of them the same in their inner consciousness – minds enlightened by souls, hearts full of the Tathagata Light. Of them it might be said not so much that they were the makers of Indian history as that they were made by world history, that is, by the power of the spirit in the region called Bharata-varsha, described as Karmabhumi, the "Land of Works". They all served humanity by sustaining India's real nature, her innate property, her spiritual law and order, which are all implicit in the term Dharma. This line of thought may appear fanciful and historically unsound. Occidental scholars complain of the lack of the sense of history in the Indian people of the past, they err in this, because they are looking for that particular type of the historical sense with which they are most familiar. Gandhiji himself has described history as understood and interpreted by Occidental culture. In this way:

History is really a record of every interruption of the even working of the force of love or of the soul... soul force being natural is not noted in history."

In this negative sense, our old records are very unhistorical; they deal mostly with actions of the soul and their emphasis is on moral forces and ideals rather than on mundane matters. The *Puranas* are history in this sense.

The difficulty of the Occidental historian reappears in a slightly altered aspect in the modern politician-British or Western-minded-who finds that Gandhiji is lacking in the political sense; for to the modern politician, the political sense expresses itself in one way and in no other. Brahmana sages at the courts of kings and emperors, like Vashistha, the adviser of Dasaratha at Ayodhya, were politicians of the highest order, but their heirs of today would not succeed in gathering sufficient votes to enter a Western parliament.

The so called inconsistencies and impracticabilities of Gandhiji are understood when we see him as a Soul, and when we take into account the fact that he is one who refuses to make compromises between his head and his heart, who declines to go against his own conscience, who views all events not from the mundane standpoint, but as an avenue for soul-learning for himself and of soul-service of others. He practises his philosophy, he lives up to his principles; and therefore he remains a puzzle of varying bafflement to all who compromise and so remain in a disintegrated state of mental confusion and of moral concessions to the flesh and to the world of the flesh.

If we clearly perceive two facts, of Gandhiji's being (1) neither a politician nor a philosopher nor a theologian, but a spiritual reformer; and (2) one who incarnates within himself the spirit of India or of Arya-Dharma (Religion of the Noble Soul) and is thus writing the chapter of present day history, we get the correct perspective of his multifarious activities.

Gandhiji is best known to the world as the political leader of India. No doubt people speak of him as a mystic and a religious man, but often his religion is looked upon as of only secondary importance, and Britishers and even many among his own countrymen err in understanding his statements because they hear and use them as if those statements were made by a patriotic politician. They overlook the significance of his rule that "politics without morality is a thing to be avoided" He is giving a new value to patriotism and to nationalism, which are root-causes of world chaos today, when he asserts, "My patriotism is subservient to my religion". He will not harm the enemy of India, because to harm anyone is irreligious.

It is therefore necessary that we enquire about the inner religion of Gandhiji. He calls himself a Hindu, but he is such only in the sense that the universal teachings expressed in Hinduism appeal to him most and most directly. He writes:

"Dharma, i.e. religion in the highest sense of the term, includes Hinduism, Islam, Christianity, etc., but is superior to them all. You may recognize it by the name of Truth, not the honesty of expedience but the living Truth that pervades everything and will survive all destruction and all transformation.

"Religion is dear to me; and my first complaint is that India is becoming irreligious. Here I am not thinking of the Hindu and Mahomedan or the Zoroastrian religion but of that religion which underlies all religions. We are turning away from God."

Gandhiji defines God as "an indefinable mysterious power

that pervades everything." He explains:

"I do perceive that, whilst everything around me is ever-changing and ever-dying, there is, underlying all that change, a living power that is changeless, that holds all together, that creates, dissolves and recreates. That informing Power or Spirit is God."

That God is triune-Sat-Chit-Ananda or Truth-Knowledge-Bliss.

"The word 'Satya' (Truth) is derived from 'Sat' which means being. And nothing is or exists in reality except Truth... And where there is Truth, there also is knowledge, pure knowledge... And where there is true knowledge, there is always bliss."

That God is "within every one" and "every man is the image of God." therefore in each one of us there exists Sat-Chit-Ananda – but only partially unfolded, for it is covered over by error and ignorance. By the power of that Deity within, ought men to endeavour to live, and when Gandhiji complains that Indians are turning away from God, he means that they are not trying to live by the Power of God within them. "Man is higher than the brute" and "has a divine mission to fulfil". "We know the earth, we are strangers to the heaven within us."

What is that higher mission of man? To find Truth by right knowledge which alone is capable of bringing lasting bliss. "To find Truth completely is to realize oneself and one's destiny, i.e. to become perfect."

But man has a lower animal nature. Imperfection is therefore stamped on the clay of which man's body is formed. The first necessary step is to recognize the existence of the latent perfection as well as the activity of the enveloping imperfection. Gandhiji puts forward, in a telling way, the work involved when we come face to face with our dual constitution – divine and demoniac. He says:

"I am painfully conscious of my imperfections and therein lies all the strength I possess, because it is a rare thing for a man to know his own limitations.

Because we do not know specifically our own limitations, we remain blind to the divinity within us. Our weaknesses raise the question of dealing with and defeating them, and naturally that question takes us to the soul and to the power of the soul within. It is the conquest of these weaknesses that makes "Life a perpetual triumph over the grave."

Now the technique of overcoming our imperfections so that the latent perfection may become manifest is given by Gandhiji in this injunction: "Develop conscious non-violence that is latent in every one of us." Note the implication – that which is latent has to be made patent by effort. How is this effort to be made?

"If man has a divine mission to fulfill, a mission that becomes him, it is that of Ahimsa (Non-Violence). Standing as he does in the midst of Himsa (Violence) he can retire into the innermost depths of his heart and declare to the world around him that his mission in this world of Himsa (Violence) is Ahimsa (Non-violence); and only to the extent that he practises it does he adorn his kind. Man's nature then is not Himsa but Ahimsa, for he can speak from experience his innermost conviction that he is not the body but Atman, and that he may use the body only with a view to self-realization."

But this resolve has to be sustained. When a person retires within, he finds both good and evil. The two minds Vohu-Nano and Akem-Mano of Zoroastrianism, are at work in him. A man's own conscience will not suffice, though it is an aspect of the spirit within. Gandhiji rightly says, "Conscience is not the same thing for all". What then shall be man's light to aid his conscience? An infallible Pope? A revealed Scripture? In what may be called a key-passage in his writings, Gandhiji says:

"I claim to have no infallible guidance or inspiration. So far as my experience goes, the claim to infallibility on the part of a human being would be untenable, seeing that inspiration too can come only to one who is free from the action of pairs of opposites, and it will be difficult to judge on a given occasion whether the claim to freedom from pairs of opposites is justified. The claim to infallibility would thus always be a most dangerous claim to make. This, however, does not leave us without any guidance whatsoever. The sum-total of the experiences of the sages of the world is available to us and would be for all time to come. Moreover there are not many fundamental truths, but there is only one fundamental Truth, which is Truth itself, otherwise known as non-violence. Finite human beings shall never know in its fullness Truth and Love, which is in itself infinite. But we do know enough for our guidance. We shall err, and sometimes grievously, in our application. But man is a self-governing being and self-government necessarily includes the power as much to commit errors as to set them right as often as they are made."

Has Gandhiji made mistake? All do. But – what is the vital factor in the committing of blunders? All men err, but how many have the powers to discern their errors? And more – how many have the courage of will to acknowledge them? One of the signs that Gandhiji is an integrated being is his habit of candid acknowledgment of his mistakes. Another is his fearless exposure of the foibles of his followers, or the slips of the members of his household, or the weaknesses of the political party to which he belongs. He is not afraid of pointing out their religious degradation to his co-religionists. Why should a man be afraid of calling a powerful imperial government "satanic" when he does not hesitate to expose himself publicly by writing about the satanic forces in his own blood, as he has done in his *Story of My Experiments with Truth?*

Also, in the above key-passage, we come upon his conception of self-government. A man governing his own being is the highest type of reformer. This concept is the base of Gandhiji's philosophy. Economic reform, political reform, social reform, religious reform, are but extensions of individual reform. For example, of the most concrete type of reform – the economic – he says:

Indian economic independence means to me the economic uplift of every individual, male and female, by his or her own conscious effort."

This conscious effort involves man's relationship to the society in which he lives. The nationalistic aspect of this economic problem is set forth in a striking way. He adds:

"Real socialism has been handed down to us by our ancestors who taught, 'All land belongs to Gopal. Where then is the boundary line? Man is the maker of that line and he can therefore unmake it.' Gopal literally means shepherd; it also means God. In modern language, it means the state, i.e. the people. That the land today does not belong to the people is too true. But the fault is not in the teaching. It is in us who have not lived up to it."

The relationship between the individual and the society in which he lives and which he affects is a family relationship. "There is no reason to believe that there is one law for families, and another for nations." Therefore, a very practical and highly important rule of public action is given thus:

"Every instance of public Satyagraha should be tested by imagining a parallel domestic case."

In other words, in dealing with public affairs, the individual must look upon the entire human kingdom as his own family. What then shall the ideal Grihastha-gentleman, who desires to practice Noblesse Oblige, do with thieves, ruffians, parasites and the like? What shall Aryannoble nations do with dictators and haters? The answer is: Make a revolution "without the element of violence in it." Shall a person or a nation allow the bully to walk over him or it? In answering this pertinent question, Gandhiji has served and is serving the whole of humanity. How?

The variety of situations which arise is innumerable; even in family relationships, the practice of non-violence requires knowledge, how to handle any particular situation according to the applied science of Satyagraha. This is no easy matter, as those who have tried it even for a short period will testify. Far more intricate is the task of a nation which plans to live and to thrive on the basis of non-violence or Satyagraha. In meeting situations as they arose in South Africa and as they have arisen in India, Gandhiji has been developing the technique of resisting evil with virtue, of meeting the mailed fist with the heart of peace. Not only in known public affairs, but in private and personal life also, week by week, in actual work, Gandhiji has been showing how to turn the Wheel of Satyagraha, of which his favourite spinning-wheel is but a material manifestation.

The culture of our modern age is not, cannot be, sympathetic to Non-violence of Satyagraha. But the failure of modern civilization is writ large, and thoughtful reformers acknowledge that if our civilization is to be salvaged, many of its old ways of doing things, its modes and its methods of life, must be abandoned.

What shall such people do?

Begin to study, in theory, the science of Satyagraha and having obtained a clear mental perception, begin to discipline themselves. Three are the forces of evil – not in the world only, but in the individual primarily. *Kama*-Lust; *Krodha*-Anger; *Lobha*-Greed: these flourish in the world because they thrive among the nations dividing that world. In each nation, they create havoc of class and caste-warfare; but their real root is in the individual. A man cannot be at peace with the world when within himself these forces are active, destroying his own peace, throwing his mind into confusion, hardening his heart against most members of the human kingdom, if not against all.

The central quality, which is ever the principle of conduct of every true Satyagrahi, is courage. Not only is that courage to be used in facing one's own lower nature, but also against the temptations which come from a world where lust is mistaken for love, and greed flourishes as a necessary force in the competition of life; where the fittest to survive are the successful competitors who use the force of wrath, however subtly disguised, against their opponents. At every turn, we need the courage of the soul that proceeds from our identification with the spirit within, which is one with the spirit of the Universe.

Not a coward's path is that of a Satyagrahi. So strongly is this brought out by Gandhiji that it is well that we should quote him on this point, which has confused many Westerners. He has written:

"I would rather have India resort to arms in order to defend her honour than that she should in a cowardly manner become or remain a helpless witness to her own dishonour."If we do not know how to defend ourselves, our women and our places of worship by the force of suffering, i.e. non-violence, we must, if we are men, be at least able to defend all those by fighting."

Some time ago, answering some Chinese visitors, Gandhiji pointed out that it was already too late for the Chinese, as a nation, to organize non-violence and to resist the evil Japan is pouring into China. The army of peace cannot be built in a day and its soldiers cannot learn the sublime art of resisting evil in as short a time as they can learn the ugly craft of handling a gun. In China it is left only to individuals to practise non-violence; and if a sufficient number of the celestial kingdom begin at once to study and to practise the truly celestial science of Satyagraha, when the time comes, and it may come any day, they will be able to save the soul of China. Gandhiji explained that "a nation's culture resides in the hearts and in the soul of its people.... Japan cannot force drugs down unwilling throats at the point of the bayonet."

He told his visitors to say this to their people: "The Japanese cannot corrupt our soul. If the soul of China is injured, it will not be by Japan." This is true of every nation; but there are nations, e.g. Britain, which can put their own affairs in order by building up quickly the Army of Peace and can thus become instrumental in saving other peoples. If Britain's armament-building programme sets other peoples following her, why could not her organized efforts at the practice of Satyagraha also energize others to do the same? Let her organize to walk "the way of peace that comes from a simple and godly life."

Gandhi's Fast for Hindu-Muslim Unity
Bishop Foss Westcott

In responding to the request for a short appreciation of some aspect of the life and work of Mr. M.K. Gandhi, I feel I cannot do better than describe the reasons which led him to undertake a fast of twenty-one days in September 1924 and the results which followed from it.

During the spring and summer of that year, Hindu-Muslim tension had grown in an alarming degree, partly as a result of the Suddhi movement which had been led by Swami Shradhanand among the nau-Muslims in the neighbourhood of Delhi. This communal friction was a cause of the deepest distress to Mr. Gandhi, with whom, as he said, Hindu-Muslim unity had been his chief concern for thirty years. As one riot succeeded another, his distress increased, till on the 17th of September, he felt himself called to undertake a fast for twenty-one days. In writing of this, he said, "My penance is the prayer of a bleeding heart for forgiveness of sins unwillingly committed". He thus identified himself with and took responsibility for the sins of which Hindus had been guilty. "To revile one another's religion, to make reckless statements, to utter untruth, to break the heads of innocent men, to desecrate temples or mosques, is the denial of God." When he announced to his friends his intention, every effort was made to induce him to abandon his fast, but he was adamant, quoting Rama's refusal to swerve from his resolve, cost what it might. His fast commenced on the 18th of September and on the same day, Hakim Ajmal Khan, Swami Shradhanand and Mr. Mohamed Ali addressed a letter to prominent Hindus and Mussalmans and others, both European and Indian, of every shade of political opinion inviting them to take part in a Peace Conference to be held at a very early date in Delhi. Nearly three hundred persons, including most of the leaders of both communities, accepted the invitation, for the deep, affectionate esteem in which Mr. Gandhi was held by all sections of India's people, and his value to them as a national asset, moved them to take any action possible to remove the cause of a fast which they feared might endanger his life. He had himself said to his friends, "I have not taken up the fast to die, but I have taken it up to live a better and a purer life for the service of the country and God. If therefore, I reach a crisis (of which humanly speaking I see no possibility whatsoever), when the choice lies between death and food, I shall certainly break the fast." The conference finally commenced its session on the 26th and was held in the Sangam Theatre. The large gathering was seated on the floor in the open space in front of the stage, upon which hung a somewhat faded drop-scene depicting Christ upon the Cross, while at the side of the stage, was an easel upon which was placed a large framed portrait of Mr. Gandhi. Mr. Mohamed Ali, as Chairman of the reception committee, welcomed those present and briefly indicated the purpose of the conference. Its scope was limited and it was to deal with the religious causes of the communal trouble, though it was recognized that there were political and economic causes as

well. Those were to be dealt with later. Pandit Moti Lal Nehru
was unanimously elected President of the conference. Its first
business, after some preliminary speeches, was to appoint a
"Subjects Committee" of some eighty members, which was to
undertake the chief burden of preparing the resolutions after
they had been drafted in a rough form by a small committee.

In a message sent by Mr. Gandhi, before the conference
commenced its labours, he urged that what was wanted was
heart unity and each must speak the truth as he saw it; even if
this involved the desecration of others' places of worship, they
must say so, and he would honour their honesty, though he
would know that in that case there was no peace for his
unhappy land. A resolution put from the Chair, endorsing Mr.
Gandhi's principles of absolute freedom of conscience in
religion, and the condemnation of the desecration of places of
worship and of the persecution of anyone who from
conscientious motives changed his religion, and of forced
conversions, was carried unanimously.

Before the inauguration of the conference, we were on all
sides reminded that Hindu-Muslim unity would not be effected
by passing resolutions, but only by a change of heart, and,
looking back over the early days of the discussions, it was just
this that, it seemed to me, was gradually effected. When we
began in the Subjects Committee to consider the resolutions
which the small committee had prepared, a bitterness and
tensity of feeling at once became obvious, with which was
associated a spirit of deep suspicion. There was a mistrust of
professions of good will, and generous advances were treated as
a means to secure some greater counter-advantages. But by the
fifth day, a definite change of spirit was in evidence, and when
Maulana Abdul Kalam Azad had delivered a speech, which by
its magnificent eloquence and generous spirit had won
unstinted admiration, a questioner, who asked him what
concession he hoped to receive in return, was greeted with
indignant exclamations from all sides of the House. It was clear

that a new spirit of tolerance was replacing the old spirit of bargaining, and differences of belief and custom were coming to be regarded as legitimate and entitled to respect. Early in the discussions, it was their rights which the speakers had emphasized, but now a sense of their responsibilities and the obligations which they entailed were in evidence.

On the eleventh day of his fast, Mr. Gandhi's condition gave cause for anxiety, and during the discussion I received an urgent note from Mr. C. F. Andrews to come at once. I thought it right to call on Dr. Abdul Rahman on my way, and he promised to make further tests that evening. This entailed a considerable wait in the house, during which Mr. Gandhi asked Mr. Andrews and myself to sing to him during his evening prayers one of our Christian hymns which had for long been a favourite with him.

> *Lead, kindly light, amid the encircling gloom*
> *Lead Thou me on;*
> *The night is dark, and I am far from home,*
> *Lead Thou me on.*
> *Keep Thou my feet; I do not ask to see*
> *The distant scene; one step enough for me.*

It was a moving experience, with the frail figure reclining on his couch in the subdued light of the room.

The doctor's report, when it came, was reassuring; the disturbing symptoms had definitely decreased, and there was no longer cause for alarm.

The results of the conference were hailed on all sides with warm approval, though it was generally recognized that the task of welding Hindu-Muslim unity must take time. This was well expressed by one of the many distinguished writers whose messages appeared in the Statesman of Calcutta on "Unity Day," October 8th. "Where political arguments, obvious and

cogent, had utterly failed, the religious emotions generated by
Mr. Gandhi's fast succeeded. There remains the yet harder task
of inducing the millions to practise toleration." That task has
not been rendered easier by subsequent political events, which
have increased political and economic tension, and the motive
with which Mr. Gandhi entered on his fast, to enthrone God in
the hearts of all men, must be accomplished if peace is to reign,
for only thus can the warring wills of men be brought under the
supreme control of the one Will of God.

Reflections on Mr. Gandhi's Leadership
H. G. Wood

The weaving of floral garlands is an Indian art and a mere
Englishman is likely to fail in attempting to offer a tribute of
respect and admiration to a great leader. If he writes with
characteristic reserve and sobriety, he will seem to be lacking in
genuine appreciation. If he lets himself go in extravagant
eulogy, he will seem to be lacking in true sincerity. Yet, however
poor and ineffective my offering may be, I cannot refuse the
invitation to join in congratulating Mr. Gandhi on attaining his
seventieth birthday. It gives me at least an opportunity of saying
something of the impression made upon me by the lead he has
given to the people of India.

Greatness in history is usually measured by the extent and
duration of a man's influence rather than by its character and
quality. It is a standard which the historian cannot neglect and
with which common sense is apt to be content. Measured by
such a standard, the world's great men today are the dictators –
Hitler, Stalin, Mussolini. The first-named, in particular, doth
bestride our little world like a Colossus. He dominates men's
minds and lives to a degree that would be ridiculous, were it
not tragic. There is undeniably some elemental greatness in a

man whose acts affect the destinies of so many peoples. Yet for the Christian, such greatness is neither ultimate nor admirable. In the time of Jesus, Alexander was universally esteemed the Great. His meteoric career as a military genius and imperial ruler gripped men's imaginations and fired their ambitions. Julius Caesar, when quester in Spain at the age of thirty-three, was smitten with remorse at the thought that he had done no great deed though he had reached the age at which Alexander died. Among the nations in the time of Jesus, those who were accounted great were those who subdued vast territories and ruled over many peoples. But Jesus set us other standards. He who would be great among you, let him be your servant. The old idolatries are not yet rooted out of men's hearts, but Napoleon did not bewitch the Europe of the nineteenth century, as Alexander captivated the imagination of the Greco-Roman world. Jesus has stained the glory of the conqueror and exalted the role of the servant. For all who come under the influence of Jesus, true greatness is seen not in those who exercise lordship, but in those who devote themselves to the poor and oppressed. A Father Damien among the lepers, a David Livingstone laying down his life in and for Africa, are recognized as the embodiments of true greatness. Among our contemporaries, genuine enduring greatness will be found in such men as W.T. Grenfell in Labrador, T. Kagawa in Japan, and Albert Schweitzer in the primeval forests of West Africa.

It is the distinction of Mr. Gandhi that he holds his place in both catalogues. He figures alike in the list of those who are politically great and in the list of those who are spiritually great. The two types of greatness do not necessarily coincide and are, in fact, not easily or often associated. That Mr. Gandhi has exerted an influence on public affairs and on the relations of India and Great Britain, which gives him a unique place in the political history of our time, reflects great credit on the people of India. They have recognized and followed a true leader. The quality of Mr. Gandhi's leadership has lifted the national movement in India to a level above that of the terrible nationalisms of the present day. It constitutes a much-needed and inspiring reaction from the political immoralism which threatens to engulf Western civilization.

Hitler and Mussolini stand for "unrestricted nationalistic egotism," and for brutal power-politics, naked and unashamed. In pursuit of what they conceive to be the interests of their own folk, they are restrained by no scruples and they acknowledge no binding moral laws. Every nationalist movement tends to run to this extreme, and acts of terrorism and crimes of political assassination have marked the struggle for liberty of most peoples. The cause of Irish independence has been marred by the activities of Irish gunmen, and terrorists degrade every cause they seek to assist. Yet when national feeling runs high, it is not easy to remember that there are things a man may not do for his country, and when leaders forget, the rank and file are not likely to be loyal to difficult standards. The Indian nationalist movement has not been free from outrages and excesses, but at least it has had a leader who has set his face against these things. At the moment, the German and Italian peoples are led by men whom no disinterested observer can respect and on whose word no one relies. Indian nationalism is still represented by one whose motives are honoured and whose sincerity is not questioned even by those who find, at times, the movements of his mind difficult to follow or who regard his actual decisions as mistaken. In consequence, the Indian nationalist movement has won a large measure of respect even from those who dislike and oppose it.

The method of non-violent non-co-operation is based on the principle of ahimsa, which plays so large a part in the religious and ethical traditions of India. Mr. Gandhi's essays in the employment of this method have thus reflected a quality of the spirit of India. Ahimsa has never been accepted in the West in the absolute form given to it in Indian thought and life. It is not likely that it will ever be accepted as an absolute, because it appears to exalt the value of life in general above the value of personality. But this application of the principle of Ahimsa in politics has given many in the West a new insight into and a new appreciation of the heart of India.

There is, however, something more in these experiments of Mr. Gandhi's in non-violent non-co-operation than a revelation of the value of a great Indian tradition. They have suggested a new technique in resisting wrongs and in advancing justice. We must not indeed make exaggerated claims for non-violence. The idea is that those who adopt the method accept suffering on others. In practice, it is very difficult to fulfil the second condition. The most obvious form of non-violent non-co-cooperation is the economic boycott, and it always involves inflicting some measure of suffering on others. Nor may we commend non-violence on the ground that it is likely to be more effective than violence. In a world where some men have erected sadism into a virtue and brutality into a system, the resort to non-violent non-co-operation is likely to result, immediately at least, in apparently futile martyrdom. But when all is said, the methods of non-violent non-co-operation are infinitely cleaner and nobler than the mass iniquities of war. And the challenge of Mr. Gandhi to our world is just this, is there not another way of resisting evil and righting wrongs than the way of brute force and the terrible weapons of modern warfare? And if there is, are not those who care for humanity bound to seek and follow it? Above all, ought not those, who profess to believe in Christ crucified, to hold themselves committed to it? Mr. Gandhi's lead comes as a challenge and gleam of hope to a world obsessed by the fear of war and preparations for war.

If Mr. Gandhi stands on a higher level than national leaders like the dictators, his position is due not only to his recognition of moral principles in the realm of political agitation but also to his being numbered with those servants of the poor and oppressed who are great when measured by Christ's standards.

After all, Mr. Gandhi's demand for swaraj has been inspired by the hope of grappling with degrading poverty in India. His main criticism of the British raj is not so much that it is British and alien as that it has neglected the poor. His positive concerns are with the uplift of the manhood of the poor, the reconstruction of village community-life, the reintegration of the outcastes in the social system. In all this, Mr. Gandhi ranks with Kagawa and Schweitzer, and he would himself acknowledge that, in part at least, he draws his inspiration from the same source as they. Here, his life and work are clearly in accord with the spirit of Him who was described as the friend of publicans and sinners. On this truer greatness, expressed in his self-sacrificing devotion to the cause of the exploited and oppressed, will rest his more enduring title to fame.

Ahimsa, the refusal to injure life, and satyagraha, the reliance on soul-force, are noble principles and they have inspired some magnificent essays in a new way of political activity. But neither principle reaches its true expression and full meaning until it is merged in the forgiveness of sins. The true foundation of politics, of a sound national life and of a genuine international order, must be sought in a readiness to acknowledge our transgressions and in a willingness to forgive those who trespass against us. Mr. Gandhi's Satyagraha comes very close to this practice of forgiveness, yet it is not its complete embodiment. More by accident than conscious design, the destinies of India and Great Britain have been strangely linked for nearly two centuries. In the British record there is much that needs to be forgiven. The relations between the peoples of India and the British have been poisoned by Imperialism, and perhaps only a complete severance of the connection can dispel the poison. And clearly the time has come when India must decide her own destiny under leaders of her own choosing. If indeed we must part, can we not part in the spirit of forgiveness and forbearance? And if we, Indians and British alike, believe sincerely and practically in the forgiveness of sins, need we part at all ? If British Imperialism and non-violent non-co-operation could both disappear and give place to a sincere and cordial partnership between India and Great Britain, between East and West, what an encouragement it might bring to a world sick and tired of national egotism! Nor can I conceive any better way of celebrating Mr. Gandhi's seventieth birthday or of thanking God for his service to his people and to mankind than the birth of that spirit of forgiveness in the hearts of both peoples which might issue in true reconciliation and enduring friendship.

Patriotism and Public Spirit
Sir Alfred Zimmern

India has been much influenced by the political thought of Europe. Yet is not Europe – the Europe of 1939 – the most politically backward of all the five Continents – with the possible exception of Africa? Are not the two distinctly political values – the two standing criteria of political well-being – Justice and Liberty, being trodden underfoot over large parts of Europe today? And is not the contempt in which they are held by the rulers of many European States, both great and small, in part – indeed, in large part – a reflection of the theories and the teaching of European political thinkers? Does not this suggest that India should look with a critical eye upon the political ideas which are wafted to her by the West wind blowing from the European peninsula?

"Ninety per cent of mankind," said President Roosevelt a year or two ago, "desire peace". The figure is probably an understatement. Why, then, is the world in a turmoil? Why cannot the peaceable ninety per cent impose their will on the turbulent ten per cent, who, as is the way with the turbulent, are not likely to be in close or cordial association in their bellicose designs?

The answer is *wrong thinking*. The ninety per cent, no doubt, have many faults. Some of them are lazy, others are cowardly, most are selfish. But these faults, some of which cancel themselves out, would not have had such disastrous results as we are witnessing if, behind them all, there was not a state of *intellectual* confusion. It is this that paralyses the attempts to form a unity among the so-called friends of Peace. It is that that enables the turbulent few to seize and keep the initiative and causes the ninety per cent to play so despicable a role.

If we reduce the political problem of today to the dimensions of a single city – say London or Delhi – we can easily see what is the right method for dealing with the type of man who is just now keeping Europe in a turmoil. Every citizen would regard such a man as Public Enemy No.1, and most able-bodied men would be ready to place themselves at the disposal of the authorities responsible for public order. The criminal intentions of the ten per cent would be checkmated by the public spirit of the remainder of the community.

Why is the same procedure not effective on the wider scale of the European Continent? Why do we see small States living in terror and some of them ruthlessly wiped off the map?

The answer is because there is not enough *public spirit* in the present-day world and, more especially, in Europe.

But are not Europeans, almost without exception, very patriotic? Are they not ready, *en masse*, to die for their respective countries? Did they not actually do so, in vast numbers, a generation ago?

Yes, but *public spirit* is not the same thing as *patriotic spirit*. Banditry in London or Delhi is put down by the public spirit of the civic community. Does such public spirit exist in the world as a whole, or in Europe? This is another way of asking whether there is, in fact, a world-community or even a European community.

Once the question is put in this form it is clear that the answer must be in the negative. The bandits are able to pursue their depredations because, although each individual householder is *patriotic* – prepared to die to defend his own house and family and property, there is an absence of public spirit in the city as a whole. Thus, the bandits can proceed at leisure from house to house until they are gorged with booty. Then they too may discover that, in spite of the success of their short-range calculations, there is something wrong about their general plan. For, in the twentieth-century world, rulers cannot maintain themselves by booty. They cannot govern indefinitely by antisocial means. They cannot ignore the elements of confidence, credit and interdependence.

But we need not trouble ourselves about the wrong political thinking of the bandits. That will become clear enough before long through the inexorable movement of events. It is the political thinking of their victims which concerns us.

There are two reasons why the individual householders cannot bring themselves to think and to act as citizens. One is rooted in custom and the other in conscious thought.

Belgians are not *accustomed* to thinking of themselves as living in the same city as Dutchmen. Holland and Belgium are two independent countries. Every Dutchman is accustomed to think in terms of Holland and every Belgian in terms of Belgium.

In this case, the custom is not of very long standing: for the Kingdom of Belgium is hardly a century old. But the very fact that it was brought into existence in the nineteenth century – that is to say, just at the time when the Industrial Revolution seemed to be establishing a world-wide system of interdependence – testifies to the strength of the desire to cling to small units, to live, as it were, by one's own fireside.

I have used the word "desire". I might have used the word "instinct". There is indeed a force lying deep in men's nature – in the nature of all but rare exceptions among mankind – which draws together like and like in small communities and sets up a barrier against what is strange or, as we say, "foreign". This is the great *psychological* obstacle, which is also (because it is inherited) a *biological* obstacle, to the development of public spirit in a large-scale world. It is psychologically and biologically easy to be *patriotic*, if the unit is small enough. Patriotism is congenial. It is difficult to be public-spirited. World-mindedness is an uncongenial attitude.

So much for the difficulty of Custom. Let us now turn to the other difficulty, the more purely intellectual obstacles to public spirit on a larger scale.

The essence of the trouble in this field is that the political doctrines of present-day Europe – the doctrines on which the statesmen and citizens of Europe have been nourished – are out of date. They no longer correspond with the conditions of the age. There is nothing final or sacred about any political doctrine. All formulations of political principle are no more than applications to existing circumstances of the great underlying political values, Justice and Freedom. Now, it is the misfortune of present day Europe that the formulations which sway the minds and hearts' of its peoples today are inappropriate to the actual situation. They date from a period when each individual political unit could afford to be self-regarding, and indeed, to a considerable extent, economically self-sufficing. The term "sovereignty", which is still dear to the lips of European statesmen and parliamentarians, dates from the sixteenth century. It was novel and indeed revolutionary then. It fitted the conditions of that age. It does not fit those of today.

The other element in the complex sentiment of European

patriotism – attachment to the *nation* – is not so old. In its present European form, it dates back to further than the last quarter of the eighteenth century. It was a few years before the French Revolution that political thinkers began to identify the State and the Nation. It was the French Revolution which clinched that identification and caused it to become the current and orthodox doctrine of the party of "Progress" throughout Europe. That it was wholly inappropriate to the conditions of a continent where nations live inextricably intermingled and where some of the most vigorous nations number no more than a few million inhabitants, mattered nothing to the theorists of the Nation-State. Thus the European street of today consists of a strange conglomeration of mansions and cottages. We call the mansions "Great Powers" and the cottages "Small Powers". But those who dwell in them are all equally in need of protection. They all need a common police force and a common fire-brigade-not to speak of a common highway.

They will not secure them until they have developed a civic consciousness. They are beginning to develop this today under the stress of suffering in some streets, and of anxiety in all.

A civic consciousness is essential as a basis for life in the twentieth-century world.

Are not great areas like North America and India further advanced than Europe in the realization of this?

If so, it is because they have either, as in North America, grown up under more modern conditions or else, as in India, benefited by the teaching of men whose thought moved habitually in a world larger and loftier than that of the parish, the province or the diplomatic ante-chamber. If Mahatma Gandhi has become one of the great figures of our generation, it is because, he is for millions, within and beyond the confines of India, the living symbol of the partnership of two powerful ideas too often divorced or even regarded as contradictory – the idea of public duty contained in the term "All India" and the idea of human brotherhood exemplified in his labours for the underprivileged and the downtrodden. Thus can the dauntless spirit of one frail mortal breathe new meanings into the familiar watchwords of Freedom and Justice.

Thanks to Gandhi
Arnold Zweig

When we emerged from the war, boundless longing filled the world. There was to be an end of the madness of bloodshed and the drunkenness which proceeded from it and the frenzy of force... Never had the spirit a greater chance, so it seemed, to assume the conduct of public affairs. The world was to be more just, more tolerant, better, more human. In the highly civilized countries of Central Europe especially in Germany, in Czechoslovakia, in Austria and Poland this, at least, was to be the fruit of the endless suffering. If the colossal sacrifice of blood could not be paid for with a radical transformation of society, as in the case of Russia, at least we were to finish with the epoch of force and henceforth reckon upon goodwill.

Then rose the star of Gandhi. He showed that a doctrine of non-violence was possible. It seemed given him to shape human society according to his teachings, in fact upon the basis that Tolstoy and Prince Kropotkin had already laid in Czarist Russia from the old doctrines of Christianity. In Germany also were representatives of such convictions. Men like Kurt Eisner and Gustav Landauer, Carl von Ossietzky, Erich Muhsam and Theodor Lessing sought nothing else. Could they fail in Germany when Gandhi succeeded in India?

Now we know the upshot of the attempt. The opponents of force, whose names we have reverently recorded above, lie one and all under the turf, violently done to death, even when, as in Ossietzky's case, tuberculosis took the place of the assassin's bullet. These murderers themselves, however, enjoy the honour and glory, as for instance the assassins of Rathenau or those who instigated the murder of Matteotti: where once a premature spirituality reigned, there now sprawls on the throne the glorification of force, its worship and perpetuation. Following a false interpretation of nature and of natural things, a one-sided interpretation of the so-called struggle for existence and the selection which it was supposed to produce, pyramids of a new Ghenghis Khan are piled up and poisoning year by year the souls of new school curricula with their doctrines, which were already false when Hammurabi compiled his code in Mesopotamia.

We need not here appeal to modern biology in order to show that the doctrines of the force worshipper are false and their interpretation of nature erroneous. Today, we would merely congratulate Gandhi upon the fact that he was born and lives in India, and has to deal with Englishmen and not with Central Europeans. For no respect for his humanity could be extorted from the animals who reign there today. We, however, gaze across at him with mournful and unenviable gratitude. Twenty years ago we took the halo that encircled him for the dawn of our new age. Today, we wonder whether it was not the dusk of that age which ended with the world war and which was followed by the wildest epoch of barbarism we could ever conceive. Even in the places where the Jewish prophets and the sublime founder of Christianity lived and roamed, terror reigns today the shedding of the blood of the unarmed and the weak, and the cult of brutality as a political weapon. Perhaps an era of the slaughtering of a peaceful population, such as the Great Powers are tolerating today in Spain and in China, is in store for the countries of the Mediterranean. Perhaps sheer delight in the bomb, which seized the Italian airmen in Abyssinia, has already encroached upon the whole circle of civilization which the proud eighteenth or nineteenth century created and led to victory in Europe. We do not know. But we, who put our strength in words, and whose lives are spent without having to resort to force, lift up our voices to greet the Mahatma across the ocean, and to thank him for confirming us in our errors and for bringing our epoch to perfection through his figure and through his life: our errors, as if Europe in the twentieth century were capable of imitating such pure doctrines and producing similar men to India and the immense empire under British rule which once saw the days of Gautama Buddha. For, in the face of world history, it will always be better to have followed the errors of civilization than the victorious gospels of the dictators, their myrmidons, and the army of slaves who lick their boots. But Gandhi, at seventy, feels himself sustained by the best forces which the race of men has ever produced, and is unwearied in completing what he began with his life. Of our discipleship he is sure.

Extracts from Letters to the Editor
(i)
From the Rt. Hon. Viscount Halifax

I wish I could have accepted your invitation to write an article for the book which you are preparing on Mr. Gandhi, and which will be eagerly read by all who know, or wish to know more of modern India. But I am afraid pressure of work makes it impossible for me to do this.

In a way, and to a degree, quite unprecedented, the strength and character of the national movement have been embodied in the person of Mr. Gandhi, whose devotion to ideals, and readiness to impose upon himself any sacrifice that he deemed necessary, have secured for him a unique position in the hearts of his fellow-countrymen.

I shall always remember the days when I worked very closely with him in a common attempt to find the way of reconciliation. Whatever may, at any time, have been the differences dividing his thought and my own, I have never failed to recognize the deep spiritual force by which he is moved, and which has always led him to count no sacrifice too great for the causes in which he believes.

(ii)
Upton Sinclair

I am very happy indeed to join with you and others in expressing my great admiration for M. K. Gandhi's personality and work. I do not agree with him in all of his ideas, and it is hardly to be expected, since we live on opposite side of the world, but his noble spirit and warm human kindness have endeared him to all humanitarians throughout the world.

(iii)
Arthur H. Compton

If you have an opportunity, I wish you would extend to Mr. Gandhi my high appreciation of what his life has meant to the world. He has helped the people of India to find their souls in an age when it is becoming more urgently necessary than ever before that we should find a way of solving vital human problems by methods of peace. Mr. Gandhi has been a pioneer in showing how these more peaceful methods may be effective.

Introduction
Mahatma Gandhi:
His Message for Mankind
Professor S. Radhakrishnan

Civilization is based on a dream. Its codes and conventions, its way of life and habits of mind are poised on a dream. When the dream prevails, civilization advances; when the dream fails, civilization goes down. When life becomes cluttered with things, when the vanities and follies of the world overtake us, when we see all around the murderous interplay of destructive forces and unnatural strivings, when we fail to see any purpose in it all, it is time we probe the human situation and find out what is wrong with it. Though we have been warned by the last war that our civilization is fragile and will break down if the present trend of human cupidity wedded to scientific genius is not checked, we seem to be confused and hesitant about the need to change the direction in which human history has been moving. When a prophet soul who is not enslaved by his environment, who is filled with compassion for suffering humanity, calls upon us to turn our backs on the present world with its conflicts and competitions, class distinctions and wars and seek the upward path, narrow and difficult, the human in us comes alive and responds. To a world lost in error and beset by the illusions of time, Gandhi announces the value of the timeless principles of the truth of God and love of fellow-men as the only basis for establishing right human relationships. In his life and message, we see the dream of civilization come true. Centuries have gone to his making and his roots are established in the ages. No wonder the world was shocked with horror and smitten with grief when it heard that the great soul, rare in any age but amazing in ours, was struck down. President Truman said that a giant among men had fallen. This little man, so frail in appearance, was a giant among men, measured by the greatness of his soul. By his side, other men, very important and famous men big in their own way, big in their space and time, look small and insignificant. His profound sincerity of spirit, his freedom from hatred and malice, his mastery over himself, his human, friendly, all-embracing charity, his strong conviction which he shared with the great ones of history that the martyrdom of the body is nothing compared with the defilement of the soul, a conviction which he successfully put to the test in many dramatic situations and now in this final act of surrender, show the impact of religion on life, the impact of the eternal values on the shifting problems of the world of time.

I. Religion and Life

The inspiration of his life has been what is commonly called religion, religion not in the sense of subscription to dogmas or conformity to ritual, but religion in the sense of an abiding faith in the absolute values of truth, love and justice and a persistent endeavor to realize them on earth. Nearly fifteen years ago I asked him to state his view of religion. He expressed it in these words: "I often describe my religion as the Religion of Truth. Of late, instead of saying God is Truth, I have been saying Truth is God, in order more fully to define my religion... Nothing so completely describes my God as Truth. Denial of God we have known. Denial of Truth we have not known. The most ignorant among mankind have some Truth in them. We are all sparks of Truth. The sum-total of these sparks is indescribable, as yet unknown Truth which is God. I am being daily led nearer to it by constant prayer."[25]

---

25 Radhakrishnan and Muirhead: Contemporary Indian Philosophy (1936), p. 21.

In the Upanishads, the Supreme is said to be Truth, Knowledge and Eternity, *satyam, jnanam, anantam, brahma*. God is the Lord of Truth, *satyanarayana*. "I am," says Gandhi, "but a seeker after Truth. I claim to have found the way to it. I claim to be making a ceaseless effort to find it. To find Truth completely is to realize oneself and one's destiny, in other words, to become perfect. I am painfully conscious of my imperfection and therein lies all the strength I possess. I lay no claim to superhuman powers: I want none. I wear the same corruptible flesh that the weakest of my fellow-beings wears and am therefore as liable to err as any." Through prayers and fasts, through the practice of love, Gandhi tried to overcome the inconsistencies of his flesh and the discursiveness of his nature and to make himself a fitter instrument for God's work. He felt that all religions, at their best, prescribe the same discipline for man's fulfillment. The Vedas and the Tipitaka, the Bible and the Koran speak to us of the need for self-discipline. The place of prayers and fasts in the lives of the Hindu sages, the Buddha and Jesus is well known. The voice of the Muezzin, which breaks the silence of the early dawn with the summons that has echoed for nearly fourteen centuries: Allahu Akbar, God is great, affirms that prayer is better than sleeping and that we should start our day with thoughts of God. The follower of Islam is called upon to pray five times a day at set hours and in prescribed words and acts and to fast one month in each year, the month of Ramadan, from sunrise to sunset without partaking of any food whatsoever.

Gandhi was convinced that all religions aim at the same goal. The inner life, the life of the spirit in God, is the great reality. All else is outside. We make much of the accessories of religion, not of religion itself. Not of the temple of God in the human spirit but of the props and buttresses which we have built round the temple for fear that it should fall. These details are moulded by the external conditions and adapted to the traditions of the people.

Hindu religious classics emphasize our duty to see all human beings in our own self, to admit their value and not judge them by external standards. India never attempted to suppress the longings of soul or the patterns of life of communities who have settled there and contributed to the richness of Indian culture.

Gandhi recalls us to the age-old tradition of India, the tradition not of mere tolerance but of profound respect for all faiths, and warns us that we should not squander away the spiritual patrimony which generations of our ancestors have built for us with so much assiduity and abnegation. When he was asked to define Hinduism, he said, "thought he was a sanatani Hindu, he was unable to define Hinduism. As a layman (who was not learned in the science of religion), he could say that Hinduism regarded all religions as worthy of all respect."[26] "Tolerance," says Gandhi, "implies a gratuitous assumption of the inferiority of other faiths to one's own, whereas ahimsa teaches us to entertain the same respect for the religious faiths of others as we accord to our own, thus admitting the imperfections of the latter." Gandhi does not claim exclusive validity for Hinduism and does not grant it to other religions. "It was impossible for me to believe that I could go to heaven or attain salvation only by being a Christian... It was more than I could believe that Jesus was the only incarnate Son of God."[27] Truth belongs to God and ideas belong to men

---

26 Harijan, February 1, 1948, p. 13

27 "Has Christianity any essential place in your theology?" askied Mr. Doke, Gandhi replied: "It is part of it. Jesus Christ is a bright revealation of God." "But not the unique revelation that he is to me?" asked Mr. Doke. "Not in the sense you mean," replied Gandhi, "I cannot set him on a solitary throne, because I believe God has been incarnate again and again." Mr. Doke continues, "I question whether any religious creed would be large enough to express his views, or any Church system ample enough to shut him in. Jew and Christian, Hindu, Mohammedan, Parsee, Buddhist and Confucian, all have their places in his heart, as children of the same Father," Doke: An Indian Patriot in South Africa, (1901), p. 90.

and we cannot be certain that our ideas have assimilated the whole truth. Whatever our religious ideas may be, we all seek to climb the hill and our eyes are fixed on the same goal. We may choose different paths and follow different guides. When we reach the top, the roads leading to it matter little if only we keep on ascending. In religion, what counts is effort.

The conception of the Indian State as a non-communal one, does not mean that it aims only at the secular ends of life, material comfort and success. It means that the State will accord free and equal treatment to all religions, to profess, practice and propagate their faiths so long as their beliefs and practices are not repugnant to the moral sense. The equal treatment of all religions imposes an obligation on the members of the different religions to practice mutual tolerance. Intolerance is a proof of incomprehension. In January 1928, Gandhi said to the Federation of International Fellowships: "After long study and experience, I have come to these conclusions, that all religions are true, are almost as dear to me as my own Hinduism. My veneration for other faiths is the same as for my own faith. Consequently, the thought of conversion is impossible...

Our prayer for others ought never to be 'God, give them the light thou hast given to me,' but 'give them all the light and truth they need for their highest development.' My faith offers me all that is necessary for my inner development, for it teaches me to pray. But I also pray that every one else may develop to the fullness of his being in his own religion, that the Christian may become a better Christian and the Mohammedan a better Mohammedan. I am convinced that God will one day ask us only what we are and what we do, not the name we give to our being and doing." At the prayer meeting on January 21, 1948, Gandhi said that he "had practiced Hinduism from early childhood. His nurse had taught him to invoke Rama when he feared evil spirits. Later on, he had come in contact with Christians, Muslims and others, and after making a fair study of other religions, had stuck to Hinduism. He was as firm in his faith today as in his early childhood. He believed God would make him an instrument of saving the religion that he loved, cherished and practised."[28]

Even though Gandhi practiced this religion with courage and consistency, he had an unusual sense of humour, a certain light-heartedness, even gaiety, which we do not associate with ardent religious souls. This playfulness was the outcome of an innocence of heart, a spontaneity of spirit. While he redeemed even the most fugitive and trivial moment from commonness, he had, all the time, a remote, far-away look. The abuses and perversities of life did not shake his confidence in the essential goodness of things, he assumed, without much discussion, that his way of life was clean, right and natural, while our way in this mechanized industrial civilization was unnatural, unhealthy and wrong.

Gandhi's religion was an intensely practical one. There are religious men who, when they find the troubles and perplexities of the world too much for them, wrap their cloaks around them, withdraw into monasteries or mountain-tops and guard the sacred fires burning in their own hearts. If truth, love and justice are not to be found in the world, we can possess these graces in the inviolable sanctuary of our souls. For Gandhi, sanctity and service of man were inseparable. "My motive has been purely religious. I could not be leading a religious life unless I identified myself with the whole of mankind; and this I could not do unless I took part in politics. The whole gamut of man's activities today constitutes an indivisible whole; you cannot divide social, political and purely religious work into watertight compartments. I do not know any religion apart from human activity.

My devotion to truth has drawn me into the field of politics;

and I can say without the slightest hesitation, and yet with all humility, that those who say that religion has nothing to do with politics do not know what religion means." Many of us who call ourselves religious maintain the stage-set of religion. We practice mechanically its rites, acquiesce passively in its dogmas. We conform to the forms as such conformity brings us social advantages or political privileges. We invoke the name of God and despise our neighbours. We deceive ourselves with empty phrases and mental cliches. For Gandhi, religion was a passionate participation in the life of spirit. It was intensely practical and dynamic. He was keenly sensitive to the pain of the world and longed " to wipe every tear from every eye." He believed in the sanctification of all life. "Politics divorced from religion" was, for him, "a corpse, fit only to be burned."

He looked upon politics as a branch of ethics and religions. It is not a struggle for power and wealth, but a persistent and continuous effort to enable the submerged millions to attain the good life, to raise the quality of human beings, to train them for freedom and fellowship, for spiritual depth and social harmony. A politician who works for these ends cannot help being religious. He cannot ignore the formative share of morality in civilization or take the side of evil against good. Owing no allegiance to the material things of life, Gandhi was able to make changes in them. The prophets of spirit make history just by standing outside history.

II. *India's Struggle for Freedom.*

It is impertinent for any man to set about reforming the universe. He must take up the work that lies nearest to hand. When, on his return from South Africa, he found the people of India suffering from mortified pride, want, pain and degradation, he took up the task of their emancipation as a challenge and an opportunity. It is wrong for the weak to submit to oppression and wrong for the strong to be allowed to oppress. No improvement, he felt, was possible without political freedom. Freedom from subjection should be won not by the usual methods of secret societies, armed rebellion, arson and assassination. The way to freedom is neither, by abject entreaty nor by revolutionary violence. Freedom does not descend upon a people as a gift from above, but they have to raise themselves to it by their own effort. The Buddha said: "Ye, who suffer, know ye from yourselves; none else compels." In self-purification lies the path to freedom. Force is no remedy. The use of force in such circumstances is foul play. The force of spirit is invincible. Gandhi said: "The British want us to put the struggle on the plane of machine-guns. They have weapons and we have not. Our only assurance of beating them is to keep it on the plane where we have the weapons and they have not." If we could combine perfect courage to endure wrong, while resisting it with the perfect charity which abstains from hurting or hating the oppressor, our appeal to the human in our oppressor would become irresistible. To a people oppressed for centuries by outsiders, he gave a new self-respect, a new confidence in themselves, a new assurance of strength. He took hold of ordinary men and women, men and women who were an incredible mixture of heroism and conceit, magnificence and meanness, made heroes out of them and organized an unarmed revolt against British rule. He weaned the country from anarchy and terrorism and saved the political struggle from losing its soul. There were occasions in India's struggle for freedom when he adopted measures which were unintelligible to the mere politician. There are great leaders who know how to bend and flatter in order to draw other men unto them. While they keep their eyes fixed upon the goal, they do not scruple about the means to reach the goal. Not so Gandhi. "If India takes up the doctrine of the sword she may gain a momentary victory, then India will cease to be the pride of my heart. I believe absolutely that India has a mission for the world; however India's acceptance of the doctrine of the sword will be the hour of my trial. My life is dedicated to the service of India through the religion of non-violence, which I believe to be the root of Hinduism." He ordered the suspension of the movement of non-co-operation when he saw that his people were not able to conform to his high standards. By his withdrawal, he exposed himself to the derision of his opponents. "Let the opponent glory in our humiliation and so-called defeat. It is better to be charged with cowardice than to be guilty of denial of our oath and sin against God. It is a million times better that I should be the laughing-stock of the world than that I should act insincerely towards myself... I know that the drastic reversal of practically the whole of the aggressive programme may be politically unsound and unwise, but there is no doubt that it is religiously sound." What is morally wrong cannot be politically right, On the evening of August 8, 1942, when what is known as the "Quit India" resolution was passed by the All-India Congress Committee, Gandhi said: "We must look the world in the face with calm and clear eyes, even though the eyes of the world are bloodshot today." When the naval disturbances started in Bombay, he scolded those who organized it: "Hatred is in the air and impatient lovers of the country will gladly take advantage of it, if they can, through violence, to further the cause of independence. I suggest that it is wrong at any time and everywhere. But it is more wrong and unbecoming in a country whose fighters for freedom have declared to the world that their policy is truth and non-violence." He had great faith that the spirit of violence "is a survival which will kill itself in time. It is so contrary to the spirit of India." "I have striven all my life for the liberation of India. But if I can get it only by violence, I would not want it." The means by which freedom is attained are as important as the end itself. An India made free through immorality cannot be really free. He conducted the struggle with the established government in India as in South Africa, without any trace of racial feeling, with civilized dignity.

The transfer of power on August 15, 1947, marked the end of struggle, It has ended in a settlement reached in a spirit of good temper and friendliness.

Freedom for Gandhi was not a mere political fact, it was a social realty. He struggled not only to free India from foreign rule but free her from social corruption and communal strife. "I shall work for an India in which the poorest shall feel that it is their country in whose making they have an effective voice; an India in which there shall be no high class and low class of people; an India in which all communities shall live in perfect harmony. There can be no room in such an India for the curse of untouchability or the curse of intoxicating drinks and drugs. Women will enjoy the same rights as men. Since we shall be at peace with all the rest of the world, neither exploiting nor being exploited, we shall have the smallest army imaginable. All interests, not in conflict with the interests of dumb millions, will be scrupulously respected. Personally, I hate the distinction between foreign and indigenous. This is the India of my dreams."[29]

Political freedom does not represent the fulfillment of a nation's dream. It only provides scope and opportunity for the renewal of a nation's life. A free India must be made a country of discerning people, cherishing the values of true civilization, peace, order, goodwill between man and man, love of truth, quest of beauty and hatred of evil.

When we scramble for power over our fellows, for power to make money, for power to make life more ugly than it is, it means that we have lost the grace of life and dignity of civilization.

Anxious to make the Indian society a truly free one, Gandhi put at the centre of his constructive programme the spinning-wheel, the removal of untouchability and communal harmony.

---

29 Young India, September 10, 1931.

Freedom is a mockery so long as men starve, go naked and pine away in voiceless anguish.

The charka or the spinning-wheel will help to redeem the common man from the evils of poverty and ignorance, disease and squalor. "Political freedom has no meaning for the millions if they do not know how to employ their enforced idleness. Eighty per cent of the Indian population is compulsorily unemployed for half the year; they can only be helped by reviving a trade that has fallen into oblivion and making it a source of new income." Gandhi stressed the use of the spinning-wheel as an occupation supplementary to agriculture.

It also serves as a check against the increasing mechanization of life. In a highly industrialized society, men's minds act like machines and not as living organisms. They are dependent on large and complicated forms of organization, capitalist combines and labour unions and they cannot influence their decisions much. Again, natural creative impulses are suppressed in millions of human beings who do one little piece of work and not the whole. There is not the sense of satisfaction in the work we do, when we do not act as responsible individuals in the society to which we belong; our lives become tiresome and meaningless and we take to wild forms of compensation for excitement and vital experience. The rich and the poor both seem to suffer in a mechanized society. The rich, men and women, seem as though they have an almost physical sense of spiritual death with their souls still and rigid. Old men starve to death, condemned to work until they can work no longer, and women are forced to undertake the most exhausting labours.

Gandhi struggled to retain the traditional rural civilization which expressed the living unity of a people harmoniously interacting on a certain soil swayed by a common feeling about life, the earth and the universe. The ambitious spirit of man feels itself strong and free in the villages with their open spaces and green belts rather than in overcrowded cities with their darkness and squalor, foul smell and stagnant air, fevers and rickets. In the village community, men feel that they are responsible individuals effectively participating in its life. When these villagers move to towns, they become restless, spiritless, and hopeless. The peasant and the weaver are displaced by the mechanic and the businessman, and to compensate for the boredom of life exciting amusements are devised. No wonder the spirit of man becomes lost in this wilderness of living. If we are to humanize society and bring moral significance to acts and relationships, we should work for a decentralized village economy where machinery could be employed so long as it does not disturb much the fundamental framework of society and the freedom of the human spirit.

Gandhi does not reject machinery as such. He observes: "How can I be against all machinery when I know that even this body is a most delicate piece of machine. What I object to is the craze for machinery, not machinery as such. The craze is for what they call labour-saving machinery. Men go on 'saving labour' till thousands are without work and thrown on the open streets to die of starvation. I want to save time and labour, not for a fraction of mankind but for all. I want the concentration of wealth, not in the hands of a few, but in the hands of all. Today, machinery merely helps a few to ride on the backs of millions. The impetus behind it all is not the philanthropy to save labour, but greed. It is against this constitution of things that I am fighting with all my might. The machine should not tend to atrophy the limbs of man... Factories run by power driven machinery should be nationalized, state-controlled. The supreme consideration is man."

"If we could have electricity in every village home, I should not mind the villagers plying their instruments and tools with the help of electricity. But then, the village communities or the state would own power houses, just as the villages have their grazing pastures... The heavy machinery for work of public utility, which could be undertaken by human labour, has its inevitable place, but all that would be owned by the state and used entirely for the benefit of the people."

As a religious and social reformer, Gandhi pricked us into a new awareness of the social evils from which we have been suffering. He exhorted us to rid religion of the many accretions with which in its long history it became encumbered, notably untouchability. Hinduism has paid a heavy price for its neglect of social responsibilities. The draft constitution for the new India aims at establishing an equitable social order in which ideals of virtue and freedom will inspire economic and political, social and cultural institutions.

Under the leadership of Gandhi, the Indian National Congress worked for friendly relations among the different religions and communities of India, for the establishment of a non-communal democratic state. He strove for a free and united India. The hour of his triumph proved to be the hour of his humiliation. The division of the country is a grievous wrong we have suffered. Our leaders, caught in a mood of frustration, tired of communal "killings," which disgraced the country for some months past, anxious to give relief to the harassed, distraught multitudes acquiesced in the partition of India against their better judgment and the advice of Gandhi. No amount of regret will bring back a lost opportunity. Mistakes of an hour may have to be atoned for by the sorrow of years. We cannot, however, build as we will but only as we can. It will take centuries of history to enable such a momentous decision as the partition of India to be properly appreciated. We have not the gift of penetrating the future. For the present however, the price of partition has not yielded communal peace, but has actually increased communal bitterness. The New Delhi celebrations on August 15th, Gandhi would not attend. He excused himself and was engaged in his lonely trek in the villages of Bengal, walking on foot, comforting the poor and the homeless, entreating them to remove from their hearts every trace of suspicion, bitterness and resentment. The large migrations, the thousands of people wandering to and fro, weary, uprooted, heavy laden, the mad career of communal violence, worst of all the spiritual degradation all around, suspicion, anger, doubt, pity, grief, absence of hope filled Gandhi with deep sorrow and led him to devote the rest of his life to the psychological solution of this problem. His fasts at Calcutta and Delhi had a sobering effect, but the evil was too deep to be cured so easily. On his seventy-eighth birthday, October 2, 1947, Gandhi said: "With every breath I pray God to give me strength to quench the flames or remove me from this earth. I, who staked my life to gain India's independence, do not wish to be a living witness to its destruction."

When last I met him early in December 1947, I found him in deep agony and determined to do his utmost to improve the relations among the communities or die in the process. Announcing his decision to undertake the fast, Gandhiji said at his prayer meeting on January 12, 1948, at Delhi. "...No man, if he is pure, has anything more precious to give than his life. I hope and pray that I have that purity in me to justify the step. I ask you all to bless the effort and to pray for me and with me. The fast will end when and if I am satisfied that there is a reunion of hearts of all communities brought about without any outside pressure, but from an awakened sense of duty. The reward will be the regaining of India's dwindling prestige and her fast-fading sovereignty over the heart of Asia and then through the world. I flatter myself with the belief that the loss of her soul by India will mean the loss of the hope of the aching, storm-tossed and hungry world. I urge everybody dispassionately to examine the purpose and let me die, if I must, in peace, which I hope is ensured. Death for me would be glorious deliverance rather than that I should be a helpless witness of the destruction of India, Hinduism, Sikhism, and Islam. Just contemplate the rot that has set in beloved India, and you will rejoice to think that there is a humble son of hers who is strong enough and possibly pure enough to take the happy step. If he is neither, he is a burden on earth. The sooner he disappears and clears the Indian atmosphere of the burden, the better for him and all concerned." He met his death while engaged in this great work. It is the cross laid on the great hearted that they exhaust themselves in sorrow and suffering so that those who come after them may live in peace and security.[30]

We are too deeply entangled in our own past misdeeds; we are caught in the web we had ourselves spun according to the laws of our own twisted ethics. Communal differences are yet a wound, not a sepsis. But wounds have a tendency to produce sepsis. If this tendency is to be checked, we must adhere to the ideals for which Gandhi lived and died. We must develop self-restraint, we must refrain from anger and malice, intemperance of thought and speech, from violence of every kind. It will be the crown of his life work, if we settle down as good neighbours and adjust our problems in a spirit of peace and goodwill. The way to honour his memory is to accept and adopt his way of approach, the way of reconciliation and sympathetic adjustment of all differences.

III. Satyagraha

When the strife of these days is forgotten, Gandhi will stand out as the great prophet of a moral and spiritual revolution without which this distracted world will not find peace. It is

---

30 On January 31st, Robert Stimson said in a news talk: "... I shall remember the eight Muslim workmen who helped build the pyre in the centre of the green common near the river Jumna. As these workmen piled up the logs of sandalwood, they told me that they loved the Mahatma because he was a true friend of the Muslims. There was an untouchable, who shyly picked up a twig before the pyre had been completed; thinking that no one was watching him, he stole forward and placed the twig on the wood that was already there. In a whisper he said: 'Gandhiji, bless me and my people.' Listener, February 5, 1948, p. 206.

said that non-violence is the dream of the wise, while violence is the history of man. It is true that wars are obvious and dramatic and their results in changing the course of history are evident and striking. But there is a struggle which goes on in the minds of men. Its results are not recorded in the statistics of the killed and the injured. It is the struggle for human decency, for the avoidance of physical strife which restricts human life, for a world without wars. Among the fighters in this great struggle, Gandhi was in the front rank.

His message is not a matter for academic debate in intellectual circles. It is the answer to the cry of exasperated mankind which is at the cross-roads-which shall prevail, the law of the jungle or the law of love? All our world organizations will prove ineffective if the truth that love is stronger than hate does not inspire them. The world does not become one simply because we can go round it in less than three days. However far or fast we may travel, our minds do not get nearer to our neighbours. The oneness of the world can only be the oneness of our purposes and aspirations. A united world can only be the material counterpart of a spiritual affinity. Mechanical makeshifts and external structures by themselves cannot achieve the spiritual results. Changes in the social architecture do not alter the minds of peoples. Wars have their origins in false values, in ignorance, in intolerance. Wrong leadership has brought the world to its present misery. Throughout the world, there seems to be a blackout of civilized values. Great nations bomb one another's cities in order to obtain the victory. The moral consequences of the use of the atom bomb may prove to be far more disastrous than the bomb itself. The fault is not in our stars but in ourselves. Institutions are of little avail unless we are trained to obey our conscience and develop brotherly love. Unless the leaders of the world discover their highest human dignity in themselves, not in the offices they hold, in the depth of their own souls, in the freedom of their conscience, there is no hope for the ordered peace of a world-community.

Gandhi had the faith that the world is one in its deepest roots
and highest aspirations. He knew that the purpose of historical
humanity was to develop a world-civilization, a world-culture,
a world-community. We can get out of the misery of this world
only by exposing the darkness which is strongly entrenched in
men's hearts and replacing it by understanding and tolerance.
Gandhi's tender and tormented heart heralds the world which
the United Nations wish to create. This lonely symbol of a
vanishing past is also the prophet of the new world which is
struggling to be born. He represents the conscience of the
future man.

For Gandhi, satya or truth is the Reality. It is God in the soul
of man. It is more potent than the sword. Truth and non-
violence, satya and ahimsa are related to each other as two
sides of one coin. If we recognize the superiority of spirit to
matter and the supremacy of the moral law, we must be able to
overcome evil through the moral power. Violence is the
ultimate expression of personality at the farthest removed from
the spirit of truth. When anyone takes to it as a first rather than
a last resort, he is deemed mad or criminal or both. Non-
violence is not limited to physical life. It is a frame of mind. To
think ill of others, to tell lies is an act of violence.

Satyagraha, or non-violence, is not for Gandhi a negative
attitude. It is positive and dynamic. It is not non-resistance or
submission to evil. It is resistance to it through love. Satyagraha
is belief in the power of spirit, the power of love by which we
can overcome evil through self-suffering and self-sacrifice. It
gives a new meaning to the temporal strivings for freedom and
peace. We must impose suffering on ourselves and not inflict it
on others. "Satyagraha is self-dependent. It does not require the
assent of our opponent before being brought into operation. It
manifests its power most strongly against an opponent who
offers resistance. It is therefore irresistible. A satyagrahi does
not know what defeat is, for he fights for truth without losing

any of his strength. Death in the struggle is release and prison a gateway wide open to liberty. And as a satyagrahi never injures his adversary and always appeals to his reason by gentle argument or to his heart by sacrifice of self, satyagraha is twice blessed; it blesses him who practises it and him against whom it is put in practice."

"My creed of non-violence is an extremely active force. It has no room for cowardice or room for weakness. There is hope for a violent man to be some day nonviolent but not for a coward. I have therefore said more than once in these pages that, if we do not know how to defend ourselves, our women, and our places of worship by the force of suffering, i.e. non-violence, we must, if we are men, be at least able to defend all of them by fighting."[31] "The world is not entirely governed by logic. Life itself involves some kind of violence, and we have to choose the path of least violence."[32] We will fight for what we believe to be right rather than abstain from violence through weakness of cowardice or selfish love of ease.

Gandhi organized an Indian ambulance corps which he led as a sergeant-major in the Boer War. He formed a stretcher-bearer unit in the Zulu rebellion of 1906. He did so because he felt convinced that the claims of Indians to the rights of citizenship entailed corresponding responsibilities. In the first great war, he took part in a recruiting campaign for soldiers on the ground that many of them refrained from joining up not because they believed in non-violence but because they were cowardly. He had always argued that death, whilst fighting with courage, was far better than refraining from its risks through fear. But for him, non-violence is the heart of religion and his many experiences strengthened his faith.

In 1938, Gandhi said: "Behind the death-dealing bomb there

---

31 *Young India*, September 16, 1927.
32 *Ibid*, September 28, 1934.

is the human hand that releases it, and behind that still is the human heart that sets the hand in motion. At the back of the policy of terrorism is the assumption that terrorism, if applied in a sufficient measure, will produce the desired result, namely, bind the adversary to the tyrant's will... I have an implicit faith-a faith that burns today brighter than ever, after half a century's experience of unbroken practice of non-violence-that mankind can only be saved through non-violence, which is the central teaching of the Bible as I have understood the Bible. Ultimately force, however justifiably used, will lead us into the same morass as the force of Hitler and Mussolini. There will be just a difference of degree. Those who believe in non-violence must use it at the critical moment. We must not despair of touching the heart even though for the moment we may seem to be striking our heads against a blind wall."

It is difficult to persuade the "advanced" nations to believe that political success can be achieved by peaceful weapons. Upton Sinclair said: "My own forefathers got their political freedom by violence; that is to say, they overthrew the British Crown and made themselves a free Republic. Also by violence they put an end to the enslavement of the black race on this continent... If there is any chance of oppressed peoples getting free by violence I should justify the use of it." Bernard Shaw points out that violence has been the scientific method of history: "It is idle in the face of history to deny these facts; it might as well be said that tigers have never been able to live by violence and that non-resistance will convert tigers to a diet of rice."[33] But these advanced thinkers, who are members of the powerful nations, now realize that the next war of atomic weapons will lead to the extermination of the human race, to the destruction of all that they wish to conserve. Wars in which lives are lost, hearts broken and minds unhinged by the million among nations which claim to be in the right, a claim which is

---

33 Rene Fulop Miller : Gandhi (1931), pp. 160-1

repudiated by the enemy are an evil and a denial of God and humanity. If Gandhi's attempts to effect changes peacefully do not succeed, we need not be disturbed. "What does it matter, then, if we perish in the attempts to apply the principle of non-violence? We shall have lived and died for a great principle."

Gandhi recognized that his followers accepted his lead for the struggle for independence but were not pledged to the adoption of non-violence in all circumstances as he himself was. Political action has to take into account the limitations of ordinary human nature and Gandhi felt that the Indian National Congress was again and again obliged to reach political decisions which did not conform to his deep convictions. When once we begin to compromise, there is no knowing where we will end. If an adherence to truth is not absolute, anything can be justified in the name of expediency. Gandhi understood the risks of adaptation of truth to the exigencies of political life and so declined to make himself responsible for the Congress decisions. He resigned his formal membership of the Congress and severed his connection with it, though he had offered advice to the Congress and assistance to it when it agreed to uphold his uncompromising honesty and truth in its actions.

Violence, himsa, is not to be confused with coercive force, or danda. There is a difference between the use of force in a state and the use of force in wars between states. The use of force is permissible when it is ordered in accordance with law by a neutral authority in the general interest and not in the interest of one of the parties to the dispute. In a well-ordered state, we have the rule of law, courts of justice, and police and prisons, but we have no international law, no international courts of justice and no international police. It is anarchy and gangster rule that prevail. Each belligerent country claims to be in the right. We may think that our cause is just. It only reflects the goodness of the human heart which seeks instinctively what is good and rejects what is bad. Even Hitler appealed to the German people in the name of the German cause, which to them seemed good. It shows the dominance in the world of the good over the evil motive. Hitler was defeated possibly because his cause was worse than ours, bad as it was. Where there is not world government, where there is no impartial court to determine what is just, no one has a right to use force to make his cause prevail over that of his neighbour. In a world where might is the basis of right, the use of force is violence and is wrong.

The root cause of wars is the anarchical world. Hitler himself is a product, not an original cause. Unless we have belief in a purpose beyond the state, the state itself is unjustly constituted. Belief in the state as the supreme object of the citizens' service may inspire a feverish fury of fanaticism but it cannot, in the present stage of human evolution, yield anything like a permanent inspiration. Supreme power is not above law. The highest law of dharma is that of which the states are the servants. When we have a world-government, with its courts of law and police, even Gandhi would permit the use of a police force on behalf of the world-government. Just as in a civilized national state, judgements of law and submission to established procedures are enforced by coercive methods, a world-government may have to restrain the aggressor nations by force. Even then, Gandhi would hold that such a world-government should be able to non-co-operate with law breakers in a non-violent manner as a resisting people can against a tyrannical government.

Gandhi has expressed in his life and teaching the ancient distinction between the functions of the teacher and the administrator, the Brahmin and the Ksatriya, the dreamer and the organizer. The teacher, the prophet, the Hindu sanyasin, the Buddhist monk, the Christian priest, should express unreservedly the truth as they see it. They should abstain from the use of force in any circumstances. They should not kill, for it is their duty to reconcile enemies and expel hate. For them, non-violence is the law of life, even in the physical sense of abstaining from the use of force. Their roots go deeper than those of the ordinary run of men, for they draw their strength from the perception of the inner beauty and purpose of things, from the invisible life which lies beyond the life of this world but which alone ennobles and explains it. But the wicked cannot be put down by a mere show of moral goodness unsupported by physical force. Christ on the Cross draws all men to himself, but that culminating act of moral stead-fastness, unsupported by force, did not prevent the crucifixion. Gandhi's case, along with a few others in history, shows that the highest wisdom is to turn the other cheek, but there is nothing to warrant the assumption that it will not be smitten. Until the whole world is redeemed, there will be the soulless, and the maintenance of the social order imposes on us the obligation to execute justice. It must be executed by spiritual persuasion where possible and by the use of force where necessary. While the teachers who accept the monastic discipline arouse us to the divine possibilities of human nature, we should also have judges and police who use force not for its own sake or for their private advantage or from a desire for revenge. They employ force under just authority and are imbued with the spirit of true non-violence or compassion. The distinctions of conduct, the complete abstention from force of the teacher who is educating us in ancient charity and disciplined co-operation and the use of force under just authority by the judges and the police, arises from the distinction of functions. Charity and justice have both a place in the imperfect human society.[34]

IV. Martyrdom

Gandhi has paid the penalty of all who are ahead of their time, misunderstanding, hatred, reaction, violent death. "The light shineth in darkness and the darkness comprehendeth it not."

---

34 See Radhakrishnan: The Bhagavadgita (1948), pp.68-69.

The struggle between light and darkness, between love and hate, between reason and unreason which is at the heart of the cosmic is shown up by this most moving tragedy of our age. We made Socrates drink death; we nailed Jesus to the Cross; we have stoned and killed our prophets. Gandhi has not escaped the fate of being misunderstood and hated. He has met his death facing the forces of darkness, of ultimate unreason, and through it has increased the powers of light, love and reason. Who knows if Christianity would have developed had Jesus not been crucified? Years ago, Romain Rolland declared that he regarded Gandhi as a "Christ who only lacked the Cross." We have now given him the Cross also. Gandhi's death was a classical ending to his life. He died with the name of God on his lips and love in his heart.[35] Even as he received the bullet wounds, he greeted his murderer and wished him well. He lived up to what he preached.

Possessed and inspired by the highest ideals of which human nature is capable, preaching and practising fearlessly the truth revealed to him, leading almost alone what seemed to be a forlorn hope against the impregnable strongholds of greed and folly, yet facing tremendous odds with a calm resolution which yielded nothing to ridicule or danger. Gandhi presented to his unbelieving world all that is noblest in the spirit of man. He illumined human dignity by faith in the eternal significance of man's effort. He belongs to the type that redeems the human race.

---

35 Cf. Gandhi's earlier statements, "The self-sacrifice of one innocent man is a million times more potent than the self sacrifice of a million men who die in the act of killing others." "I hope that there will be non-violent non-co-operators enough in India of who it will be written "they suffered bullets without anger and with prayer on their lips even for the ignorant murderer'." Harijan, February 22, 1948. On January 20, 1948, when a misguided youth threw a bomb, Gandhi told the Inspector-General of Police '"not to harass him in any way. They should try to win him over and convert him to right thinking and doing...' Gandhi warned his hearers against being angry with the accused." Harijan, February 1,1948, p. 11.

If Gandhi was able to rid himself of all rancour and hatred, to develop that flame of love which burnt up all impurities, if he feared no evil even though he walked in the valley of the shadow of death, if he represented to us the eternal voice of hope, it is because he believed in the heritage of India, the power of the inward life of spirit. When problems, material and spiritual, crowded upon him, when conflicting emotions shook him, when troubles oppressed him, he retired at will into the retreats of the soul, into the secret corridors of the self to gain strengh and refreshment. His life has revived and refreshed our sense of the meaning and value of religion. Such men who are filled with spiritual poise and yet take upon themselves the burden of suffering humanity are born into the world at long intervals.

We have killed his body, but the spirit in him, which is a light from above, will penetrate far into space and time and inspire countless generations for nobler living.

> *yad-yad vibhutimat sattvam*
> *srimad urjitam eva va*
> *tad-tad eva'vagaccha tvam*
> *mama tejo amsasambhavam*

Whatever being there is endowed with glory and grace and vigour, know that to have sprung from a fragment of My splendour – Bhagavadgita X. 41.

Tribute to Gandhi
Professor G.D.H. Cole

There are two kinds of human greatness, in the sense in which greatness is a quality to be admired. One kind, the purely intellectual or artistic, isolates its possessor, however much he may be appreciated or extolled. The other kind unites, by making the person in whom it is found a representative figure, in whom many men and women find their own emotions and sentiments expressed, not in mere words, but in the art of living itself. I do not deny that this second kind of greatnness – can sometimes be found in artists or writers, as well as in men of action; but it is found more often – not that it is found often at all – in the doer than in the philosopher or the maker of beautiful things.

Gandhi was pre-eminently a great man of this second kind. His greatness, and his hold on the hearts of his people and of the world, lay in his power of identifying himself with the common men and women of his own community and of making this identification felt by those to whom it applied. When I say "his own community," I do not mean merely the Hindus, though to them his appeal was most entire: I mean Indians of every spot, Mussalmans as well as Hindus, and all the rest of that vast commingling of peoples that makes up the Indian nation, and is nonetheless a nation because its members quarrel or because it is today driven in twain against its manifest destiny and common well-being. Gandhi was the grand representative figure of Indian unity; and it was for that unity, and because of his unfailing belief in it, that he died.

A man so representative of India could not be easy for the West to understand – even for those in and of the West who most deeply admired him. Few Westerners can think or feel as he felt and thought – or, even if at bottom the thoughts and feelings are the same, as proceeding from a common source of human nature, the words and symbols which express them are so different as to put immense barriers in the way of understanding. The life of the West, and the language of intercourse based upon it, are pre-dominantly extrovert: Western Christianity, despite its origin in the East, has been adapted to this habit of mind, which has been characteristic of Europe, or at any rate of Western Europe, ever since the end of the Middle Ages. We cast even our introverted thoughts and feelings, when we express them, into the mould of an extroverted way of living. He cast his social thinking, and his feeling for personal perfection, which he called, in his *Autobiography,* his "experiments with truth." Truth, for him, was not a thing external, to be acquired and assimilated from the environment: it was something within him, subjective as well as objective, to be lived personally, and uattainable except by being so lived. This comes out continually both in his *Autobiography,* to which I turned back first when I was asked to write this appreciation, and in his story of his struggles in South Africa and his more occasional writings. In order to pursue truth, he had to live it; and this involved him, in the midst of his eminently practical campaignings, in an unceasing enndeavour after personal perfection through truth in behaviour, in small things no less than great.

By the Western student, this attitude of Gandhi's can easily be mistaken at times for egoism. He seems to be bothering so much about his own soul, as if that mattered far above his practical success in the public work he was seeking to do. Yet, in truth, no man was ever less egoistic, in any bad sense of the word. Gandhi troubled about his own soul because he identified its purity and truth with the causes for which he was fighting. Very likely no Indian needs to remind himself of this, or is put off or misled at all by this way of feeling. I confess I am put off by it, not just once but again and again, until I have been at the pains of trying to place myself in his mind. The causes in which I believe always present themselves to me as outward things, belonging to an external world of experience; whereas Gandhi saw them as within himself, to be carried to success by an internal process of purification as well as by overt acts.

These two aspects, the internal and the external, came together as one and the same things, in many of his overt proceedings. When he fasted, it was not only as a man doing penance for others whom he identified with himself: it was, beyond this, a purification of the cause. But there was also

another aspect to his fasting – a deep-seated asceticism and a
belief that the road to purification lay through the complete
conquest of desire. Of course, there have been, and there still
are, ascetics in the West; but the ascetic ideal, in the form in
which it presented itself to Gandhi, has characteristics which, I
think, very few men or women who have been brought up in
the Western tradition can understand. In his *Autobiography*, the
hardest passages for the Western reader are those in which he
discusses his relations with his wife and children – I do not
mean primarily in connection with the institution of child-
marriage, but rather where he is speaking of his attitude to
sexual relations and to the upbringing of his children. Can it
really be the ideal, in the relation between husband and wife,
that desire should play no part? What of the woman's point of
view in such a matter, as well as the man's? And, in respect of
the children, were their claims as individuals sufficiently taken
into account? My feelings on these points may be due to failure
to understand: but I cannot here escape from a sense of
something lacking in the warmth of common humanity in
Gandhi's ideal, which can never be made consistent, as far as it
prevails, with the creation of a satisfactory human society. If
the answer is that the ascetic ideal, in its completeness, is put
forward not for the ordinary man but only for the exceptional
"saint," I cannot but answer that my ideal of sainthood is the
ordinary human way of living raised to a higher plane not
something essentially other and inconsistent with it.

Dismiss this, reader, if you will as the outcome of a failure to
comprehend. It may be so: at all events, it does not make me
think of Gandhi less as a representative man. Without this
quality of representation through indentification, he could
neither have done what he did nor been followed as he was
followed. The struggle in South Africa, on behalf of the Indians
there, illustrates this at a hundred points. It was an immense
personal achievement which owed its quality above all else to
Gandhi's astonishing power of making himself one with those

for whom he was contending, and therewith permeating the entire cause with his own sincerity and respect for truth.

The same qualities went with him back to India and marked from first to last his relation to the Indian Congress and to the other national leaders. Among them he had surely most in common with Gokhale, to whom he often paid generous tribute. In seeking to act for India, he had necessarily to face much wider and more complex issues than had arisen out of his South African campaign. Quite apart from the question of ending British rule and restoring self-government to the peoples of India, he had to face the question of the pattern of living that it would be best for these peoples to pursue. On this issue, Indian Nationalism was already speaking with many voices; and Gandhi, if I understand him aright, was distinctive in the line which he took. On the one hand, appreciating the common element in all religions above the differences and eager to purify Hinduism of those elements in which it was a practical denial of the common brotherhood of man, he found himself opposed to the traditionalist and conservative groups among his co-religionists, both politically and in terms of ultimate philosophy. He set out to struggle for an India in which men of all religions could live side by side, not merely with mutual toleration, but as brothers; and this required both a changed attitude of Hindu to Muslim and of Muslim to Hindu and the denial of caste as an unscaleable barrier between man and man. On the other hand, he did not agree with those who wished India, in learning the lessons of Western civilization, to forget its own and to re-model itself on the basis of a Western pattern of values. His ideal for India involved neither riches, however distributed, nor armed strength. It called for simplicity of living and for reliance on moral as against physical force. One aspect of this ideal led him to khaddar and insistence on the panchayat as a foundation for simple community living: out of the other aspect emerged the policy of non-violent non-co-operation, or rather of non-violence with non-co-operation as one of its manifestations in action. This attitude necessarily put him in fundamental antagonism to all the thoroughgoing Westerners – to millowners and steel magnates dreaming of intensive capitalist industrialisation on the one hand, and on the other, to Marxists dreaming of a social revolution to be followed up by a similar in industrialization under proletarian control. Not that he fought outright either mill-owners or Marxists, or was without influence upon either, despite the depth of the ideological conflict between him and them. He could not wish to fight them, because he wanted India to be independent and united, not disrupted by internal conflicts either during the struggle for independence or after it had been won. He did, however, oppose them both by living as well as preaching his own ideal, which involved that India, while learning from the West, should assimilate what of Western thought or practice could help it to develop its own different way of life – not allow itself to be assimilated to the West in violation of its own nature and tradition.

Independent India has now to find its way, without Gandhi's living help, of resolving this ideological conflict. Gandhi's approach to a solution of it found the easiest response in the village rather than in the town, or, if in the town, more among the village-minded than among the wholly urbanised inhabitants. His influence was paramount in bringing the peasants to Congress as an active force, and in combating the tendency to regard the peasant as incapable of helping positively to shape the national destiny. In reading, not long ago, certain reports of the Indian National Congress on economic and industrial policy, I was struck by the extent to which the conclusions were blurred by a sheer failure either to choose between the policy of developing village industries and that of large-scale industrialization on the model of the West, or to harmonize the two lines so as to assign to each its place within a coherent national plan. I felt sure that there is a way of reconciling the two courses, and that village development, based on low expenditure of capital and high use of labour, has a great part to play in the coming campaign against primary poverty. The notion that India can be lifted speedily to a level with the great industrialized countries by intensive capital investment is unrealistic. It could be achieved only by impossible feats of abstinence by a rapidly growing population that is already, perforce, quite abstinent enough, or, theoretically, by immense borrowings of capital from abroad, mainly from the United States. It is fantastic to suppose that loans could be procured on anything approaching the requisite scale; and if they could, their effect would be again to forfeit India's independence. I am not suggesting that India does not need capital development: plainly it does, most of all for irrigation and hydro-electric installations, for improved transport facilities, and, up to a point, for the expansion of engineering and other advanced industries. But all that can be done in these way will, for a long time, make only a small impact on the poverty of the people – and therewith a great inroad on their ways of living – unless it is combined with the development of village industries and village construction designed to make better use of the abundant resources of labour rather than to rely mainly on methods which require expensive machines to do the work of men and women.

In this connection, Gandhi's influence was, I feel sure, wholly salutary. It was good economics as well as good sociology. It pointed the way both to successful warfare upon primary poverty and to the preservation of the essential structure of the Indian ways of life.

For Gandhi, this economic policy, like everything else, was an outgrowth of his religious attitude. In his vision there was one God, whom men worshipped under many different names and forms and in diverse ways. This God was hardly at all a personal being, in any ordinary sense of personality. Gandhi's God was rather a principle of unity, of meaning, and of value; and the forms of worshipping this God embodied aspects of truth, commingled in every religion with much of falsehood and bigotry that he sought to purge away. His aim was not that all men, or even all Indians, should worship this God in the same form or by like observances, but that they should unite in recognizing all their Gods and worships as aspects and ways of approach to the same essential truth.

To the civilizations of the West, his attitude was partly the same, but in part different. In Western ways of life, he was ready to recognize the same commingling of partial truth with manifest error as he saw among his own people; but as an Indian, deeply conscious of his oneness with the peoples and the traditions of India, he could never identify himself with the values of the West as he could with those of every Indian community. The Western values he could see and to some extent appreciate, but could never share. They remained always external to him, and largely incompatible with his own values. And so it comes about, that when it falls to me, whose values are thoroughly Western, to pay tribute to Gandhi's greatness, the sense of externality is bound to be present; for, though I can appreciate, identification is wanting, and I cannot even wish that it were there. I say this, because it helps to explain the imperfections of this essay, which has been written not out of any feeling of competence for the task, but in response to a request which I felt unable to refuse without seeming reluctant to pay my poor tribute, beside others, on the grave of veritable greatness and magnificence of social spirit.

Gandhi[36]
Rt. Hon. Sir Stafford Cripps

This afternoon I have been asked to say a few words to you

---

36 Speech at a service of intersession for the people of India in Westminister Abbey on February 17, 1948.

about Mahatma Gandhi.

He started life in the way that any of us might have started. He studied to become a lawyer and in the course of those studies, he became a student of the Middle Temple here in London, where he was later qualified by being called to the Bar. In his later years, he looked back on those days with no regret and often spoke to me about them. He was proud of his legal qualifications and used to recount the early triumphs that he had when he went to practise in South Africa.

It was there first that he came into contact, in an intimate way, with the difficulties of his own people. He became the Indians' and the Poor Man's Lawyer and had his mind strengthened in the will and the purpose of his leading his people out of their bondage into freedom.

Already his deep religious conviction of non-violence had taken shape, based upon the policy pursued in the great days of Hinduism in India.

Non-violence for him was not a negative policy; it was much more than that. It was the determination that the power of love should triumph, a determination based upon a deep and unshakable belief in that power. It was by that power of love that he was determined to liberate his country, and for that purpose he returned to India and spent many years walking up and down its length and breadth preaching his gospel of freedom through love and non-violence.

He never took the view that he must divorce his religion from his everyday life. Religion was his life and his life was religion. When he saw injustice or when he thought the time ripe for some advance of his people towards their freedom, he applied his beliefs by action. He knew, as no other man perhaps has ever known, the spirit and character of the Indian people of all races and creeds. He understood how self-sacrifice appealed to them and he made his own self-sacrifice the central feature of all his actions. He lived the simplest of lives, surrounded by an ever-growing band of devoted followers. His food, his clothing, his lodgings were all of the simplest.

He indulged in no luxuries and did without many things that most of us would regard as necessities.

His most powerful weapon with his own people was his willingness to fast, taking upon himself the sins of others and thus doing penance for them.

He was never arrogant, but he had a stubborness of determination which it was impossible to overcome, when once he was convinced as to the rightness of his course.

He was no simple mystic; combined with his religious outlook was his lawyer-trained mind, quick and apt in reasoning. He was a formidable opponent in argument and would often take up the attitude that his views and the policy he was advocating had come to him in his meditations from God and then no reasoning upon earth could make him depart from them. He knew he was right. It was by prayer and meditation that his mind was often made up and not by reasoning with his fellow men.

He stood out head and shoulders above all his contemporaries as one who believed and who fearlessly put his beliefs into practice. I know of no other man in our time, or indeed in recent history, who so fully and convincingly demonstrated the power of the spirit over material things.

In his religion, he was most catholic in outlook. A sincere Hindu, he did not seek to convert others to his religions, for he recognised the value of all true religions in the influence they could bring to bear on men's lives. But he expected others to live up to their own religious beliefs as he lived up to his.

He felt no religious or racial opposition to Muslims, Christians or any others. He had, as he himself said, sought to absorb all that was best from other religions and he asked others to examine Hinduism to see whether there was not something of value that they could take from it.

He stuck firmly to his own views as to the way in which Indian freedom should come, but he always tried his utmost to avoid all communal feeling and rivalries.

It was in a supreme effort to heal the differences between Hindu, Mussulman and Sikh that he was engaged at the time of his death. It was the greatest task that he has ever undertaken, and in it he had already had a large measure of success. Almost alone, he quelled the disturbances in Bengal, which but for the force of his character and teaching, would undoubtedly have led to disasters as serious as those in Punjab.

His attitude to the British as individuals was always one of friendliness, and even so far as that somewhat impersonal entity the British people he has no wishes except for their happiness. Many people will remember his visit to Lancashire at a time when there was bitter feeling against the Indians over the affairs of the cotton industry. He walked as was his custom amongst the workers, and by his personality and sympathy, met with almost universal acclaim. His personality was magnetically attractive, especially in those intimate personal talks to which he gave so much of this time. He was truly the friend of everyone he met.

I certainly always found him a good and faithful friend upon whose word I could rely. It was at times difficult for me to see things through his eyes and to follow his reasonings. But then I had a Western European background of thought while he was steeped in the philosophy of India and the East. He took a strong view, however, of what he regarded as the unsympathetic and wrong attitude of successive British Governments in their policies, and he found it hard to realize after the war that there had been a great change of outlook in this country, though I believe that he was finally convinced of this after the visit of the

Cabinet delegation to India in 1946. The fact that he resisted by his policy of non-co-operation the British-controlled Indian Government was the natural, and I would say proper reaction of a keen Indian nationalist bent upon winning the freedom of his people by non-violent means. I feel fairly certain that any of us who had encountered similar circumstances in our own country would have taken action of the same kind, had we had his spiritual force and his political determination.

He stands out as a great example of spiritual strength which should help to guide us – as well as his own people – in the difficult years that lie ahead.

His passage from us is a loss to all the world, for where can we find today the leaders who are able to emphasize, by their own life and actions, the overpowering force of love in solving our difficulties? And yet, that is the doctrine which Christ taught us and which we as Christians profess.

May not the whole world learn from his life something of fundamental value. That it is idle to try and save overselves from destruction by the use of force and that our greatest weapon of salvation is the supreme and redeeming power of love.

It is our earnest prayer, that in his own country, his example of patience, tolerance and love of his fellow men may live on to bring their peoples through the troubled times which now beset them into that fair and happy future which was ever his wish and for which he so steadfastly worked and sacrificed throughtout life.

No words could perhaps better sum up his spirit than those of Thomas a Kempis:

"Love feels no burdens, thinks nothing of trouble, attempts what is above its strength, pleads no excuse of impossibility; for it thinks all things lawful for itself and things possible.

"It is therefore able to undertake all things, and it completes many things and brings them to a conclusion where he who does not love faints and lies down."

Mahatma Gandhi
E.M. Forster

The organizers of this meeting (of Cambridge Majlis) have asked me, before I call on the principle speakers, to pay a short tribute myself. In doing so, I do not desire to emphasize the note of grief. Grief is for those who knew Mahatma Gandhi personally, or who are close to his teaching. I have neither of those claims. Nor would it be seemly to speak with compassion and pity of him, as that the blow has fallen. If I have understood him rightly, he was always indifferent to death. His work and the welfare of others was what mattered to him, and if the work could have been furthered by dying rather than living, he would have been content. He was accustomed to regard an interruption as an instrument, and he remarks in his Autobiography that God seldom intended for him what he had planned. And he would have regarded death, the supreme interruption, as an instument, and perhaps the supreme one – preferable to the full 125 years of life for which, in his innocence, he had hoped. The murder seems so hideous and senseless to us – as an English friend of mine put it, one would have liked the old Saint to fade away magically. But we must remember that we are looking at it all from outside; it was not a defeat to him.

"But although neither grief nor pity are in place this evening, we may well entertain a feeling of awe and a sense of our own smallness. When the news came to me last week, I realized intensely how small I was, how small those around me were, how impotent and circumscibed are the lives of most of us spiritually, and how in comparison with that mature goodness, the so-called great men of our age are no more than blustering school-boys. Read the newspapers tomorrow, see what they advertise and whom, observe the values they imply and the actions they emphasize. Then think anew of the career and character of Mahatma Gandhi and the feeling of awe will return with a salutary shock. Today – we are inventive and adaptable, we are stoical and learning to bear things, our young men have acquired what may be termed the "returned warrior" attitude, and that is all very well. But we are losing the sense of wonder. We are forgetting what human nature can do, and upon what a vast stage it is set. The death of this very great man may remind us, he has indicated by his existence, possibilities still to be explored.

His character was intricate, and this is not the place to analyse it. But all who met him, even the critical, have testified to the goodness in it, a goodness irradiated by no ordinary light. His practical teachings the doctrine of non-violence and the doctrine of simplicity, symbolized by the spinning-wheel proceeded from that goodness, and it also inspired his willingness to suffer. He was not only good. He made good and ordinary men all over the world now look up to him in consequence. He has placed India on the spiritual map. It was always on that map for student and the scholar, but the ordinary man demands tangible evidence, spiritual proofs of moral firmness, and he has found them in the imprisonments, the fastings, the willingness to suffer, and in this death. The other day, I passed a taxi-rank, and heard the drivers talking to one another about "Old Gandhi" and praising him in their own way. He would have valued their praise. He would have valued it more than any tribute the scholar or the student can bring. For it sprang from simplicity.

"A very great man" I have called him. He is likely to be the greatest of our century. Lenin is sometimes bracketed with him, but Lenin's kingdom was of this world and we do not know yet what the world will do with it. Gandhi's was not. Though he impinged upon events and influenced politics, he had his roots outside time, and drew strength thence. He is with the founders of religion, whether he founds a religion or not. He is with the great artists, though art was not his medium. He is with all the men and women who have sought something in life that is neither chaos nor mechanism, who have not confused happiness with possessiveness, or victory with success, and who have believed in love.

Mahatma Gandhi
Professor L. W. Grensted

Occasionally, very occasionally, a piece of news comes to us with a curious timeless quality, a blending of shock and of significance which seems, from the first moment when we hear it, to have been always true, part of the eternal meaning of the world. Sometimes such news is concerned with matters intimate and personal to ourselves, and its message is for ourselves, and its message is for ourselves alone, hardly to be conveyed to others. Sometimes, perhaps not so often, it comes to us from the affairs of a wider world, with a message that many can read, though some may understand it better than others, and few, it may be, can understand it in full. Perhaps in these cases, too, there is always some element of intimacy, of a personal concern which has behind it not only interest but a quality of identification, so that that which happened does not merely concern us, for indeed such concern may be quite remote, but has in some deep sense happened to us. Such news as that speaks to us not only of current history but of the eternal things, and of the eternal things we too are part. And such, to an Englishman living in Oxford, was the news of Gandhi's death.

It was not, for me, the news or the death of a friend, for I had never met Gandhi, though I know more than one of those to whom his friendship meant a great deal, and though I have cared much about India, her culture, her hopes, and her many problems, it would be presumptuous to say that I know anything about her beyond the barest superficialities, for I have never been farther east than Switzerland, and Lucerne is no more Oriental than Oxford itself. But upon the Sunday of that fateful weekend, when we did not yet know what tragic forces might be let loose in India and Pakistan, I found it impossible, in preaching to a Christian congregation, to take any other subject than Gandhi's life and death, and it was a moving experience to be asked, that same evening, to join with Indian students in Oxford in their tribute of respect and sorrow, and to try to express to them and through them to India the sympathy of their Western and Christian friends. Nor was it difficult for me, as a christian, to try to convey that message, for I could say, with perfect sincerity, that the life of Gandhi was one in which some of the essential elements in the teaching of Christ were expressed with a consistency that puts most of us Christians to shame, and that when I thought of the principles for which he cared and about which his whole life was built into a single pattern, my own faith had acquired a new meaning and a new challenge from this man who would not call himself a Christian, but who greatly honoured Christ. I shall not easily forget that evening, the hushed sincerity of students of many nationalities, the scent of the sandalwood, the dim spaces of the great Law Library in All Soul's College, and the strong sense that life, as well as death, was abroad in the world and with power.

Now, writing after a little time has passed, I can try to set down, rather more dispassionately, what it was in Gandhi that made him so impressive and challenging a figure to myself and to many who, with me, knew little of the political and social problems among which his work was done. Perhaps I can sum it up in a single comment. His greatness, for history will surely rank him among its great men, lay not in his achievement but in his character. His achievement was in fact considerable, and that is in it-self a matter of some moment, for sanctity and effectiveness have not always gone hand in hand; but it is not his achievement that has impressed the world but something in himself. His achievement, indeed, still stands under the judgment of history, and he would be the first to say, as he said so often, that his mistakes must come under that judgement as well as his true insights. But the spirit which was in him lives on, making and shaping history, and it is there that his claim to greatness is assured.

He was, of course, Indian of the Indians, for all his early background of legal training and Western culture. The very spirit of India lived in him, and it was for India, the India of his vision, that he lived and died. Of his hopes and plans for India, it is not for me, a Westerner, to judge. What has always been impressive is the manner in which he sought to turn those hopes into realities. It can seldom have been true of any politician that political action and the inmost spirit of religion were so deeply blended into a unity, and it is that unity that India of today is seeking to translate into outward fact. And if many of us here in England are watching that great experiment with hope and with goodwill, it is largely to Gandhi that our hope and goodwill are due.

Let me try to analyse the things that I have found so significant in his actions and in his character.

The first I have already mentioned. He was completely free from that self-protective face-saving which cannot admit mistakes. His own admissions of error in judgment and in policy have often been quoted. He was as far as possible from being the self-styled religious leader who claims finality for his own version of the truth. As a result, he was frequently perplexing alike to his own followers and to politicians who

tried to deal with him, but nobody could ever dispute his
sincerity. And though he had more than one afterthought as to
the rightness of some particular line of action, he had none as
to his own personal methods and obligations in trying to carry
it out, and he demanded from his friends and followers nothing
that he did not demand with even more rigour from himself.

That this led him to accept a rule of life of great simplicity and
austerity, and to follow it through with a light-hearted freedom
and happiness, and a strong sense of fun, to which all his
friends have borne witness, does not mark him out very
strongly from the great company of those, Eastern and Western
together, who have taken this particular way, and found it
good. More striking, and to a Westerner more difficult to
interpret, was his use of fasting as a means of influencing the
course of events and of forcing a rapid decision in a crisis. The
history of hunger-striking in the West has not been a happy
one, and it has been employed for many ends, not all
commendable. Its history in the East, so far as I understand it,
has been even more unhappy, and all too intimately bound up
with beliefs which were quite foreign to Gandhi's nature. But as
he interpreted it and used it, the fast was undoubtedly raised to
a higher level. It became symbolic of his whole-hearted desire
to take upon himself the responsibility and cost of the actions
of others, and though he used it, as others have done, to bring
pressure upon those whose actions he wished to influence, it
was not the least of his achievements that he freed it from all
suspicion of rancour and bitterness, and indeed always
maintained the friendliest of relations with those against whose
policy the fast was directed. His fast involved no curse, except,
it may be, a taking of the curse upon himself.

This brings me to those aspects of his life that are most
significant of all. I can recall nobody who has gone so far to
make Christ's way of life evident and effective in the sphere of
world politics. To me a Christian, he seems not only to have
drawn the very spirit of his teaching from the Gospels but to

have read his Hindu sacred books in the light of Christ. Hinduism can fairly claim him as its own, but the spirit that was in him was drawn from that deepest ground of all religions, the place where they meet. Certainly, he was as ready to challenge certain aspects of Hindu orthodoxy by his championship of the outcast as he was to reject the claims of a Christianity that was not prepared to make good its faith in the actual stress of life. Jesus and Gautama were both rebels, by the religious conventions of their day. Gandhi, neither Christian nor Buddhist, would have been at home with either of them, and his whole political life was effective simply because he put religion at the heart of politics, not, as so many have done, going apart into the desert or "into the forest" to find his soul's freedom, but taking the faith which he had found out into the world to prove itself and to win freedom for others.

It was wholly consistent with this attitude that his devotion to India and his passionate desire for her freedom should have been completely free from a blind and fulsome patriotism. He demanded for India the best from the world, but still more from herself. He won his hold over his own countrymen by asking of them self-sacrifice to the utmost limit. Freedom, history tells us, has never come without the shedding of blood. "But remember: it must be your own blood. Never a drop of anyone else's blood." To students shouting a welcome, he replied in hardly more than a sentence, calling for prayer that India might be not as she is but as God means her to be. In his last fast, the seven conditions of repentance which he asked were laid upon India alone, none on Pakistan.

He was often criticized, both in India and in England, on the ground that whatever he might say, his policy did actually lead to outbreaks of violence. His reply was characteristic. He accepted imprisonment gladly, cheerfully, and without the shadow of a suggestion that he was being treated unjustly or being made a martyr. When prosecuted as an agitator, he immediately assumed full responsibility for actions which his followers had committed in flagrant disobedience to his instructions, and asked that the most severe sentence of the law should be inflicted upon himself. He was the despair of governors and administrators, for no administrative action could touch the deep principles of his conduct, or break his friendly concurrence in the disciplinary action which, as he freely admitted to them, they were bound to take. In effect, there was little difference in status or in actual power between Gandhi in prison and Gandhi free. For he knew no power save that of the spirit, and for the spirit, prison bars have no meaning, save the positive and creative meaning that sacrifice prevails. Few things were more impressive about him than his complete fearlesness and his complete disregard of personal danger of suffering.

Behind this lay the immensely rich interpretation which he gave to ahimsa. For him, this opened out into a complete gospel of non-violence, and of respect for all men. He was as wholly at home among the poor in the East End of London as he was in India. His concern for the outcast was not a mere sentimentalism but an expression of his whole conception of the sacredness of life. A friend of his had said that his two passions were peace and the poor, but these two, were in truth, one. He was a lover of men, and because he loved them, he must fight for them, and use no other weapons than those of the spirit, lest force destroy love.

Now he has gone, and, as I said on that first Sunday after his death, "it was good and well that at the last he should come to his end not by some chosen fast, but by meeting the unreason of the universe and saluting it, so signifying that, at the last, unreason and tragedy itself shall be tranaformed by the conquest of unresisting love. He is not dead. The death which he has died has but set him free, and today we of the West salute an India reborn, an India in which his spirit lives, and of which we shall not live to see the full fruition."

M.K. Gandhi
Rt. Hon. Lord Halifax

I shall always be thankful for the opportunity of knowing and being, I hope, a friend of Mr. Gandhi. Since the tragedy of his assassination, so much has been spoken and written of the qualities in him that seemed to the particular observer to be pre-eminent, that every country of the world has become, to a great extent, familiar with this most remarkable human figure. And as with all great men, different aspects stand out for different people. That which gave him his exceptional position in India was something different from that which won for him the admiration of friends in Western countries, which is another way of saying that the man himself was larger than any of the attempts made to paint his portait.

There was a directness about him which was singularly winning. But this could be accompanied by a subtlety of intellectual process which could sometimes be disconcerting. For to appreciate what was passing in his mind it was necessary, if not to start from the same point, at least to understand very clearly what was the starting point for him. And this was nearly always very human and very simple.

I remember when I first went to India talking about him to C. F. Andrews, who I imagine was closer to him than any other Britisher. He said, as indeed was very clear when it came to the Round Table Conference, that Mr. Gandhi cared little for constitutions and constitutional forms. What he was concerned with was the human problem of how the Indian poor lived. Constitutional reform was important and necessary for the development of India's personality and self-respect; but what really mattered were the things that affected the daily lives of the millions of his fellow countrymen salt, opium, cottage industries and the like.

I have no doubt this was true, and though it was easy to smile at the devotion of Mr. Gandhi to the spinning wheel, while Congress was largely dependent for its funds upon the generosity of wealthy Indian mill-owners, the wheel, none the less, stood for something very fundamental in his philosophy of life.

He was the natural knight-errant, fighting always the battle of the weak against suffering and what he judged injustice. The rights of Indians in South Africa, the treatment of Indian labourers in the indigo fields in India, the thousands rendered homeless by the floods of Orissa, and above everything, the suffering arising from communal hatreds – all these were in turn a battlefield on which he fought with all his strength for the cause of humanity and right.

As I look back upon the talks that I had with him in Delhi in the spring of 1931, two conversations stand out in my recollection. They have always seemed to me a better interpretation of his mind and method than anything else, as showing the way the idealist and realist could meet.

The first related to his demand, as part of the arrangement to be made on the cessation of civil disobedience, for an enquiry into the actions of the police over the last twelve months. I resisted this on various grounds, pointing out to him among other arguments that I had no doubt the police, like everybody else, had made mistakes, but that it was quite futile to attempt twelve months later to get accurate information of what might have passed in some local brawl or minor riot. All that we should achieve would be to exacerbate tempers on both sides. This did not satisfy him at all, and we argued the point for two or three days. Finally, I said that I would tell him the main reason why I could not give him what he wanted. I had no guarantee that he might not start civil disobedience again one of these days, and if and when he did, I wanted the police to have their tails up and not down. Whereupon his face lit up and he said: "Ah, now Your Excellency treats me like General Smuts treated me in South Africa. You do not deny that I have an equitable claim, but you advance unanswerable reasons from the point of view of government why you cannot meet it. I drop the demand."

The other incident was of the same date, and illustrates, if I was correctly informed, both the quality of Mr. Gandhi's courage and sense of honour. After we had made our so-called Irwin-Gandhi Pact, he came to me the next morrning and said that he wished to talk about another matter. He was just going off to the meeting of the Congress at Karachi, which he hoped would ratify our agreement, and he wished to appeal for the life of a young man called Bhagat Singh who had been recently condemned to death for various terrorist crimes. He was himself opposed to capital punishment, but that was not now in debate. If the young man was hung, said Mr. Gandhi, there was a likelihood that he would become a national martyr and the general atmosphere would be seriously prejudiced. I told him that while I quite appreciated his feeling in the matter, I also was not concerned with the merits or demerits of capital punishment, since my only duty was to work the law as I understood it. On that basis, I could not conceive anyone who had more thoroughly deserved capital punishment than Bhagat Singh. Moreover Mr. Gandhi's plea for him was made at a particularly unfortunate moment. For it so happened that on the previous evening, I had received his appeal for a reprieve which I had felt bound to reject, and he was accordingly due to be hung on Saturday morning (the day of our conversation being, if I remember rightly, Thursday). Mr. Gandhi would be getting to Karachi for the meeting of Congress in the afternoon or evening of Saturday after the news would have come through, and the coincidence of date from his point of view, could therefore hardly be more difficult.

Mr. Gandhi said that he greatly feared, unless I could do

something about it, that the effect would be to destroy our pact.

I said that it would be clear to him there were only three possible courses. The first was to do nothing and let the execution proceed, the second was to change the order and grant Bhagat Singh a reprieve. The third was to hold up any decision till after the Congress meeting was well over. I told him that I thought he would agree that it was impossible for me, from my point of view, to grant him his reprieve, and that merely to postpone decision and encourage people to think that there was such a chance of remission was not straightforward or honest. The first course alone, therefore, was possible in spite of all its attendant difficulties, Mr, Gandhi thought for a moment and then said: "Would Your Excellency see any objection to my saying that I pleaded for the young man's life?" I said that I saw none, if he would also add that from my point of view he did not see what other course I could have taken. He thought for a moment, then finally agreed, and on that basis went off to Karachi. There it happened much as anticipated; the news had come through, many of the crowd were in a highly emotional state, and I was told afterward that he was quite roughly received. But when he had opportunity, he spoke in the sense agreed between us.

The two episodes that I have quoted will suffice to show on the personal side what reason I had to value his friendship, and I can think of no person whose undertaking to respect a confidence I should ever have been more ready to take than his.

Measured by our standards, the abrupt, cutting short of such a life is an immeasurable disaster for the country that he loved. But those who know best what he achieved, and what he might still have achieved in life, will pray that an even richer harvest of understanding may be the fruit of death that closed a life devoted as was his to service and so willingly surrendered.

On Mahatma Gandhi
S. I. Hsiung

In post-war England, certain shortages were no less, if not more serious than in the days of conflict. Among the cereals, rice was one of those things which people in Europe could manage to do without and so had disappeared from the market for many years. I and my family, being brought up on it, felt the shortage very much. But through the kindness of some privileged compatriots, we were about to have a real Chinese luncheon with rice on January 30, 1948. Friends and family were with me around the table in our quiet home in Oxford. But we never knew what we were eating during that meal. A few minutes before we started, we heard on the wireless that Mahatma Gandhi had just been assassinated.

None of us have had the pleasure and honour of knowing Mahatma Gandhi personally. Neither are we specially interested in world politics. Not only I myself, but all my children in Oxford confine our work to literary subjects. "What do you think of the news that Hitler has just died?' One of my children who lectures on English literature was asked by a friend. The answer was polite but firm. "Pardon my ignorance in these matters. Perhaps one of my brothers is sufficiently interested in it to discuss it with you." We had to change the subject.

But the death of Mahatma Gandhi shocked us. We felt the loss as if someone very very dear and very very close to us had just been killed. For days, that desolate feeling continued in our minds. The world seemed to us much poorer after his assassination. It was an irreparable loss, not only to India, but also to mankind.

In China, there are two Indians whose names have impressed every single citizen; that of Buddha and Gandhi. They lived thousands of years apart, but their greatness has been, is, and will forever be there, leaving no gap anywhere. We, who have suffered indescribable hardships during the past decades, know what it has been for India, for her people and for her leaders. The respect we have for merely a national hero, a political genius, or a man of great integrity, could be limited. But the reverence we have for Mahatma Gandhi's spiritual greatness is unbounded. To us, his place is among the saints and sages who live immortally in our mind.

Was it not Confucius who said: "Once a man has contrived to put himself right, he will find no difficulty at all in being a politician. But if he cannot put himself right, how can he hope to succeed in putting others aright?" And Mahatma Gandhi said of himself: "My devotion to truth has drawn me into the field of politics," and "Politics bereft of religion are a death-trap, because they kill the soul."

The spirit of humanity which urged Mahatma Gandhi to revive village industry whilst military conquests were the sole aim of other national leaders can be compared with the teachings of Mencius. Two thousand years ago, there was a certain Chinese king who wanted to make war so that his kingdom might become a great empire. Mencius told him that he was like a man who wanted to climb a tree to catch fish. According to Mencius, the only way a king could bring prosperity to the world was by "planting mulberry trees in homesteads of five acres so that men of fifty could wear silk" and by "breeding poultry and swine so that men of seventy could eat meat."

The founder of our Taoist School, Lao Tze who was the elder contemporary of Confucius, taught us that "of all things, soldiers are instruments of evil, hated by men" and that "A victory should be celebrated with Funeral Rites." He also preached that "by doing nothing, everything is done" and that "he who conquers the world often does so by doing nothing."

In the present world, no heads of state would hear of that. They acted directly opposite such theories. But Mahatma Gandhi, alone, preached and acted the doctrines of non-violence and non-resistance.

That is why we Chinese will eternally place him side by side with those greatest men in the history of mankind.

A Note on Gandhi
Aldous Huxley

Gandhi's body was borne to the pyre on a weapons carrier. There were tanks and armoured cars in the funeral procession, and detachments of soldiers and police. Circling overhead were fighter planes of the Indian Air Force. All these instruments of violent coercion were paraded in honour of the apostle of non-violence and soulforce. It was an inevitable irony; for by definition, a nation is a sovereign community possessing the means to make war on other sovereign communities. Consequently, a national tribute to any individual – even if that individual be a Gandhi – must always and necessarily take the form of a display of military and coercive might.

Nearly forty years ago, in his *Hind Swaraj*, Gandhi asked his compatriots what they meant by such phrases as "Self-Government" and "Home Rule." Did they merely want a social organization of the kind then prevailing, but in the hands, not of English, but of Indian politicians and administrators? If so, their wish was merely to get rid of the tiger, while carefully preserving for themselves its tigerish nature. Or were they prepared to mean by "swaraj" what Gandhi himself meant by it – the realization of the highest potentialities of Indian civilization by persons who had learnt to govern themselves individually and to undertake collective action in the spirit and by the methods of satyagraha?

In a world organized for war it was hard, it was all but impossible, for India to choose any other nations. The men and women who had led the non-violent struggle against the foreign oppressor suddenly found themselves in control of a sovereign state equipped with the instruments of violent coercion. The ex-prisoners and ex-pacifists were transformed overnight, whether they liked it or not, into jailers and generals.

The historical precedents offer little ground for optimism. When the Spanish colonies achieved their liberty as independent nations, what happened? Their new rulers raised armies and went to war with one another. In Europe, Mazzini preached a nationalism that was idealistic and humanitarian. But when the victims of oppression won their freedom, they soon became aggressors and imperialists on their own account. It could scarcely have been otherwise. For the frame of reference within which one does one's thinking, determines the nature of the conclusions, theoretial and practical, at which one arrives. Starting from Euclidean postulates, one cannot fail to reach the conclusion that the angles of a triangle are equal to two right angles. And starting from nationalistic postulates, one cannot fail to arrive at armaments, war and an increasing centralization of political and economic power.

Basic patterns of thought and feeling cannot be quickly changed. It will probably be a long time before the nationalistic frame of reference is replaced by a set of terms in which men can do their political thinking non-nationalistically. But meanwhile, technology advances with undiminished rapidity. It would normally take two generations, perhaps even two centuries, to overcome the mental inertia created by the ingrained habit of thinking nationalistically. Thanks to the application of scientific discoveries to the arts of war, we have only about two years in which to perform this herculean task. That it actually will be accomplished in so short a time seems, to say the least, exceedingly improbable.

Gandhi found himself involved in a struggle for national
independence; but he always hoped to be able to transform the
nationalism in whose name he was fighting to transform it first
by the substitution of satyagraha for violence and second, by
the application to social and economic life of the principles of
decentralization. Up to the present, his hopes have not been
realized. The new nation resembles other nations inasmuch as it
is equipped with the instruments of violent coercion. Moreover,
the plans for its economic development aim at the creation of a
highly industrialized state, complete with great factories under
capitalistic or governmental control, increasing centralization
of power, a rising standard of living and also, no doubt (as in
all other highly industrialized states) a rising incidence of
neuroses and incapacitating psychosomatic disorders. Gandhi
succeeded in ridding his country of the alien tiger; but he failed
in his attempts to modify the essentially tigerish nature of
nationalism as such. Must we therefore despair? I think not.
The pressure of fact is painful and, we may hope, finally
irresistible. Sooner or later it will be realized, that this dreamer
had his feet firmly planted on the ground, that this idealist was
the most practical of men. For Gandhi's social and economic
ideas are based upon a realistic appraisal of man's nature and
the nature of his position in the universe. He knew, on the one
hand, that the cumulative triumphs of advancing organization
and progressive technology cannot alter the basic fact that man
is an animal of no great size and, in most cases, of very modest
abilities. And, on the other hand, he knew that these physical
and intellectual limitations are compatible with a practically
infinite capacity for spiritual progress. The mistake of most of
Gandhiji's contemporaries was to suppose that technology and
organization could turn the petty human animal into a
superhuman being and could provide a substitute for the
infinities of a spiritual realization, whose very existence it had
become orthodox to deny.

For this amphibious being on the borderline between the

animal and the spiritual, what sort of social, political and
economic arrangements are the most appropriate? To this
question, Gandhi gave a simple and eminently sensible answer.
Men, he said, should do their actual living and working in
communities of a size commensurate with their bodily and
mental stature, communities small enough to permit of genuine
self-government and the assumption of personal responsibilities, federated into larger units in such a way that the
temptation to abuse great power should not arise. The larger a
democracy grows, the less real becomes the rule of the people
and the smaller the say of individuals and localized groups in
deciding their own destinies. Moreover love, and affection are
essentially personal relationships. Consequently, it is only in
small groups that Charity, in the Pauline sense of the word, can
manifest itself. Needless to say, the smallness of the group in no
way guarantees the emergence of Charity between its members;
but it does, at least, create the possibility of Charity. In a large,
undifferentiated group, the possibility loes not even exist, for
the simple reason that most of its nembers cannot, in the nature
of things, have personal reations with one another. "He that
loveth not knoweth not God; for God is love." Charity is at
once the means and the end of spirituality. A social
organization, so contrived that, over a large field of human
activity, it makes the manifestation of Charity impossible, is
obviously a bad organization.

Decentralization in economics must go hand in hand vith
decentralization in politics. Individuals, families and small co-
operative groups should own the land and instruments
necessary for their own subsistence and for supplying a local
market. Among these necessary instruments of production,
Gandhi wished to include only hand tools. Other decentralists –
and I for one would agree with them – can see no objection to
power-driven machinery provided it be on a scale commensurate with individuals and small co-operative groups. The
making of these power-driven machines would, of course,

require to be carried out in large, highly specialized factories. To provide individuals and small groups with the mechanical means of creating abundance, perhaps one-third of all production would have to be carried out in such factories. This does not seem too high a price to pay for combining decentralizaion with mechanical efficiency. Too much mehanical efficiency is the enemy of liberty because it leads to regimenation and the loss of spontaneity. Too little efficiency is also the enemy of liberty, because it results in chronic poverty and anarchy. Between the two extremes, there is a happy mean, a point at which we can enjoy the most important advantages of modern technology at a social and psychological price which is not excessive.

It is interesting to recall that, if the great apostle of Western democracy had had his way, America would now be a federation, not merely of forty-eight states, but of many thousands of self-governing wards. To the end of a long life, Jefferson tried to persuade his compatriots to decentralize their government to the limit. "As Cato concluded every speech with the words, *Carthago delenda est*, so do I every opinion with the injunction, 'Divide the counties into wards.'" His aim, in the words of Professor John Dewey, "was to make the wards 'little republics, with a warden at the head of each, for all those concerns which being under their eye, they could better manage than the larger republics of the county or State'. In short, they were to exercise directly, with respect to their own affairs, all the functions of government, civil and military. In addition, when any important wider matter came up for decision, all wards would be called into meeting on the same day, so that the collective sense of the whole people would be produced. The plan was not adopted. But it was an essential part of Jefferson's political philosophy." And it was an essential part of his political philosophy, because that philosophy, like Gandhi's philosophy, was essentially ethical and religious. In his view, all human beings are born equal, inasmuch as all are the children of God. Being the children of God, they have certain rights and certain responsibilities – rights and responsibilities which can be exercised most effectively within a hierarchy of self-governing republics, rising from the ward through the state to the Federation.

"Other days," writes Professor Dewey, "bring other words and other opinions behind the words that are used. The terms in which Jefferson expressed his belief in the moral criterion for judging all political arrangements and his belief that republican institutions are the only ones that are legitimate, are not now current. It is doubtful, however, whether defence of democracy against the attacks to which it is subjected does not depend upon taking, once more, the position Jefferson took about its moral basis and purpose, even though we have to find another set of words in which to formulate the moral ideal served by democracy. A renewl of faith in common human nature, in its potentialities in general and in its power in particular, to respond to reason and truth, is a surer bulwark against to – talitarianism than in demonstration of material success or devout worship of special legal and political forms."

Gandhi, like Jefferson, thought of politics in moral and religious terms. That is why his proposed solutions bear so close a resemblance to those proposed by the great American. That he went further than Jefferson – for example, in recommending economic as well as political decentralization and in advocating the use of satyagraha in place of the ward's "elementary exercises of militia" – is due to the fact that his ethic was more radical and his religion more profoundly realistic than Jefferson's. Jefferson's plan was not adopted; nor was Gandhi's. So much the worse for us and our descendants.

Mahatma Gandhi
Kingsley Martin

When I first saw Mahatma Gandhi at the Round Table Conference in 1931, I asked how far he was saint and how far astute politician. Later, I realized that the question was unanswerable: the two aspects were inextricably blended in a singular complex character. In India, saints can be politicians just as they could in medieval Europe. The ascetic interpreter of sacred writings may win for himself a place in a still largely religious community which no politician can hope to achieve in the sceptical and mechanized West. Gandhi differs from all the other unclothed holy men whom you may meet anywhere in India because his religious inspiration had survived a lawyer's training, a wide reading of Western books, a knowledge of the world and ruthless examination by his own powerful intellect. It is this constant testing and application of religious principle by the process of reason that fascinates me in Gandhi.

The Mahatma never hid the process of his thought or the difficulties he found in reaching his conclusions. In private conversation, he was always ready to argue, and laughingly admitted inconsistencies. *Harijan* is unlike any other newspaper I know in that Gandhi there sought only truth and exposed his own inner conflicts. I think he would have admitted that his political position was not always satisfactory, particularly in the difficult period before his imprisonment in 1942, when he had parted company from his old friend Rajagopalchari, and was never sure how far he could carry his followers in non-violent resistance to an expected Japanese invasion. He was apt to get cross with simple-minded followers who assumed that once they had subscribed to the doctrine of ahimsa, everything would be easy. He told them roundly that he had never found any of his problems simple. The principle was clear enough; its application to the social and political tangle was an affair of the intellect.

You could trust the Mahatma not to be caught by humbug. He at once saw through the pretensions of Oxford Groupers and advocates of "moral rearmament" who came to see him. Listening to God, he told them in *Harijan*, implies "fitness to listen." How easy to say to oneself that one is listening-in to God! What was the use of British imperialists telling him that India should repent? "It does not lie in the mouth of the debtor to say he will not pay till the creditor pays or purifies himself." And then he made the shrewd comment, so reminiscent of Tolstoy, and so fundamental to the understanding of his own asceticism: "Peace and a high standard of living are incompatible." If a man encumbers himself with property, then he cannot do without police. By the same token, an Empire implies soldiers and war.

Gandhi's fasts were peculiarly unintelligible to English people. They are part of an Indian tradition; Gandhi himself remarked that he imbibed the idea of the fast with his mother's milk. She herself used, to fast if one of the children were ill. The value of the Mahatma's fasts lay in their religious appeal; they were not intended as a method of coercion. The first object of a fast was self-purification. To embarrass the Government or to have effect on those against whom he fasted was a secondary consideration. He also declared that he never fasted against his enemies; he hoped "to move to action those who bear affection towards me." But he said he did not really know how his fasts worked; he merely knew from experience that they did. I suppose one would be oversimplifying if one said that the fast was to make clear the truth for which he was prepared to die, and thereby to persuade those against whom it was directed to reconsider their position and ask themselves whether they might not be wrong. As a sacrificial act, the fast to the death is comparable with the death on the Cross. And yet, as with other problems raised by the unique life of the Mahatma, it was sometimes difficult to distinguish between this religious act and a very effective and more mundane form of coercion. Gandhi denied that he ever intended to coerce. In the case of his fast, which was designed to persuade Ambedkar and the untouchables, it must, I think, be admitted that its speedy effect was due to the knowledge that Gandhi's death would produce extremely unpleasant results for the recalcitrants. Gandhi, however, repudiated this explanation of his success. His object, he said, was not to coerce enemies, but "to sting into action the many who have taken pledge to remove untouchability."

The Mahatma could claim to have won a more remarkable and satisfying victory in the fast that ended the communal riots in Bengal. I arrived in the East just when his final fast, the object of which was to end the violence of the Hindus against the Muslims in Delhi, had been completed. It was a fast that nearly ended in death, and the Mahatma only called it off when he had the assurance of all those in a position to give it that everything would be done to make life tolerable to Muslims in Delhi. It is not true that its only effect was to force Patel and others to pay the 50 crores of rupees owed to Pakistan. It also changed the atmosphere in Delhi. Muslims were able to walk about in Delhi, at any rate by day, without fear of a Sikh kripan in the back, and I was myself present at the Muslim festival at Mehrauli, which could not have been held at all if Gandhi had not made its untroubled celebration a condition of ending his fast. The last time I saw Gandhi alive was at the prayer meeting he held at Mehrauli, with an audience of some four thousand eager and anxious Muslims.

Gandhi was a politician. He did not wish to die in his fasts, and he chose the occasion for them after much consideration of the political situation. Indeed, I am reminded in all the Mahatma's actions, of a passage in Bernard Shaw's *St. Joan*, where Dunois, her fellow commander-in-chief, remarks that he would have thought her "a bit cracked" if he had not noticed that she gave very sensible reasons for what she did, though he heard her telling others she was only obeying the voice of St. Catherine. To which St. Joan replied that "the voices come first;

and to find the reasons after." So with Gandhi; the religious mystic relied on intuitions, but he was quite sufficiently astute to act only on those intuitions which his reason confirmed. What a good idea, for instance, is the day of silence! How beneficial a weekly day of silence would be for many other politicians in Delhi, not to speak of London also! An Indian politician is surrounded, to an even greater extent than one in the West, with people who believe that he should be accessible to everyone. They claim the right of entry into his house; they assume that it is his duty to listen to their complaints; to meet their wives and families; to discuss with them the affairs of the realm. These obligations press heavily on Indian leaders, whose time is already too fully engaged with the job of administration, with making speeches and with party politics. The day of silence meant that Gandhi was able, for one day a week, to be inaccessible to the intruder. It meant that he had time to think, to plan ahead, to prepare his mind for the burdensome decisions that had to be made. Similarly, many have misunderstood his advocacy of the spinning wheel. It has seemed to be mystical nonsense and an impractical proposal for retarding the industrial progress of India. It was, of course, a symbol of the Mahatma's protest, in which he represented millions of people everywhere against the machine age to which India, almost alone among the great nations of the world, has not yet succumbed and from which he desired to save it. But as always with Gandhi, the spinning-wheel had an immediate practical significance. He knew that the Indian villager would have more independence, political and economic, if he was not bound to buy the textiles imported from the West. Again, Indian politicians, even more than those of the West, must waste their strength in long journeys, tiring to the nerves and disturbing to the digestion. Hung with garlands when they arrive at the station, they are swept away to vast feasts, after which they are expected to make lengthy speeches. An intimate friend of Gandhi's, who suffered from this kind of life, remarked to me on the sound practical sense that Gandhi had shown in restricting himself to five simple and basic foods. Since it was known that he was an ascetic who would not eat the curries and other luxuries set before him, he did not offend his hosts, but on the contrary, gained credit for an asceticism which kept him alert and fit when others tended to get stout and lethargic. I think that the Mahatma himself would have accepted some such explanation of his actions, and I doubt whether he himself could have disentangled the complex relation of political acumen and religious inspiration.

I had my last talk with Gandhi on the Monday before his assassination. He had completely recovered from his fast; his mind was as agile as when I first knew him. He was perhaps rather more authoritative, and less legalistic, in argument. As always, he was prepared precisely to explain the nature of his doctrine. He had publicly expressed his deep disappointment, and indeed his misery of soul, at the revelation of the Indian mind after the withdrawal of British control. I asked him whether his recent confession of failure, as expressed in *Harijan*, involved any revision of his doctrine of ahimsa. He explained that his doctrine had never changed, but that he had discovered, to his sorrow, that passive resistance, designed to dislodge the British from India, had been merely the weapon of the weak and not the genuine ahimsa which relies only on truth, love and sacrifice. He had made this distinction, he told me, as early as the days of his first struggles in South Africa when he repudiated the idea that he supported "passive resistance." He never believed in passivity, nor did he ever believe in what is today called "appeasement." His advice to mankind is that in any dispute, one must first establish the truth and purify one's own motives. Then one must stand by the truth, by ahimsa, if one believes in it and has trained oneself for that method of resistance. He, more than once surprised the world, by saying that for those who are not ready for ahimsa, violent resistance is better than cowardly submission to evil.

Whether ahimsa is externally successful clearly depends on whether the opponent has a conscience. I read in *Harijan*, "Our triumph consists in being in prison for no wrong whatever." In the struggle against the British, persecution had to become a regular part of life. In the absence of violent resistance "the wrong-doer wearies of wrong doing." So when Bernard Shaw remarked that "the vegetarianism of the sheep makes no appeal to the tiger," Gandhi replied that he did not believe that "the British are all tiger and no man." He was willing to admit the peculiar difficulty of applying ahimsa in a case like that of the Nazis who were trained to enjoy the suffering of others, and who killed six million Jews who did not threaten them. But he could fairly claim that even the non-violence of the weak had had its effect when used against the British people who disliked the use of lathis against unarmed resisters. Indeed, British officials have admitted that if the technique of passive resistance had been more constantly and persistently used by the Indians, the British might have been driven out of India at an earlier stage. But this, the Mahatma had discovered, had never really been ahimsa. Passive resistance is a weapon which can be used with effect by those who could resort to force, to persuade the aggressor to desist from evil. Ahimsa, in a sentence, involves first personal purity of motive and the complete admission of the truth; secondly, after all concessions that should be made injustice to the opponent had been made, ahimsa requires a completely firm stand on a point of principle where the opponent is clearly in the wrong. Victory may then be achieved by love, even if the individual who uses ahimsa may have to die before he has convinced his enemy. This doctrine, the Mahatma admitted, had not been generally understood by the millions who had passively resisted the British.

At this point I raised what has always seemed to me the essential weakness of Gandhi's philosophy. I said that while fully appreciating this doctrine, which was not very different from the teaching of Christ as I had learnt to understand it in my childhood, it still appeared to me in its most perfect form to provide no answer for those who undertook the task of government. I could see well enough that ahimsa could defeat an aggressive power, but when those who had won were confronted with the task of government, they would be taking over a machine which, by its very nature, involved the use of force. How would the Mahatma, for instance, use ahimsa in the immediate issue of Kashmir? He replied that he believed it possible for a government to use ahimsa, and quoted Tolstoy's story of Ivan the Fool. He added that Sheikh Abdullah could use ahimsa in Kashmir if he believed in it. "I would use it," he said, "against the tribesmen and I believe successfully. But Sheikh Abdullah does not believe in ahimsa." "Do you not," I asked, "sometimes give practical advice on political matters where the doctrine of ahimsa does not arise?" He laughed. "I most certainly do," he said, and the conversation switched into a highly realistic and practical discussion of the political issues in Kashmir.

This was very characteristic of the Mahatma. Conversation with him about political matters did not follow the normal course because he insisted on getting the principle straight and refusing to compromise upon it. He would apparently stand pat on a point of principle until he was sure either of the goodwill of his adversary – which happened when the Cabinet mission finally persuaded him of its sincerity – or, as in this case of Kashmir, until agreement had been reached that the ideal solution must be, for the moment, left out of the question. He would then suddenly, and often to the surprise of a Westerner used to laying down principles only to compromise in their application, switch off completely to a highly realistic discussion in which the principle appeared to be forgotten. Perhaps the right way to put it is that he was more determined than other people are to consider a problem on two levels. He took as it were, his bearings by laying down the principle. He could always return to it. If that course was blocked, he would trim his sails, with the result that while still pretending to seek the ideal, he might find that he had lost sight of his objective: he preferred, if he could not sail straight to the goal, to accept the lower level of practical politics and frankly to give advice on the basis of expediency. Not having lost his bearings by tacking, he could always start again on the true course.

Two things were at once borne in upon me during the dramatic days following the Mahatma's assassination. The first was the dependence of other Indian leaders on his advice and consultation. His prestige was so great, his position so impregnable, that the leaders of very political persuasion regarded him as their guru. They relied on him perhaps too much, and some of them may find a greater political stature of their own now that they have lost their mentor. One remarkable and I think unique feature of his position as "father" of the new India, was that he possessed an extraordinary intelligence service, since everyone from the humblest to the greatest came and poured out to him their troubles, both personal and political. I know of no similar case in politics. A junior civil servant could complain to Gandhi of misbehaviour of his Minister, and Gandhi would take the matter up with the Minister, who could raise no objection to criticism having been made without his knowledge, and through these unofficial channels. This strange, personal and unifying influence has now disappeared from Indian politics, with results that are not easy to assess.

Hindu-Muslim peace was only one of the causes to which the Mahatma devoted his life. He had dedicated his life earlier to the causes of untouchability, khadi and village regeneration. He died, I know, with a sense of failure. Too few of his followers understood ahimsa, and too few of them were sufficiently trained in its application. He had had many converts to non-violence, but with the departure of the British, it has been made manifest that they had understood the passive resistance of the

weak and not the non-violence of the strong. That the British
had left India without violence was, he admitted, a remarkable
achievement. He had made, he told Edgar Snow in the last
weeks of his life, "a kind of contribution" to the world by
showing that non-violence was a political means and not only a
matter of personal ethics. He was aware that the forces of
passion and violence were growing in the new India. Ahimsa,
he said, could never be defeated since it was a state of mind
which was in itself a victory and which could have only good
spiritual results in others even if it did not win external victory.
But the immediate challenge was the communal struggle. When
he had recovered from his Delhi fast, he wished to go to
Pakistan and appeal to his friends there. He was well aware
that he might not live to do this; the bomb that was thrown
during his fast was sufficient warning of the fanaticism of the
extremer sort of Hindu. He remarked, only the day before his
murder, that it would always be easy to kill him at one of his
prayer-meetings. So it proved. But his death started a legend
and Gandhi today stands among the celestial hierarchy in the
minds of Indians. In his remarkable broadcast, spoken with
deep emotion on the night of the assassination, Pandit Nehru
used the occasion to rally all the forces of tolerance and
righteousness. For the moment, at any rate, the Mahatma's
death confirmed the lessons of his fasts and reinforced the
hopes of communal peace. Whatever happens in India and
Pakistan, Gandhi's contribution will not be lost. There is a
danger, of course, that his legend may be perverted; when the
saint dies there are always those who glorify his memory in
order that the world may the more readily forget what he
taught. But they never wholly succeed. Even in the case of
Christianity, where the wrangles of the Church and the
pronouncements of Popes have done so much to pervert the
lesson of the Cross, the contents of Christ's teaching have
continuously broken through ecclesiastical obscurantism,
inspiring and refreshing his disciples. Gandhi's life and death

will similarly remain a witness to the faith that men may still overcome misery, cruelty and violence by Truth and Love.

The Challenge of Gandhi
John Middleton Murry

I do not think that any serious student of Gandhi's teachings would deny that *Hind Swaraj* is the fundamental document. It is a strangely lucid and impressive little book which, one feels, was the outcome of some profound experience of illumination such as seems to have been the common destiny of all great religious teachers. And, in particular, it has a marked affinity in the vehemence of its repudiation of Western civilization, with the discourse which was the outcome of Rousseau's illumination on the road to Vincennes. The place of Rousseau's natural man, uncorrupted by civilization, is taken in Gandhi's mind by the Indian peasant, who has the advantage over Rousseau's conception of being a reality. Not, of course, that, as shallow critics pretend, Rousseau's natural man was a mere romantic fiction: he was a normative ideal, which is a very different thing. But, for Gandhi, the normative ideal of the man uncorrupted by civilization actually existed. There were hundreds of millions of them in the villages of India living lives of communal fraternity, of frugality, of simple duty deeply rooted in an enduring religious faith, for who the Westernization of the thin stratum of Indian intellectuals was a remote happening which did not really concern them. And Gandhi's conception of Hind Swaraj (Indian home-rule) was, in essence, a spiritual reconquest of the corrupted Westernizers by the great body of this truly self-governing people – a reconquest to be achieved by a spiritual regeneration of the Westernizers themselves, through a recognition of their own corruption, and a humble reidentification of themselves with the true civilization of the Indian villager. "Civilization," said Gandhi, "is that mode of conduct which points out to man the path of duty." That path was being followed, and had been followed for centuries, by the Indian peasant.

In other words. Gandhi conceived it as his function to become the explicit consciousness of the wisdom that underlay the ancestral life of India, and to convert to it that thin upper stratum of educated Indians who had from motives, good or bad, suffered themselves to be perverted by the achievements and the values of Western civilization. In the traditional economic organization and the folkways of India, he saw the actual working of the soul-force which he desired consciously to use at once as a spiritual discipline for the individual and as a means of liberating India from the alien industrial civilization which Britain, with the connivance of her own educated classes, had imposed upon her. It is important to realize that, in Gandhi's philosophy, the soul-force is nothing recondite.

Thousands, indeed tens of thousands, depend for their existence on a very active working of this force. Little quarrels of millions of families in their daily lives disappear before the exercise of this force... History does not and cannot take note of this fact. History is really a record of every interruption of the even working of the force of love or the soul. History, then, is a record of an interuption of the course of nature. Soul-force, being natural, is not noted in history. That is a profound and illuminating saying, though the usual difficulties about the conception of nature may be raised. But it is perfectly clear from the context that, for Gandhi, a natural society is one based on a deeprooted religious tradition which, over long centuries, has shaped a tenacious pattern of daily life. This is found pre-eminently in India. Indian civilization was stable, in contrast to the essentially unstable industrialized civilization of the West.

At moments, in *Hind Swaraj*, Gandhi perhaps intoxicated by his own rediscovery of his own own great country, romanticizes it. He will not convince the critical reader when, for example, he declares:

It was not that we did not know to invent machinery; but our forefathers knew that, if we set our hearts after such things, we should become slaves and lose our moral fibre. They, therefore, after due deliberation, decided that we should only do what we could do with our hands and feet.

The notion that the sages of India, after due deliberation, at some remote period of time, consciously and purposefully rejected the technological achievements which were afterwards to be discovered and exploited by the men of Western Europe is certainly mythical; but if we take the statement in the spirit and not in the letter, it does convey an important truth, namely, that the supremely conservative civilization of India, in spite of all its aberrations and deformities, is based on a religious wisdom which has made a deliberate choice, and chosen spiritual rather than material things. The contrast, in this respect, between India and Western civilization is deeply impressive, and Gandhi is fully justified in driving it home even at the cost of violence to historical truth. Although at no point in history was India actually capable of the technological discoveries made in the West, and refused to make them, she did make a religious and metaphysical choice which rendered her incapable of those discoveries. Behind this fact, undoubtedly lies a profound difference between the ethos of Christianity and Hinduism, on a discussion of which we forbear to enter here.

But *Hind Swaraj* makes it crystal clear that Gandhi's rejection of Western civilization is quite radical, and that it is completely mistaken to regard his repudiation of the applied arts and sciences of Europe as a quirk of temperament. He is entirely serious about it, for it is an integral part of his whole religious philosophy. Western civilization is, for him, the outcome of a rejection of spiritual truth, and a consequent concentration on material things, which cannot but be disastrous. When he peremptorily declares that "Machinery represents a sin," he intends the word "sin" to be taken with the utmost rigour.

There is, therefore, at least a superficial paradox in Gandhi's having become so deeply involved in a movement of national liberation after the European pattern of the nineteenth century. His leadership of that movement had its justification, for him, in that the removal of British control was the indispensable condition of the return of India to her own natural and traditional life. It was primarily as the imposers and disseminators of the sinful Western civilization that the British had to be ousted. But such a motive was radically different from that of a majority of Congress members who only desired to be masters in their own house, while retaining all the techniques of the Western civilization. The two purposes were antithetical and their alliance adventitious. Hence Gandhi's unique position. He was essentially a great religious reformer, a renovator of Hinduism, but by no means a revolutionary one, but rather a teacher of a new path to spiritual perfection that branched off from a familiar road. The enormous strength of his position as a politician lay in the fact that in the eyes of the Indian peasant, he was a saint. He, and not the largely Westernized Congress, had the masses of India behind him. Though it would be unfair to many of his brilliant and devoted supporters among the Congress politicians to represent them as restive under his leadership, for they also recognized his spiritual *authority* as well as his incomparable influence over the Indian people, it is necessary to emphasize the fundamental divergence of aims and values that existed between a majority of the Congress and himself.

Were the aims and values of Gandhi practicable, or were they romantic: an example of what Toynbee in his *Study of History* calls "archaicism" that impossible effort at reversion to the past whose effects, Toynbee shows, are only more revolutionary? I doubt whether any Indian would feel capable of answering that question with any confidence: and it would obviously be ridiculous for me to attempt to do so. Nevertheless, the question is of such importance for an estimate of Gandhi's eventual status that one cannot refrain from speculating upon it.

But first, we need to be clear as to the path along which Gandhi wanted to lead India. His rejection of Western civilization was fundamental to his religious and philosophical position. Nevertheless, it would be a caricature of his views to represent him as determined, if and when he gained the power to do so, to root out the railways from India and destroy the cotton mills, even though that seems to follow directly from his doctrine when it is taken literally. But, in the first place, it follows from his doctrine that he could not even aim at power in that sense. The dictatorial power of a Stalin or a Hitler was completely alien to him; but hardly less alien was the constitutional political authority of a Nehru. Gandhi sought and achieved only the power of the wise man, the sage, the religious and spiritual leader, who persuades people by his teaching and example of what it is right for them to do. Being absolutely convinced that the pursuit of material goods is wrong, that frugality and austerity is right, he rejected entirely the idea that the problem of India was to raise "the standard of living" by industrialization. He was thus implacably and equally opposed to Capitalism, Socialism and Communism, because he denied the spiritual validity of the end which is common to all those types of economic and political organizations – namely, an increase in the production and consumption of material goods.

Not that he acquiesced in the great poverty of the Indian masses. He regarded that as something to be remedied, as soon as possible and by practical means. But it is of cardinal importance to realize that a condition of life which would, by Western standards, be still one of abject and deplorable poverty was to Gandhi the rightful standard of human living. Thus, his practical aim was to raise the standard of the Indian peasant living from grinding and wasteful poverty to decent, happy and holy poverty. He believed that that had been the condition of the peasant in the old days, but that the former equilibrium had been destroyed by the British conquest; and, above all, by the imposition of Lancashire cotton upon India. Hence came his insistence on the revival of village spinning and weaving as a precursor to the general improvement of the village hand-economy.

It seems to me, that it is impossible even for the professional economist, who is not entirely enslaved to abstractions, to deny that the Charka movement was inspired by great practical wisdom. From the strictly economic point of view, the most urgent problem of India is the universal under-employment of the peasant. Because of the climatic conditions and the smallness of his holding (which is estimated to average under 3 acres) it is reckoned that for about four months in the year the peasant has nothing to do. To provide him with useful work that calls for a minimum of capital outlay is a crying need; the hand-spinning of cotton would provide it. Even though the end-product is more expensive in terms of money than the machine-made fabric, that is not an objection to the method as a means of enabling the under-employed peasant to use his wasted time in clothing himself. Similarly, comparisons between the cost in man-hours of khaddar and the machine-made cloth are totally irrelevant. Millions of man-hours are running to waste in the villages: the problem is to make them immediately productive with the minimum of capital outlay.

From this point of view, it seems to an outsider that the Charkha movement is abundantly justified, and deserves all the stress that Gandhi placed upon it. But the question to be answered is whether it is to be regarded as a short term expedient, or the foundation of a permanent policy? Though it is clear enough that in *Hind Swaraj*, Gandhi regarded the return of India to a hand-economy as a spiritual and moral good, and was indeed contemplating as desirable a complete rejection of machinery and, indeed, of Western science, it is doubtful whether he had fully thought out his position. Thus he made a famous exception to his indictment of machinery in favour of the sewing-machine, probably because it was hand or foot-driven; and he seems to have envisaged the manufacture of such machines in national factories, under good conditions. Generalizing from this instance, we may perhaps conclude that Gandhi would have accepted such machines as would strengthen and not disrupt the village-economy. Negatively, therefore, they must not be power-driven; positively, they must not create or prolong under-employment. It is a difficult economic conception to work out in theory; but, providing one accepts as fundamental the idea of a self-subsistent and fully employed village-community as the vital organic unit of the distinctive Indian civilization, it is probably capable of realization by a people for whom ethical conceptions, rooted in a living religious tradition, are decisive. It should permit a certain, but strictly limited, raising of the material standard of living, and it might well achieve a degree of simple human happiness of "joy in widest commonalty spread" on which Western civilization seems to have turned its back for ever. What it would not permit is that a nation, even if, like India, it were of continental size, should become a great power – or, indeed, any kind of power, except a spiritual one.

Gandhi's economic conception of India is pacifist through and through. Thus Gandhi's pacifism differs totally from the pacifism that has developed in Western civilization, in the main, as a corollary of economic individualism. Gandhi's pacifism, being based on an explicit renunciation of the pursuit of material goods, is much more impressive and respectable than Western pacifism which expects, at once, to maintain and even increase its standards of material living and to escape the obvious consequences of that preference of material to spiritual ends.

That is not to suggest that Gandhi's thought is innocent of Western affiliation. The influences of Thoreau and Tolstoy, in particular, are manifest, and were openly acknowledged by him. But whereas those prophets are quite eccentric to the main direction of Western thought, as assimilated by Gandhi, they are linked to the age-old and continuous religious tradition of India. Voices crying in the wilderness of America and Russia are transformed in Gandhi into the utterance of the soul of vast people. It is by no means inconceivable that Gandhi, after his heroic and symbolic death, may become the central figure and guiding spirit of a spiritually renovated India, which will, in a spirit of contented renunciation, pacifically oppose to the material values of the industrial civilization its own spiritual life-mode. It is very hard for a Westerner to contemplate such a possibility, though it is certainly not alien to his own nominal religion of Christianity. Unfortunately, his own religion really is nominal. It has long since ceased to have any control over the automatism of material progress and material disaster; it merely endorses the one and deplores the other. This is not intended as a criticism. The question, whether a technological civilization is really compatible with any religion at all, is one that requires even in its Christian members, an almost super-human detachment to ask with the necessary rigour, and an almost superhuman wisdom to answer. It is a question which obviously undercuts the conspicuous and alarming antitheses of the present time: Those between Capitalism and Communism, and Democracy and Communism. These are antitheses within the technological civilization itself: on both sides of which it is taken for granted that technology is a good and necessary thing which bestows material benefits which are, self-evidently, the summum bonum for the vast majority of human beings. Thus, it is anxiomatic for the statesmen of the West that the attack of Communism can only be successfully repelled by raising the material standards of the West to a point which Communism cannot practically achieve. This may be true, and the material achievement may be possible. But, if and when it is achieved, will Western humanity be out of the wood, or further lost in it?

Will it be even less capable than it is today of contentment and peace?

Gandhi had a plain and forthright answer to this question. Peace is radically incompatible with the fundamental restlessness sometimes called the "divine discontent" – presumed and inspired by technology. For peace is an attitude, a way of life of the individual human person based on a religious choice – a renunciation of material things in favour of spiritual things a renunciation that must be made in fact by the vast mass of the people to whom he belonged, in virtue of a living and all pervasive religious tradition. I do not know whether Gandhi was right or wrong. Still less can I conjecture whether India will follow him. But I have no doubt that the challenge he made to the West was that of a very great soul indeed, in whom the metaphysical and religious genius of India spoke with new authority.

The perfect Artist
Jawaharlal Nehru

Nineteen-sixteen. Over thirty-two years ago. That was when I first saw Bapu, and an age has gone by since then. Inevitably one looks back and memories crowd in. What a strange period this has been in India's history, and the story, with all its ups and downs and triumphs and defeat, has the quality of a ballad and a romance. Even our trivial lives were touched by a halo of romance, because we lived through this period and were actors, in greater or lesser degree, in the great drama of India.

This period has been full of wars and upheavals and stirring events all over the world. Yet events in India stand out in distinctive outline because they were on an entirely different plane. If a person studied this period without knowing much of Bapu, he would wonder how and why all this happened in

India. It is difficult to explain it; it is even difficult to understand by the cold light of reason why each one of us behaved as he or she did. It sometimes happens that an individual or even a nation is swept away by some gust of emotion or feeling into a particular type of action, sometimes noble action, more often ignoble action.

The surprising thing about India during this period was not only that the country, as a whole, functioned on a high plane, but also that it functioned more or less continuously for a lengthy period on that plane. That, indeed, was a remarkable achievement. It cannot easily be explained or understood, unless one looks upon the astonishing personality that moulded this period. Like a colossus he stands astride half a century of India's history – a colossus not of the body but of the mind and spirit.

We Feel Orphaned

We mourn for Bapu and feel orphaned. Looking back at his magnificent life, what is there to mourn for? Surely to very, very few human beings in history could it have been given to find so much fulfilment in their own lives. He was sad for our failures and unhappy at not having raised India to greater heights. That sadness and unhappiness are easy to understand. Yet who dares say that his life was a failure? Whatever he touched, he turned into something worthwhile and precious. Whatever he did yielded substantial results, though perhaps not as great as he hoped for. One carried away the impression that he could not really fail in anything that he attempted. According to the teachings of the Gita, he laboured dispassionately without attachment to results and so results came to him.

During his long life, full of hard work and activity and novel adventures out of the common rut, there is hardly any jarring note anywhere. All his manifold activities became progressively

a symphony, and every word he spoke and every gesture that he
made fitted into this, and so unconsciously he became the
perfect artist, for he had learnt the art of living, though the way
of life he had adopted was very different from the world's way.
It became apparent that the pursuit of truth and goodness
leads, among other things, to this artistry in life.

As he grew older, his body seemed to be just a vehicle for the
mighty spirit within him. Almost, one forgot the body as one
listened to him or looked at him, and so where he sat became a
temple and where he trod was hallowed ground.

Died a Martyr

Even in his death, there was a magnificence and complete
artistry. It was from every point of view a fitting climax to the
man and to the life he had lived. Indeed, it heightened the
lesson of his life. He died a martyr to the cause of unity to
which he had always been devoted and for which he had
worked unceasingly, more especially during the past year or
more. He died suddenly as all men wish to die. There was no
fading away of the body or a long illness or the forgetfulness of
the mind that comes with age. Why, then, should we grieve for
him? Our memories of him will be of the Master whose step
was light to the end, whose smile was infectious and whose
eyes were full of laughter. We shall associate no failing powers
with him of body or mind. He lived and he died at the top of
his strength and powers, leaving a picture in our mind and in
the mind of the age that we live in that can never fade away.

The picture will not fade. But he did something much more
than that, for he entered into the very stuff of our minds and
spirits and changed them and moulded them. The Gandhi
generation will pass away, but the stuff will remain and will
affect each succeeding generation, for it has become a part of
India's spirit. Just when we were growing poor in spirit in this
country, Bapu came to enrich us and make us strong, and the

strength he gave us was not for a moment or a day or a year, but it was something added on to our national inheritance.

Bapu has done a giant's work for India and the world and even for our poor selves, and he has done it astonishingly well. And now it is our turn not to fail him or his memory, but to carry on the work to the best of our ability and to fulfil the pledges we have so often taken.[37]

"Be Not Afraid"

...And then Gandhi came. He was like a powerful current of fresh air that made us stretch ourselves and take deep breaths; like a beam of light that pierced the darkness and removed the scales from our eyes; like a whirlwind that upset many things, but most of all the working of people's minds. He did not descend from the top; he seemed to emerge from the millions of India, speaking their language and incessantly drawing attention to them and their appalling condition. Get off the backs of these peasants and workers, he told us, all you who live by their exploitation; get rid of the system that produces this poverty and misery. Political freedom took new shape then and acquired a new content, much that he said we only partially accepted or sometimes did not accept at all. But all this was secondary. The essence of his teaching was fearlessness and truth, and action allied to these, always keeping the welfare of the masses in view. The greatest gift for an individual or a nation, so we had been told in our ancient books, was abhaya (fearlessness), not merely bodily courage but the absence of fear from the mind. Janaka and Yajnavalkya had said, at the dawn of our history, that it was the function of the leaders of a people to make them fearless. But the dominant impulse in India, under British rule, was that of fear-pervasive, oppressing, strangling fear; fear of the army, the police, the widespread

---

37 Harijan, February 15, 1948.

secret service; fear of the official class; fear of laws meant to suppress and of prison; fear of the landlord's agent; fear of the moneylender; fear of unemployment and starvation, which were always on the threshold. It was against this all-pervading fear that Gandhi's quiet and determined voice was raised: "Be not afraid." Was it so simple as all that? Not quite. And yet, fear builds its phantoms which are more fearsome than reality itself, and reality, when calmly analysed and its consequences willingly accepted, loses much of its terror.

So suddenly, as it were, that black pall of fear was lifted from the people's shoulders, not wholly of course, but to an amazing degree. As fear is close companion to falsehood, so truth follows fearlessness. The Indian people did not become much more truthful than they were, nor did they change their essential nature overnight; nevertheless, a sea-change was visible as the need for falsehood and furtive behaviour lessened. It was a psychological change, almost as if some expert in psychoanalytical methods had probed deep into the patient's past, found out the origins of his complexes, exposed them to his view, and thus rid him of that burden.

We did not grow much more truthful, perhaps, than we had been previously, but Gandhi was always there as a symbol of uncompromising truth to pull us up and shame us into truth. What is truth?

It is not surprising that this astonishingly vital man, full of self-confidence and an unusual kind of power, standing for equality and freedom for each individual, but measuring all this in terms of the poorest, fascinated the masses of India and attracted them like a magnet.

He seemed to them to link up the past with the future and to make the dismal present appear just as a stepping stone to that future of life and hope. And not the masses only but intellectuals and others also, though their minds were often troubled and confused and the change-over for them from the habits of a lifetime was more difficult. Thus he effected a vast psychological revolution not only among those who followed his lead but also among his opponents and those many neutrals who could not make up their minds what to think and what to do."[38]

Gandhi
Herman Ould

The biographers of Mohandas Karamchand Gandhi will have a hard task to separate fact from fiction, hearsay from truth. Even in his lifetime, Gandhi took on something of the character of a mythological figure: a symbol, an image to point to or swear by, one endowed with almost miraculous gifts and powers. Many a time I have myself invoked his name to clinch an argument or to point a moral, particularly during the 1914-1918 War, when I called myself a pacifist. My pacifism was ostensibly inspired by the teachings of Jesus Christ, as expounded by Leo Tolstoy. I say ostensibly, because I have since come to believe that great teachers do not hand over their teachings, but only raise into consciousness, ideas and tendencies which lie embedded in their pupils' own minds. Whether this is so or not, it is certainly true that when the First World War broke out, I was already wedded to the ideal of non-resistance and non-violence and looked upon Gandhi as one of the most notable exponents of the faith. Because he was teaching and acting in accordance with my own beliefs, I accepted him whole, without question.

During the course of the thirty years which followed, my mind and character inevitably underwent certain changes: I hope I became less dogmatic and more tolerant, less prone to generalize and readier to admit the sincerity of those whom I regarded as mistaken: and when the English press recorded, from time to time, the deeds and words of Gandhi, I found myself sometimes inclined to be critical of his deeds and sceptical of his teachings. The deeds seemed to me somewhat too spectacular, the teachings somewhat too rigid. I readily admitted that imperfect knowledge of all the circumstances made judgement difficult, if not impossible, and that an Englishman who had never lived in India and had little more than the average Englishman's acquaintance with Indians, would be unlikely to form an accurate estimate of Gandhi's contribution to the Indian question. I did not, of course, wish to sit in judgement; nevertheless, I was conscious of responding less sympathetically to the Mahatma's call.

It was not until I went to India, in 1945, and spent some three months going from place to place and meeting all sorts and conditions of people, that I began to see Gandhi in true perspective. It would be absurd to say that he was a typical Indian: great men of the stature of a Gandhi are not typical of any country or time, they are unique. Nevertheless, he was a true Indian, and only India could have produced him. It is highly improbable that his peculiar force and influence would have thrived in Europe as they did in a country which, notwithstanding its age-long history and great traditions has a population that is largely illiterate and is essentially simple. Subtle and complex though his own character was, Gandhi's message to his people was direct and simple, and expressed without ambiguity. There can be no doubt that the progress of Western civilization has led to a high degree of sophistication and scepticism, and it is unlikely that Gandhi's message, conveyed in terms so simple, would have had the power to sway the people of Europe, or of those countries whose stock is mainly European. Indeed, I frequently met among the younger generation of educated Indians, particularly among those engaged in industries where political theories were much discussed, the same kind of scepticism concerning the Mahatma's teachings as I should expect to find in similar circles in Europe. The very word 'Mahatma' was often spoken by these young men with a curled lip and a half-sneering smile.

But in general, I found the name of Gandhi pronounced with awe and received with respect. The Indian's capacity for reverence is far greater than the Englishman's and whereas the average Englishman would be inclined to deny that reverence was called for by any other man, but should be reserved for God and the saints, the average Indian seems always eager to find a person to revere and will not hesitate to lavish awed veneration on very dubious specimens of sainthood. Why, even I found it necessary to discourage discipleship! In an atmosphere were such a thing as this is possible, how natural that a Gandhi should awaken a glow of worship in the hearts of millions of his countrymen! He stood, for, them, as the great spokesman of their aspirations: the Voice of India, the voice, above all, of the inarticulate millions of Indians who had come to believe that freedom from British rule meant freedom indeed.

When I was in Bombay, I had an opportunity of experiencing this upsurging of mass emotion. An Indian friend of mine, frankly calling himself a follower of the Mahatma, came to me one day with the exciting news that Gandhi would shortly be spending a day in Bombay. He was very anxious that I should come face to face with one whom he regarded with such reverence and promised to do his best to arrange an interview. My friend was a truly saintly person to whom I was sincerely attached, and I was loathe to upset him by displaying less enthusiasm than the occasion seemed to call for, but I felt compelled to say that the last thing I wished was to inflict my presence on a man who was always besieged by people of all kinds, many of whom, no doubt, had greater claims to his attention than I. I was quite content to admire at a distance. But my friend had made up his mind, and a few days later, I heard that the Mahatma would see me if I could come to Petit

Hall where he was staying and accompany him to his usual prayer meeting.

Even before we were in sight of the great house, I was aware of the tense atmosphere that seemed to pervade the whole district. Apart from a number of cars on their way to Petit Hall, there was very little ordinary traffic in the streets, which were lined with boy scouts standing at attention. In the large hall of the house, we found a number of men of a type only to be found in India – large-eyed, smooth-faced, dreamy-looking creatures, dressed in the long white garment that goes well with their dark skins. They told us that the Mahatma would soon be emerging, but they sent in my name to him.

As we entered the ante-room, I received my first shock, for my friend murmured something about taking off one's shoes. Now I had often enough taken off my shoes on entering a mosque, and this had not come amiss to me, for a mosque is the house of God, but something in me revolted against removing my shoes in the presence of another human being, however worthy of respect. I was spared a decision, luckily, by the appearance, of the Mahatma himself, accompanied by a number of men and women. The atmosphere of awe was almost tangible. Voices were hushed; all eyes were turned on Gandhi, who was accompanied by his wife and a young girl, on both of whom he leaned. Before introducing me to him, my friend had prostrated himself before the Mahatma and kissed his feet – an action which I found distasteful. When Gandhi heard my name, he returned my clasped-hand salute which had become second nature to me and then with a smile he shook hands with me, European fashion, but said nothing. By this time we were moving in a kind of procession to the door, Gandhi still leaning on the young girl and followed by a row of women in white saries and the men who had been awaiting him.

As we proceeded down the path lined by boy scouts, who saluted us, our numbers swelled and I found myself at the head of a procession some fifty or sixty strong. The Mahatma indicated to me that I should stay by his side, and turning to me, he pursed his lips and tapped them with his index finger. "He means it is his silence day," explained Mrs. Gandhi, and my friend walking behind me murmured reverently that although Gandhi could not speak to me I might speak to him. I confess the situation embarrassed me. If I had been alone with Gandhi, or anybody else, I might have been induced to speak in the hope of interpreting his reactions by the look in his eyes; but walking down a public thoroughfare, with policemen keeping the crowd at a distance, and boy scouts extending their staves in salute, I felt quite incapable of uttering a monologue for which I was unprepared. I decided that my time would be more profitably spent in observing the Mahatma, who seemed to be in excellent health. Supported by the two women, he held himself very erect; his body was taut and wiry, and his rather spindly legs were quite equal to carrying him along at a good pace. He wore a dhoti and a shawl and no shoes. His bare body was glowing like polished copper and his shiny head was bald and shaven. Although he did not speak, his rather small shrewd eyes were active, to charm, to please, to impose silence, to admonish, but chiefly or so it seemed to me, to charm.

We drew near the grounds of the mansion where the prayer meeting was to be held, the crowd grew considerably, and the guard of scouts and policemen was in closer formation. A platform had been erected behind the house, facing a green sward going down to the sea. On the platform were a couple of couches covered with white material and a large square cushion on which Gandhi sat crosslegged; behind him, an erection of pillows, against which, however, he did not lean. He sat there, like an ancient sculpture, his eyes closed, motionless, and praying out from the dais some hundreds of people, men, women and children, were assembled, most of them sitting on the grass.

The service began by somebody intoning a hymn, in the

somewhat whiney voice characteristic of Indian sacred singing,
further sang a phrase which was repeated by the congregation
as they clapped their hands rhythmically. There were amplifiers,
but I don't think they were in use. A carpet had been spread
near the platform on which I was invited to squat, but I
remained standing, looking at the immobile figure on the dais,
impressed by the profile with its thrusting lower lip, the very
symbol of determination. All around me was a lively excited
crowd; reporters and photographers were everywhere, as well
as men with movie-cameras; there were hawkers with
sweetmeats and flowers; one wild-eyed woman carried a vessel
containing a mixed assortment of foods, a handful of which she
offered me; but a journalist at my elbow told me not to eat it,
so with tact I allowed the wet and sticky mess to trickle
through my fingers. The service over, the autograph-hunters
crowded round the Mahatma and those who were lucky
enough to get his signature paid five rupees to the Harijan
fund. Reporters besieged me too, begging for interviews. What
was my opinion of the Mahatma? They drew a blank, but I
heard from them and from others a series of little stories of
Gandhi which revealed the attitude of awe which they shared
with my saintly friend and with the masses surrounding us.
One eager young man declared, as if he had just worked out
the discovery himself that Gandhi was democratic, aristocratic,
plutocratic: democratic – as witness his signing of autograph
books; aristocratic – for he was truly noble; and even
plutocratic – for did he not use even millionaires for the Cause?

In the light of this incident – not in itself greatly to my taste –
I seemed to attain a cleare understanding of Gandhi. Certain
things about him, his methods and his aims, I had always taken
for granted. His love for India and his conviction that her
freedom from British rule was essential; his genuine belief in a
policy of non-violence; his genuine advocacy of civil
disobedience. One might doubt the wisdom of any or all of
these beliefs, but I, for one, never doubted that Gandhi was

sincere in his enthusiasm for them. Where for me, doubt crept in was concerning the methods by which he sought to further them. Civil disobedience was a course of action with which I was familiar, for in the 1914-1948 War, I had been a conscientious objector and had refused to obey the law which would have led me into the army, but in doing this, I had involved nobody but myself and any ill consequences of my act of disobedience were borne by me alone; whereas Gandhi not only himself refused to obey, but was the direct cause of thousands of others behaving similarly. When I read the accounts of lathi charges against unresisting men and women who had been inspired by Gandhi to embarrass the British authorities by accepting inevitable suffering, my admiration for the courage of these simple people was boundless, but I found it difficult to exonerate Gandhi from being the cause of it.

His interpretation of the doctrine of non-violence seemed to me similarly faulty. To undertake a fast "to the death if necessary" as a protest against a Government's behaviour, or in order to arouse a sense of shame in warring communities, is an action requiring great courage and steadfastness, but it is essentially an act of violence – a threat which cannot be justified by its results because it has no relation to the offence against which it is intended to be a protest. It is an act that would be as effective in an unjust cause as in a just cause.

But Gandhi sincerely believed in those methods and so far as one knows suffered no qualms in applying them; for him, therefore, the important thing was to make them effective. And during my few months in India, and particularly when I saw for myself how the populace responded, I came to realize with what consummate skill and knowledge, the Mahatma worked on the susceptibilities of his own people, leading them in the direction which he honestly believed to be the way of righteousness. Protest as he might against being called saint, it was because he was profound. He lived in the utmost simplicity, identifying himself with the simple life of the vast

millions of the subcontinent; his asceticism was an attribute of
sainthood with which their religious beliefs made them familiar,
and his willingness to fast, unto death if required, was a form
of vicarious sacrifice which inspired them with awed love.

Last Day
Vincent Sheean

Professor Radhakrishnan knows better than anybody else what
must be the progression and modulation of ideas in a Western
mind confronted with the phenomenon of Mahatma Gandhi.
So very much of what went into the formation of the
Mahatma, historically and spiritually, is unfamiliar to the West,
so much of the essence is misunderstood or susceptible of
misunderstanding, and there is such a large area of experience
peculiar to the Indian consciousness through the ages, that alike
in learning, in perception and in experimental equipment both
conscious, and unconscious the Westerner is at a disadvange.
Gandhi transcended our categories and transvaluated our
values. It also appears to me and again Professor
Radhakrishnan is the best judge – that he did the same to
Indian categories and values. Thus in considering what he was,
did and taught, we all of us have to rise far above our ordinary
circumvallations, our prisons large and small, to a level at
which it is possible to contemplate selfless purity as a force in
the world-not, that is, withdrawn from life but deeply and
widely effective in it.

Some awareness of what this might or could be brought me to
India at the end of 1947. I had been there before and had been
certain, not without discomfort, that someday I must go back
again to learn what it was. Arriving first at Karachi, I stayed
there for some time, only hastening my progress when the
papers reported that Gandhi was about to begin a fast to

ensure the safety of the Muslims in Delhi. This fast began on January 13, 1948. I arrived in New Delhi on January 14th and waited. Any fast at Gandhi's age was the occasion for great anxiety, but also it seemed certain, or at least probable, that unprecedented efforts would be made to induce him to break it. (He did not make conditions, of course, in begining the fast – it was as always a form of prayer and atonement.) The conditions were made on the following Saturday night (January 18th) when a group of thirty Hindu leaders, representing every group and organization, including ultra-nationalists, visited him to ask what would convince him of their good intentions. It was then that he named seven conditions looking toward the security of life and worship for the Muslims of Delhi. These conditions were pledged by the thirty leaders, and at noon on Sunday, Gandhi ceased fasting.

During this period I had been reading and waiting. I was not wholly unprepared for a decisive experience of some kind: 'Gandhi had been a sort of magnetic force in my own consciousness, as in so many others,' for years (I think since the Salt March). It appeared to me that he had entered upon his theophanic moment on August 15th, when power was transferred into Indian hands, and he spent the day in silence, meditation, spinning and prayer. The question in my mind was only how long the theophanic moment would last: that is to say, how long it would be before the inevitable martyrdom. I half-expected it in September in Calcutta (I was in Vermont, but I was extremely aware of what he was doing by means of the BBC). It was in the inner logic and organic development of the whole drama of his life. What is more, I had made no secret of this view, either in New York or among friends in Delhi after my arrival there. I say all this only to indicate how and why my first conversation with him – which, with my feeling of approaching climax, I felt might be the last – had such tensity for me. I went to the prayer-meeting at Birla House after his fast had ended, but made no attempt to see Gandhi or speak to him until Mr. Nehru told me he was well enough for such a conversation.

When I went into that garden room at Birla House which has been so often described, it was my feeling that this might be my only chance to talk to him. I had wanted to go to Wardha for years, but there appeared no chance of this now. Gandhi was immensely occupied; he was unhappy over all that had happened since August 15th; and the dark forces were gathering near. Under the circumstances, I had no desire to ask about temporary things, however important. I did not want to speak of India or any other country, time or place. Twenty-five years of too much concern with the world in general had brought me here to ask older questions: What is the truth? What is action ? What is the fruit of action? Is there a righteous battle? How can a righteous battle produce a disastrous result? The frame into which these questions fitted with extraordinary propriety had fallen under my hand by chance in a bookshop a few days before. It was the Gandhi Gita – his *Anasaktiyoga*, the way of selflessness – as translated into English by Mahadev Desai from Gandhi's Gujarati translation and notes. The conversation dealt with these subjects only. Gandhi knew at once that I was desperately serious and that his answers meant more to me than any others I ever expected to get. I did not tell him until much later in the talk that these questions referred to our war against Hitler and its result, and he may indeed have had some other conflict in mind: it was restricted, however, to the battlefield of Kurukshetra. In this conversation he went farther than in any other of which I can find record in absolute non-violence, in identification of ends with means, and in the insistence upon renunciation. I realize now that he could see my awful need and wanted to help me. At one point, he sent for a copy of the *Isa Upanishad*, but it was brought only in Sanskrit; he told me that if I could not find a copy in English, he would get one for me the next day. He then read the first sloka of the *Isa* to me and explained it in his own words: Renounce the world and receive it back again as the gift of God. There were points of some philosophical interest: he would not permit me to use the word "illusion" as a translation of *maya,* for example, and we settled upon "appearances." Atomic energy, electromagnetic diffusion and all the kindred phenomena, including the possible dissolution of this universe, he viewed with the utmost tranquility. (I did not know then, as I know, how explicit they are in the Upanishads). At the end of the conversation, which I have hardly indicated in this paragraph, he told me that I could come to him every day at Birla House and he would see me after the evening prayer – that I could indeed move into the house if I liked-and that in a few days he was going to Wardha, where I could come with him and continue my questions.

On the second day, my questions were upon the possibility of conflict between truth and non-violence, which he refused to admit. As I was going away, he told me that we might pursue the subject on the next day, but I remarked that I was then going to Amritsar with Mr. Nehru. He raised his two hands in the air and said "Go, go." These were the last words I heard him say, because on my return from Amritsar two days later, it was January 30th. On that day, I proposed to drop the truth-ahimsa discussion (it was specifically on the milk vow and I felt that it gave him pain) and proceed to the next subject, which was *The Kingdom of God is Within You,* Tolstoy's late work which had influenced him greatly, years before. I wanted to find out how the sermon on the Mount seemed to him, at the end of a long life profoundly influenced by it, in the social relation to which Tolstoy had wished to make it the only guide. He was twelve minutes late to the prayer ground having, as I learned afterwards, spent the afternoon on the new constitution of India and other grave subjects – and walked into the sunset at 5.12 precisely. As he came to the top of the steps, which lead to the rectangular prayer ground at the end of the garden, I heard the four small, dark explosions. I was only a few yards away, but there were people between me and Gandhi. I did not see him. It can be imagined how overwhelming was the impression made by the sound of these explosions, since I had known, for a long time, that they would come. It is possible that I lost consciousness very briefly; at any rate something of an extraordinary nature happened, because I did not see them carry him away or, in fact, anything else of consequence. The only way I can describe it is by likening it to an earthquake, in which, very probably, little is seen but much felt. I was in that garden for an hour and a half before a friend and colleague came and took me away; but most of what I remember is what went on in my own mind.

Afterwards I went to the Jumna bank every day to hear the chanting of the Gita, and then to the last prayer meeting at Birla House beside his ashes on February 12th, and then on the special train with the ashes down to the confluence of the rivers at Allahabad. Afterwards, it was my task, as it still is, to make an attempt towards the understanding of what he said to me, of what the concatenation of the external circumstances meant, and of what might have been the continuation or amplification of the brief lessons I had received from him.

The testimony I can and will give, when I get it all into order, will be much more detailed and comprehensive than I can indicate here, but one thing in it is quite certain and was certain in the first few minutes: Gandhi was in no sense and in no way whatsoever afraid. I believe he never had been. He has often been called indomitable. I should say rather that he was inexpugnable – there was no place or approach by which he could be attacked, assaulted or seriously injured, much less conquered. (The body is irrelevent here in fact he told me it was "a prison"). At the very outset of our first talk, as we walked up, and down the blue carpet, he said he wanted me to understand one thing clearly. "I am ill," he said. "I sent for the best doctors obtainable. I have a fever. They give me injections of Sulpha drugs and thereby saved my life. This proves nothing.

It may be that it was better for humanity for me to lose my life. Is that clear? If it is not perfectly clear, I will repeat it."

I said that I believed I understood it. We then began to speak of the Gita and he did not refer to the subject again but to me, at any rate, there was no doubt of what he meant (there had not been since August 15th: that was in fact why I left America to go there). Now, this inexpugnable fearlessness is itself based upon the Gita, the Upanishads and other influences (including the sermon on the Mount) and also must have been in his character from the beginning: yet according to his own teaching it was developed by constant effort throughout a long life. I find in his printed work, a progression as steady as it was long. Never before had he said according to anything I can find in print-that violence was wrong at all times and places and could have no good results. The battlefield of Kurukshetra was in the heart of man: means and ends could not be differentiated. He also affirmed that even if his interpretation of the Gita should be disproved by all the scholars, he would still believe it. The absolute purity, fearlessness and selflessness of these statements shook me so in that first conversation, that I could hardly make my way out of the dark garden afterwards. I did not think either of Jesus or the Buddha then (it is only since that I have discovered some extraordinary likeness of concept in "resist not evil"). Also, I do not think that Gandhi thought of them at the time. He was answering straight from the formulable essence of his being. Never in my life have I found anybody else of whom this could be said. No external detail had any existence for him while his mind contemplated the subjects I had come to lay before him – the subjects which, after all, constituted the final essence of his own life's aspiration.

His interpretation of the Gita, although sustained and amplified by Mahadev Desai, does not, I believe, engage much support amongst scholars. Sri Aurobindo Ghose certainly does not agree that Kurukshetra is in the heart of man; in his *Essays on Gita* he most definitely states it to be a field of physical carnage, terrible in the extreme. This is also what any ordinary reader is bound to assume. But Gandhi's view arose from the depths of his own soul and was supremely true for him; therefore, when he stated it to me after a long life which had been from beginning to end all sacrifice and selfless struggle, I was bound to see it, as I do now, under the aspect of truth. If the self rises to realization (as I must confess I feel that Gandhiji's did) then this becomes true, Kurukshetra is in the heart of man and the karma-yogin translates it into pure and absolute non-violence. It may not be objectively the fact for ordinary mortals, but it is the karma-yogin's truth as embodied in the life, teaching and death of Mahatma Gandhi.

I have also found much to reflect upon in his attitude towards the *Isa Upanishad*. The sovereign influence upon his development, I believe, falls into two categories, the first of which is canonical and the second, intellectual. The sermon on the Mount, as we know, came to him at about the same time as the *Gita*, but it reached him in the beautiful language of the King James version, whereas the *Gita*, at that time, was accessible to him only in Sir Edwin Arnold's metrical translation. (He was then about twenty). It is hardly surprising that under these circumstances the sermon on the Mount had an even more powerful influence, in spite of the fact that it is canonically Christian and Gandhiji was profoundly Hindu. The *Gita* then came to him in its full power when he was fifty-four, during the three weeks' fast at Delhi (1924) when the late Pandit Malaviya chanted it to him in Sanskrit many times. For the rest of his life, he read, studied and memorized the *Gita* in Sanskrit, finding in those organ harmonies ever greater splendour. The last nineteen verses of the second chapter of the *Gita* were always chanted at his prayer meeting, morning and evening. It seems to have become subtly blended with the sermon on the Mount in his consciousness, so that his interpretation, as he told me, was criticized as being unduly swayed. And yet, in that conversation of January 27th, when he felt that I needed a truth within his reach, what he sought to give me was – going behind and perhaps above the *Gita* – the *Isa Upanishad*. And although he had undoubtedly known it all his life, he told me he had "found" it (how well I recognized what he meant by the use of that word !) in 1946, when he wanted some authority to use in convincing Christian audiences in Travancore.

The secular intellectual influences upon his development are secondary, in my opinion, to these great canonical guides. Perhaps what gave the Sermon on the Mount and the Gita their decisive power over his spirit was precisely their lack of canonical investiture in his own eyes. He was not a Christian any more than he was a Buddhist; and although, as a Hindu and a Vaishnavite, he may have given canonical authority to the Gita more or less in spite of himself, the fact is that he did not consciously attribute divine origin to the Mahabharata or the Ramayana: he told me so. He spoke of them as "significant fictions." Thus the two great religious scriptures came to him fresh and new, not as imposed or revealed truths, but naturally and as if by his own spontaneous discovery.

The secular intellectual influences seem to have been chiefly Ruskin who led him to co-operative labour and the spinning-wheel-and Tolstoy The Ruskin discovery is well and fully treated in his own autobiography, but it is to me regrettable indeed that I had no chance to ask him about *The Kingdom of God is Within You*. I cannot believe that in retrospect he would have found it to be as convincing as it seemed to him when he was young. Obviously, if the battle of Kurukshetra is in the heart of man, then Tolstoy's view, at its highest philosophical pitch, was correct; but Tolstoy's whole argumentation was on the plane of social and political arrangements, in which it is difficult indeed to see how men can get along without forms of co-ercion and visible imposed order. But this subject was not to be touched, nor was the one we might have reached on the Sunday – Jesus of Nazareth as an artist. This was an idea of his developed in an interview in 1924, and my wish to have him discuss it further was based upon the concept (in my own mind, not in Gandhi's words of 1924) that the creative genius which he indicated for both Jesus and Muhammad, which was in fact akin to his own, arose from a very special aptitude for collaboration with destiny. I had intended to ask him, for example, why Jesus went to Jerusalem at a time when he must have known quite clearly that it would mean his death. I wanted the Mahatma to differentiate for me between the collaboration with destiny-i.e. significant sacrifice, teaching by death and suicide. (He had already told me, with a very wise and emphatic look through his spectacles, that he could not commit suicide, which in view of the extremes to which he had gone on various occasions in fasting, demanded some elaboration). In speaking to him of Jesus as artist, in other words, I might have learned something about his own unfaltering advance towards martyrdom.

I say "might have." There could be no certainty in the matter, for the fact is that in spite of his extraordinary serenity and elevation of mind, his pervading sanity, his indefatigable practical activity and insistence upon common sense, the Mahatma might not have been wholly conscious of his own collaboration with destiny. He was, after all, a genius, one of the greatest in all history, and the primary characteristic of genius appears to be a creative power arising at least partly from the unconscious. Thus it seems probable that when he performed the Salt March, he was not aware of all the reverberant symbolizations and significances attached to it in all languages, places and times, although he clearly realized that it transcended the Indian languages and was thus of primary importance in the awakening of the Indian people. (Mrs. Naidu, who followed him then in making salt and going to jail, told me that at the time she had not known its full power as symbol, nor had he explained it to her; it was a thing done, and realization came afterwards.)

In any case, the further questions and answers were not to be, and my effort to explore these meanings must be based upon what we had been able to touch in two conversations. This may seem too slight and small a foundation for any contribution of value to the subject, and yet coming as they did in a nexus of circumstances which can hardly be explained or even believed on any materialist hypothesis, they must be offered as part of the general cogitation.

Mahatma Gandhi
Thakin Nu

In a world still darkened with intolerance, greed and hatred despite two major catastrophes, the life and teachings of Mahatma Gandhi shine as a solitary beacon of light. The suffering and destruction resulting from two World Wars waged during the span of twenty-five years would, one might expect, have sufficed to induce a sense of sobriety in the minds of the nations, and incline them to the pursuit of the ideals of purity, self-denial and non-violence which Mahatmaji practised and propagated. But the end of World War II merely seemed to have signalled a return to the selfishness, intolerance and disunity which caused the War itself. In his own country, Mahatma Gandhi's lofty idealism and practice of his teachings raised the fight for freedom to a spiritual level, and made India's claim to independence irresistible, by all standards. In the world at large, his teachings constituted a challenge to the law of the jungle and greed for the neighbour's land which largely characterized man's actions in the international sphere. His death at the hands of a fanatic thus stunned not only India but the world; it seemed as if the edifice of love and peace which he had so carefully built up would crash and the harmony which he had inspired disappear. But the potency of his idealism proved far stronger than death at the assassin's hand and Mahatma Gandhi's teachings continue to inspire the lives and emotions of millions all over the world and millions yet unborn will in their turn derive the same inspiration therefrom.

Mahatma Gandhi's passionate search after truth, and his absolute sincerity of purpose, have inspired me from childhood. It has been my ardent desire to live as a disciple in his ashram for at least a year and imbibe his teachings more thoroughly than can ever be possible through study of published writings, but circumstances ordained otherwise. I was determined, however, to see him once, and the kind invitation which Pandit Jawaharlal Nehru extended to come to visit India offered the opportunity for which I longed so much. I offered Mahatmaji a *khamauk* – the Burmese peasant's hat – which he gracefully accepted, and I spent some time looking for the kind he preferred. When at last I found one, I flew it to him in the charge of my friend U Ohn, but alas! even as the plane carrying the offering of a humble disciple was on its way to Delhi, the assassin's bullet pierced his fragile body and deprived mankind of one of its greatest sons. The *khamauk* was placed as an offering at his cold feet, and symbolized for me the determination unto death to apply his teachings of love, purity and sacrifice in the service of our masses.

Three of Mahatma Gandhi's ideals made a special appeal to be as a Buddhist and as a humble seeker after Truth. One was the ideal of absolute chastity, which he not only preached but practised unswervingly during the greater part of his life. By agreement with his wife that their marriage should henceforth be devoid of any sexual element, he had killed the lust of his flesh and the sexual side of life had no longer any meaning for him. Purity of body sprang from purity of mind. He was Mahatma – one who had conquered his lust.

The second ideal is one which many have been able to follow – the ideal of poverty. He possessed no personal property beyond what is permitted of hermits and recluses, namely a roof over his head and clothing of the simplest kind just enough to ward off heat and cold. His food in his later years was also of the simplest – dates and goat's milk. Wealth and comfort had no meaning for him and he eschewed everything that was beyond the bare necessities of life.

The third ideal, which I specially admire, is that of absolute non-violence or ahimsa. Mahatmaji's view was that nothing justifies violence, that violence should be conquered with non-violence, hatred with love, pride with meekness. This doctrine is not new to the world. It had been preached by the Buddha, Christ and founders of other religions. Mahatmaji revived this doctrine in a world that had forgotten it, a world where might was right, where strong nations subjugated the weak by force and where imperialism and capitalism, taking shelter behind tanks and bayonets, overawed mankind. Mahatmaji's originality lay in the application of this doctrine to the practical problems of a nation which had been enslaved and was the victim of a ruthless racial and economic domination. India could have revolted and pitted violence against violence, but success was uncertain; whether successful or not, a revolution by force would have entailed bloodshed, misery and suffering. It would also have laid a trail of racial hatred stretching far into the future.

Through the preaching of these three ideals, and their consistent practice in his daily life, Mahatmaji welded together the disunited masses of India into a powerful force which successfully battled against imperialism and won for their country its rightful place amongst free nations. A people which had all but forgotten its glorious past and the teachings of her philosophers, and whose lives were dominated by a mass of disunited, selfish trends, once more found its voice and, realizing its own strength, shook India out of her slumbers. The great change which came over the consciousness of the Indian masses in the twenties of this century is a measure of the potency of Mahatma Gandhi's idealism.

Early in his life, Mahatmaji had applied satyagraha or non-violent disobedience to the problem of the Indian settlers in South Africa. He relinquished his large income as a barrister and led the Indians in a campaign of non-violent resistance to unjust laws. It succeeded partially. Complete success was unobtainable because not all followed the doctrine or were prepared to suffer the extreme hardships which he himself endured willingly. But he knew that his method must in the end break the bonds of racial slavery. Even in his early days in South Africa, he had coupled his campaign of non-violent resistance with the doctrine of absence of hatred. In the Boer War, he raised and commanded a Red Cross unit, organized a plague hospital when the disease broke out in Johannesburg and he led a stretcher-bearer party during the Natal revolt of 1908.

In India, to which he returned in 1914, he found a wider field for the practice of satyagraha in the first campaign following the repressive Rowlatt Acts of 1919, but alas! his followers were not all able to make their non-violence absolute and in the end, in the Punjab and elsewhere, the campaign ended in failure.

But the seed had been sown and the idea of non-violent non-co-operation spread. The great civil disobedience campaign of 1930 began with the mass violation of the salt laws, and if it did not force the withdrawal of the British from India, it shook the stability of the imperial power and numbered its days. If fully followed and by all Indians, the campaign of non-violent disobedience could not fail to succeed. It was the weakness of human nature and not any inherent defect in the method that led to the failure of that campaign. In the end, it was the seed which the great Indian leader had implanted in the minds of his people that made their demand for independence irresistible.

Among the great causes with which Mahatmaji's name will

ever be linked is that of the Harijans. India was fighting against a ruling caste of conquerors from another clime, but within herself, Hindu India maintained an ancient caste system which forbade the "depressed" classes even to tread on the shadows of men of higher castes, or to use the wells and temples used by them. This was contrary to Mahatmaji's conception of humanity and to his doctrine of universal love. His powerful intellect and saintly influence were therefore harnessed to the cause of the Harijan. It became the mission of his life to purge Hinduism of this feature. The struggle had not ended when he died, though he had compelled the Congress to adopt it as an integral part of its programme. Mahatmaji, who considered all men equal and brethren, be they Muslim or Hindu, European or Jew, had thus laid the seeds of reform, and in time, they will flower and bring victory to the Harijan cause.

Mahatma Gandhi is dead; millions mourn his loss. But the noble ideals he implanted in the minds of men and women, the ideals of absolute purity in conduct, absolute love to friend and foe, poverty and the total abolition of class distinctions between man and man and woman and woman, will live and bring humanity nearer to the goal of universal love and universal peace.

How Gandhi Helped Me
Sybil Thorndike

It is strange to observe how often the doctrine of one's own Church is illuminated by someone from outside someone from another form of faith. This has been my own experience; and the one who has helped me to clarify my thoughts about the doctrine of the Church to which I think I should rather say he has helped me to see Christianity more clearly, which is a broader view than that of any particular Church or branch of

Christianity. By his writing, by his political actions and life, and by his personal attitude to life, he has witnessed for the Faith – the Faith in God, and as one reads and re-reads the New Testament one is conscious how very near he was to the teaching of our Lord, Jesus Christ. One always knew that Gandhi would take what we call the Christian attitude in any difficult situation, and this made him such a true guide to us Church people. It has always been a puzzle to me, since childhood, how any one sect, any one form of faith can be so certain that in its present state it contains the whole Truth, for one has found so often that other people's forms of religion can be like a signpost along the road we are travelling. This Gandhi has clarified for me.

I could not help feeling how wonderful was the service in Westminster Abbey, that day of the Memorial Service in his honour, after his death. Gathered together were Christians of different sects – Hindus were there, Buddhists, Muslims, and there may have been many more, I only speak of those I saw and knew – all of us joined together with one idea, to give thanks to God for a saintly life we had been privileged to know. An Indian friend was talking to me afterwards, and saying how splendid it would be if periodically, once a year perhaps, there could be some such service where we could all concentrate on those things in which we are agreed, and forget for a short while our differences as Gandhi was able to, and that is why he helped us so much to realize our oneness with other human beings, other nations to realize the Fatherhood of God – the brotherhood of mankind, and these things – these good things we must hold on to even when we quarrel about our differences.

Gandhi, too, has helped me to understand more fully many of the doctrines in my own Church, such as the teachings about the Blessed Virgin Mary, the teaching about meditation, confession, contemplation – not in the orthodox Church way perhaps, but by his vision I have been able to see more clearly the Church's vision.

His teaching on the merging of matter and spirit – his insistence on the quiet hours of thinking and prayer – his humility, these are aids we have received from this great saint whom we all seem to know so well even if we have never met him personally. His writings and sayings are so intimate and sincere that one feels one has really talked to him, and one is enabled to know somehow what way he would advise through certain hard problems.

For many of us, he has been as it were an Interpreting of Christ and the gratitude we feel for his way of life will, we hope, make us strive personally for that same deep knowledge of God in our work, in our politics in our personal relationships.

His death is not a passing away, but a passing forward, he is treading out the path that the saints have all trod to make our travelling more sure, and lead us to a better state. Those who were his friends still reflect in their lives something of his goodness, and help us, sinners and strugglers, by their example aid their shining light.

Gandhi's Message to the World
Roy Walker

It is perhaps typical of our way of looking at things that when we see an Indian and an Englishman together, the first thing we notice is the different colour of their skins and the last thing we observe is the "fundamental affinity between British and Indian reactions, physical, mental, emotional and even spiritual" to which no less experienced an observer than Lord Pethick-Lawrence has recently testified. In somewhat the same way, the first thing we notice about the cultures of India and the West is the difference, and very often we do not penetrate to the level where community of insight and aspiration is to be found. Yet a culture may be likened to a language. It is the apt means of communication for a certain people or peoples in a given era of human history, and although language reacts on thought, conditioning what can be clearly expressed, it is broadly true that all languages provide the means of expressing all important truths. One of the great needs of our time is for what may be called cultural linguists, men not only of learning, but of insight sufficient to interpret East and West to each other; men, in short, like the late Ananda K. Coomaraswamy. The danger of allowing this function to fall into incapable hands is great. Already identities are being lost in a great boiling together of traditions. It is as though, having made the simple discovery that every flower in a garden has its own beauty, the gardener should resolve to graft them all together and so produce one really good flower, or shall we say a flower to end flowers. The contrary danger is an obstinate cultural provincialism, whose self-respect is usually centred in the dogmatic belief that its own particular civilization is the "best", not only for its own people, but for everyone else. This is a fault common in the West, and the root of much prejudice against open-hearted reception of the world-message of Mahatma Gandhi. "That sort of thing may be all very well in India," people will say, "but I can't see it happening over here." Or, "Non-violence worked with the British, because we are by and large a tolerant and just people. It couldn't work against people like the Nazis or long-range weapons of mass-destruction like the atom bomb."

Yet Gandhi is not so much an Eastern as a universal figure; his philosophy and example are essentially valid for all humanity or none, because they work at a level deeper than that at which cultural, social, and technological variations are of conclusive importance. To judge Gandhian pacifism irrelevant because Gandhi was an Indian is not much more sensible than objecting to Marxism at the outset on the score that Marx was a

German. Five questions, all obvious but seldom put, will decide whether or not the Gandhian example is of universal significance: (1) What were the sources of Gandhi's beliefs? (2) What were those beliefs? (3) What had Gandhi himself to say about the world beyond India? (4) What is the judgement of competent opinion? (5) What is the response of individual conscience? I will try to indicate in what direction answers to these questions may be found.

Gandhi was a Hindu. But it was essential to his position that "though religions are many, Religion is one." "My Hinduism is not sectarian. It includes all that I know to be best in Islam, Christianity, Buddhism, and Zoroastrianism." It is therefore incorrect to speak of the New Testament and other scriptures as secondary influences on Gandhi. The three other formative influences from literary sources were the Christian pacifism of Tolstoy as expressed in *The Kingdom of God is Within You*: the visionary communism of Ruskin's *Unto This Last* (which the author considered his finest work): and the mystical anarchism of Thoreau's essay on *Civil Disobedience,* which supplied not only the name but much of the substance of this advanced phase of assertive non-violent direct action. It is a fact, to which the present world crisis adds solemn significance, that of the three important modern influences on this great Indian, one was a Russian, one an Englishman, and one an American. Moreover, Gandhi's development took place not in India, but in London and South Africa. It was in London that he read for the first time, and in the English verse translation of his friend Sir Edwin Arnold, his favourite Hindu scripture, *Bhagvad Gita*: and that he changed from a man restrained from meat-eating only by a vow given to his mother, which he fully intended to set aside after his parents' death, to a vegetarian by choice and principle – a transformation brought about by reading Henry Salt's *Plea for Vegetarianism* and other vegetarian books and by his association with the London Vegetarian Society, on whose Executive he served and to whose weekly newspaper he contributed his first published articles early in 1891. In the long struggle for Indian rights in South Africa that ended for the time being just before the outbreak of the First World War, Gandhi's thought reached maturity, and there is nothing essentially new after the little book he wrote on the voyage back to South Africa, *Hind Swaraj*, Indian Home Rule, published in 1909. Most of Gandhi's struggles were against European opponents, usually the British. That alone would make them highly relevant to the West, in as much as they reveal the reactions of Western statesmen and peoples to non-violent methods of resolving conflict.

No adequate account of Gandhi's outlook can be given here, but the proposition that "Religion is one" is the root of the matter. "I enter politics only in so far as it develops the religious faculty in me," he said. His political decisions were valid by their spiritual content, not by objective tests of expediency alone. This spiritual content is of universal relevance. It may be necessary to study the circumstances of a struggle to see the spiritual significance of a particular decision; once seen the essential human gesture can be recognized and reversed. The criticism of Gandhi as "an astute politician" – implying not the relevance of goodness to large-scale human problems, but a Jekyll and Hyde combination of saint and party-boss – is absolutely false; indeed many of Gandhi's major decisions from the halting of the Non-Co-operation campaign as it moved forward into Civil Disobedience to his deliberate absence from Delhi on village work in Bengal while the fate of India was being settled with the Cabinet Mission, are flatly incomprehensible as judgements of political expediency. Gandhi would have agreed with William Blake: "Religion is politics and politics is brotherhood."

Gandhi's references to the world beyond India, and to the West in particular, leave no doubt that he regarded his beliefs as relevant to other civilizations. It is important to realize that his doctrine of Swadeshi, or reliance on and working through the immediate environment, was a discipline that limited him to advice and action within the context of Indian affairs for the greater part of his public life; but he always looked outwards to the horizons of the globe itself. What he wrote in *Harijan* a few months before his death was not at all different from what he had written in *Young India* in the early twenties: "I said at the Asiatic Conference that I hoped the fragrance of the non-violence of India would permeate the whole world. I often wonder if that hope will materialize." During his visit to England in 1931, he advised non-co-operation with the dole system to the British unemployed and in Switzerland, on his way home, he told Pierre Ceresole that he believed the people of Europe were capable of non-violent action, but that the sort of leadership the times called for was lacking. He later advised the Jews in Central Europe to use corporate non-violence against Nazi persecutions; he advised Czechoslovakia to defend her freedom against German invaders by non-violence in 1939, and made similar suggestions to Poland in response to Paderewski's appeal to him later in the same year. To Britain, at war, he addressed in 1940, an appeal to cease fighting by force of arms and to take up non-violent struggle for justice. Non-violence was the whole tenor of his appeal to the Great Powers met at San Francisco to form the United Nations Organization, and his only answer to the atom bomb. Unquestionably, Gandhi did not regard his beliefs as relevant only to Asiatic conditions.

But was he right ? Reviewing a discussion of non-violence by Radhakrishnan recently, the *Times Literary Supplement* conceded that "Here indeed we may learn something from the East..." Aldous Huxley, in his essay *Science, Liberty and Peace* made some amends for an eloquent silence about Gandhi in his earlier works, answering those "who think that the record of Gandhi's achievements is irrelevant to the historical and psychological situation of the industrial West" with the forecast, "In the years ahead it seems possible that satyagraha may take root in the West..." Dr. G. N. Dhawan, MA, PhD., in the first full length study of *The Political Philosophy of Mahatma Gandhi* (1946) judges it to be "the most original contribution of India to political thought and political practice." "In group relations, even more than in individual life, conflicts and violence have become chronic today and threaten the very existence of civilized life. In satyagraha, Gandhi has given to the world a technique for fighting, in a creative, constructive way, aggression and exploitation in inter-group and international relations." The list could be swelled with the names of Krishnalal Shridharani, Bart de Ligt, and almost all the distinguished people who contributed to the first edition of this volume. Appraisal and discussion are, of course, a vital part of the process of understanding the life and inspiration of a man who, by any standard, was one of the greatest of the age, and by my criteria the greatest. But Gandhi's own words, brought home to us again and with new poignancy by the grand and terrible manner of his death, are wise. "Abstract truth has no value, unless it incarnates in human beings who represent it by proving their readiness to die for it." How far has the truth of non-violence been successfully incarnated in the West as yet, not only in the private lives of a few exceptionally wise and gifted men, but in the historic struggles of our time? I think there is little doubt that the most significant example was the magnificent resistance to the Quisling regime and the German occupying force offered by the Norwegian people during the years 1940-45. The resistance began, of course, with a brief military struggle, and was chequered towards the end with increasing sabotage and terrorism mostly organized from abroad. Yet, not only in my own Gandhian appraisal, but in the longer work by a non-pacifist Member of Parliament, William Warbey, it is recognized that the resistance was predominantly non-violent and remarkably successful.

The last of my five questions was: What is the response of

individual conscience? In many ways, it is the most important question of all. Gandhi has already been surrounded by our commentaries, explanations and adaptations, overlaid by our tributes. We mean well, but we come between you and the man himself and that is not good. The best advice is to seek out something that Gandhi himself has written; no easy matter in these days when almost every worthwhile book is out of print, but most libraries have one or more of C.F. Andrew's versions of Gandhi, or some other compilation. Before you have read many pages you will know that the man whose mind and personality you have sought out had the gift-not in the least a literary one-of speaking simply and directly to the humanity that is common to us all. It is because he has this quality in pre-eminent degree that he is the only valid world figure today. There has been much talk, some of it positively superstitious, of tapping the power of non-violence in the West; few statesmen and religious leaders have cared to recognize that Gandhi's power was in his appeal to the best in human nature, and that the ability to evoke response grew with the confidence of the common people, that Gandhi had indeed renounced war, that non-violence was his final creed for all occasions. Now that atomic and bacteriological warfare threaten all with annihilation, and the last vestige of "defensive war" has disappeared for ever, the world waits, with the sands running out, for spiritual and political leaders in both East and West, who will learn from Gandhi the indispensable condition on which influence for good is granted to men.

(Extracts from Mahatma Gandhi's Writings and Speeches)

I

Hinduism

I call myself a Sanatani Hindu, because:

(1) I believe in the Vedas, the Upanishads, the Puranas and all that goes by the name of Hindu scriptures, and therefore in avatars and rebirth;

(2) I believe in the Varnashrama Dharma in a sense, in my opinion, strictly Vedic, but not in its present popular and crude sense;

(3) I believe in the protection of the cow in its much larger sense than the popular;

(4) I do not disbelieve in idol worship.

The reader will note that I have purposely refrained from using the word divine origin in reference to the Vedas or any other scriptures. For I do not believe in the exclusive divinity of the Vedas. I believe the Bible, the Koran and the Zend Avesta to be as much divinely inspired as the Vedas. My belief in the Hindu scriptures does not require me to accept every word and every verse as divinely inspired. Nor do I claim to have any firsthand knowledge of these wonderful books. But I do claim to know and feel the truths of the essential teaching of the scriptures. I decline to be bound by any interpretation, however learned it may be, if it is repugnant to reason or moral sense. I do most emphatically repudiate and claim (if they advance any such) of the present Sankaracharyas and Shastris to give a correct interpretation of the Hindu scriptures. On the contrary,

I believe that our present knowledge of these books is in a most chaotic state. I believe implicitly in the Hindu aphorism, that no one truly knows the Shastras who has not attained perfection in Innocence (Ahimsa), Truth (Satya) and Self-control (Brahmacharya) and who has not renounced all acquisition or possession of wealth. I believe in the institution of gurus, but in this age millions must go without a Guru, because it is a rare thing to find a combination of perfect purity and perfect learning. But one need not despair of ever knowing the truth of one's religion, because the fundamentals of Hinduism, as of every great religion, are unchangeable and easily understood. Every Hindu believes in God and His oneness, in rebirth and salvation. But that which distinguishes Hinduism from every other religion is its cow protection, more than its Varnashrama.

Varnashrama is, in my opinion, inherent in human nature and Hinduism has simply reduced it to a science. It does attach to birth. A man cannot change his Varna by choice. Not to abide by one's Varna is to disregard the law of heredity. The division, however, into innumerable castes is an unwarranted liberty taken with the doctrine. The four divisions are all sufficing.

I do not believe that inter-dining or even inter-marriage necessarily deprives a man of his status that his birth has given him. The four divisions define a man's calling, they do not restrict or regulate social intercourse. The divisions define duties, they confer no privileges. It is, I hold against the genius of Hinduism to arrogate to oneself a higher status or assign to another a lower. All are born to serve God's creation, A Brahman with his knowledge, a Kshatriya with his power of protection, a Vaishya with his commercial ability, and a Shudra with bodily labour. This, however, does not mean that a Brahman, for instance, is absolved from bodily labour or the duty of protecting himself and others. His birth makes a Brahman predominantly a man of knowledge, the fittest by heredity and training to impart learning to others. There is nothing, again, to prevent the Shudra from acquiring all the knowledge he wishes. Only, he will best serve with his body and need not envy others their special qualities for service. But a Brahman who claims superiority by right of knowledge falls and has no knowledge. And so with the others who pride themselves upon their special qualities. Varnashrama is self-restraint and conservation and economy of energy.

Though, therefore, Varnashrama is not affected by inter-dining or inter-marriage, Hinduism does most emphatically discourage inter-dining and inter-marriage between divisions. Hinduism reached the highest limit of self-restraint. It is undoubtedly a religion of renunciation of the flesh so that the spirit may be set free. It is no part of a Hindu's duty to dine with his son. And by restricting his choice of a bride to a particular group, he exercises rare self-restraint. Hinduism does not regard a married state as by any means essential for salvation. Marriage is a fall even as birth is a fall. Salvation is freedom from birth and hence death also. Prohibition against inter-marriage and inter-dining is essential for a rapid evolution of the soul. But this self-denial is no test to Varna. A Brahman may remain a Brahman, though he may dine with his Shudra brother, if he has not left off his duty of service by knowledge. It follows from what I have said above that restraint in matters of marriage and dining is not based upon notions of superiority. A Hindu who refuses to dine with another from a sense of superiority misrepresents his Dharma.

Unfortunately today Hinduism seems to consist merely in eating and not eating. Once I horrified a pious Hindu by taking toast at a Mussalman's house. I saw that he was pained to see me pouring milk into a cup handed by a Mussalman friend, but his anguish knew no bounds when he saw me taking toast at the Mussalman's hands. Hinduism is in danger of losing its substance, if it resolves itself into a matter of elaborate rules as to what and with whom to eat. Abstemiousness from intoxicating drinks and drugs and from all kinds of foods, especially meat, is undoubtedly a great aid to the evolution of the spirit, but it is by no means an end in itself. Many a man eating meat and with everybody, but living in the fear of God, is nearer his freedom than a man religiously abstaining from meat and any other things, but blaspheming God in every one of his acts.

The central fact of Hinduism, however, is cow-protection. Cow-protection, to me, is one of the most wonderful phenomena in human evolution. It takes the human being beyond his species. The cow, to me, means the entire sub-human world. Man through the cow is enjoined to realize his identity with all that lives. Why the cow was selected for apotheosis is obvious to me. The cow was, in India, the best companion. She was the giver of plenty. Not only did she give milk, but she also made agriculture possible. The cow is a poem on pity. One reads pity in the gentle animal. She is the mother of millions of Indian mankind. Protection of the cow means protection of the whole dumb-creation of God. The ancient seer, Whoever he was, began with the cow. The appeal of the lower order of creation is the gift of Hinduism to the world. And Hinduism will live so long as there are Hindus to protect the cow.

I can no more describe my feeling for Hinduism than for my own wife. She moves me as no other woman in the world can. Not that she has no faults. I dare say she has many more than I see myself. But the feeling of an indissoluble bond is there. Even so I feel for and about Hinduism with all its faults and limitations. Nothing elates me so much as the music of the *Gita* or the *Ramayana* by Tulasidas, the only two books in Hinduism I may be said to know. When I fancied I was taking my last breath, the *Gita* was my solace. I know the vice that is going on today in all the Hindu shrines, but I love them in spite of their unspeakable failings. There is an interest which I take in them and which I take in no other. I am a reformer through and through. But my zeal never takes me to the rejection of any essential thing of Hinduism. I have said I do not disbelieve in idol worship. An idol does not excite any feeling of veneration in me. But I think that idol worship is part of human nature. We hanker after symbolism. Why should one be more composed in a church than elsewhere? Images are an aid to worship. No Hindu considers an image to be God. I do not consider idol worship a sin.

It is clear from the foregoing that Hinduism is not an exclusive religion. In it there is room for the worship of all the prophets of the world. It is not a missionary religion in the ordinary sense of the term. It has no doubt absorbed many tribes in its fold, but this absorption has been of evolutionary, inperceptible character. Hinduism tells everyone to worship God according to his own faith or Dharma, and so it lives at peace with all the religions.

That being my conception of Hinduism, I have never been able to reconcile myself to untouchability. I have always regarded it as an excrescence. It is true that it has been handed down to us from generations; but so are many evil practices even to this day. I should be ashamed to think that dedication of girls to virtual prostitution was a part of Hinduism. Yet it is practised by Hindus in many parts of India. I consider it positive irreligion to sacrifice goats to Kali and do not consider it a part of Hinduism. Hinduism is a growth of ages. The very name Hinduism, was given to the religion of the people of Hindusthan by foreigners. There was no doubt at one time that the sacrifice of animals was offered in the name of religion. But it is not religion, much less is it Hindu religion. And so also it seems to me, that when cow protection became an article of faith with our ancestors, those who persisted in eating beef were excommunicated. The civil strife must have been fierce. Social boycott was applied not only to the recalcitrants, but their sins were visited upon their children also. The practice which had probably its origin in good intentions hardened into usage and even verses crept into our sacred books giving the practice a permanence wholly undeserved and still less justified. Whether my theory is correct, or not, untouchability is repugnant to reason and to the instinct of mercy, pity or love. A religion that establishes the worship of the cow cannot possibly countenance or warrant a cruel and inhuman boycott of the human being. And I should be content to be torn to pieces rather than disown the suppressed classes. Hindus will certainly never deserve freedom nor get it, if they allow their noble religion to be disgraced by the retention of the taint of untouchability. And as I love Hinduism dearer than life itself, the taint has become for me an intolerable burden. Let us not deny God by denying to a fifth of our race the right of association on an equal footing.

(From *Young India,* October 6, 1921)

II

The Place of Jesus

For many years, I have regarded Jesus of Nazareth as one among the mighty teachers that the world has had, and I say this in all humility. I claim humility for this expression because this is exactly what I feel. Of course, Christians claim a higher place for Jesus of Nazareth than I, as a non-Christian and a Hindu, am able to feel. I purposely use the word "feel" instead of "give", because I consider that neither I nor anybody else can possibly arrogate to himself the claim of giving a place to a great man.

For the great teachers of mankind have not had their places given to them. That place has belonged to them as a matter of right, as a matter of service; but it is the privilege of the lowest and humblest amongst us to feel certain things about them. The relation between ourselves and the great teachers is somewhat after the style of the relation between wife and husband. It would be a terrible thing, a tragic thing, if I were to argue out intellectually for myself what place I was to give to the wife of my heart. It is not, indeed, a matter of my giving at all. She takes the place that belongs to her and a matter of right in my heart. It is a matter purely for feeling. Thus I can say that Jesus occupies in my heart the place of one of the great teachers who have made a considerable influence on my life.

I say to the seventy five per cent of Hindus receiving instruction in this college that your lives also will be incomplete unless you reverently study the teaching of Jesus. I have come to the conclusion in my own experience that those who, no matter to what faith they belong, reverently study the teaching of other faiths, broaden instead of narrowing their own hearts. Personally I do not regard any of the great religions of the world as false. All have served to enrich mankind, and are now even serving their purpose. A liberal education should include, as I have put it, a reverent study of all other faiths.

The message of Jesus is contained in the Sermon on the Mount, unadulterated and taken as a whole. Even in connection with the sermon on the Mount, my own humble interpretation of the message is in many respects different from the orthodox. When I was prematurely discharged from jail, C.F. Andrews, than whom I do not own on this earth a closer friend, showed me a letter addressed by the bishops to their flock. It may be presumptuous for me to say so, but I did not agree with their interpretation of Christ's words.

One's own religion is after all a matter between oneself and one's Maker. But if I feel impelled to share my thoughts with you, it is because I want to enlist your sympathy in my search for truth, and because so many Christian friends are deeply interested in my thoughts on the teachings of Jesus and wish to know what place I give to Jesus in my heart.

If, then, I had to face only the sermon on the Mount and my

own interpretation of it, I should not hesitate to say, "Oh, yes, I am a Christian." But I know that at the present moment, if I said any such thing, I would lay myself open to the gravest misinterpretation.

But negatively I can tell you that to my mind much of that which passes for Christianity is a negation of the Sermon on the Mount. Please mark my words carefully. I am not at the present moment speaking especially of Christianity as it is understood in the West. I am painfully aware of the fact that conduct everywhere falls far short of belief. Therefore I do not say this by way of criticism. I know from the treasures of my own experience that, although I am every moment of my life trying to live up to my professions, nevertheless my conduct falls short of these professions. Far therefore be it from me to say this in a spirit of criticism. But I am placing before you my fundamental difficulties with regard to the appearance of Christianity in the world and the formulation of Christian beliefs.

There is one thing which came forcibly to me in my early studies of the Bible. It seized me immediately when I read one passage. The text was this: "Seek ye first the kingdom of God and His righteousness, and all other things will be added unto you." I tell you that if you will understand, appreciate, and act up to the spirit of this passage then you will not even need to know what place Jesus, or any other teacher, occupies in your heart or my heart. If you will do this moral scavenger's work, so as to clean and purify your hearts and get them ready, you will find that all these mighty teachers will take their places without any invitation from us. That, to my mind, is the basis of all sound education. The culture of the mind must be subservient to the culture of the heart. May God help you to become pure!

When I began as a prayerful student to study Christian literature in South Africa in 1893, I asked myself again and again, "Is this Christianity?" And I could only say, "No, no.

Certainly this that I see is not Christianity." And the deepest in me tells me that I was right; for it was unworthy of Jesus and untrue to the sermon on the Mount.

I claim to be a man of faith and prayer, and even if I were to be cut to pieces, I trust God would give me the strength not to deny Him, but to assert that He is. The Mussalman says, "He is, and there is no one else." The Christian says the same thing, and so does the Hindu. If I may venture to say so, the Buddhist also says the same thing, only in different words. It is true that we may each of us be putting our own interpretation on the word "God". We must of necessity do so; for God embraces, not only this tiny globe of ours, but millions and billions of such globes and worlds beyond worlds. How can we, little crawling creatures, possibly measure His greatness, His boundless love, His infinite compassion? So great is His infinite love and pity that He allows man insolently to deny Him, to wrangle about Him, and even to cut the throat of his fellow-man!

Thus, though we may utter the same words about God. they may not bear the same meaning for us all. But what does that matter? We do not need to proselytize either by our speech or by our writing. We can only do so really with our lives. Let our lives be open books for all to study.

Would that I could persuade all my missionary friends to take this view of their mission! Then there would be no distrust, or suspicion, or jealousy, or dissension amongst us in these religious matters, but only harmony and peace.

Because of its Western, external appearance, we in India have come to distrust the Christian missionary endeavour that has reached us from the West.

The one deduction I would like you students to draw from all this is that you yourselves should not be torn from your moorings; and those from the West should not consciously or unconsciously lay violent hands upon the manners and customs of this country, in so far as they are not repugnant to fundamental morality. Do not confuse Jesus's teaching with what passes as modern civilization. I ask you who are missionaries, pray do not do unconscious violence to the people among whom you cast your lot. It is no part of your call, I assure, you, to tear up the lives of the people of the East by their roots. Tolerate whatever is good in them. As Christ said to us all: "Judge not, that ye be not judged. Forgive, and it shall be forgiven you. For with what measure ye mete, it shall be measured to you again."

In spite of your belief in the greatness of Western civilization, and in spite of your pride in all your achievements, I plead with you to exercise humility. I ask you to leave some room for honest doubt. Let us simply each one live our life: and if ours is the right life, where is the cause for hurry? It will react of itself.

By all means drink deep of the fountains that are given to you in the sermon on the Mount; but then you will have to take up sackcloth and ashes also with regard to failure to perform that which is taught in Christ's sermon, For the teaching of the sermon was meant for each and every one of us. You cannot serve both God and Mammon. God the compassionate and the merciful, who is tolerance incarnate, allows Mammon to have his nine days' wonder. But I say to you, students and youths, fly from that self-destroying but destructive show of Mammon which I see around me today. For you cannot, serve Mammon and God together.

(From an address to members of a college at Colombo. See
C.F. Andrews, *Mahatma Gandhis Ideas*, pp.92-7)

III

Among Evangelical Christians

Mr. Baker was getting anxious about my future. He took me to
the Wellington Convention. The Protestant Christians organize
such gatherings every few years for religious enlightenment, or
in other words, self-purification. One may call this religious
revival. The Wellington Convention was of this type. The
chairman was the famous divine, the Reverend Andrew
Murray. Mr. Baker had hoped that the atmosphere of religious
exaltation at the convention and the enthusiasm and
earnestness of the people attending it would inevitably lead me
to embrace Christianity.

But his final hope was the efficacy of prayer. He had an
abiding faith in prayer. It was his firm conviction that God
could not but listen to prayer fervently offered. He would cite
the instances of men like George Muller of Bristol, who
depended entirely on prayer even for his temporal needs. I
listened to his discourse on the efficacy of prayer with unbiased
attention, and assured him that nothing could prevent me from
embracing Christianity, should I feel the call. I had no
hesitation in giving him this assurance, as I had long since
taught myself to follow the inner voice. Therefore I delighted in
submitting myself to it. To act against it would be difficult and
painful to me.

So we went to Wellington. Mr. Baker was hard put to it in
having "a coloured man" like me for his companion. He had to
suffer inconveniences on many occasions entirely on account of
me. We had to break the journey on the way, as one of the days
happened to be a Sunday, and Mr. Baker and his party would
not travel on the sabbath. Though the manager of the station
hotel agreed to take me in after much altercation, he absolutely
refused to admit me to the dining-room. Mr. Baker was not the

man to give way easily. He stood by the rights of the guests of a hotel. But I could see his difficulty. At Wellington also I stayed with Mr. Baker. In spite of his best efforts to conceal the little inconveniences he was put to, I could see them all.

This convention was an assemblage of devout Christians. I was delighted at their faith. Here I met personally the Reverend Andrew Murray and saw that many were praying for me. Some of their hymns I liked; they were very sweet.

The convention lasted for three days, I could understand and appreciate the devoutness of those who attended it. But I saw no reason for changing my belief. It was impossible for me to believe that I could go to heaven or attain salvation only by becoming a Christian. When I frankly said so to some of the good Christian friends, they were shocked. But there was no help for it. My difficulties lay deeper. It was more than I could believe, that Jesus was the only incarnate son of God, and that only he who believed in him would have everlasting life. If God could have sons, all of us were his sons. If Jesus was like God, or God Himself, then all men were like God and could be God Himself. My reason was not ready to believe literally that Jesus by his death and his blood redeemed the sins of the world. Metaphorically, there might be some truth in it. Again, according to Christianity, only human beings had souls, and not other living beings, for whom death meant complete extinction; while I held a contrary belief. I could accept Jesus as a martyr, an embodiment of sacrifice, and a divine teacher, but not as the most perfect man ever born. His death on the cross was a great example to the world, but that there was anything like a mysterious or miraculous virtue in it my heart could not accept. The pious lives of Christians did not give me anything that the lives of men of other faiths had failed to give. I had seen in other lives just the same reformation that I heard of amongst Christians. Philosophically, there was nothing extraordinary in Christian principles. From the point of view of sacrifice, it seemed to me that the Hindus greatly surpassed the

Christians. It was impossible for me to regard Christianity as a perfect religion or the greatest of all religions.

(In South Africa about 1893. See C. F. Andrews, *Mahatma Gandhi* – His Own Story, pp. 139-41)

IV

Christianity and Hinduism

Not many of you know that my association with Christians – not Christians so-called but real Christians – dates from 1889, when as a lad I found myself in London; and that association has grown riper as years have rolled on. In South Africa, where I found myself in the midst of inhospitable surroundings, I was able to make hundreds of Christian friends. I came in touch with the late Mr. Spencer Walton, Director of the South Africa General Mission, and later with the great divine, the Rev Andrew Murray, and several others.

There was even a time in my life when a very sincere and intimate friend of mine, a great and good Quaker, had designs on me. He thought that I was too good not to become a Christian, I was sorry to have to disappoint him. One missionary friend of mine in South Africa still writes to me and asks me, "How is it with you?" I have always told him that so far as I know it is all well with me. If it was prayer that these friends expected me to make. I was able to tell them that every day the heartfelt prayer within the closed door of my closet went to the Almighty to show me light and give me wisdom and courage to follow that light.

In answer to promises made to one of these Christian friends of mine, I thought it my duty to see one of the biggest of Indian Christians, the late Kali Charan Bannerjee. I went to him with an absolutely open mind and in a receptive mood, and I met him also under circumstances which were most affecting. I found that there was much in common between Mr. Bannerjee and myself. His simplicity, his humility, his courage, his truthfulness – all these things I have all along admired. He met me when his wife was on her death-bed. You cannot imagine a more impressive scene, a more ennobling circumstance. I told Mr. Bannerjee: "I have come to you as a seeker" – this was in 1901 – "I have come to you in fulfilment of a sacred promise I have made to some of my dearest Christian friends that I will leave no stone unturned to find out the true light." I told him that I had given my friends the assurance that no worldly gain would keep me away from the light if I could but see it. Well, I am not going to engage you in giving a description of the little discussion that we had between us. It was very good, very noble. I came away, not sorry, not dejected, not disappointed, but I felt sad that even Mr. Bannerjee could not convince me. This was my final, deliberate striving to realize Christianity as it was presented to me.

Today my position is that, though I admire much in Christianity, I am unable to identify myself with orthodox Christianity. I must tell you in humility that Hinduism, as I know it, entirely satisfies my soul, fills my whole being, and I find a solace in the *Bhagavad Gita* and *Upanishads* that I miss even in the sermon on the Mount. Not that I do not prize the ideal presented therein; not that some of the precious teachings in the sermon on the Mount have not left a deep impression upon me; but I must confess to you that when doubt haunts me, when disappointments stare me in the face, and when I see not one ray of light on the horizon, I turn to the *Bhagavad Gita*, and find a verse to comfort me; and I immediately begin to smile in the midst of overwhelming sorrow. My life has been full of external tragedies, and if they have not left any visible and indelible effect on me, I owe it to the teachings of the *Bhagavad Gita*.

I have told you all these things in order to make absolutely clear to you where I stand, so that I may have, if you will, closer touch with you. I must add that I did not stop studying the Bible and the commentaries and other books on Christianity that my friends placed in my hands; but I said to myself that if I was to find my satisfaction through reasoning, I must study the scriptures of other religions also and make my choice. And I turned to the Koran. I tried to understand what I could of Judaism as distinguished from Christianity. I studied Zoroastrianism. And I came to the conclusion that all religions were right, and every one of them imperfect, because they were interpreted with our poor intellects, sometimes with our poor hearts, and more often misinterpreted. In all religions, I found to my grief that there were various and even contradictory interpretations of some texts, and I said to myself, "Not these things for me. If I want the satisfaction of my soul I must feel my way. I must wait silently upon God and ask Him to guide me." There is a beautiful verse in Sanskrit which says, "God helps only when man feels utterly helpless and utterly humble." When I was studying Tamil I found in one of the books of Dr. Pope, a Tamil, proverb which means, "God helps the helpless." I have given you this life-story of my own experience for you to ponder over.

You, the missionaries, come to India thinking that you come to a land of heathen, of idolaters, of men who do not know God. One of the greatest Christian divines, Bishop Heber, wrote two lines which have always left a sting with me: "Where every prospect pleases and only Man is vile." I wish he had not written them. My own experience in my travels throughout India has been to the contrary. I have gone from one end of the country to the other, without any prejudice, in a relentless search after Truth, and I am not able to say that here in this fair land, watered by the great Ganges, the Brahmaputra, and the Jumna, man is vile. He is not vile. He is as much a seeker after truth as you and I are, possibly more so.

This reminds me of a French book translated for me by a French friend. It is an account of an imaginary expedition in search of knowledge. One party landed in India and found Truth and God personified in a little pariah's hut. I tell you there are many such huts belonging to the "untouchables" where you will certainly find God. They do not reason, but they persist in their belief that God is. They depend upon God for His assistance and find it, too. There are many stories told throughout the length and breadth of India about these noble untouchables. Vile outwardly as some of them may be, there are noblest specimens of humanity in their midst. But does my experience exhaust itself merely with the untouchables? No, I am here to tell you that there are non-Brahmins today in India who are embodiments of self-sacrifice, godliness, and humanity. There are Brahmins who are devoting themselves body and soul to the service of untouchables, but with execration from orthodoxy. They do not mind it because in serving pariahs they are serving God.

I can quote chapter and verse from my experience. I place these facts before you in all humility for the simple reason that you may know this land better, the land which you have come to serve. You are here to find out the distress of the people of India and remove it. But I hope you are here also in receptive mood, and if there is anything that India has to give you, you will not stop your ears, you will not close your eyes and steel your hearts, to receive all that may be good in this land. I give you my assurance that there is a great deal of good in India.

Do not flatter yourselves with the belief that a mere recital of that celebrated verse in St. John makes a man a Christian. If I have read the Bible correctly, I know many men who have never known the name of Jesus Christ, men who have even rejected the official interpretation of Christianity, but would nevertheless, if Jesus came in our midst today in the flesh, be probably owned by him more than many of us. I therefore ask you to approach the problem before you with open-heartedness and humility.

It has often occurred to me that a seeker after truth has to be silent. I know the wonderful efficacy of silence, I visited a Trappist monastery in South Africa. A beautiful place it was. Most of the inmates of that place were under a vow of silence. I inquired of the Father the motive of it, and he said that the motive is apparent. We are frail human beings. We do not know very often what we say. If we want to listen to the still small voice that is always speaking within us, it will not be heard if we continually speak. I understand that precious lesson. I know the secret of silence.

I have told my missionary friends, "Noble as you are, you have isolated yourselves from the people whom you want to serve." I cannot help recalling to you the conversation I related in Darjeeling at the Missionary Language School. Lord Salisbury was waited upon by a deputation of missionaries in connection with China and this deputation wanted protection. I cannot recall the exact words, but give you the purport of the answer Lord Salisbury gave. He said: "Gentlemen, if you want to go to China to preach the message of Christianity, then do not ask for assistance of the temporal power. Go with your lives in your hands, and if the people of China want to kill you, imagine that you have been killed in service of God!" Lord Salisbury was right. Christian missionaries come to India under the shadow, or, if you like, under the protection of a temporal power, and it creates an impassable bar.

If you give me statistics that so many orphans have been reclaimed and brought to the Christian faith, I would accept them; but I do not feel convinced thereby that this is your mission. In my opinion, your mission is infinitely superior to that. You want to find true men and women in India; and if you want to do that, you will have to go to the lowly cottages – not to give them something, but it might be to take something from them. A true friend, as I claim to be of the missionaries of

India and of the Europeans, I speak to you what I feel from the bottom of my heart. I miss receptiveness, humility, willingness on your part to identify yourselves with the masses of India. I have talked straight from my heart. May I find a response from your hearts?

(Address delivered to the Christian missionaries assembled in Calcutta on July 28, 1925. See C. F. Andrews, *Mahatma Gandhis* Ideas, pp. 71-77.)

V

Ideals for the Ashram of Soul-force

No work done by any man, however great, will really prosper unless it has a distinct religious backing. But what is Religion? I for one would answer: "Not the Religion you will get after reading all the scriptures of the world. Religion is not really what is grasped by the brain, but a heart grasp."

Religion is a thing not alien to us. It has to be evolved out of us. It is always within us: with some, consciously so; with others, quite unconsciously. But it is always there. And whether we wake up this religious instinct in us through outside assistance or by inward growth, no matter how it is done, it has got to be done, if we want to do anything in the right manner, or to achieve anything that is going to persist.

Our Scriptures have laid down certain rules as maxims of human life. They tell us that without living according to these maxims, we are incapable of having a reasonable perception of Religion. Believing in these implicitly, I have deemed it necessary to seek the association of those who think with me in founding this institution. The following are the rules that have been drawn up and have to be observed by everyone who seeks to be a member.

The first and foremost is

The Vow of Truth

Not simply as we ordinarily understand it, not truth which merely answers the saying, "Honesty is the best policy," implying that if it is not the best policy we may depart from it. Here Truth, as it is conceived, means that we may have to rule our life by this law of Truth at any cost; and in order to satisfy the definition, I have drawn upon the celebrated illustration of the life of Prahlad.[39] For the sake of Truth, he dared to oppose his own father; and he defended himself, not by paying his father back in his own coin. Rather, in defence of Truth as he knew it, he was prepared to die without caring to return the blows that he had received from his father, or from those who were charged with his father's instructions. Not only that, he would not in any way even parry the blows; on the contrary, with a smile on his lips, he underwent the innumerable tortures to which he was subjected, with the result that, at last, Truth rose triumphant. Not that he suffered the tortures because he knew that some day or other in his very lifetime he would be able to demonstrate the infallibility of the Law of Truth. That fact was there; but if he had died in the midst of tortures he would still have adhered to Truth. That is the Truth which I would like to follow. In our Ashram, we make it a rule that we must say "No" when we mean No, regardless of consequences.

Then we come to the

Doctrine of Ahimsa

Literally speaking, Ahimsa means "non-killing." But to me, it

---

39 The story of the young boy Prahlad, who suffered for the truth's sake, is one of the most famous in ancient Indian literature. It is well known by every Indian child – just as the story of George Washington is famous in the West.

has a world of meaning, and takes me into realms much higher, infinitely higher. It really means that you may not offend anybody; you may not harbour an uncharitable thought, even in connection with one who may consider himself to be your enemy. To one who follows this doctrine, there is no room for an enemy. But there may be people who consider themselves to be his enemies, so it is held that we may not harbour an evil thought even in connection with such persons. If we return blow for blow we depart from the doctrine of Ahimsa. But I go farther. If we resent a friend's action, or the so-called enemy's action, we still fall short of this doctrine. But when I say we should not resent, I do not say that we should acquiesce; by the word "resenting" I mean wishing that some harm should be done to the enemy; or that he should be put out of the way, not even by any action of ours, but by the action of somebody else, or, say by divine agency. If we harbour even this thought we depart from this doctrine of non-violence. Those who join the Ashram have literally to accept that meaning.

This does not mean that we practise that doctrine in its entirety. Far from it. It is an ideal which we have to reach, and it is an ideal to be reached even at this very moment, if we are capable of doing so. But it is not a proposition in geometry; it is not even like solving difficult problems in higher mathematics – it is infinitely more difficult. Many of us have burnt the midnight oil in solving those problems. But if you want to follow out this doctrine, you will have to do much more than burn the midnight oil. You will have to pass many a sleepless night, and go through many a mental torture, before you can even be within measurable distance of this goal. It is the goal, and nothing less than that, which you and I have to reach, if we want to understand what a religious life means.

A man who believes in the efficacy of this doctrine finds in the ultimate stage, when he is about to reach the goal, the whole world at his feet. If you express your love-Ahimsa in such a manner that it impresses itself indelibly upon your so-called enemy, he must return that love. Under this rule, there is no room for organised assassinations, or for murders openly committed, or for any violence for the sake of your country or even for guarding the honour of precious ones that may be under your charge. After all that would be a poor defence of their honour. This doctrine tells us that we may guard the honour of those under our charge by delivering our own lives into the hands of the man who would commit the sacrilege. And that requires far greater courage than delivering of blows. If you do not retaliate, but stand your ground between your charge and the opponent, simply receiving blows without retaliating, what happens? I give you my promise that the whole of his violence will be expended on you, and your friend will be left unscathed. Under this plan of life, there is no conception of patriotism which justifies such wars as you witness today in Europe.

Then again there is

The Vow of Celibacy

Those who want to perform national service, or to have a gleam of the real religious life, must lead a celibate life whether married or unmarried. Marriage only brings a woman closer to man, and they become friends in a special sense, never to be parted either in this life or in the lives to come. But I do not think that, in our conception of marriage, our lusts should enter. Be that as it may, this is what is placed before those who come to the Ashram. I do not deal with it at any length.

Then we have, further,

The Vow of the Control of the palate

A man who wants to control his animal passions easily does so if he controls his palate. I fear this is one of the most difficult vows to follow. Unless we are prepared to rid ourselves of stimulating, heating, and exciting condiments, we shall certainly not be able to control the overabundant, unnecessary, and exciting stimulation of the animal passions. If we do not do that, we are likely to abuse the sacred trust of our bodies that has been given us, and to become less than animals and brutes, eating, drinking, and indulging in passions which we share with animals. But have you ever seen a horse or cow indulging in the abuse of the palate as we do? Do you suppose that it is a sign of civilization, a sign of real life, that we should multiply our eatables so far that we do not even know where we are; and seek dishes until at last we have become absolutely mad and run after the newspaper sheets which gives us advertisements about these dishes?

Then we have once more

The Vow of Non-Thieving

I suggest that we are thieves in a way. If I take anything that I do not need for my own immediate use and keep it, I thieve it from somebody else. It is the fundamental law of Nature, without exception, that Nature produces enough for our wants from day to day; and if only everybody took enough for himself and nothing more, there would be no pauperism in this world, there would be no man dying of starvation. I am no Socialist, and I do not want to dispossess those who have got possessions; but I do say that personally those of us who want to see light out of darkness have to follow this rule. I do not want to dispossess anybody; I should then be departing from the rule of Non-violence. If somebody else possesses more than I do, let him. But so far as my own life has to be regulated, I dare not possess anything which I do not want. In India we have got many millions of people who have to be satisfied with one meal a day, and that meal consisting of a Chapatti containing no fat in it and a pinch of salt. You and I have no right to anything that we really have until these many millions are clothed and fed. You and I, who ought to know better, must adjust our wants, and even undergo voluntary privation in order that they may be nursed, fed and clothed.

Then there is the "Vow of Non-Possession," which follows as a matter of course, and needs no further explanation at this point, where only a brief summary of various difficulties and their answer is being given.

Then I go to

The Vow of Swadeshi

The vow of Swadeshi is a necessary vow. We are departing from one of the sacred laws of our being when we leave our neighbourhood and go out somewhere else in order to satisfy our wants. If a man comes from Bombay and offers you wares, you are not justified in supporting the Bombay merchant so long as you have got a merchant at your very door, born and bred in Madras.

That is my view of Swadeshi. In your village, you are bound to support your village barber to the exclusion of the finished barber who may come to you from Madras. If you find it necessary that your village barber should reach the attainments of the barber from Madras, you may train him to that. Send him to Madras by all means, if you wish, in order that he may learn his calling. Until you do that, you are not justified in going to another barber. That is Swadeshi. So when we find that there are many things that we cannot get in India we must try to do without them. We may have to do without many things; but, believe me, when you have that frame of mind, you will find a great burden taken off your shoulders, even as the Pilgrim did in that inimitable book *Pilgrim's Progress*. There came a time when the mighty burden that the Pilgrim was carrying unconsciously dropped from him, and he felt a freer man than he was when he started on the journey. So will you feel freer men than you are now, if immediately you adopt this Swadeshi life.

We have also

The Vow of Fearlessness

I found, through my wanderings in India, that my country is seized with a paralysing fear. We may not open our lips in public: we may only talk about our opinions secretly. We may do anything we like within the four walls of our house; but those things are not for public consumption.

If we had taken a vow of silence I would have nothing to say. I suggest to you that there is only one whom we have to fear, that is God. When we fear God, then we shall fear no man, however high-placed he may be; and if you want to follow the vow of Truth, then fearlessness is absolutely necessary. Before we can aspire to guide the destinies of India we shall have to adopt this habit of fearlessness.

And then we have also

The Vow Regarding the "Untouchables"

There is an ineffaceable blot that Hinduism today carries with it. I have declined to believe that it has been handed down to us from immemorial times. I think that this miserable, wretched, enslaving spirit of "untouchableness" must have come to us when we were at our lowest ebb. This evil has stuck to us and still remains with us. It is, to my mind, a curse that has come to us; and as long as that curse remains with us, so long I think we are bound to consider that every affliction in this sacred land is a proper punishment for the indelible crime that we are committing. That any person should be considered untouchable because of his calling passes my comprehension; and you, the student world, who receive all this modern education, if you become a party to this crime, it were better that you received no education whatsoever.

Education through the Vernaculars

In Europe every cultured man learns, not only his own language, but also other languages.

In order to solve the problem of language in India, we in this Ashram must make it a point to learn as many Indian vernaculars as possible. The trouble of learning these languages is nothing compared to that of mastering English. How dare we rub off from our memory all the years of our infancy? But that is precisely what we do when we commence our higher life through the medium of a foreign tongue. This creates a breach for which we shall have to pay dearly. And you will see now the connection between this education and untouchability, this persistence of the latter in spite of the spread of knowledge and education. Education has enabled us to see the horrible crime, but we are seized with fear, and therefore we cannot take this doctrine to our homes.

The Vow of Khaddar[40]

You may ask, "Why should we use our hands?" You may say, "Manual work has got to be done by those who are illiterate. I can only occupy myself with reading literature and political essays." We have to realize the dignity of labour. If a barber or shoemaker attends a college, he ought not to abandon his profession. I consider that such professions are just as good as the profession of medicine.

Last of all, when you have conformed to these rules you may come to

---

40 Khaddar is home-spun and home-woven cloth. The vow Khaddar would be to spin with one's own hands and to wear nothing but home-spun garments.

The Religious use of Politics

Politics, divorced from religion, has absolutely no meaning. If the student would crowd the political platforms of this country, that is not necessarily a healthy sign of national growth; but this does not mean that you, in your student life, ought not to study politics. Politics are a part of our being; we ought to understand our national institutions. We may do this from our infancy. So, in our Ashram, every child is taught to understand the political institutions of our country and to know how the country is vibrating with new emotions, with new aspirations, with new life. But we want also the steady light, the infallible light of religious faith; not a faith which merely appeals to the intelligence, but a faith which is indelibly inscribed on the heart. First we want to realize our religious consciousness, and immediately we have done that, the whole department of life is open to us; and it should then be a sacred privilege of all, so that when young men grow to manhood, they may do so properly equipped to battle with life. Today what happens is this: much of the political life is confined to the students, but immediately they cease to be students, they sink into oblivion, seeking miserable employments, knowing nothing about God, nothing of fresh air or bright light, or of real vigorous independence, such as comes out of obedience to those laws that I have placed before you on this occasion.

(See C. F. Andrews, *op. cit.*, pp. 101-11.)

VI

"To Every Englishman" (1920)

DEAR FRIEND,

I wish that every Englishman may see this appeal, and give thoughtful attention to it.

Let me introduce myself to you. In my humble opinion, no
Indian has co-operated with the British Government more than
I have for an unbroken period of twenty-nine years of public
life in the face of circumstances that might well have turned any
other man into a rebel. I ask you to believe me when I tell you
that my co-operation was not based upon the fear of the
punishments provided by your laws or any other selfish
motives. It was free and voluntary co-operation, based on the
belief that the sum total of the British Government was for the
benefit of India. I put my life in peril four times for the sake of
the Empire: at the time of the Boer War, when I was in charge
of the Ambulance Corps whose work was mentioned in
General Buller's dispatches; at the time of the Zulu Revolt in
Natal, when I was in charge of a similar corps; at the time of
the commencement of the late war, when I raised an ambulance
corps, and as a result of the strenuous training had a severe
attack of pleurisy; and lastly in fulfilment of my promise to
Lord Chelmsford at the War Conference in Delhi, I threw
myself in such an active recruiting campaign in Khaira District,
involving long and trying marches, that I had an attack of
dysentery which proved almost fatal. I did all this in the full
belief that acts such as mine must gain for my country an equal
status in the Empire. So last December, I pleaded hard for a
trustful co-operation. I fully believed that Mr. Lloyd George
would redeem his promise to the Mussalmans, and that the
revelations of the official atrocities in the Punjab would secure
full reparation for the Punjabis. But the treachery of Mr. Lloyd
George and its appreciation by you, and the condonation of the
Punjab atrocities have completely shattered my faith in the
good intentions of the Government and the nation which is
supporting it.

But, though my faith in your good intentions is gone, I
recognize your bravery; and I know that what you will not
yield to justice and reason, you will gladly yield to bravery.

See what the British Empire means to India:

(1) Exploitation of India's resources for the benefit of Great Britain.

(2) An ever-increasing military expenditure and a Civil Service which is the most expensive in the world.

(3) Extravagant working of every Department in utter disregard of India's poverty.

(4) Disarmament and therefore emasculation of a whole nation lest an armed nation might imperil the lives of a handful of you in our midst.

(5) Traffic in intoxicating drugs and liquors for the purpose of maintaining a top-heavy administration.

(6) Progressively repressive legislation in order to suppress an ever-growing agitation seeking to express a nation's agony.

(7) Degrading treatment of Indians residing in British Dominions.

(8) Total disregard of our feelings by glorifying the Punjab Administration and flouting the Mohamedan sentiment.

I know you would not mind if we could fight and wrest the sceptre from your hands. You know we are powerless to do that; for you have ensured our incapacity to fight in open and honourable battle. Bravery on the battlefield is thus impossible for us. Bravery of the soul still remains open to us.

> (*see* C. F. Andrews, *op. cit.* pp. 239-41. A report of the Trial Speech below will be found in the same book)

VII

The Doctrine of the Sword (1920)

In this age of the rule of brute force, it is almost impossible for anyone to believe that anyone else could possibly reject the law of the final supremacy of brute force. And so I receive anonymous letters advising me that I must not interfere with the progress of non-co-operation, even though popular violence may break out. Others come to me and, assuming that secretly I must be plotting violence, inquire when the happy moment for declaring open violence is to arrive. They assure me that the English will never yield to anything but violence, secret or open. Yet others, I am informed, believe that I am the most rascally person living in India, because I never give out my real intention and that they have not a shadow of a doubt that I believe in violence just as much as most people do.

Such being the hold that the doctrine of the sword has on the majority of mankind, and as success of Non-co-operation depends principally on absence of violence during its pendency and as my views in this matter 'affect the conduct of a large number of people, I am anxious to state them as clearly as possible.

I do believe that, where there is only a choice between cowardice and violence, I would advise violence. Thus when my eldest son asked me what he should have done had he been present when I was almost fatally assaulted in 1908, whether he should have run away and seen me killed or whether he should have used his physical force which he could and wanted to use, and defended me, I told him that it was his duty to defend me even by using violence. Hence it was that I took part in the Boer War, the so called Zulu rebellion and the late war. Hence also do I advocate training in arms for those who believe in the method of violence. I would rather have India resort to arms in order to defend her honour than that she should, in a cowardly manner, become or remain a helpless witness to her own dishonour.

But I believe that non-violence is infinitely superior to violence, forgiveness is more manly than punishment (*ksama virasya bhusanam*). Forgiveness adorns a soldier. But abstinence is forgiveness only when there is the power to punish; it is meaningless when it pretends to proceed from a helpless creature. A mouse hardly forgives a cat when it allows itself to be torn to pieces by her. I therefore appreciate the sentiment of those who cry out for the punishment of General Dyer and his ilk. They would tear him to pieces if they could. But I do not believe India to be helpless. I do not believe myself to be a helpless creature. Only I want to use India's and my strength for a better purpose.

Let me not be misunderstood. Strength does not come from physical capacity. It comes from an indomitable will. An average Zulu is any way more than a match for an average Englishman in bodily capacity. But he flees from an English boy, because he fears the boy's revolver or those who will use it for him. He fears death and is nerveless in spite of his burly figure. We in India may in a moment realize that one hundred thousand Englishmen need not frighten three hundred million human beings. A definite forgiveness would therefore mean a definite recognition of our strength. With enlightened forgiveness must come a mighty wave of strength in us, which would make it impossible for a Dyer and a Frank Johnson to heap affront upon India's devoted head. It matters little to me that for the moment I do not drive my point home. We feel too down-trodden not to be angry and revengeful. But I must refrain from saying that India can gain more by waiving the right of punishment. We have better work to do, a better mission to deliver to the world.

I am not a visionary. I claim to be a practical idealist. The religion of non-violence is not meant merely for the Rishis and saints. It is meant for the common people as well. Non-violence is the law of our species as violence is the law of the brute. The spirit lies dormant in the brute and he knows no law but that of physical might. The dignity of man requires obedience to a higher law to the strength of the spirit.

I have therefore ventured to place before India the ancient law of self-sacrifice. For Satyagraha and its off-shoots, non-co-operation and civil resistance are nothing but new names for the law of suffering. The Rishis who discovered the law of non-violence in the midst of violence, were greater geniuses than Newton. They were themselves greater warriors than Wellington. Having themselves known the use of arms, they realized their uselessness and taught a weary world that its salvation lay not through violence but through non-violence.

Non-violence in its dynamic condition means conscious suffering. It does not mean meek submission to the will of the evil-doer, but it means the putting of one's whole soul against the will of the tyrant. Working under this law of our being, it is possible for a single individual to defy the whole might of an unjust empire to save his honour, his religion, his soul and lay the foundation for that empire's fall or its regeneration.

And so I am not pleading for India to practise non-violence, because it is weak. I want her to practise non-violence being conscious of her strength and power. No training in arms is required for realization of her strength. We seem to need it, because we seem to think that we are but a lump of flesh. I want India to recognize that she has a soul that cannot perish and that can rise triumphant above every physical weakness and defy the physical combination of a whole world. What is the meaning of Rama, a mere human being, with his host of monkeys, pitting himself against the insolent strength of ten-headed Ravan surrounded in supposed safety by the raging waters on all sides of Lanka? Does it not mean the conquest of physical might by spiritual strength? However, being a practical man, I do not wait till India recognizes the practicability of the spiritual life in the political world. India considers herself to be powerless and paralysed before the machine guns, the tanks and the aeroplanes of the English. And she takes up non-co-operation out of her weakness. It must still serve the same purpose, namely, bring her delivery from the crushing weight of British injustice, if a sufficient number of people practise it.

I isolate this non-co-operation from Sinn Feinism, for it is so conceived as to be incapable of being offered side by side with violence. But I invite even the school of violence to give this peaceful non-co-operation a trial. It will not fail through its inherent weakness. It may fail because of poverty of response. Then will be the time for real danger. The high-souled men, who are unable to suffer national humiliation any longer, will want to vent their wrath. They will take to violence. So far as I know, they must perish without delivering themselves or their country from the wrong. If India takes up the doctrine of the sword, she may gain momentary victory. Then India will cease to be the pride of my heart. I am wedded to India, because I owe my all to her. I believe absolutely that she has a mission for the world. She is not to copy Europe blindly. India's acceptance of the doctrine of the sword will be the hour of my trial. I hope I shall not be found wanting. My religion has no geographical limits. If I have a living faith in it, it will transcend my love for India herself. My life is dedicated to the service of India through the religion of non-violence, which I believe to be the root of Hinduism.

VIII

The Trial Speech (1922)

Before I read this statement, I would like to state that I entirely

endorse the learned Advocate-General's remarks in connection
with my humble self. It is the most painful duty with me, but I
have to discharge that duty knowing the responsibility that
rests upon my shoulders and I wish to endorse all the blame
that the learned Advocate-General has thrown on my shoulders
in connection with the Bombay, Madras and Chauri Chaura
occurrences. Thinking over these deeply and sleeping over
them, night after night, it is impossible for me to dissociate
myself from the diabolical crimes of Chauri Chaura, or the mad
outrages of Bombay. He is quite right when he says that, as a
man of responsibility, a man having received a fair share of
education, having had a fair share of experience of this world, I
should have known the consequences of every one of my acts. I
know that I was playing with fire. I ran the risk, and if I was
set free, I would still do the same. I have felt it this morning
that I would have failed in my duty, if I did not say what I said
here just now.

I wanted to avoid violence; I want to avoid violence. Non-
Violence is the first article of my faith. It is also the last article
of my creed. But I had to make my choice. I had either to
submit to a system which I considered had done an irreparable
harm to my country, or incur the risk of the mad fury of my
people bursting forth, when they understood the truth from my
lips. I know that my people have sometimes gone mad. I am
deeply sorry for it, and I am therefore here to submit, not to a
light penalty, but to the highest penalty. I do not ask for mercy.
I do not plead any extenuating act. I am here therefore, to
invite and cheerfully submit to the highest penalty that can be
inflicted upon me for what in law is a deliberate crime, and
what appears to me to be the highest duty of a citizen. The only
course open to you, the Judge, is as I am just going to say in my
statement, either to resign your post or inflict on me the
severest penalty, if you believe that the system and law you are
assisting to administer are good for the people. I do not expect
that kind of conversion but by the time I have finished with my

statement, you will perhaps have a glimpse of what is raging within my breast to run this maddest risk which a sane man can run.

I owe it, perhaps, to the Indian public and to the public in England that I should explain why from a staunch Loyalist and co-operator I have become an uncompromising, disaffectionist and non-co-operator. To the Court, too I should say why I plead guilty to the charge of promoting disaffection towards the Government established by law in India.

My public life began in 1893, in South Africa, in troubled weather. My first contact with British authority in that country was not of a happy character. I discovered that as a man and an Indian I had no rights. More correctly, I discovered that I had no rights as a man, because I was an Indian.

But I was not baffled. I thought that this treatment of Indians was an excrescence upon a system that was intrinsically and mainly good. I gave the Government my voluntary and hearty co-operation, criticizing it freely where I felt it was faulty, but never wishing its destruction.

Consequently, when the existence of the Empire was threatened in 1899 by the Boer challenge, I offered my services to it, raised a volunteer ambulance corps, and served at several actions that took place for the relief of Ladysmith. Similarly in 1906, at the time of the Zulu revolt, I raised a stretcher-bearing party and served till the end of the "rebellion." On both these occasions I received medals, and was even mentioned in dispatches. For my work in South Africa I was given by Lord Hardinge a Kaiser-i-Hind Gold Medal. When the war broke out in 1914 between England and Germany, I raised a volunteer ambulance corps in London, consisting of the then resident Indians in London, chiefly students. Its work was acknowledged by the authorities to be valuable. Lastly, in India, when a special appeal was made at the War Conference in Delhi in 1918 by Lord Chelmsford for recruits, I struggled at the cost of my health to raise a corps in Khaira, and the response was being made when the hostilities ceased and orders were received that no more recruits were wanted. In all these efforts at service, I was actuated by the belief that it was possible by such service to gain a status of full equality in the Empire for my countrymen.

The first shock came in the shape of the Rowlatt Act, a law designed to rob the people of all real freedom. I felt called upon to lead an intensive agitation against it. Then followed the Punjab horrors, beginning with the massacre at Jallianwalla Bagh and culminating in crawling orders, public floggings, and other indescribable humiliations. I discovered, too, that the plighted word of the Prime Minister to the Mussalmans of India, regarding the integrity of Turkey and the holy places of Islam, was not likely to be fulfilled. But in spite of forebodings and the grave warnings of friends, at the Amritsar Congress in 1919, I fought for co-operation and for working the Montagu-Chelmsford reforms, hoping that the Prime Minister would redeem his promise to the Indian Mussalmans, that the Punjab wound would be healed and that the reforms, inadequate and unsatisfactory though they were, marked a new era of hope in the life of India.

But all that hope was shattered. The Khilafat promise was not to be redeemed. The Punjab crime was white-washed; and most of the culprits not only went unpunished, but remained in service, continued to draw pensions from the Indian revenues, and in some cases were even rewarded; I saw, too that not only did the reforms not mark a change of heart, but they were only a method of further draining India of her wealth and of prolonging her servitude.

I came reluctantly to the conclusion that the British connection had made India more helpless than she ever was before, politically and economically. A disarmed India has no power of resistance against any aggressor if she wanted to engage in an armed conflict with him. So much is this the case that some of our best men consider that India must take generations before she can achieve the Dominion status. She has become so poor that she has little power of resisting famines.

Before the British advent, India spun and wove, in her millions of cottages, just the supplement she needed for adding to her meagre agricultural resources. This cottage industry, so vital for India's existence, has been ruined by incredibly heartless and inhuman processes, as described by English witnesses.

Little do town dwellers know how the semi starved masses of India are slowly sinking of lifelessness. Little do they know that their miserable comfort represents the brokerage they get for the work they do for the foreign exploiter, that the profits and the brokerage are sucked from the masses. Little do they realize that the Government established by law in British India is carried on for this exploitation of the masses. No sophistry, no jugglery in figures, can explain away the evidence that the skeletons in many villages present to the naked eye. I have no doubt whatsoever that both England and the town dwellers of India will have to answer, if there is a God above, for this crime against humanity which is perhaps unequalled in history.

The law itself in this country has been used to serve the foreign exploiter. My unbiased examination of the Punjab Martial Law cases has led me to believe that at least ninety-five per cent of convictions were wholly bad. My experience of political cases in India leads me to the conclusion that in nine out of every ten cases, the condemned men were totally innocent. Their crime consisted in their love of their country. In ninety-nine cases out of a hundred, justice has been denied to Indians as against Europeans in the courts of India.

This is not an exaggerated picture. It is the experience of almost every Indian who has had anything to do with such cases. In my opinion, the administration of the law is thus prostituted, consciously or unconsciously, for the benefit of the exploiter.

The greater misfortune is that the Englishman and their Indian associates in the administration of the country do not know that they are engaged in the crime I have attempted to describe. I am satisfied that many Englishmen and Indian officials honestly believe that they are administering one of the best systems devised in the world, and that India is making steady, though slow, progress. They do not know that a subtle but effective system of terrorism, together with an organized display of force on the one hand, and the deprivation of all powers of retaliation or self-defence on the other, have emasculated the people and induced in them the habit of simulation. This awful habit has added to the ignorance and the self-deception of the administrators.

Section 124, A, under which I am happily charged, is perhaps the prince among the political sections of the Indian Penal Code designed to suppress the liberty of the citizen. Affection cannot be manufactured or regulated by law. If one has no affection for a person or system, one should be free to give the fullest expression to his disaffection, so long as he does not contemplate, promote, or incite to violence. But the section under which Mr. Banker and I are charged is one under which mere promotion of disaffection is a crime. I have studied some of the cases tried under it, and I know that some of the most loved of India's patriots have been convicted under it. I consider it a privilege, therefore, to be charged under that section.

I have endeavoured to give in their briefest outline the reasons for my disaffection. I have no personal ill will against any single administrator, much less can I have any disaffection towards the King's person. But I hold it to be a virtue to be disaffected towards a Government, which in its totality, has done more harm to India than any previous system. India is less manly under the British rule than she ever was before. Holding such a belief, I consider it to be a sin to have affection for the system. And it has been a precious privilege for me to be able to write what I have in various articles rendered in evidence against me.

In fact, I believe that I have rendered a service to India and England by showing in non-co-operation the way out of the unnatural state in which both are living. In my humble opinion, non-co-operation with evil is as much a duty as is co-operation with good. But in the past, non-cooperation has been deliberately expressed in violence to the evildoer. I am endeavouring to show to my countrymen that violent non-co-operation only multiplies evil and that, evil can only be sustained by violence. Withdrawal of support of evil requires complete abstention from violence.

Non-violence implies voluntary submission to the penalty for non-co-operation with evil. I am here, therefore, to invite and submit cheerfully to the highest penalty that can be inflicted upon me for what in law is a deliberate crime, and what appears to me to be the highest duty of a citizen. The only course open to you, the Judge, is either to resign your post and thus dissociate your self from evil if you feel that the law you are called upon to administer is an evil and that in reality I am innocent; or to inflict on me the severest penalty, if you believe that the system and law you are assisting to administer are good for the people of this country, and that my activity is therefore injurious to the common weal.

IX

Speech at the London Round Table Conference (1931)

Prime Minister and Friends, I wish that I could have done without having to speak to you, but I felt that I would not have been just to you or just to my principles if I did not put in what may be the last word on behalf of the Congress. I live under no illusion. I do not think that anything that I can say this evening can possibly influence the decision of the Cabinet. Probably the decision has been already taken. Matters of the liberty of practically a whole continent can hardly be decided by mere argumentation, even negotiation. Negotiation has its purpose and has its play, but only under certain conditions. Without those conditions, negotiations are a fruitless task.

The Congress represents the spirit of rebellion. I know that the word "rebellion" must not be whispered at a Conference which has been summoned in order to arrive at an agreed solution of India's troubles through negotiation. Speaker after speaker has got up and said that India should achieve her liberty through negotiation, by argument, and that it will be the greatest glory of Great Britain if Great Britain yields to India's demands by argument. But the Congress does not hold that view quite. The Congress has an alternative which is unpleasant to you.

I heard several speakers and let me say I have endeavoured not to miss a single sitting: I have tried to follow every speaker with the utmost attention and with all the respect that I could possibly give to these speakers saying what a dire calamity it would be if India was fired with the spirit of lawlessness, rebellion, terrorism and so on. I do not pretend to have read history, but as a schoolboy I had to pass a paper in history also, and I read that the page of history is soiled red with the blood of those who have fought for freedom. I do not know an instance in which nations have attained their own without having to go through an incredible measure of travail. The dagger of the assassin, the poison bowl, the bullet of the rifleman, the spear and all these weapons and methods of destruction have been up to now used by what I consider blind lovers of liberty and freedom, and the historian has not condemned him. I hold no brief for the terrorists.

I have mentioned these things to show that for the sake of liberty people have fought, people have lost their lives, people have killed and have sought death at the hands of those whom they have sought to oust. The Congress devises a new method not known to history, namely, that of civil disobedience, and the Congress has been following that method up. But again I am up against a stone wall and I am told that that is a method that no government in the world will tolerate. Well, of course, the governments may not tolerate, no government has tolerated open rebellion. No government may tolerate civil disobedience, but governments have to succumb even to these forces, as the British Government has done before now, even as the great Dutch Government after eight years of trial had to yield to the logic of facts. General Smuts is a brave General, a great statesman and a very hard taskmaster also, but he himself recoiled with horror from even the contemplation of doing to death innocent men and women who were merely fighting for the preservation of their self-respect, and the things which he had vowed he would never yield to, in the year 1908, reinforced as he was by General Botha, he had to do in the year 1914 after having tried these civil resisters through and through. And in India, Lord Chelmsford had to do the same thing; the Governor of Bombay had to do the same thing at Borsad and Bardoli. I suggest to you, Prime Minister, it is too late today to resist this, and it is this thing which weighs me down, this choice that lies before them, the parting of the ways probably. I shall hope against hope, I shall strain every nerve to achieve an honourable settlement for my country, if I can do so without having to put the millions of my countrymen and countrywomen and even children through this ordeal of fire. It can be a matter of no joy and comfort to me to lead them on again to a fight of that character, but if a further ordeal of fire has to be our lot, I shall approach that with the greatest joy and with the greatest consolation that I was doing what I felt to be right, the country was doing what it felt to be right; and the country will have the additional satisfaction of knowing that it was not at least taking lives, it was giving lives; it was not making the British people directly suffer, it was suffering.

Whilst there is yet a little sand left in the glass, I want you to understand what this Congress stands for. My life is at your disposal. The lives of all the members of the Working Committee, the All India Congress Committee, are at your disposal. But remember, that you have at your disposal the lives of all these dumb millions. I do not want to sacrifice those lives if I can possibly help it. Therefore please remember that I will count no sacrifice too great if by chanee I can pull through an honourable settlement, you will find me always having the greatest spirit of compromise, if I can but fire you with the spirit that is working in the Congress, namely, that India must have real liberty. Call it by any name you like: a rose will smell as sweet by any other name, but it must be the rose of liberty that I want and not the artificial product. If your mind and the Congress mind, the mind of this conference and the mind of the British people, mean the same thing by the same word, then you will find the amplest room for compromise, and you will find the Congress itself always in a compromising spirit. But so long as there is not that one mind, that one definition; not one implication for the same word that you and I and we may be using, so long there is no compromise possible. How can there be any compromise as long as we each one of us has a different definition for the same words that we may be using? It is impossible, Prime Minister. I want to suggest to you, in all humility, that it is utterly impossible then to find a meeting ground. To find a ground where you can apply the spirit of compromise. And I am very grieved to have to say that up to now I have not been able to discover a common definition for the terms that we have been exchanging during all these weary weeks.

I was shown last week the Statute of Westminister by a sceptic, and he said: "Have you seen the definition of

'Dominion'?" I read the definition of "Dominion," and naturally I was not at all perplexed or shocked to see that the word "Dominion" was exhaustively defined, and it had not a general definition but a particular definition. It simply said: the word "Dominion" shall include Australia, South Africa, Canada and so on, ending with the Irish Free State. I do not think I noticed Egypt there. Then he said: "Do you see what your Dominion means?" It did not make any impression upon me. I do not mind what my Dominion means or what complete independence means. In a way, I was relieved. I said I am now relieved from having to quarrel about the word "Dominion," because I am out of it. But I want complete independence, and even so, so many Englishmen have said: "Yes you can have complete independence, but what is the meaning of complete independence?" and again we come to different definitions. Therefore, I say the Congress claim is registered as complete independence.

One of your great statesmen, I do not think I should give his name, was debating with me, and he said: "Honestly, I did not know that you meant this by complete independence." He ought to have known, but he did not know, and I shall tell you what he did not know. When I said to him, "I cannot be a partner in an Empire," he said, "Of course, that is logical." I said, "But I want to become that. It is not as if I shall be if I am compelled to, but I want to become a partner with Great Britain. I want to become a partner with the English people; but I want to enjoy precisely the same liberty that your people enjoy, and I want to seek this partnership not merely for the benefit of India and not merely for mutual benefit; I want to seek this partnership in order that the great weight that is crushing the world to atoms may be lifted from its shoulders."

This took place ten or twelve days ago. Strange as it may appear, I got a note from another Englishman whom also you know and whom also you respect. Among many things, he writes: "I believe profoundly that the peace and happiness of mankind depend on our friendship," and as if I would not understand that, he says, "your people and mine." I must read to you what he also says. "And of all Indians you are the one that the real Englishman likes and understands."

He does not waste any words on flattery, and I do not think he has intended this last expression to flatter me. It will not flatter me in the slightest degree. There are many things in this note which, if I could share them with you, would perhaps make you understand better the significance of this expression, but let me tell you that when he writes this last sentence he does not mean me personally. I personally signify nothing, and I know I would mean nothing to any single Englishman; but I mean something to some Englishmen because I represent a cause, because I seek to represent a nation, a great organization which has made itself felt. That is the reason why he says this.

But then, if I could possibly find that working basis, Prime Minister, there is ample room for compromise. It is friendship I crave. My business is not to throw overboard the slave holder and tyrant. My philosophy forbids me to do so, and today, the Congress has accepted that philosophy not as a creed, as it is to me, but as a policy, because the Congress believes that it is the right and best thing for India, a nation of 350 millions to do. A nation of 350 million people does not need the dagger of the assassin, it does not need the poison bowl, it does not need the sword the spear or the bullet. It needs simply a will of its own, an ability to say "No", and that nation is today learning to say "No".

But what is it that that nation does? Summarily, or at all to dismiss Englishmen? No. Its mission is today to convert Englishmen. I do not want to break the bond between England and India, but I do want to transform that bond. I want to transform that slavery into complete freedom for my country. Call it complete independence or whatever you like, I will not quarrel about that word, and even though my countrymen may dispute with me for having taken some other word, I shall be able to bear down that opposition so long as the content of the word that you may suggest to me bears the same meaning. Hence, I have times without number to urge upon your attention that the safeguards that have been suggested are completely unsatisfactory. They are not in the interests of India.

Three experts from the Federation of Commerce and Industry have in their own manner, each in his different manner, told you out of their expert experience how utterly impossible it is for any body of responsible Ministers to tackle the problem of administration when eighty percent of India's resources are mortgaged irretrievably. Better than I could have shown to you they have shown, out of the amplitude of their knowledge, what these financial safeguards mean for India. They mean the complete cramping of India. They have discussed at this table financial safeguards, but that includes necessarily the question of Defence and the question of the Army. Yet, while I say that the safeguards are unsatisfactory, as they have been presented, I have not hesitated to say, and I do not hesitate to repeat, that the Congress is pledged to giving safeguards, endorsing safeguards which may be demonstrated to be in the interests of India.

At one of the sittings of the Federal Structure Committee, I had no hesitation in amplifying the admission and saying that these safeguards must be also of benefit to Great Britain. I do not want safeguards which are merely beneficial to India and prejudicial to the real interests of Great Britain. The fancied interests of India will have to be sacrificed. The illegitimate interests of Great Britain will also have to be sacrificed.

I will not be baffled. I shall be here as long as I am required because I do not want to revive civil disobedience. I want to turn the truce that was arrived at, at Delhi, into a permanent settlement. But for heaven's sake give me, a frail man, sixty two years gone, a little bit of a chance. Find a little corner for him and the organization that he represents. You distrust that organization though you may seemingly trust me. Do not for one moment differentiate me from the organization of which I am but a drop in the ocean. I am no greater than the organization to which I belong. I am infinitely smaller than that organization; and if you find me a place, if you trust me, I invite you to trust the Congress also. Your trust in me otherwise is a broken reed. I have no authority save what I derived from the Congress. If you will work the Congress for all it is worth then you will say goodbye to terrorism; then you will not need terrorism. Today you have to fight the school of terrorists which is there with your disciplined and organized terrorism, because you will be blind to the facts or the writing on the wall. Will you not see the writing that these terrorists are writing with their blood? Will you not see that we do not want bread made of wheat, but we want bread of liberty; and without that liberty there are thousands today who are sworn not to give themselves peace or to give the country peace.

I urge you then to read that writing on the wall. I ask you not to try the patience of a people known to be proverbially patient. We speak of the mild Hindu, and the Mussalman also by contact, good or evil, with the Hindu has himself become mild. And that mention of the Mussalman brings me to the baffling problem of minorities. Believe me, that problem exists here, and I repeat what I used to say in India I have not forgotten those words that without the problem of minorities being solved there is no Swaraj for India, there is no freedom for India. I know that; I realize it; and yet I came here in the hope perchance, that I might be able to pull through a solution here. But I do not despair of some day or other finding a real and living solution in connection with the minority's problem. I repeat what I have said elsewhere, that so long as the wedge in the shape of foreign rule divides community from community and class from class, there will be no real living solution, there will be no living friendship between these communities. It will be after all and at best a paper solution. But immediately you withdraw that wedge the domestic ties, the domestic affections, the knowledge of common birth do you suppose that all these will count for nothing?

Were Hindus and Mussalmans and Sikhs always at war with one another when there was no British rule, when there was no English face seen there? We have chapter and verse given to us by Hindu historians and by Mussalman Historians to say that we were living in comparative peace even then.

This quarrel is not old; this quarrel is coeval with this acute shame. I dare to say it is coeval with the British advent, and immediately this relationship, the unfortunate, artificial, unnatural relationship between Great Britain and India is transformed into a natural relationship, when it becomes, if it does become, a voluntary partnership to be given up, to be dissolved at the will of either party, when it becomes that, you will find that Hindus, Mussalmans, Sikhs, Europeans, Anglo-Indians, Christians, Untouchables, will all live together as one man.

I want to say one word about the Princes, and I shall have done. I have not said much about the Princes, nor do I intend to say much tonight about the Princes, but I should be wronging them, and I should be wronging the Congress if I did not register my claim, not with the Round Table Conference, but with the Princes. It is open to the Princes to give their terms on which they will join the Federation. I have appealed to them to make the path easy for those who inhabit the other part of India, and therefore I can only make these suggestions for their favourable consideration, for their earnest consideration. I think that if they accepted, no matter what they are, but some fundamental rights as the common property of all India, and if they accepted that position and allowed those rights to be tested by the court, which will again be of their own creation, and if they introduced elements only elements of representation

on behalf of their subjects, I think that they would have gone a
long way to conciliate their subjects. They would have gone a
long way to show to the world and to show to the whole of
India that they are also fired with a democratic spirit, that they
want to become constitutional monarchs even as King George
of Great Britain is.

Sir, a note has been placed in my hands by my friend, Sir
Abdul Qaiyum, and he says, will not I say one word about the
Frontier Province? I will, and it is this. Let India get what she is
entitled to and what she can really take, but whatever she gets,
whenever she gets it, let the Frontier Province get complete
autonomy today. That Frontier will then be a standing
demonstration to the whole of India, and therefore the whole
vote of the Congress will be given in favour of the Frontier
Province getting Provincial autonomy tomorrow. Prime
Minister, if you can possibly get your Cabinet to endorse the
proposition that from tomorrow, the Frontier Province becomes
a fullfledged autonomous Province, I shall then have a proper
footing amongst the Frontier tribes and convene them to my
assistance when those over the border cast an evil eye on India.

Last of all, my last is a pleasant task for me. This is, perhaps,
the last time that I shall be sitting with you at negotiations. It is
not that I want that. I want to sit at the same table with you in
your closets and to negotiate and to plead with you and to go
down on bended knee before I take the final leap and final
plunge. But whether I have the good fortune to continue to
tender my co-operation or not does not depend upon me. It
largely depends upon you. But it may not even depend upon
you. It depends upon so many circumstances over which
neither you nor we may have any control whatsoever. Then let
me perform this pleasant task of giving my thanks to all, from
their Majesties down to the poorest men in the East End, where
I have taken up my habitation.

In that settlement, which represents the poor people of the

East End of London, I have become one of them. They have accepted me as a member, and as a favoured member of their family. It will be one of the richest treasures that I shall carry with me. Here, too, I have found nothing but courtesy and nothing but a genuine affection from all those whom I have come in touch. I have come in touch with so many Englishmen. It has been a priceless privilege to me. They have listened to what must have often appeared to them to be unpleasant, although it was true. Although I have often been obliged to say these things to them they have never shown the slightest impatience or irritation. It is impossible for me to forget these things. No matter what befalls me, no matter what the fortunes may be of this Round Table Conference, one thing I shall certainly carry with me – that is, that from high to low I have found nothing but the utmost courtesy and the utmost affection. I consider it was well worth my paying this visit to England in order to find this human affection. It has enhanced, it has deepened my irrepressible faith in human nature that although Englishmen and Englishwomen have been fed upon the lies that I so often see disfiguring your Press, that although in Lancashire, the Lancashire people had perhaps some reason for becoming irritated against me, I found no irritation and no resentment even in the operatives. The operatives men and women, hugged me. They treated me as one of their own. I shall never forget that.

I am carrying with me thousands upon thousands of English friendships. I do not know them, but I read that affection in their eyes, as early in the morning I walk through your streets. All this hospitality, all this kindness will never be effaced from my memory, no matter what befalls my unhappy land. I thank you for your forbearance.

(*Indian Round Table Conference Proceeding*, 1932, H. M. Stationery Office, pp. 389-99, abbreviated.)

X

On God (1931)

There is an indefinable mysterious Power that pervades everything. I feel it, though I do not see it. It is this unseen Power which makes itself felt and yet defies all proof, because it is so unlike all that I perceive through my senses. It transcends the senses. But it is possible to reason out the existence of God to a limited extent.

Even in ordinary affairs, we know that people do not know who rules or why and how he rules; and yet they know that there is a power that certainly rules. In my tour last year in Mysore, I met many poor villagers, and I found upon inquiry that they did not know who ruled Mysore; they simply said some god ruled it. If the knowledge of these poor people was so limited about their ruler, I who am infinitely lesser in respect to God than they to their ruler need not be surprised if I do not realize the presence of God, the King of kings.

Nevertheless I do feel, as the poor villagers felt about Mysore, that there is orderliness in the universe; there is an unalterable Law governing everything and every being that exists or lives. It is not a blind law; for no blind law can govern the conduct of living beings; and thanks to the marvellous researches of Sir J. C. Bose, it can now be proved that even matter is life.

That Law, then, which governs all life, is God. Law and Law-giver are one. I may not deny the Law or the Law-giver because I know so little about it or him. Just as my denial or ignorance of the existence of an earthly power will avail me nothing, even so my denial of God and His law will not liberate me from its operation; whereas humble and mute acceptance of divine authority makes life's journey easier even as the acceptance of earthly rule makes life under it easier.

I do dimly perceive that whilst everything around me is ever changing, ever dying there is underlying all that change a Living Power that is changeless, that holds all together, that creates, dissolves, and recreates. That informing Power or Spirit is God; and since nothing else that I see merely through the senses can or will persist, He alone is.

And is this power benevolent or malevolent? I see it as purely benevolent. For I can see that in the midst of death, life persists; in the midst of untruth, truth persists; in the midst of darkness, light persists. Hence I gather that God is Life, Truth, Light. He is Love. He is the supreme Good.

But He is no God who merely satisfies the intellect, if He ever does. God, to be God, must rule the heart and transform it. He must express Himself in every smallest act of His votary. This can only be done through a definite realization more real than the five senses can ever produce. Sense perceptions can be, and often are, false and deceptive, however real they may appear to us. Where there is a realization outside the senses, it is infallible. It is proved, not by extraneous evidence, but in the transformed conduct and character of those who have felt the real presence of God within.

Such testimony is to be found in the experiences of an unbroken line of prophets and sages in all countries and climes. To reject this evidence is to deny oneself.

This realization is preceded by an immovable faith. He who would in his own person test the fact of God's presence can do so by a living faith: and since faith itself cannot be proved by extraneous evidence, the safest course is to believe in the moral government of the world, and therefore in the supremacy of the moral law, the law of Truth and Love. Exercise of faith will be the safest where there is a clear determination summarily to reject all that is contrary to Truth and Love.

I confess that I have no argument to convince through reason.

Faith transcends reason. All I can advise is not to attempt the impossible. I cannot account for the existence of evil by any rational method. To want to do so is to be coequal with God. I am therefore humble enough to recognize evil as such: and I call God long suffering and patient precisely because He permits evil in the world. I know that He has no evil in Himself; and yet if there is evil he is the author of it and yet untouched by it.

I know, too, that I shall never know God if I do not wrestle with and against evil, even at the cost of life itself. I am fortified in the belief by my own humble and limited experience. The purer I try to become the nearer to God I feel myself to be. How much more should I be near to him when my faith is not a mere apology, as it is today, but has become as immovable as the Himalayas and as white as the snows on their peaks ?

APPENDIX II

World Homage

Mr. Horace Alexander, *Society Of Friends,*

When we see the history of this age in its true proportions, I believe it will be seen that Mahatma Gandhi has been, in a very profound sense, the truest friend of England, the faithful friend, who has helped the English people to see the facts and to turn away from evil policies.

In the course of Gandhiji's long life, many English men and women have been privileged to count themselves amongst his host of friends from the early days in South Africa, when Henry Polak and others supported the Satyagraha movement. On through the long years of his intimate friendship with C. F. Andrews, and right to the end of his life, he was surrounded by English friends. In the last few weeks, he was nursing an English friend at Birla house.

The long struggle against British power never led to alienation from English people. Not only did he count several Viceroys and other British rulers as friends, but even among those who were his close intimates, among those who ran to him with all their problems and difficulties, among those who loved to call him "Bapu", not a few were English men and women.

He himself has often declared how much he owed to British influence. His friends would sometimes complain that he was too British in his insistence on punctuality, his slavery to his watch. But there were many other characteristics too, where the influence of English thought was manifest. I think that most English people who met him found him a very easy and understandable person, at any rate in the affairs of ordinary everyday life, though in other ways, his deep metaphysical reasonings could be very baffling to the Anglo Saxon mind.

I had occasion only the other day to say to him, "You know, I think you are more pro-British than I am," to which he replied, "You may well say that."

Rt. Hon. L. S. Amery

The spirit of our age has been directed almost entirely to material schemes of social betterment, to mechanical projects for the prevention of war by the methods of war. We are beginning to doubt increasingly whether the methods will, in fact, preserve us from the atomic bomb or ensure peace and contentment in our midst. May the better line of approach not be that of the social reformer, who in his own person preached the happiness of the simple life and the human dignity of the untouchables; of the opponent of British rule in India, who yet understood and even loved the English people; of the devout Hindu, who yet sought spiritual communion both with Christianity and with Islam; of the pacifist, who believed that peace could only be won by the conversion of the individual soul to the hatred of war? (*Sunday Chronicle*, February 1, 1948)

Rajkumari Amrit Kaur

In the twinkling of an eye, our greatest and most beloved leader, our friend, philosopher and guide, was taken away from us. More than leader, he was a father to us all. Not for nothing did we call him "Bapu." And we are today orphans. It is impossible to estimate his loss at this critical juncture in our society. I am sure that we shall miss his wise counsel more and more as days pass by. He has led as faultlessly to our goal of political independence. The communal strife that started almost immediately after August 15th wounded him to the depths.

An India wedded to violence he could not tolerate. He saw the moral deterioration in us, and as a loving father he again unwearyingly pointed out to us the right way.

With his infinite love, he was trying to quench the anger that raged in many breasts. He was the one thing that stood between us and disaster, for lawlessness and disorder and hate and violence can lead nowhere else.

The fury of a madman has taken his frail body from our midst, but who can kill his spirit? He can never die, and we shall continue always to feel his presence near us and we shall, I hope, be truer to him now than when he was with us.

He has won the martyr's crown. His soul is at rest. But he had to offer the supreme sacrifice for us. Let us not forget our guilt. Every true Indian must hang his head in utter shame that one of our own had fallen so low as to put an end to his precious life. May God forgive him, and may we try to forgive the assassin as surely Bapu must have forgiven him and loved him even as he was firing at him.

Bowed down with grief as we are, and enveloped as we are since yesterday in the black clouds of despair, let each one of us pledge ourselves not to give way to either.

Let us have the strength to follow the path of truth and love which he would have had us follow and thereby in God's good time, wipe out the ghastly stain which has today tarnished the fair name of this country. May God have mercy on us all and give us the strength to be true to Bapu and thus build up the India of his dreams. (API)

Rt. Hon. Clement Attlee

Everyone will have learnt with profound horror of the brutal murder of Mr. Gandhi. I know that I am expressing the views of the British people in offering to his fellow countrymen our deep sympathy in the *lots* of their greatest citizen. Mahatma Gandhi, as he was known in India, was one of the outstanding figures in the world today, but he seemed to belong to a different period of history. Living a life of extreme asceticism, he was revered as a divinely inspired saint by millions of his fellow countrymen. His influence extended beyond the range of his co-religionists and, in a country deeply driven by communal dissension, he had an appeal for all Indians. For a quarter of a century, this one man has been the major factor in every consideration of the Indian problem. He had become the expression of the aspirations of the Indian people for independence, but he was not just a nationalist. His most distinctive doctrine was that of non-violence. He believed in a method of passive resistance to those forces which he considered wrong. He opposed those who sought to achieve their ends by violence and when, as too often happened, his campaigns for Indian freedom resulted in loss of life owing to the undisciplined action of those who professed to follow him, he was deeply grieved. The sincerity and devotion with which he pursued his objectives are beyond all doubt. In the latter months of his life, when communal strife was marring the freedom which India had obtained, his threat to fast to death resulted in the cessation of violence in Bengal, and again recently brought about a change in the atmosphere. He had, besides, a hatred of injustice and strove earnestly on behalf of the poor, especially of the depressed classes of India. The hand of a murderer has struck him down and a voice which pleaded for peace and brotherhood has been silenced, but I am certain his spirit will continue to animate his fellow countrymen and will plead for peace and control.

Sri. Aurobindo

I would have preferred silence in the face of these circumstances that surround us. For any words we can find fall flat amid such happenings. This much, however, I will say, that the light which led us to freedom, though not yet to unity, still burns and will burn on till it conquers. I believe firmly that a great and united future is the destiny of the nation and its peoples. The power that brought us through so much struggle and suffering to freedom will achieve also, through whatever strife or trouble, the aim which so poignantly occupied the thoughts of the fallen leader at the time of his tragic ending; as it brought us freedom it will bring us unity. A free and united India will be there and the Mother will gather around her sons and weld them into a single national strength in the life of a great and united people.

M. George Bidault

The world had heard today one of the saddest tidings of our time. He, who only a few days ago showed that good-will and renunciation would conquer hate and ambition, has left us, struck down by a madman. Not only his own people will mourn him but all those who believe in the possibility of brotherly understanding. Mr. Gandhi gave the example of an obstinate, an absolute search for love of mankind, whatever their race or religion. France stands tonight at the bier of this great man, fallen victim to the violence against which he always fought. May his sacrifice crown his lifework.

Mr. W. J. Brown

Today we mourn the death of Gandhi, the strangest combination of mystic, saint and practical politician that possibly the world has ever known. Those who understood him grieve for the passing of a spirit unique in our day, who dared in the press of practical things, to base his life in the world on the categorical imperatives of Eternity. And even those for whom a Gandhi is among those things "too high, too deep for them to understand" are aware that it was no ordinary man, however "great" who died the other day, and that something of ponderous import has happened in the world, beyond the categories of ordinary events. Only the long perspective of Time, which sets in proportion the clamouring and contesting events of the past and makes of the chaos of things an ordered picture, will enable both to see the death of Gandhi as the perfectly timed thing that it was.

Nor, in the sense of tragedy, was the manner of his death other than the most potent and the most fitting. We humans are so composed that we can't appreciate mass tragedy. Tragedy has to be reduced in scale, presented on a small stage, contracted to the case of one man or one woman, for us to realize it in all its intensity. When we read of the death of thousands in battle, or in drownings at sea, or in mine disasters, the impression made upon our minds is less than that made, say by the sight of a little child run over in the street outside our door. That is why the assassination of Gandhi will be remembered in the centuries to come when the memory of all the mass atrocities of the past few months is, in retrospect, no more than a dark blur.

Faith Made Immortal

There is another thing. To live for a faith is noble. To die for it may be to make the faith immortal. For the willingness to die is all. Without that utter and final willingness to stake life itself on his own perceptions of truth, the last guarantee of a man's ultimate sincerity is lacking in the eyes of other men. When that willingness to die is demonstrated in a single act of tragedy such as happened the other day in a garden in Delhi, the impression lasts through the centuries. They say that as Gandhi was carried from the garden to the house there was on his dying face an expression of deep peace. It was all finished! The years of austerity, asceticism and self denial, the decade of battle with the strongest of Imperialisms, which he himself equipped with nothing but the sword of the spirit, the pitched battles with followers who, seeing the end, forgot that the choice of the means determines the end, and that their choice of means would destroy the end. And finished the self doubt of the shrinking saint who did not dare to be unfaithful; the differences with friends and colleagues; the mourning over sheep unwilling to be led by the shepherd; the everlasting heartbreak at the heart of things. The long task was finished; and the end was peace.

I dare hope that may be the end in India, too. Not immediately, perhaps, but soon. To the Mohammedan, no less than to the Hindu. Gandhi was a saint. Whenever, from now on, man lifts his hand against his fellowman in India, aye, and perhaps elsewhere too, the memory will be evoked of a man who lived his life, who fasted nigh unto death, and then faced and accepted death, that man might lift his hand against his fellow no more. That memory may prove more powerful than politics, more strong than the argument that crime breeds crime for ever or that the "good republic" cannot be built on mutual murder. In his life, the single spirit of Gandhi was more potent than the strength of an Empire. It stood up to and defeated the conquerors of one-fourth of the globe. In death, that spirit may assume a wider dominion over the hearts of men than in life it did over their bodies.

"Nothing is here for tears," save, indeed, those tears which come when, after long strain and anguish, the assurance of triumph speaks in the hearts of men.

(*Time and Tide*, February 7, 1948)

Madame Pearl S. Buck

The death of Mahatma Gandhi by violence struck a blow not only to India's rising prestige in the West but to the whole cause of freedom of peoples.

Today, the enemies of this cause rejoice while others mourn the passing of one of the greatest men of human history. We sorrow because this death, so cruelly and blindly committed, casts its shadow upon all who stand for world peace and co-operation.

The responsibility now rests upon India to make the death of Mahatma Gandhi a rallying point for fresh determination to carry out the principles for which he died. Our profound condolence goes first to Nehru. He stands alone today against the dark sky of India. What will India do with Nehru? For her own sake before the world, let India support Nehru. There is no other who can take his place at this hour.

India has become the symbol of a people freed from foreign rule, but in spite of continuing strife, Mahatma Gandhi's recent fast won deep respect for India. Never had his spiritual prestige and India's risen so high in the U.S.A. as during the past month.

Mahatma Gandhi's death comes at a strategic moment, and respect is increased to reverence for a martyr. Everything now depends upon the people of India. The world watches and waits.

News Chronicle

The darkness which is over the earth today is but a deepening of the shadow which has fallen across all generations of men. The murder of Mahatma Gandhi is something far more terrible than any political crime. It belongs to the supernatural realm of high religious tragedy.

The hand that killed the Mahatma is the same hand that nailed the Cross; it is the hand that fired the faggots; it is the hand that through the ages has been growing ever more mighty in war and less sure in the pursuit of peace. It is your hand and mine.

But let there be no despair because this thing has happened.

We are the children of our generation in whom faith is not yet greater than fear. This fear, that fails to understand and quails before the great demands of the spirit, takes refuge in the material and things when it has killed the flesh that it has won its victory.

But where is the Victory? Gandhi in his long life did so much to increase the power of faith. It was he, who more than any other man we have known in modern times made it clear that fear can be conquered and that it is faith which endures.

What may happen now in India the mind hardly dares to contemplate. It may be that the folly of mankind is so far from having run its course that the death of the man of peace will open the floodgates of bloodshed. If this crowning disaster comes about, it will be truly said that in our age, men plumbed the depths of human conduct.

Yet after the work of Gandhi, it is not presumptuous to hope for a miracle. It may be that the death of this leader, who was held in so much reverence by so many millions, will raise men to heights they have not hitherto attained. It may be that the love against which the gun has no power will evoke out of this great tragedy the beginnings of peace and unity for India. Men have been shocked into sublimit, before.

Whatever happens, this is certain. The example and teaching of Mahatma Gandhi have left indelible marks upon our times. We of this generation have to make that choice between material and moral forces which is also the choice between the death and the life of the human species. By the perfection of our instruments of destruction, we have laid this duty unavoidably upon ourselves.

It is only through the lives of such as Gandhi that we can hope to discharge it. We are weak in resolution and in understanding. We have to borrow strength from those who have it more abundantly. We need guidance, and beacons to show the path which we must take.

To the most turbulent age the earth has ever seen, both these things have been given in the person of the greatest Indian of our day. In moments of stress, perception is often more sure than at any other time. Now, in the pain of Gandhi's death, it is possible to realize how lasting and how strong is the faith which he preached. Now we can see that the light which was kindled in the East has not been put out, but is made one with the "white radiance of eternity."

In that light, many feet will walk in certainty and safety. And
from the faith which burns there, untold thousands of men will
find the strength which can abate the storms in the human
heart and turn it toward that fuller life, the knowledge of which
is our distinctive heritage.

*The grass withereth, the flower fadeth: but the word... shall
stand for ever.*

(January 31, 1948)

Mr. Arthur Shirley Cripps

HOMAGE TO MAHATMA GANDHI

News that God's Will was Peace you brought,
Peace, which both Church and State betray,
God's Will, which this world sets at nought.
Resist not sin in sin's own way!
Resist not! Rather fast and pray!
Such wisdom from your lips we sought.
Will faithless men your slayer slay-
Forgetful of that Faith you taught?

You have not fought as we have fought:
No weapons helped you win the day :
No force of arms availed you aught:
Peace was your strength, and Hope your stay:
Good in unnumbered hearts you wrought-
Bidding us Hate by Love repay!

(The Sunday Mail, S. Rhodesia, February 15, 1948)

Rt. Hon. Sir Stafford Cripps

The assassination of Mahatma Gandhi is a tragedy of the
deepest intensity for India and the world. He had exercised a

most powerful influence for peace in the tense situation which has ruled since the coming of independence and the loss of that strong and calming personality in these critical times will be deplored by all who seek for a peaceful solution of the world's difficulties.

To his friends, the loss will be even greater. His faith in non-violence was expressed not only in words but in his actions and in the self sacrifice which he showed throughout his life.

There has been no greater spiritual leader in the world in our time. His loss will mean a setback and discouragement for those who, like him, believe above all in the spiritual values.

Manchester Guardian

A leader who shows perfect courage perfect honesty, and absolute freedom from envy, hatred, malice, and all uncharitableness does not live in vain. To India, Mr. Gandhi gave a new standard of courage and virtue in public life. India knows the value of that gift, and shudders to see it imperiled by the demoralizing forces of communal strife. To the West, he is not merely the man who risked his life and his political influence rather than acquiesce in the continuance of a time-honoured system of social oppression. He is, above all, the man who revived and refreshed our sense of the meaning and value of religion. For though he had not the all-comprehending intellect or the emotional riches which can construct a new philosophy or a new religion, yet the strength and purity of his moral urge were clearly derived from deep religious feelings which neither claimed for his own religion nor allowed to the religions of others an exclusive right of access to the divine.

(January 31, 1948)

Lord Halifax

The news of Mr. Gandhi's murder is the news of a great tragedy to India and to the cause for which, at any time, he was willing to give his life.

No one has tried to serve India with greater devotion, and his friends in India and elsewhere will only hope that the lesson and effect of his tragic death may be to bring all his countrymen to understand and practise the principles that he so constantly and faithfully preached.

I suppose there can be few men in all history who, by personal character and example, have been able so deeply to influence the thought of their generation.

Mr. Donald Harrington

Prayer

O God, our hearts are full of anguish. For again among us, Caesar has conquered; armed violence has had its way; the armoured car and the iron curtain their victory. The warrior has swept away the peacemaker and the little father, who loved all men, who walked with the humblest, who lifted up the lowliest, who trusted his enemies, who forgave those who tried to kill him, is gone.

Make us remember in this hour, O God, how we left him to fight alone for our peace-how we laid the chastisement of our peace upon his frail, little brown body. Make us remember that though we are glad to sing his glory today, we followed him not, nor did the things which he said. Had a few of us who honour him today shared the cross he bore, perhaps he need not have died.

Yea, O God, he hath borne our sorrows and by his pangs have we been healed. We all like sheep had gone astray, and he took up himself the iniquities of us all, and this is the condemnation, that thy light came into our world, but we preferred our darkness.

Yet we know, O God, that Gandhiji is not dead. His spirit

singeth still within our souls, and dwelleth on high with thee in glorious brightness. And we too can turn again from the ways of hate and greed and war to the way of thy spirit. He can repent us of our warlike madness and turn to the way of thy forgiveness and love.

And as the little Father of India blessed his assassin, so would we forgive in his name all our enemies, all the sad and violent wanderers in the way of wickedness, all the unrepentant and criminal – so would we also sacrifice that love might dwell upon the weary face of earth.

(Memorial Service, Community Church, New York City, February 1, 1948)

Hearst Press, U.S.A.

Too Few such Men in History

The assassination of Gandhi has had an emotional impact upon the world of today that has no parallel in human history since the similar martyrdom of Lincoln, and it menaces the peace of the world today in a manner probably not equaled by any act of violence against any man since the assassination of Sarajevo.

Gandhi was not simply a great man, but a good man, and as sorrowing people of many nations will know, the combination of the qualities of greatness and goodness in man is too rarely achieved and too little appreciated.

There have been too few such men in human history and they have so often been sorely and cruelly dealt with by the men of their times. So it has been with Gandhi who loving all men and leading the infinite wisdom of his great mind and the incalculable greatness of his gentle spirit to the enrichment and enlightenment of his fellow beings, is now destroyed in a physical sense by the insensate act of a man for whom, even the instant before death, the sign of forgiveness was made. But

Gandhi himself is not destroyed, or his noble work, or his beloved name, or his honoured place in the affections of the world today and in the eternal annals of history.

It is only the life of Gandhi which is at an end, for there is no work of destruction which could be wrought against the edifice of kindness and dignity, reason and justice, which he patiently and selflessly erected for the good of India and the peace of the world hour upon hour and day upon day and year upon year throughout the prolific time of his fruitful life.

Dr. John Haynes Holmes

When all the kings and princes and great captains of our time, who make so much noise and occupy so central a place upon the stage, when these have long since been forgotten, every one of them, the Mahatma will still be known and revered as the greatest Indian, since Gautama the Buddha, and as the greatest man since Jesus Christ.

Gandhi gave to the Indian people the weapons where-with to carry on their fight, weapons of unimaginable power, weapons that guaranteed eventful victory and in Gandhi's own time, praise be to God, won the victory that he could see. Gandhi's programme of non-violent resistance is unprecendented in the history of mankind. The principle itself, resist not evil and love your enemies, is nothing new. It is at least as ancient as the teachings of Jesus of Nazareth in the Sermon on the Mount. But Gandhi did what had never been done before. Up to this time the practice of these non-resistant principles had been limited to single individuals, or to little groups of individuals. Gandhi worked out the discipline and the programme for the practising of this particular kind of principle by unnumbered masses of human beings. He worked out a programme, in other words, not merely for any individual, or a small group of individuals, but for a whole nation, and that, I say to you, is something new in the experience of man.

I can best sum up the significance of this second period of Gandhi's life, which ended on the 15th day of August 1947, with the triumph of Indian freedom, by quoting to you a remarkable paragraph from a book entitled *The Tragedy of Europe*, written by a great scholar, Dr. Francis Neilson. This is the way he puts it: "Gandhi," he says, "is unique. There is no record of a man of his position challenging a great empire. A Diogenes in action, a St. Francis in humility, a Socrates in wisdom, he reveals to the world the utter paltriness of the methods of the statesman who relies upon force to gain his end. In this contest, spiritual integrity triumphs over the physical opposition of the forces of the state." That was Gandhi's triumph. That was his achievement. That marks his place in history.

(Memorial Service, Community Church,
New York City, February 1, 1948)

The Mahatma's secret was the spirit. He believed that spirit is a reality. He trusted it as more potent than the sword. He lived in it as love in the midst of hate, as forgiveness in the midst of vengeance, as good in the midst of evil. The spirit which is God within the soul of man – this can overcome the world. Here was Gandhi's secret, which he called "truth". In his own faith and practice, he proved it to be truth; and we must accept it if we would live. It is the atom bomb or Gandhi choose ye this day which ye will serve!

(University of Chicago Round Table, February 1, 1948)

Mr. Laurence Houseman

Gandhi's fast was a triumph, a great victory for Peace the influence of a single man's devotion to the way of truth on the minds of millions of his fellow countrymen committed to a fierce racial conflict, for which there seemed to be no solution. Was his death a defeat? At short range it might seem so; for the immediate result was a renewed outbreak of violence and bloodshed.

But this will not be the first time in the history either of religion or politics, when a blind deed of hatred and misunderstanding, inflicting death on one who had done nothing to deserve it, has formed the crowning point to a great life of spiritual revelation and service to God and man and has demonstrated more than anything else could do, the meaning of that life-its profound and fundamental difference from the general character of the mass mentality which formed its environment.

That difference was expressed in what immediately followed when Gandhi fell by the hand of his assassin. His last gesture was a gesture of courteous acceptance of the death that had been dealt him by a fellow countryman and one, nominally, of his own religion; the immediate reaction of the surrounding spectators was a frenzied attempt to wreak vengeance on the murderer.

So, at the very moment of his death, in their misguided love for him, his followers forsook his example and teaching; for in that act of violence there was more likeness between them and the man whom they hated, than between them and the man whom they loved.

And that likeness and unlikeness applies to the whole world today in its social organization, and its lack of faith in the power of good over evil.

Gandhi would have wished that his murderer should go unpunished. It cannot be done; we have not the moral background to make it possible: and this wish of the man we love and revere that his murderer should be forgiven must go unfulfilled.

Here, then we have demonstrated how pathetically and morally helpless we are, without a general change of heart, both individually and in our social structure, to follow the example and teaching of the man whose loss we mourn today as the greatest of all our contemporary leaders in the Way of Truth, which is also the way, and the only way, of Peace.

It is a strange paradox in the problem of human nature, that of this man, whom millions love and revere, and whom many more have now come to respect, we cannot yet be faithful followers. Society is not yet shaped for it: only if we love all men, the good and the bad, as Gandhi loved them, can we afford socially 'to forgive our criminals, internationally to lay down our arms and renounce war.

When, between the two world wars the worst wars that the world has ever known Gandhi came to this country for the Round Table Conference, I had the honour the greatest honour that has ever come to me, to take the chair at the great meeting of welcome held at Friend's House, London. And to Gandhi I then said: "Mr. Gandhi, you are a strange man; you are so simple that you puzzle people: you are so honest that men doubt you".

That is still true: the spiritual simplicity of Gandhi seems utterly out of place in the over sophisticated world of today: his honesty too uncompromising to form the basis for any practical policy.

Yet the sword of his spirit pierces to the very heart of the moral problem with which modern civilization is now confronted, and unless something of that spirit is accepted and made practical politics, civilization as we know it may be doomed.

Dr. Syud Hussain

The saviour of India has been crucified. He is gone. India will eternally walk under the shadow of his cross. No more tragic and unspeakable thing has ever happened to any nation than has befallen this unhappy and helpless people.

Not only our light has gone out, but the purest spiritual flame in the world has been extinguished especially at a time when its radiance and warmth were at their highest. He was affectionately called "Bapu." More millions have been truly orphaned by his passing than by that of any other figure in recorded history.

In this hour of national dislocation, let us try and pay humble homage to his sacred memory by remembering and practising his eternal gospel of Truth and Non-violence, and by re-dedication to the service of India even as he had served.

Mr. Fernand Van Langenhove

A tragic event dominates our thoughts. We have met today (in the Security Council) under the spell of emotion which has gone through the world at the death of Mr. Gandhi.

We know what this event represents and particularly for the populations of India. In the name of the Security Council, I express to the Indian representative, to his Government and his entire nation, our profound sympathy and the sorrow which we feel at the act of a madman.

Mr. Gandhi gave to the world a great lesson.

Few people have shown such absolute devotion to the generous ideas to which he had vowed himself. On many occasions, he offered the sacrifice of his life so that these ideas might triumph.

From the distance he appeared to us to be already above this world as a great symbol. He represented in the highest degree and in its most noble aspect, the spirit of the independence of his people.

He lived long enough to see India become fully sovereign. But he represented something more the idea of non-violence which is the very principle which inspires our organization.

This alone would justify the respect in which we will hold his memory. He represented also the spirit of unity, understanding and fraternity. For these reasons, his name was on several occasions brought into our debates. Somehow we felt that in our efforts for pacification and mutual understanding, we had in him a great ally.

Chief Rabbi D.H.M. Lazarus

On behalf of British Jewry I wish to convey my deepest sympathy and sorrow at the tragic death of Mr. Gandhi. The loss of one whose saintly character and lifelong devotion to the cause of peace will cause his name always to be remembered, is irreparable.

Not only India but the whole world saw his ideals, difficult as they were of attainment, the only practical means of reaching the ultimate aim of humanity, a lasting peace and friendship among peoples of all races and creeds.

General Douglas MacArthur

Nothing more revolting has occurred in the history of the modern world than the senseless assassination of this venerable man. He had come through time and circumstances and his oft repeated ideologies are to be regarded as the very symbol and apotheosis of peace.

That he should die through violence is one of those bitter anachronisms that seem to refute all logic. In the evolution of civilization, if it is to survive, all men cannot fail eventually to adopt his belief that the process of mass application of force to resolve contentious issues is fundamentally not only wrong and useless, but contains within itself the germ of self-destruction.

Mahatma Gandhi, however, was one of those prophets who lived far ahead of time.

Mr. Milton Mayer

This old man had no possessions; he had no position. His life was worth nothing to him; and his death did not bother him. But the world was shaken because, without an army, a navy, an air force, without a stick or a stone, without power or patronage, he pulled down the pillars of an empire and brought freedom to a sub-continent of four hundred million unarmed people.

To most white men, he was a comical, certainly an unrealistic figure. Alongside the strong men of our age – the Roosevelts, Churchills, and Stalins – he was unimpressive in his shawl and his loincloth. But the meek were once told that they would inherit the earth; and now men everywhere are wondering whether this meekest of men may not have been the strongest man of our age. Millions of people followed him without benefit of promise of benefit. They followed him to prison and to prayer and to freedom.

Jesus said, "If My Kingdom were of this world, then would my servants fight." Gandhi's kingdom was of this world, and still his servants would not fight. Gandhi adapted Holy Writ to statesmanship, and in this strict sense, I think, we have to say that he was the first Christian politician since Jesus – Washington, Jefferson and Lincoln not excepted.

All armed ideologies, including our own, fall together, all bosses who believe in force and all workers who believe in force fall together. If Jesus is right, if Gandhi is right, then Roosevelt and Hitler fall together and Wallace and Taft, and Truman and Stalin. If Gandhi is right, all those who believe that force and pressure and power will carry the day are wrong, and always have been, even though some of them would use force for good rather than for evil purposes.

This, if it is true, is terrible to contemplate. The fate of Churchill's world empire and of Hitler's world slavery is before our eyes. If Gandhi is right, and if mankind survives in the spirit of love, then the ruins of democracy by force and communism by force will both bear their blackened testimony to the rightness of the Christian politician.

But this means a revolution much more radical than any of the revolutionaries have ever suggested. It means that we must change the whole order of personal and political life or change nothing.

(University of Chicago Round Table,
February 1, 1948)

Rt. Hon. Lord Mountbatten

The Governor-General, Lord Mountbatten, broadcasting from New Delhi on February 12th, said that the death of Mahatma Gandhi came with a shock of personal bereavement to millions of people in every part of the civilized world. Not only those who worked with him throughout his life, or who, like myself, had known him for a comparatively short time, but people who had never met him, who had never seen him or had even read one word of his published works, felt as if they had lost a friend.

"Dear friend," that is how he would begin his letters to me, and how I used to address him. And that is how I and my family will always think of him.

I met Gandhiji for the first time in March last year, for my first act on arriving in India was to write to him and suggest we should meet at the earliest possible moment and at our first meeting we decided the best way we could help one another deal with the tremendous problems ahead was to maintain constant personal contact. The last time he came to see me was a month ago, a few minutes after the prayer meeting at which he had announced he would fast unto death unless communal harmony was restored. The last time I saw him in his life was when my wife and I went to visit him on the fourth day of his fast. During the ten months we had known one another, our meetings had never been formal interviews; they were talks between two friends and we had been able to establish a degree of confidence and understanding which will remain treasured in my memory.

Gandhi, man of peace, apostle of ahimsa, died by violence as a martyr in the struggle against fanaticism that deadly disease that has threatened to jeopardize India's new-found freedom. He saw that this cancer must be rooted out before India could embark on the great task of nation-building which lies ahead.

Our great Prime Minister, Pandit Nehru, has set us the high aim of a secular democratic State wherein all can lead useful, creative lives, and in which a genuinely progressive society can be developed, based on social and economic justice; and the best tribute we can pay to Gandhiji's memory is to turn our hearts and our minds and our hands to building such a society upon the foundations of freedom that he so firmly laid during his lifetime. Gandhiji will have rendered his last and greatest service of all to the people he loved so well if the tragic manner of his death has shocked and spurred us into sinking all differences and joining in a sustained united effort beginning here and now. Only in this way can his ideal be realized and India enter into her full inheritance.

Moustapha El Nahas

The assassination of the great spiritual leader Mahatma Gandhi has deeply affected my friends and myself as it has the people of the Nile Valley. The death of the man of love and peace at the hands of a dastardly murderer adds to our affliction and bereavement and the great loss incurred by his disappearance is not limited to India and the East alone, but is felt in every corner of the world, for in truth he belonged to all mankind.

The selflessness, devotion and sacrifice of Mahatma Gandhi in the cause of love and goodwill shall remain an eternal example along the course of time. I myself keep many cherished memories of the great leader whose magnificent fight for the liberty of his country was contemporaneous with our own struggle since the very beginning of our great revolution.

My personal relations with him have made me appreciate even more the greatness of his personality and the elevation of his moral character. He was the strongest pillar of love and peace.

Mrs. Sarojini Naidu

There is no occasion for me to speak today. The voice of the world in many languages has already spoken, and proved that Mahatma Gandhi was a world figure, loved and worshipped by all those who have a sense of ideals, of righteousness, right doing and peace.

Mahatma Gandhi's first fast, with which I was associated, was for the cause of Hindu-Muslim unity. It had the sympathy of the entire nation. His last fast was also for the cause of Hindu-Muslim unity, but the whole nation was not with him in the fast.

It had grown so divided, so bitter, so full of hate and suspicion, so untrue to the tenets of all the various creeds in this country that it was only those who understood Mahatma Gandhi that realized the meaning of that fast.

Alas, for the Hindu community, that the greatest Hindu ever born, the only Hindu who was absolutely true to the doctrines, ideals and philosophy of Hinduism, should have been slain by the hand of a Hindu.

Should Not Desert Him

Some of us have been closely associated with him that our lives and his life were an integral part of one another. Some of us are indeed dead, with him. Some of us, indeed have had vivisection performed on us by his death, because the fibres of our being, our muscles, veins and hearts and blood were all intertwined with his life. But we will be acting as deserters if we were to yield to despair, if we were to believe that he is dead, if we were to believe that all is lost because he has gone.

Of what avail will be our faith, our loyalty to him, if we dared to believe that all is lost because his body is gone from our midst? Are we not here, his heirs, his spiritual descendants, legatees of his great ideals, successors of his great work?

The time is over for private sorrows. The time is over for beating of breasts and tearing of hair. The time is here and now to stand up and say, "We take up the challenge with those who defied Mahatma Gandhi."

We are his living symbols; we are his soldiers, we are the carriers of his banner before an embattled world. Our banner is truth, our shield is non-violence our sword is the sword of the spirit that conquers without blood. Shall we not follow in the footsteps of our master, shall we not obey the mandates of our father; shall we not be his soldiers, and carry his battle to triumph; shall we not give the world the completed message of Mahatma Gandhi? Though his voice will not speak again, have we not a million, million voices to bear his message to the world? And not only in this world of our contemporaries, but in the world, generation after generation?

Here and now, I for one before the world that listens to my quivering voice, pledge myself as I pledged myself more than thirty years ago, to the service of the Mahatma.

What is death? My own father died, and just before his death he said: "There is birth; there is no death. There is only the soul seeking higher and higher stages of the truth."

Gandhiji Has Risen Again

Mahatma Gandhi, whose frail body was committed, to the flames yesterday, is not dead. Like Christ of old, on the third day he has risen again, in answer to the cry of his people and the call of the world for the continuance of his guidance, his love, his service and inspiration.

It is right that the cremation took place in the midst of the dead Kings who are buried in Delhi, for he was the Kingliest of all Kings. It is right also that he who was the apostle of peace should have been taken to the cremation ground with all the honours of a great warrior. Far greater than all warriors who led armies to battle was this little man, the bravest, the most tried friend of all. Delhi has become the centre and the sanctuary of the great revolutionary who emancipated his enslaved country from foreign bondage, and gave to it its freedom and its flag.

May the soul of my master, my leader, my father, rest not in peace. Not in peace, my father, do not rest. Do not rest. Keep us to our pledge. Give us the strength to fulfil our promise, your heirs, your descendants, your students, guardians of your dreams, fulfillers of India's destiny.

Pandit Jawaharlal Nehru

The light has gone out of our lives and there is darkness everywhere. I do not know how to tell you. The father of the nation is no more. Now that the light has gone out of our lives, I do not quite know what to tell you and how to say it. Our beloved leader is no more. We who have seen him for these many years, cannot turn to him any longer for advice or to seek solace and that is a terrible blow not only to me but also to the millions and millions of this country.

A madman has put an end to his life... There is bound to be anger as well as sorrow in the heart of the nation. But none of us dare misbehave.

We have to behave like strong and determined people, determined to face all perils that surround us, determined to carry out the mandate that our great teacher and our great leader has given us, remembering always that if, as I believe, his spirit looks upon us and sees us, nothing would displease his soul so much as to see we have indulged in any small behaviour or any violence.

The best prayer we can offer him and his memory is to dedicate ourselves to truth and to the cause for which this great countryman of ours lived and for which he died.

Pandit Nehru's Tribute In Dominion Parliament, February 2, 1948.

We praise people in well-chosen words, and we have some kind of measure for greatness. How shall we praise him and how shall we measure him? For he was not of the common clay of which all of us are made. He came and lived a fairly long span of life, and has passed away. No words of praise of ours in this House are needed, for he has had greater praise in his life than any living man. In his history and during these two or three days since his death he has had the homage of the world. What can we add to that? How can we praise him? How can we have been children of his, and perhaps more intimately children of his than children of his body, for we have all been in some greater or smaller measure children of his spirit, unworthy as we were. Yet he would not have us feel this way after all that glory that we saw for all these years. That man with divine fire changed us also, and such as we are we have been moulded by him during these years, and out of that divine fire many of us also took a small spark which strengthened and made us work to some extent on the lines that he fashioned. And so if we praise him our words seem rather small, and if we praise him, to some extent, we praise ourselves. Great men and eminent men have monuments in bronze and marble set up for them, but this man of divine fire managed in his lifetime to become enmeshed in millions and millions of hearts, so that all of us become somewhat of the stuff that he was made of, though to an infinitely lesser degree. He spread out over India, not in palaces only or in select places or in assemblies, but in every hamlet and hut of the lowly and those who suffer. He lives in the hearts of millions, and he will live for immemorial ages.

What, then can we say about him except to feel humble on this occasion, to praise him? We are not worthy to praise him whom we could not follow adequately and sufficiently. It is almost doing him an injustice just to pass him by with words, when he demanded work and labour and sacrifice from us in large measure. He made this country during the last thirty years or more attain to heights of sacrifice which in that particular domain have never been equalled elsewhere. He succeeded in that, yet ultimately things happened which no doubt made him suffer tremendously, though his tender face never lost its smile. He never spoke a harsh word to anyone, yet he must have suffered, suffered for the failings of this generation whom he had trained, suffered because we went away from the path that he had shown us, and ultimately because the hand of a child of his (for he, after all, is as much a child of his as any other Indian), the hand of that child of his struck him down.

Long ages afterwards, history will judge this period that we have passed through. It will judge its successes and failures. We are too near it to be proper judges and to understand what has happened and what has not happened. All we know is that for the moment there is darkness, not so dark certainly, because when we look into our hearts we still find the living flames exist. There will not be darkness in this land. We shall be able with our effort, by praying to him and following his path, to illumine this land again, small as we are, but still with the fire that he instilled into us. He was perhaps the greatest symbol of the India of the past, and, may I say, of the future, that we could have. We stand on this perilous age of the present between that past and the future. We face all manner of perils, and the greatest peril is sometimes the lack of faith which comes to us as a sense of frustration, that comes to us as a sinking of the heart and of the spirit, that comes to us when we see Ideals go overboard, when we see the great things that we talked about somehow pass into empty words and life take a different course. Yet I do believe that perhaps this period will pass soon enough.

Great as this man of God was in his life, he has been great in his death, and I have not a shadow of doubt that by his death he has served a great cause, as he served it throughout his life. We mourn him, we shall always mourn him, because we are human and cannot forget our valued master. But I know that he would not like us to mourn him. No tears came to his eyes when his dearest and closest went away. Only a firm resolve to preserve and to serve the great cause that he had chosen. So he would chide us if we merely mourn. That is a poor way of doing homage to him. The only way is to express our determination, to pledge ourselves anew, to conduct ourselves so and to dedicate ourselves to the great task which he undertook and which he accomplished to such a large extent. So we have to work, we have to labour, we have to sacrifice, and thus prove to some extent at least worthy followers of his.

He has gone, and all over India there is a feeling of having been left desolate and forlorn. All of us sense that feeling, and I do not know when we shall be able to get rid of it. Yet together with that feeling there is also a feeling of proud thanksgiving that it has been given to us of this generation to be associated with this mighty person in ages to come. Centuries, and it may be millenniums after us, people will think of this generation when this man of God trod the earth. They will think of us, who, however small could also follow his path, and they will probably tread on the holy ground where his feet had been. Let us be worthy of him. Let us always be so.

R T. Hon. Philip Noel-Baker

This tragic event has taken from us a man venerated not only in his own country but by men of all the world.

Mr. Gandhi was a man whose greatness belonged not only to his lifetime but to history. Never was the spirit of love and brotherhood, of which he was the supreme advocate and is now the martyr, more solely needed than today alike in the Indian sub-continent as throughout the world.

For half a century his inspiration has been unfailing and in the past year it perhaps attained its supreme expression.

His death must bring home to us all the peril in which we stand from which the issue can only be won by following the precepts on which his whole life was founded.

No one in modern history has exercised such influence over the minds of men by his individual strength of character, his purity of motive and selfless devotion to the cause in which he believed.

I believe that like other prophets his greatest work is still to come.

R. T. Hon. Lord Pethick-Lawrence

WE MUST DO HOMAGE BY DEEDS

Gandhiji was deeply loved. He will be deeply mourned. He is no longer with us in the flesh, but his spirit endures. What was the secret of his power over the hearts and minds of men and women? In my opinion it was the fact that he voluntarily stripped himself of every vestige of the privilege that he could have enjoyed on account of his birth, means personality and intellectual preeminence and took on himself the status and infirmities of the ordinary man.

When he was in South Africa as a young man and opposed the treatment of his fellow-countrymen in that land, he courted for himself the humiliation of the humblest Indian that he might in his own person face the punishment meted out for disobedience. When he called for non-cooperation with the British in India he himself disobeyed the law and insisted that he must be among the first to go to prison. When he declaimed against the adoption by India of Western industrialism he installed a spinning wheel in his own house and laboured at it daily with his own hands. When he set out to combat inter communal violence he faced death by starvation in an act of penance for the error and sin of the community of which he was himself a member.

He never claimed to be any other than an ordinary man. He acknowledged his liability to error and admitted that he had frequently learnt by his mistakes. He was the universal brother, lover, and friend of poor, weak, erring, suffering humanity. Let us all do homage to his spirit, not by words alone but by dedicating our lives as he did to the pursuit of truth, the love of our fellow men the healing of the wounds of nations.

Mr. Reginald Sorensen

I am quite sure he himself would desire that all who knew and loved him should neither seek revenge nor allow themselves to be obsessed by the nature of his parting.

His life was so dominated by a sense of eternal values that it would be incongruous for us to do otherwise than feel gratitude at a life lived so richly in service to his fellows.

The influence he has had not only in India but upon our modern age is beyond calculation, for he bore witness to the power of the spirit and sought to implement this in his political activity.

Whether we agree in all respects with him or not, we cannot withhold our sense of indebtedness to him.

Mr. H.S. Suhrawardy

I feel as if the bottom of the world has fallen out. Who is there who will now assuage the anguish of the oppressed, who is there who will now wipe their tears? To him we had learnt to turn for guidance and for advice in all our difficulties and he never failed us.

Weep, India, weep until thy heart breaks, for extinguished is the light that shed Truth and Justice, a deep love for humanity and transcendental sympathy for the forlorn and the friendless. May we take his teachings to heart, and in the midst of our gloom and despair, endeavour to put into practice those grand tenets of peace and love of mankind for which he gave his life.

I am sure he sees what we do; let us try to fulfil his cherished dream of Hindu Muslim unity and oneness of mind and spirit in the common service of Humanity.

New York Times

A light has gone out. The rest remains for history's inexorable hand to write down.

A hush will go round the world today as Gandhi's frail body is borne to the banks of the sacred river Jumna, there to be turned to ashes.

Out of the ashes we do not know what flowers will spring. But this we do know; that saintly man, who preached non-violence, is dead by violence. Those who saw him cut down believe that with a last gesture of forgiveness he forgave his last enemy. His undying spirit speaks now to all India and the world.

He has left as his heritage a spiritual force that must, in God's good time, prevail over arms and armaments and dark doctrines of violence.

(January 31, 1948)

President Truman

Gandhi was a great Indian nationalist, but at the same time he was a leader of international stature.

His teachings and his actions have left a deep depression on millions of people.

He was and is revered by the people of India and his influence was felt not only in the affairs of Government but also in the realm of the spirit. Unhappily, he did not live to witness the full realization of those ideals for which he struggled, but his life and his work will be through the years to come the greatest monument to him.

His selfless struggle for the betterment of his people will, I am sure, endure as an example for India's leaders, many of whom are his disciples.

I know that not only the people of India but also all peoples will be inspired by his sacrifice to work with increased vigour toward brotherhood and peace which the Mahatma symbolized...

I am deeply grieved by the news of the assassination of Mohandas Gandhi, and I send you and the Government and people of India my sincere condolences.

As a teacher and leader, his influence made itself felt not only in India but everywhere in the world and his death brings great sorrow to all peace loving people.

Another giant among men has fallen in the cause of brotherhood and peace.

I know that the peoples of Asia will be inspired by his tragic death to strive with increased determination to achieve the goals of co-operation and mutual trust for which the Mahatma has now given his life.

Mr. Eamon De Valera

In its later phases, our own struggle for freedom and that of India have coincided. Our people felt they were brothers in a common cause and wished each other well.

The Indian people are bereaved tonight and we grieve with them. They have lost a leader who brought them to their present freedom. Our prayer is that the sacrifice of his life, by which he gave to his country this last full measure of devotion, will bring to the Indian people that brotherly peace which was so dear to him. The loss is not India's alone: the world has lost a great leader whose influence will long survive his death.

Mr. U. Win, *Burmese Ambassador In India*

The world has suffered an irreparable loss today. The Father of the Indian Nation is now no more. He has become a victim of forces of evil. We now see to what length such forces of evil will go. We are completely stunned by this most cowardly act and unexpected tragedy. Just as Jesus Christ suffered to save erring humanity so has Mahatmaji suffered now. To us Burmans, it is more than a national loss no less painful than the loss of our own leaders last July. The Burmese people had a special reverence for Mahatmaji. The world has lost its greatest man in history, the living personification of Love and Truth.

The light has gone from this world. Let us rekindle this torch by following Mahatmaji's example and pray that the national unity and communal harmony which has been so dear to Mahatmaji will be achieved over his death bed.

Mr. Lin Yu-tang

Mahatma Gandhi was the only modern saint and prophet which his country produced. Only in a country like India or in Asia could a man achieve tremendous political power because of spiritual power. Indians must decide the possibility of war. I hope peace will prevail. Such a phenomenon as Mahatma Gandhi could not be possible in the Western world. It should convince Westerners not to interfere in Oriental politics.

Sir M. Zafrullah Khan

On behalf of the Government and people of Pakistan and my own desire, I associate myself with the tributes paid by the members of the Council to the memory of one who illustrated the noblest ideals of enlightened Hinduism in the present age.

His tragic death constitutes as grievous a loss to Pakistan as to India. Indeed, it is an irreparable loss to the cause of peace throughout the world.

Mr. Gandhi was beloved by hundreds of millions deeply revered by all who heard his name. One of his many claims go greatness was the faculty which always enabled him to win through to sanity in every one of the crises which he faced during his life.

It was inconceivable that anybody would wish to do him harm.

The irony is that he should have fallen by the hand of an assassin. The poignancy and tragedy is enhanced by the realization that he was the keystone of the arch that is at this moment subject to so many stresses.

The keystone has been removed by a dastardly hand. It is difficult to assess what this disaster may portend. Yet one should be permitted to indulge the hope and utter the prayer that, through the supreme sacrifice, Mr. Gandhi may have accelerated the achievement of those ideals for which his whole life was dedicated.